The Sons of Molly Maguire

The Sons of Molly Maguire

The Irish Roots of America's First Labor War

Mark Bulik

Fordham University Press | New York   2015

Library of Congress Cataloging-in-Publication Data

Bulik, Mark.
  The Sons of Molly Maguire : the Irish roots of America's first labor war / Mark Bulik.
— First edition.
    pages cm
  Includes bibliographical references and index.
  ISBN 978-0-8232-6223-6 (cloth : alk. paper)
  1. Molly Maguires (Organization) 2. Coal miners—Pennsylvania—History. 3. Irish Americans—Pennsylvania—History. 4. Irish Americans—Pennsylvania—Social conditions. I. Title.
  HV6452.P4M63 2015
  364.10609748—dc23

                        2014029715

Printed in the United States of America
17 16 15   5 4 3 2 1
First edition

to the memory of my grandfather
James J. O'Connor
a breaker boy and a book lover

Contents

Illustrations follow page 182

The Sons of Molly Maguire

Part I

Introduction: The Fountainhead

We behold a stream as deep as it is dark, which indicates, by its continuous current, that it is derived from an unfailing fountain, and which however augmented by the contributions of other streams of bitterness, must be indebted for its main supply to some abundant and distant source. Where, then, is the wellhead to be found?

—Richard Lalor Sheil, on Irish secret society violence

The Schuylkill River earns its name in the rugged, coal-laden hills north and west of Minersville, Pennsylvania. Arendt Corssen of the Dutch East India Company dubbed the river "Skokihl," Dutch for "hidden stream," in the 1600s, and its West Branch rises as two all but invisible creeks that meander through Foster and Cass Townships in Schuylkill County.[1]

One of the creeks, the West-West, begins in the hills above the village of Forestville, whispering its way down through a quiet, fern-lined hollow where the waters pool below a series of falls. Over the eons the action of water flowing over rock ate through the ridge, exposing seams of hard coal, or anthracite. The ridge came to be known as Mine Hill.

Deep in the hollow, near one of the falls, a broad, flat rock bears the chiseled names of long-dead coal miners—S. Lynch, C. J. Lynch, W. J. Dormer, E. P. O'Brien, and P. J. Doyle—and the year, 1886. Their families had come from Ireland decades before to mine the coal, creating Forestville, where the stream tumbles out of Mine Hill. Over the course of half a century, miners tore more than a million tons out of the Forestville Colliery.[2]

Today, the mine is gone. The village consists of a sprinkling of houses, the Forestville Citizens Fire Company, and a barely noticeable bridge that carries Forest Lane over the creek.

From Forestville, the stream winds south to an even smaller hamlet, Phoenix Park, which shares the name of that vast green expanse in Dublin where Irish radicals assassinated London's chief secretary and undersecretary in 1882, amid Ireland's last great land war. It was there, on the banks of the West-West, that mine workers like Pat Lynch voiced their bitterness about mean-spirited bosses, abysmal conditions, and miserly pay in a ballad, "The Phoenix Park Colliery":

> It stands right there in Phoenix Park
> You all may know it well
> Although it stands in Phoenix Park
> It may as well stand in hell.
>
> ...There's "Snipey" Dormer, the breaker boss
> A snip of a man, they say;
> He wants you to work as hard as a mule
> For ninety cents a day.[3]

Lynch knew all about abysmal conditions in the Phoenix Park breaker, a vast structure where the coal was sorted outside the mine; he had worked there for years as a young man. In 1958, after singing the ballad for a folklorist, he recounted how his older brother, Pete, slipped as he was working as a slate picker, or "breaker boy," at Phoenix Park. Pete took a long fall and was impaled on a stalagmite of ice that had formed as water dripped from the breaker, he said. It was the darkest of winter days, December 22, 1896. Pete was just thirteen years old; Pat, seven months.

"They tell me I was the last one he touched before going to work," Lynch recalled. "He was killed that day in the mines."[4]

From Phoenix Park, the Schuylkill moves south to its junction with the Muddy Branch flowing down from Branchdale. The waters are then deflected eastward by Sharp Mountain, and eventually join with others to become something like a river.

The second creek, the West Branch, rises miles to the north in Foster Township and flows largely unseen beside the road between Glen Carbon and Heckscherville, two tiny collections of houses notable for the lilting brogue that was still to found among some older residents through the end of the twentieth century. To mapmakers this is the Heckscherville Valley, but the locals use another name: Irish Valley. The stream runs east through Cass Township, between Broad Mountain and Mine Hill, past slag heaps and strip mines, by Clover Fire Company and St. Kieran's Catholic church, to Coal Castle.

There it turns to the south, through Mine Hill Gap, wandering past another sprinkling of houses, Duncott, where Bill Keating composed that quintessential hard-coal ballad, "Down, Down, Down," in the dank gloom of the Oak Hill Colliery. It is the bitter, comic lament of a hung-over miner, to be sung as work boots tap barroom sawdust, in a voice lubricated by whiskey and porter and seasoned by the cadences of the ould sod:

> The Oak Hill officials are foxy galoots
> With company-store tyrants they're all in cahoots;
> With the gangways a river, you're bound to buy boots
> While you're down, down, down.
>
> ... All I drew for a year was a dollar or three.
> Those company-store thieves made a pauper of me.[5]

Below Duncott, the stream gains strength as it enters its first real town, Minersville, then turns toward the Schuylkill County seat, Pottsville. But before reaching Pottsville, the stream merges with the West-West and flows through a gap in Sharp Mountain. The west and east branches of the Schuylkill, in turn, join a few miles to the south at the twin boroughs of Cressona and Schuylkill Haven. From there, the waters run south, tamed partly by a canal, into the history of the industrial revolution. For coal dug in Schuylkill County fired the forges of Reading, Phoenixville, and Philadelphia, turning the lower Schuylkill Valley into the workshop of an emerging nation.

But something more than a river was born in those rugged hills above Minersville. For just as the hidden stream gave rise to the mines, the coal industry spawned a hidden by-product of its own along the westernmost reaches of the Schuylkill—the Molly Maguires, a secret society of assassins rooted in the north of Ireland. The emergence of the Mollies on the banks of the West Branch and their prolonged battle with the mine owners became one of the most sensational newspaper stories of the nineteenth century. Indeed, the Mollies fired the first shots in America's labor wars. Observers ranging from the socialist leader Eugene Victor Debs to leading historians like Samuel Eliot Morison, Henry Steele Commager, and William E. Leuchtenburg agreed that it was the Molly Maguires who gave the United States its first glimpse of class warfare.[6]

The spark for all this trouble was the Civil War, which created a labor shortage and increased demand for coal. For the first time, the mine workers had the upper hand in dealing with management. They exploited it with a strike that soon became intertwined with violent resistance to the draft. In May 1862 troops occupied Heckscherville and Forestville during a mine strike. In the fall, the draft led to a new strike, with opponents of conscription staging a paramilitary march from mine to mine. And in December 1862, strikers invaded the Phoenix Park Colliery uttering a peculiar battle cry: "Molly Maguire!" If the name mystified some managers, it was well-known to their Irish workforce as a secret society in the Ulster borderlands that wreaked bloody vengeance on landlords and their agents for evicting tenant farmers during the potato famine of the 1840s.

In Coal Castle, on January 2, 1863, five assassins gunned down a disabled Union Army veteran in his home. A little over a week later, two of the victim's acquaintances were shot and wounded as they walked on the road that parallels the West Branch between Heckscherville and Coal Castle. These shootings were the first in a long series of attacks that inspired Arthur Conan Doyle to write that Sherlock Holmes classic, *The Valley of Fear.*

In 1865, a mine boss was gunned down in broad daylight near Branchdale. The following year, a Heckscherville mine superintendent was killed by three gunmen on the road between Pottsville and Minersville. The gunmen fled toward Minersville—and Cass Township, where the slain mine boss had provided quarters for an army of occupation just a few years before.

The wellhead of this Civil War violence in the hills outside Minersville is nearly as obscure as the origins of the Schuylkill there. The secret society at the center of it all left no records, and had two contradictory identities. Its public face was the Hibernian order, a politically active fraternal organization of Irish Americans pledged to benevolence and mutual aid. The hidden side was the Molly Maguires, a smaller group within the Hibernians that used anonymous threats and assassination in a long battle with the mining companies and their allies in government. There was no group called the "Molly Maguires" separate and apart from the Hibernians— the name simply came to designate a subset of the order (itself a subset of the larger Irish community) that was willing to resort to violence and intimidation.

When twenty reputed Mollies were hanged, the subject became taboo for many in the anthracite region. The silence was deep, pervading, reflexive—a part of the culture. In Schuylkill County, where company houses, company stores, company police, and company spies created a state as totalitarian as any this nation has known, people learned to talk all day without giving away things like names. Pat Lynch was happy to regale the folklorist George Korson with stories of life and death in the mines, but when he was asked who had taught him "The Phoenix Park Colliery" half a century before, the old reflexes kicked in: "I hesitate to mention his

name."[7] The song, like many miners' ballads, was inherently subversive—
what good could come from the naming of names, even as late as 1958?

Much of what is known about the Mollies was gleaned from investigations and trials conducted in the 1870s, more than a decade after the initial
outbreaks of conspiratorial violence. Those records offer a wealth of detail
on the period 1874–76, but far less on the 1860s, when the Mollies emerged
along the West Branch. And the sources of those records—undercover detectives hired by the coal companies, and trials where coal company executives served as prosecutors—present their own problems.

Given the nature of the evidence and the emotions involved, it is hardly
surprising that there has been little agreement about the events that led to
the deaths of dozens of men on both sides of the anthracite region's sectarian and social divide in the years 1863–75. Early apologists for the prosecution portrayed the hanged Irishmen as primitive terrorists who applied
Old World methods of resistance to a New World where such practices were
no longer needed.[8] Marxists and socialists saw the executed men as labor
martyrs—indeed, looking back on the hangings decades later, Debs called
the dead men "the first martyrs of the class struggle in the United States."[9]
Some Irish Americans have likewise defended them as the victims of a coal
company conspiracy.[10]

Today, the only consensus is that there is no consensus. Donald Miller
and Richard Sharpless summed it up in their book *The Kingdom of Coal*:
"On the question of the very existence of a society called the Molly Maguires, even professional historians have been unable to give an incontrovertible verdict . . . And as to whether the anthracite Irishmen were class heroes
or cutthroat vigilantes concerned more with getting even than with getting
fair treatment for their brethren—well, the answer still depends, in the region at least, on which side your ancestors took."[11]

The lack of consensus about the Molly Maguires may in part reflect the
fact that for a century after the organization first appeared in Pennsylvania,
many writers tended to view the violence in a primarily American context,
rather than an Irish one. Until about twenty-five years ago, two of the most
important (if elusive) elements of the anthracite troubles—their Civil War
origins and their roots in the peasant mores of the Ulster borderlands—
were often glossed over. In recent decades there have been big strides on
both fronts. In 1990 the historian Grace Palladino published *Another Civil
War*, a groundbreaking study of the labor troubles in the West Branch region during the 1860s. And the historian Kevin Kenny framed the anthracite violence in an Irish context in his 1998 book *Making Sense of the Molly
Maguires*.[12] My work augments theirs, exploring in detail the relationship

between Irish folk culture and the Mollies—a link so profound in famine-era Ireland that it echoed across the Atlantic during the Civil War.

The key to understanding what happened in the anthracite region in the 1860s is the realization that it was one of the few rural areas of the United States where Irish Catholic immigrants settled in such concentrated numbers that they retained the folk culture of the Irish countryside. Indeed, the Mollies were but one aspect of a transplanted culture that included the Irish language (most of the Mollies were Gaelic speakers), keening and wake games, belief in fairies, and holiday customs like mummery.

What follows is an attempt to explain and place in an Irish context the draft resistance, labor unrest, military occupation, and premeditated murder that wracked the anthracite region during and immediately after the Civil War—to show why the violence broke out when it did and how it did.

It is also an attempt to set the record straight, for much of what we think we know about the origins of the Molly Maguires is unproven at best, and wrong at worst. The name almost certainly does not come from an old widow evicted from her Irish farm by a callous landlord. There is no contemporary evidence whatsoever that the organization was founded in the County Longford village of Ballinamuck in the 1830s, as the Irish Mollies claimed, or near Carrickmacross in County Monaghan in 1843, as a landlord's agent famously claimed. The Jeremiah Reilly who in that same period supposedly transplanted the organization to Cass Township, Pennsylvania, does not appear in any records from that time and place. And the first victim of cold, calculated Molly violence was not a mine boss, but an Irish mine worker.

Last but not least, this book is an attempt to examine some of the consequences of the violence. For the impact of the West Branch troubles, like the river itself, did not remain dammed up in the hills of Cass Township. The effects of the conflict flowed out, slowly at first, but gaining strength over time, widening and deepening, forever altering the industrial landscape of eastern Pennsylvania and areas far beyond.

My journey tracing the course of those troubles is nearly as long and twisted as the river itself. It began with a discussion of family history. My mother was born on the banks of the West-West, into an extended clan of Lynches and O'Connors. As a young girl she was lulled to sleep on summer nights by the soft babble of water over rock outside her bedroom window. It was the sound of the Schuylkill a few feet away, still small enough to jump, slowly cutting its way into Mine Hill. Her ancestors had come from Ulster, and worked the Forestville mines for generations.

Pat Lynch, whose rendition of "The Phoenix Park Colliery" is now in the Library of Congress, was her uncle—so was his brother Pete, who died in the breaker. Like all the Lynches and O'Connors of that generation, Pat died before I was old enough to ask him about the Molly Maguires, and why they first turned up at Phoenix Park when his father was a young mine laborer there.

To find the answers my older relatives might have supplied, I have haunted Harrisburg archives and Minersville cemeteries; dug through military correspondence in the National Archives and old newspapers in the Library of Congress in Washington; read crumbling reports of long-forgotten crimes in Dublin, compared the texts of mummers plays outside Belfast, and visited a museum in the home of a murdered landlord in County Roscommon. I have examined Pinkerton detective reports in Wilmington, Delaware; pored over court records in Pottsville and trial transcripts in Jim Thorpe, Pennsylvania; checked out census data in Philadelphia and coal company correspondence in New York; and toured Irish battlefields.

The result may not be an "incontrovertible verdict" that finally lays to rest all the controversy about one of the longest and most murderous industrial conflicts the nation has ever seen. But it does strip away some of the gray mist of myth, misinformation, and propaganda that has long shrouded the origins of the Molly Maguires. Here, then, is the story of when, where, how, and why the first of America's labor wars began.

1

"A Slumbering Volcano"

Subterranean spirits might dwell in burning mountains, or occupy themselves in mining ... Many Irish legends relate to such. They may appear as Daome-Shi [fairies], dressed in green, with mischievous intent.

—James Bonwick

The first of the assassinations came at the dawn of the year, in the middle of the day, in the shadow a burning mountain. The last came nearly thirteen years later, on a December night as black as anthracite. Both killings involved teams of gunmen, opening fire in the home of an Irish immigrant. In many ways, the murders were mirror images of each other—the bookends of a shadowy struggle that left dozens dead in the hard-coal fields of northeastern Pennsylvania in the latter half of the nineteenth century.

Those marked for death in the two attacks stood on opposite sides of that struggle. The first victim was a former militiaman whose murder was blamed on a violent secret society. The last victims were a member of that secret society and his pregnant sister-in-law. A militia unit's second-in-command was implicated in the killings.

In neither case was anyone ever brought to justice. For generations, the exact motives have remained a mystery.

The first killing took place in a valley that was often swathed in sulfurous fumes. The fire in the burning mountain had blazed long and deep, but when exactly it erupted remains something of a mystery. One account says it all began in the darkest recesses of winter, on December 13, 1840; another claims it was 1835. Local folklore is short on specifics but long on atmosphere.

The miners were going for a vein of anthracite so thick it was known as "the jugular" near the village of Coal Castle, Pennsylvania, in the Heckscherville Valley of Schuylkill County. In 1932, an eighty-six-year-old resident of the valley told a folklorist that water trickling down into a mine had frozen, turning the underground chambers into a palace of shimmering black ice, with frozen stalactites reaching down from the roof and crystals coating the anthracite walls. The miners, so the story goes, lit a fire on a Saturday to melt the ice, then left, returning on Monday to find the shaft and the face of the coal seam ablaze. The local newspaper, relating the story decades after the fact, reported that two of the miners entered the burning pit to retrieve their tools, never to return.[1]

While the newspaper said it was common practice to set fires in grates to prevent mine water from freezing, *Scientific American* blamed the blaze on "careless miners." The phrase had very specific legal ramifications. Because carelessness by a miner—any miner, not just the dead one—could absolve a mine operator of liability for a fatal accident, "careless miner" became a stock phrase for those who would have otherwise borne the responsibility.[2]

However and whenever it started, the underground fire burned for years, at times leaving the valley below and the hidden stream that ran through it enveloped in steam and smoke.

"It has even roasted the rocky strata above it, destroying every trace of vegetation along the line of the breast, and causing vast yawning chasms, where the earth has fallen in, from which issue hot and sulfurous fumes, as from a volcano," one observer wrote in the 1843. Elsewhere, the fire hollowed out portions of the hill. Anyone traversing those areas ran the risk of plunging through the upper crust, perhaps three or four feet, into pits of ash up to one hundred feet deep. The fire was "still burning, like a slumbering volcano," in 1855.[3]

By June 21, 1861, when David J. Kennedy painted a watercolor of the scene, *Mine Hill Gap and Burning Mountain*, there was just the barest hint of the underground fire—a bare patch and two bare trees on the mountain in the background—but there was also the suggestion of a more recent conflagration. A rifleman in blue appears along the rail line through the gap, though it is not clear whether he is a Union Army soldier on patrol or simply a hunter, out for a stroll in the lingering light of the summer solstice.[4]

For the Irish immigrants who dominated the valley, the underground inferno was a mixed curse. By 1858, word had spread that sulfur-laden water from the burning mine cured rheumatism, restored twisted limbs, and even rejuvenated a broken-down old colliery mule. People from far and wide made the pilgrimage to Coal Castle to cure their afflictions.

In that sense, the mine water was akin to the holy wells of Ireland that were said to effect miraculous cures, and when some enterprising miners decided to sell barrels of the stuff for profit, the older Irish of the area were aghast at the sacrilege. Holy wells were not to be profaned—indeed, it was said they could lose their powers if desecrated by a murder nearby. So perhaps the fate of the burning mine's healing waters should come as no surprise. "The day came when their misgivings were realized," the folklorist George Korson wrote of the Irish. "The snow no longer melted on the mountain in the winter. Its water became like any other sulfurous mine water. The magic mine had grown cold!"[5]

It was here in the shadow of Mine Hill, where miracles were born of fire and brimstone and peasant belief clashed head on with the capitalist spirit, that one of the century's most sensational campaigns of cold, calculated killing began, on a winter's day just about a quarter century after the start of the mine fire. It was these burning hills that gave birth to the Molly Maguires of Pennsylvania.

What defined a Molly Maguire was the resort to conspiratorial violence— during the potato famine in Ireland, teams of Mollies, often dressed as women, had murdered grasping Irish landlords and local magistrates with ruthless efficiency. That sort of organized, premeditated violence claimed its first life in this country on January 2, 1863, in the village of Coal Castle, under that "smoldering volcano" at Mine Hill Gap.*

The Mollies would gain infamy in Pennsylvania for killing mine bosses, but the man gunned down in Coal Castle that day was an Irish-born mine worker, James Bergen, a wounded Union soldier who had spent his entire life under a series of rumbling volcanoes.

Bergen was born in Ireland around 1833, almost certainly near Castlecomer, County Kilkenny, a coal-mining center. Castlecomer natives, several named Bergen, poured into Coal Castle and other mining villages along the western branches of the Schuylkill River in the years before the Civil War. Local tradition holds that a Heckscherville mine operator, William Payne, went to Ireland in 1845 to recruit men from Queen's and Kilkenny Counties to dig Schuylkill anthracite, which was similar to the hard coal the Irishmen mined.[6]

Bergen was born in a period when poverty, not Britain, was the true ruler of rural Ireland. The authorities labored mightily, and with only middling success, to stem an epidemic of violence by secret peasant societies that, like the Mollies, were intent on enforcing traditional notions of the

---

* The fatal beating of a Carbon County mine boss, Frank Langdon, in June 1862 would later be described as the first Molly murder, but it occurred outside a tavern, and the weapons used, sticks and stones, were not the choice weapons of Molly assassins. The killing, neither cold nor calculated, was linked to the Mollies only fifteen years afterward, when it served the purposes of a coal company.

social contract. In the early 1830s, when Bergen was born, the coal fields of Queen's County and County Kilkenny were beset by a secret society called the Whitefeet, which sought to improve conditions for miners and peasants. In November 1831, a band of Whitefeet clashed with the police on the border between the two counties. When several members of the group were arrested, a crowd attempted to rescue them. In the ensuing battle, between seven and ten people were killed, and up to fifty were wounded.[7]

For all the violence, the real horror came just as Bergen reached puberty, with the failure of the potato crop from 1845 to 1850. The great famine decimated agrarian Ireland. It is estimated that more than a million died, and more than a million emigrated.

Among the immigrants were many Bergens. Some had already made it to Pennsylvania by 1850—the census for that year shows five families listed variously as Bergan, Bergen, and Bergin living in close proximity in the Heckscherville Valley in Cass Township. At least one head of a Coal Castle household, Michael Bergin, had been married in Castlecomer. Up the valley in Heckscherville lived William Bergan, a native of County Kilkenny.[8] The overlap in children's given names suggests that many of the Bergen families were related. The men were all Irish-born miners or mine laborers. And they soon learned of the dangers that smoldered deep below the surface.

In June 1853, John Bergen, sixteen, was driving a mule in a Heckscherville mine when a fellow worker began teasing the beast. Annoyed, the boy offered some fighting words, whereupon his antagonist hit him in the forehead with a pick, killing him, according to the local paper. The attacker escaped.[9]

It is possible that the killing was not isolated. Just a month before John Bergen was killed, the newspaper reported that a James Burger has been shot in the jaw at Payne's Mines—another name for Heckscherville—after an altercation with an Arthur O'Neal.[10] John Bergen's father was named James, and the newspaper sometimes rendered the family's last name with an "r" instead of an "n," in which case the victim in the shooting might have been John Bergen's father.

The motive for this violence, if it was connected, remains murky, though regional rivalries may have played a role. The Bergens were from southern Ireland, and the mid-May shooting involved a man with a distinctly northern name—O'Neal. There was certainly tension in Cass Township between natives of the various parts of Ireland. Almost a year to the date after the O'Neal shooting, a riot erupted in Mackeysburg, at the western end of the Heckscherville Valley, between "Far-downs," or Ulstermen, and natives of

Connacht, the western Irish province.[11] And various early accounts about the origins of the Molly Maguires, including one written by a Schuylkill County resident, speak of tensions or "a feud" between Kilkenny natives and those from other counties in Ireland.[12]

John Bergen's family left the area after his killing, but a second James Bergen stepped into this violent world sometime between 1850 and 1855, settling just down the road from Heckscherville in Coal Castle. The village had about seventy homes in 1845, but that number swelled with the influx of famine immigrants over the next ten years.[13]

Nicknamed "Yellow Boy" for his fair hair and complexion, Bergen, like most of his neighbors in the predominately Irish Cass Township, worked in the anthracite mines. Though his new life was hard and dangerous, Bergen found time for romance and the military. By about 1855 he had found a wife, Elizabeth; they had a daughter the following year. Bergen also volunteered as a private in the Columbian Infantry, an almost entirely Irish American militia unit based in Glen Carbon, just up the valley on the other side of Heckscherville.[14] The names on its rolls—Brennan, Lawler, Tobin, Mealy, O'Brien, Whelan, and, of course, Bergen—suggest that the bulk of the unit were natives of Kilkenny and Queen's Counties.

As the crisis between the North and South mounted in the late 1850s Bergen's family continued to grow. By 1860, he and Elizabeth had three children ranging in age from four years to six months.[15]

With the eruption of the Civil War, Bergen's unit was mustered into service on April 21, 1861, as Company C of the 5th Pennsylvania Infantry. The regiment had some trouble reaching Washington—Confederate sympathizers in Maryland were suspected of sabotaging the train tracks—but on April 27, the 5th Pennsylvania arrived in the nation's capital, where it was greeted by President Lincoln.[16] The regiment was in service for three months. During the first battle of Bull Run it was on outpost duty in Alexandria, Virginia, and mustered out in late July, without seeing any real fighting.

Bergen missed combat at the front, but it appears he found some at home. A James Bergen went on trial on December 4, 1861, in Schuylkill County court for assault and battery with intent to kill in an incident involving a John Curran. Though the motive for the crime is unclear, it is all but certain that defendant James Bergen was Pvt. James Bergen. The names of two witnesses in the case—William Brennan and Matthew Maley—match those of privates in Bergen's unit, Company C. A jury convicted Bergen on December 7, but his sentence was suspended.[17]

In Coal Castle on November 24, Pvt. Bergen enrolled in the 48th Pennsylvania Infantry, a new regiment raised entirely in Schuylkill County. He was mustered in on December 23 at Hatteras Inlet, North Carolina.[18] The timing is consistent with the trial and its outcome, and strongly suggests that Bergen was allowed to avoid punishment by reenlisting.

The bargain proved a poor one. The 48th fought in some of the bloodiest battles of the war—Fredericksburg, Antietam, and Petersburg. In the spring of 1862, the regiment saw action at New Bern, North Carolina. The 48th was pulled out of the Carolinas in early July for duty in Virginia, and on August 29, at 2:25 P.M., it went into the line at the Second Battle of Bull Run. The 48th spearheaded a three-regiment assault on Stonewall Jackson's Confederates, who were holding a line along an unfinished railroad cut in a wooded area.

Capt. James Wren, commanding Company B, described what happened next in a vivid diary entry: "We was ordered to cease firing & then ordered to fix baynet & we Charged the Cut & routed the enemy out of the Cut & we held the Cut & we war advancing beyond the Cut when a masked battrey opened and drove us Back into the Cut & while we were advancing beyond the Cut, our Left was unsupported and the enemy got around our left & got in our rear & we then had a fire to Contend against in front and rear."[19]

The regiment made its way back to Union lines, but lost seven dead and sixty-one wounded.[20] Among the injured was James Bergen. Hospitalized for a time with a wounded arm, he eventually returned to his wife, Elizabeth, and their three children in Coal Castle. As with the two men who reentered the burning mine in Coal Castle twenty-five years before, going back proved a fatal mistake.

Capt. Wren had recorded in his diary on May 6, 1862, after a heavy storm the day before, that the slaves around New Bern "have a Kind of superstition that thear was a heavy battle Fought yesterday, which caused the trouble of the elements."[21] May 5 did indeed mark the beginning of a battle, for as Wren, Bergen, and the rest of the regiment sought shelter from torrential rains at Fort Totten, North Carolina, 1,500 mine workers went on strike for higher pay throughout the West Branch region of Schuylkill County, which includes Cass, Foster, Reilly, and Branch Townships. Led by men who preferred to remain in the shadows, the walkout was the spark for a long conflagration.

By the end of the week, a front-page headline in Philadelphia was trumpeting "The War at the Coal Mines." With no settlement several days into the strike, the largely Irish workers stopped the pumps that prevented water from flooding the mines. The governor of Pennsylvania dispatched more than eight hundred troops from Philadelphia to occupy the mining villages of Heckscherville and Forestville, where the strikers were reported to be heavily armed. A settlement was reached before there were any clashes, but sporadic labor trouble continued through early July.[22]

Thus, the Cass Township to which the Bergen returned after he was wounded in August was a far different place than the one he had left. If the intervention of troops in a labor dispute had helped sour many Cass Township residents on Union blue, the launching of a state militia draft a few months later completed the job. Benjamin Bannan, the Pottsville newspaper publisher appointed to administer the draft in Schuylkill County, was a Radical Republican and proud bigot with intimate ties to the coal industry. The son of a Protestant Ulsterman, he hated Irish Catholics, Democrats, and unions, and conceived a special loathing for Cass Township, where all three flourished.

To Bannan, the militia draft was a handy broom for sweeping troublesome union activists and Irish Catholic Democrats from the mining villages along the West Branch into the maw of a bloody civil war, where they would have no chance to either strike or vote. With the connivance of Republican state officials, Bannan set unusually high quotas for Cass Township. At a time when soldiers in the field were denied the franchise, he then urged that the draft be held before a crucial election, to ensure a Republican victory.[23]

Shredding the anthracite region's frayed social contract, the political abuse of conscription by Bannan proved a catastrophic miscalculation. For among the bulwarks of the Irish community in Schuylkill County was the Hibernian Benevolent Society, a fraternal group rooted in the Catholic secret societies of northern Ireland, which had long experience in fighting precisely this sort of official persecution.

A direct ancestor of the Hibernians—a secret society called the Defenders—had led resistance to a militia draft in Ireland in the 1790s, when miners opposed to conscription shut down and threatened to flood collieries in the Kilkenny coal fields.[24] When the Defenders were suppressed after joining the United Irishmen in the great, failed uprising of 1798, they evolved into another secret society, the Ribbonmen. An American branch of the Ribbonmen—the Hibernians—was founded in 1836 by Irish immigrants in Schuylkill County and New York City. The anthracite Hibernians quickly became involved in Democratic politics and labor issues, and they appear to have been the driving force behind the May strike.

Bannan's political manipulation of the 1862 draft thus forced some Schuylkill County Hibernians back into their old role as outlawed defenders of the oppressed. The new militancy quickly became evident. In October

1862, Gov. Andrew Curtin of Pennsylvania wrote the War Department in Washington about organized draft resistance in Schuylkill County by up to one thousand armed men, many of whom feared that freed slaves would take their jobs in the mines. Hundreds of armed miners marched through Cass Township that month, shutting down the collieries, and newspapers suggested that a shadowy organization was behind the trouble.[25]

To avert open warfare, local officials, with Washington's support, drew up affidavits stating that Cass Township's quota had been filled by volunteers who joined military units from adjacent towns, such as the Ringgold Rifles of Minersville, the Minersville Artillerists, and James Bergen's old unit, the Columbian Infantry of Glen Carbon.

Bannan's attempt to dragoon his political and economic foes had failed, for the time being. He retreated to his newspaper, damning the Cass Irish and their political leaders as Southern sympathizers, and urgently calling for martial law.

In the wake of the successful draft resistance, new labor troubles wracked the West Branch region. By December 1862, strikers were using the name "Molly Maguire"—a nickname for the Hibernians—as both a battle cry and a signature on "coffin notices," or death threats aimed at mine bosses. Amid the industrial chaos, signs of a crackdown loomed clear.

On December 27, 1862, Bannan's newspaper, the *Miners' Journal*, announced the appointment of Charlemagne Tower as provost marshal to enforce future drafts in Schuylkill County. It described Tower as "a firm, conscientious gentlemen" who would "discharge the duties of his office with zeal and fidelity." He was also a coal baron who only a few years before, during a stint as Schuylkill County district attorney, had prosecuted striking Irish miners on conspiracy charges, ensuring that future strikes could succeed only if they were, in fact, a conspiracy.

On January 1, 1863, the Emancipation Proclamation took effect, worsening the fears of many West Branch residents that if they were drafted freed slaves would replace them in the mines. The very next day, "Yellow Boy" Bergen's luck finally ran out. It had carried him through the great famine, years of work in notoriously dangerous mines, and a cataclysmic civil war. It would not survive Schuylkill County politics. On Friday, January 2, five strangers entered the Bergen home, asking for ale. It seems the wounded veteran and his wife had opened an unlicensed beerhouse, or "shebeen." (Cass Township boasted scores of such establishments, and an Elizabeth Bergen stood trial in June 1863 on charges of selling liquor without a license.)[26]

When Bergen told the five strangers there was no ale to be had, three drew revolvers and fired, hitting him in the abdomen. They fled, cheering for the president of the Confederacy, Jefferson Davis—an odd utterance for frustrated tipplers, but one that makes perfect sense were the victim killed because he was a two-fisted supporter of the government in an area up in arms against conscription.

Bergen, gutshot, died in agony three days later.[27] He was buried in the old hillside cemetery behind St. Vincent's Church in Minersville. A simple stone marks his grave: "Jas. Bergen, Co. E, 48th Pa. Infantry." An inquest conducted by the Schuylkill County coroner, W. B. Johnson, concluded that Bergen had been shot "by unknown persons."[28]

No charges were ever brought in the case, but a series of attacks in the ensuing days point to a motive.

One week after the Bergen shooting, a gang of forty men attacked the home of John McDonald, between Coal Castle and Heckscherville. McDonald hid in a nearby mine, but the attackers warned his wife they would kill him if they caught him.[29] A John McDonald had served as a private with Company F of the 16th Pennsylvania Infantry, a three-month regiment mustered in at nearby Minersville in April 1861.

Two days after McDonald's home was attacked, two men were shot as they walked together on the road between Heckscherville and Glen Carbon. One was identified as James O'Connor. James Bergen had a neighbor in Coal Castle named James O'Connor, a twenty-five-year-old carpenter with political connections. His brother Patrick, with whom he lived, had served as the township auditor in 1853, and Patrick O'Connor's tavern served as the polling place for north Cass Township.[30]

O'Connor was shot in the hand and legs. His companion, identified only as "Curry of Glen Carbon," was shot in the lung. The latter's first name may be lost, but there was only one family of Currys listed in Foster Township in the 1860 census, and all four of its adult sons—Michael, Daniel, Thomas, and John—had served in military units with Bergen. Both of the Currys in the 48th Regiment, Thomas and John, had been wounded at the Battle of Fredericksburg in December 1862. John was sent to a military hospital in Reading, Pennsylvania, just south of Schuylkill County, and went AWOL on January 2, 1863—the very day that his old comrade was gunned down in Coal Castle. Perhaps he had heard the news, and felt compelled to discover why the valley he called home was turning against soldiers in Union blue.[31]

Whatever Curry's first name, he had served with Bergen and belonged to a family with government and management sympathies—Daniel Curry was a young colliery superintendent at the time of the shooting, and raised a volunteer company about six months later to help repel Lee's invasion of Pennsylvania.[32] The victim was shot as he spoke with a politically connected neighbor of Bergen's, barely a week after a slaying with strong political overtones. He was the third soldier attacked over the course of nine days in a short stretch of the Heckscherville Valley.

Popular tradition attributed the attacks on Bergen, McDonald, Curry, and O'Connor to the Molly Maguires, but the few historians who mentioned the incidents were stumped. Francis P. Dewees, writing in 1877 about the shooting of O'Connor and Curry, said, "The whole affair is a mystery." He may have missed the connection with the Bergen killing because of a typo—a chronology in his book, the first on the subject, placed the killing in 1864.

J. Walter Coleman, writing in 1930s, pointed out that Bergen, McDonald, O'Connor, and Curry were all of Irish extraction: "The fact that the attacks occurred within a radius of a few miles may indicate that the assailants had a common plan, or belonged to a single organization. On the other hand, there is no apparent reason an Irish gang would have singled out these members of their own race as victims."[33]

In light of their service records and the recent military occupation of Cass Township, the reason they were singled out seems clear—three of the four were Union Army veterans living in an area where government troops had suppressed a strike just months before, and where a new military crackdown seemed imminent.

Bergen had also belonged to a militia unit that was dominated by Kilkenny men, at a time and in a place when there were tensions between natives of that county and some other elements of the Irish community. What is more, he likely alienated his own comrades with the 1861 attempted murder case—two testified against him—and angered the Irish community at large by joining the Union Army to evade punishment. If the Mollies wanted to make an example of a soldier, they could have picked no more isolated a victim for their first cold-blooded killing.

One intriguing hint that the Bergen slaying was committed on behalf of the community, as a form of folk justice, lies in its timing (on the day after New Year's) and its circumstances (a visit by a band of men to a home).

For generations, secret society assassins in Ireland had targeted those perceived as breaking society's rules with attacks that took place around— but rarely on—festive holidays like New Year's or Halloween. The killers' timing and their disguises—women's clothing, straw clothing, blackface or whiteface—were meant to signal that the killers were acting on behalf of the community, for it linked them to a far more benevolent custom in the Irish countryside: mummery.

Well into the twentieth century, bands of Irish mummers promoted community cohesion by visiting homes during the Christmas season, dressed as women, or in straw, or with painted faces. They solicited drinks, food, and money in return for the performance of a "combat play" that always included the killing of one character. The money was used to pay for a community party, and admitting the mummers to one's home affirmed one's acceptance of the rules of communal life in the Irish countryside. During the potato famine, men in costumes identical to the mummers began visiting homes in the same region, at the same time of year, demanding a contribution to help the starving. They were Molly Maguires, members of the last of Ireland's great peasant conspiracies, and when they did not get what they wanted, the killing became very real.

Mummery had long flourished in Pennsylvania. But in the years just before the Civil War, a peculiar form of mummery, one rooted in opposition to compulsory militia service, had appeared in Schuylkill County. So, too, had assassination on behalf of the community, by Irishmen in disguises that mimicked those of the Irish mummers. The first such killing involved a man who, like Bergen, was thought to have evaded justice for a violent crime against an Irishman. It took place on December 30, 1846, nearly sixteen years to the day before Bergen was slain. The killer had a face as white as a mime's.

The link between festive custom and early Molly Maguire violence is thrown into sharp relief by another killing in the hard-coal fields in 1863. The victim, George K. Smith, was a mine superintendent from Audenried, Carbon County, just over the Schuylkill County line. Like Bergen, he was an isolated and belligerent supporter of the government in an area that had been occupied by government troops. Like Bergen, he was killed in his home by a band of men around a holiday.

On November 5, less than a week after Halloween, several men with false whiskers and blackened faces burst into Smith's home and shot him dead. This time there was no doubt about who was behind the crime: "Molly McGuires on the Rampage" read a front-page headline in the New York Times. Fifteen years later, a witness told a Carbon County court that Smith was killed because he was helping the government enforce the draft, and that the organization behind the killing went by three names—the Hibernians, the Molly Maguires, and the Buckshots.[34]

Thus the real mystery to emerge from the January 1863 killing of James Bergen in Cass Township is not so much why he was gunned down, or even who was behind the attack, which set the mold for future Molly Maguire killings in the coal fields. The real—and far deeper—mystery is threefold: What was the relationship between the holiday festivities of groups like the mummers and the holiday mayhem of a secret society like the Molly Maguires? How was that organization transplanted from Ireland to the hills of northeastern Pennsylvania? And why did it emerge when it did, and where it did? The answers to the first two questions lie in the blood-soaked soil of Ulster.

Part II

2

The Black Pig's Realm

So it was prophesied . . . that no rebellion ever was or could be of any use
that did not commence in the Valley of the Black Pig.

—William Carleton

Ireland's greatest river rises from the Shannon Pot, a small spring-fed pool
nestled in the lap of Cuilcagh mountain, which straddles the border between the Irish Republic and Northern Ireland in the far west of County
Cavan.

Trees climb into the mountain mists as cows and sheep graze the thin
fields around the pool. Nearby stands an abandoned cottage, a mute reminder of the struggle against evictions here on the eve of the potato famine. It is a high, lonesome place, lost to time and haunted by dark legend.

The wellspring and the river are said to be named for Sionna, the grand-
daughter of the great sea god Lir. The legends vary, but they all have Sionna
drowning, usually at an undersea well of wisdom—the fountainhead of
all knowledge—with her body bobbing up from that hole in the earth
here, the Shannon Pot. The notion that the spring is connected to some vast,
hidden world survives—neighbors believe it is linked by an underground
stream to the Claddach, the river that flows from the Marble Arch Caves
just over the mountains in neighboring County Fermanagh. They tell
stories of how chaff tossed into the Claddach will bubble forth from the
Shannon Pot.[1]

In Irish, Cavan means "the hollow place."

From its source in the parish of Glangevlin, the Shannon runs southwest through the ancient kingdom of Breifne, to Dowra, on the Cavan/
Leitrim County line, where there stands a remnant of the Black Pig's Dyke,
an intermittent earthwork named for the enchanted boar that legend says
used its tusks to furrow the Ulster border. Running the length of the island,
from County Down to Donegal Bay, the dyke dates to 95 B.C.E. and sealed

the few entrances to Ulster left by the hills, bogs, and lakes. Scientists have found evidence that suggests a link between these frontier fortifications and Emain Macha, the fortress of ancient Ulster's renowned warrior brotherhood, the Red Branch.[2]

From Dowra the river flows into Lough Allen, which is sandwiched between Slieve Anierin, or the iron mountain, in Leitrim and the coal-rich Kilronan Mountain in County Roscommon. The river emerges from the lake near Drumshanbo and continues south, forming the border between Counties Roscommon and Leitrim, and later, Longford, before flowing south to the sea.

The Shannon's watershed, in its upper reaches, roughly approximates the realm of another mythical Irishwoman whose name has long been associated with untimely death—Molly Maguire. The violent secret society that came to be called the Molly Maguires was born in the Ulster borderlands of western Cavan and Leitrim, the offspring of a clash between English commerce and Gaelic tradition. The mystique that the Mollies created for themselves utilized motifs that dated back centuries in the folklore and mythology of the region: holiday bloodshed, men seeking vengeance in women's clothes, the slain rising to fight again, and the mythical black pig, which legend linked to Gaelic Ireland's final uprising against the English.

The Mollies' first recorded murder, in Garadice, County Leitrim, took place on January 29, 1845, two days before an important peasant holiday, within a good walk of the site in Ireland most closely linked to blood sacrifice. Magh Slécht ("the plain of adoration") near Ballymagovern in western Cavan was so named because it was there that a legendary king, Tigernmas, and his subjects were said to have ensured the fertility of their fields by sacrificing animals or the first-born child of every family.[3] The sacrifices were offered on Samhain, November 1, the ancient Celtic Halloween, to the idol Crom Cruach:

In dark November
When the two worlds were near each other
He glittered among his subjects,
Blood-crusted, insatiable.[4]

The grimmest tale of Magh Slecht tells how Tigernmas and two-thirds of his followers were slaughtered there by Crom on the eve of Samhain.[5]

It sometimes seems that in the Ulster of old, no holiday went unsanctified with blood. Near Magh Slecht is the town of Ballyconnell, a Molly Maguire stronghold that was named for Conall Cernach, a Red Branch hero who is said to have been slain there by warriors from the kingdom of Connacht on another holiday, Beltane, or May 1.*

Conall Cernach's friendly rivalry with the greatest of Ireland's legendary heroes, Cuchulain, figures in another tale of festive bloodletting, "Bricriu's Feast." At a lavish dinner, a dispute erupts among the Red Branch warriors over who will get the "champion's portion." In the challenges that ensue, Cuchulain decapitates an opponent, only to see him rise, pick up his head, and walk away, returning the next day to fight again.[6] The death-and-resurrection theme echoes down through the ages, in the Arthurian tale "Sir Gawain and the Green Knight," and in a nineteenth-century ghost story from Sligo that relates how, after a man named McMurrough killed a landlord's agent in a duel involving a stick and a sword, the agent's ghost returned to battle McMurrough once more as he wandered the borderlands, a fugitive from justice.[7] Likewise, a Molly Maguire ballad celebrating a sensational murder in 1845 tells how the ghost of the victim, named Bell, "came back from hell" to fight another battle with his killer, Pat Dolan, while Dolan was on the run. The Bell killing took place on June 22, the day after the summer solstice.

The Mollies' proclivity for dressing as women when they sought vengeance evokes another tale linked to the Ulster–Connacht wars, the death of Conn of a Hundred Battles. Conn is credited with forming a central monarchy over Connacht and Meath at Ulster's expense around 200 C.E. According to several versions of the tale, the king of Ulster, seeking to avenge the death of his father, sent dozens of assassins dressed as women to the hill of Tara, the seat of the high kings, where they killed Conn as he prepared to celebrate the triennial festival of Tara. The festival is central to the plot, and one version makes clear that it coincided with Samhain, or Halloween.[8] Conn's descendants, the O'Neills, would get their revenge by conquering the north and ruling it for a thousand years.

Finally, the black pig and its link to Gaelic Ireland's last uprising against the English feature prominently in the tales the Mollies wove about where their movement was born—the hamlet of Ballinamuck. In Irish the name is

* The official history of the Ancient Order of Hibernians rather fancifully traces the organization's lineage to Conall Cernach and the Red Branch order via Rory O'Moore, the seventeenth-century Irish patriot. In volume 1 of his *History of the Ancient Order of Hibernians and Ladies' Auxiliary*, 4 vols. (New York: National Board of the AOH, 1923), O'Dea devotes an entire chapter to O'Moore, saying he was not only descended from Conall, but saw the Red Branch as the model for seventeenth-century Irish resistance to the English.

"Beal Atha na Muice," or "the mouth of the ford of the pig." According to legend, a local man had stopped the black pig from rooting up the border there by striking it on the head with a stone. Eighteen centuries later, the last battle of the 1798 uprising was fought there, and the Gaelic-speaking rebels were slaughtered. In claiming that their movement was born in Ballinamuck, the Mollies were saying that they were the men of '98, risen from the dead to fight again. The notion may seem fantastical, but in 1848, as the Mollies were murdering landlords, an expert on Irish folklore noted the following folk belief about the fairies of Ireland:

> The Tuatha-de-Dananns
> By force of potent spells and wicked magic
> Could raise a slaughtered army from the earth
> And make them live, and breathe, and fight again.[9]

A harmless bit of folklore, perhaps, except that violent secret societies were sometimes referred to as "the fairies."[10]

These motifs from ancient Ulster—the black pig, holiday sacrifice, killers dressed as women, and dead men rising to fight again—were transmitted to the modern era by the oral tradition of the borderlands, most conspicuously in the age-old folk dramas of the mummers and wren boys. Both were pegged to the most important holiday of the year and featured men dressed as women. The sacrifice of a wren was central to the wren boy's performance. The mummers play always featured combat, a killing, and the dead man rising to fight again.

Mummery was a form of trick or treat, an ancient play performed by amateur troupes who visited nearby homes during the Christmas season. The costumes included straw clothing and blackface. The performance was simple—two champions would fight with swords, one would be killed, and a female character would raise money to pay a doctor, who would resurrect the slain man with the words "Rise up dead man and fight again." In addition to echoing "Bricriu's Feast," the action ties the play to ancient agricultural myths of the vegetation god who is wounded, dies, and is resurrected, invariably with the aid of a woman.[11] The symbolism was clear to a peasant audience—a man dressed in straw is cut down, just like a crop being harvested. He rises again, just as the crops do.

The mummers were rewarded for the performance with drinks and money—the payment to "the doctor"—which they used to throw a party. Inviting all the households they had visited, they annually cemented the bonds of community.

The Molly Maguires worked so hard to expropriate the legitimacy of the mummers—dressing in identical costumes, appearing at the same time of year, utilizing the same motifs—that there is every reason to suspect that there was a good deal of overlap between the two groups. Both the festive groups and the secret society tended to attract young, unmarried men. Statistics on agrarian crime for 1844–45 show that while the Mollies were active in the same winter months as the mummers, a curious cease-fire seems to have been declared in exactly those weeks when the mummers traditionally made their rounds. Both before and after the Mollies, there is evidence of connections between violent secret societies and festive groups. Indeed, in the folklore of the western Cavan and south Fermanagh borderlands, the lines between entertainers, rebels, and outlaws were often blurred beyond recognition.

Consider the tales about the rebel bandit "Souple" Corrigan that were collected by the folklorist Henry Glassie for a study of a south Fermanagh region within sight of Cuilcagh. Corrigan was part of a band headed by "Black Francis" McHale that operated in the heartland of the Maguire clan, between the Cavan highlands and the waters of Fermanagh's Lough Erne, in the days when the Catholic Church was all but banned. Like Robin Hood, the outlaws are said to have robbed the rich, in this case the descendants of English conquerors and settlers, to help the poor native tenant farmers who had trouble paying their rent.

The story goes that in one such raid, on an abbey confiscated by the English, Black Francis was captured because he had delayed his getaway in order to upbraid a gang member who had insulted a woman. Corrigan escaped, and disguised himself as a woman to watch the public hanging of Black Francis.

According to another story, Corrigan and a fiddler slipped into the English barracks in Enniskillen in disguise one Christmas Eve, and, as they entertained the drinking troops, learned of a planned government raid on a Mass to be said that night on the slopes of Cuilcagh. The two men headed for the mountain and prepared a successful ambush of the English—"mowed them down," as one man put it, an interesting turn of phrase given the harvest symbolism of the mummers play.[12]

The stories, with their talk of cross-dressing, entertainment, Christmas revelry, and killing, neatly mesh the rebel tradition with some of the key elements of mummery—and the older legends of pagan holiday mayhem.

Even the region's most prominent saint, Mogue, has links to tales of festive bloodshed. Mogue was said to have lived, died, and been buried at Magh Slecht, the old pagan killing ground of Crom Cruach. Emigrants believed that clay from his grave site would guarantee a calm ocean passage, and so little bits of Magh Slecht were carried aboard ships to America.[13] In the full circle of Breifne folk culture, the ancient traditions were never really forgotten—they were sublimated into Christian holidays, the folk drama of the mummers, the tales of Souple Corrigan mowing down his enemies on Christmas Eve. Samhain became All Hallows' Eve. Imbolc, an old festival that began at sunset on January 31 to mark the start of spring, morphed into St. Brigid's feast day on February 1; Lughnasa, an ancient August 1 festival often associated with Crom, became Garland Sunday at the end of July. And on the eve of the famine, the dark old ways came bubbling back to the surface in the form of the Molly Maguires, like so much Fermanagh chaff welling up in the Shannon Pot.

The Red Hand

The mummers play was brought to Ireland by settlers from England and Scotland, and caught on largely because it was so similar to the performances of the wren boys. This pattern—invasion and cultural accommodation—had been going on centuries.

The very symbol of Ulster stems from tales of one such conquest, by the O'Neills of Connacht. According to legend, an O'Neill and a rival chieftain agreed that the man whose hand first touched Ulster's soil would rule it. In the ensuing race, the O'Neill saw his boat slipping behind, and desperate to claim the north as his own, drew a sword and slashed off his own hand, flinging it to shore moments before his rival touched land.[14] Thus a red hand, severed at the wrist, became not just part of the heraldry of the O'Neills and other northern families, but the enduring icon of Ulster, a metaphor for all those invaders who sacrificed some vital part of themselves to possess the soil of the north.

Often what the invaders lost was their very identity. The Vikings raided Ireland and eventually settled there, but were absorbed by the native Irish. The Normans invaded in the twelfth century, and they, too, were eventually subsumed, but not before forcing the Irish chieftains to pay homage to the English crown. In 1316, Robert the Bruce brought over mercenaries from the Hebrides and over the years more followed, aligning themselves with the O'Neills. These mercenaries, or gallowglass, became the Irish MacSweeneys, MacCabes, MacRorys, and MacSheehys.[15]

Over the centuries, England's influence grew, until by the late sixteenth century Ulster remained the last stronghold of Ireland's Celtic aristocracy. The tensions of the Reformation added a religious dimension to the growing divide between London and the earls of Ulster. In the early 1590s, Hugh

Maguire, the lord of Fermanagh, launched a desperate stand against the English. He was joined by Red Hugh O'Donnell, the earl of Tyrconnell, and Hugh O'Neill, the earl of Tyrone. The northern chieftains held out for years, then suffered a crushing defeat on Christmas Eve, 1601, at Kinsale in County Cork, where three thousand Spaniards had landed to assist them.

O'Donnell sailed into exile and died, to be succeeded as head of his clan by Rory O'Donnell. Maguire and O'Neill retreated to the north, where they were eventually forced to submit to the English.

The terms left them in possession of many of their lands, but the independence of Ulster had ended forever. On September 14, 1607, Rory O'Donnell, O'Neill, Maguire, and ninety-seven other northern chieftains sailed from the aching beauty of Donegal's Lough Swilly into voluntary exile on the continent.

"The flight of the earls" set the stage for one last invasion. The English government, determined to subdue Gaelic Ulster once and for all, decided to "plant" the province with settlers from England and Scotland. With the seizure of the land of the departed earls, half a million acres were thrown open to this newest invasion.

By 1630, four thousand English and Scottish families had arrived.[16] Over the next eighty-five years, the numbers multiplied, despite a number of bloody and unsuccessful insurrections that fostered a siege mentality among the settlers. Here was a group that would not be readily absorbed by the native Irish. The settlers' icons became the Red Hand of Ulster and William of Orange on a white horse at the Battle of the Boyne, where the Protestant invader crushed the hopes of Catholic Ireland in 1690.

By 1715, just before the floodgates of Scots–Irish immigration to America opened, Protestants—mostly Anglicans and Presbyterians—accounted for 27 percent of Ireland's population, with the vast majority in the Northeast. The plantation of Ulster had created a new border, between the Catholic south and the heavily Protestant north, which in some ways corresponded with the old Black Pig's Dyke. Counties Antrim and Down were predominantly Protestant, but Counties Armagh, Cavan, Monaghan, Fermanagh, Tyrone, and Donegal held large numbers of Catholics. In south Ulster, Protestants generally occupied the fertile drumlins, or low hills. Catholics were consigned to the higher elevations like Tullyhaw or the marshy lowlands of south Fermanagh and Cavan.

Just below Ulster, Counties Leitrim, Roscommon, Longford, and Louth were a Catholic sea dotted with Protestant islands—the estates of the landlords. As E. Estyn Evans put it, "The interactions of physical, historic and economic factors have kept alive the suspicions of an ancient frontier."[17]

Just as the old frontier was given new meaning, so, too, were some of the old legends. In the half century before the great famine ended, assassins dressed as women would again stalk the border, foreign armies would once more swarm by the Black Pig's Dyke, and blood would again be shed near Magh Slecht, the sacrificial altar to that ancient idol, Crom Cruach.

If Irish history was a nightmare, as James Joyce so famously wrote, it was a recurring one along the Ulster border.

The Unvanquished

Viewed from the top, Catholic Ireland in the mid-eighteenth century was a conquered, colonized nation. In 1750 the Catholic majority owned just 5 percent of the country's land. Catholics were banned from holding public office, practicing a profession, voting, and owning guns. Catholic bishops and clergymen were banished. The very term "Protestant Ascendancy" reflected the lack of a place for Catholics at the upper levels of Irish society.

But viewed from the bottom levels, Ireland remained largely unvanquished. For peasants in the countryside, English rule was distant and had a negligible impact on day-to-day matters connected to wresting a living from the soil. Though they lamented the flight of the earls in song and showed deference to the dispossessed descendants of the Gaelic aristocracy who remained, the majority of peasants held tenaciously to their traditional customs and lifestyle, to their language and their God.

The English conquest had succeeded in imposing political rule on the Irish, but not in changing the communal culture of the peasantry. In this, the remnants of the old landholding families, a sort of Catholic descendancy, played an important role. Serving as "an underground gentry," they helped preserve popular culture as patrons of poets, pipers, bards, and mummers.[18] It was from this alternative culture—Gaelic, communal, and traditional—that new challenges to English law would spring for generations after the mid-1700s.

The English had recognized from the first that they could not hold Ireland without transforming its culture. "We must change their course of government, clothing, customs, manner of holding land, and habit of life," Sir George Carew said of the Irish during the Elizabethan era. "Otherwise it will be impossible to set up in them obedience." Sir George knew of what he spoke, having played a crucial role in the defeat of O'Neill and the plantation of Ulster.[19]

Nearly three hundred years later, another Englishman acknowledged the failure of Carew's program and took steps to undo it. "Old Irish ideas were never supplanted except by the rude hand of violence," said William

Gladstone, the Liberal prime minister for much of the late nineteenth century who pushed through two Irish land reform acts. He decried "laws written on the State Book, but never entering into the heart of the Irish people."[20]

The failure of English law and English culture to enter the hearts of the Irish people stems in part from the fact that from the time of Carew to the era of Gladstone, the English language never managed to fully conquer Ireland. Gaelic was marginalized, but in those margins it survived as a repository for the legends of old. It has been argued that the structure of the Irish language reflected and reinforced a collective, dependent, and conservative outlook. A part of the Gaelic speaker's worldview was the notion that action should be anonymous and collective. Glimpses of that worldview survived the switch to English; in south Fermanagh, for example, to "join" work means to begin it—the assumption being that work cannot be begun alone.[21]

For many peasants, anonymity and collectivism were reinforced by their vast distance from the landlords whose soil they depended on for sustenance. Absentee ownership and the middleman system ensured that there were many levels between the men who owned the soil and those who actually tilled it. A Frenchman who toured Ireland in 1796 described the arrangement: "A rich man, unwilling to be at any trouble, lets a large tract of country to one man, who does not intend to cultivate it himself, but to let it out to three or four others; those who have large shares farm them to about a score, who again let them to about a hundred comfortably situated peasants, who give them at an exorbitant price to about a thousand poor laborers, whom necessity obliges to take their scanty portion at a price far beyond its value."[22]

At the very bottom of this system were the landless agricultural laborers who depended on the seasonal rental of small pieces of land for growing potatoes. The system, called conacre, ensured the laborers food and employment when land was scarce but labor was not.[23]

The collective nature of the Irish peasant's communal lifestyle is perhaps best illustrated by the rundale–clachan system of land use. Under rundale, a handful of leaders from a small cluster of houses, or "clachan," might jointly lease land on behalf of twenty or more households, then divide it into two or three categories, based on its quality, and apportion some of each category to their fellow tenants.[24] The land was periodically redistributed—in some areas, every three years—by the leaders, or "head of quarters." All the cattle grazed together, in mountainous areas unsuited for farming and in the fields after harvest.

There were two problems with clachans, as far as the authorities and the landlords were concerned. The first was that the degree of autonomy and peasant solidarity they fostered was considered to be inherently subversive. One such community in County Monaghan, Blackstaff, near Carrickmacross, was broken up in part because of "the dangers apprehended from this irregular union of a number of families during the disturbed period of 1798." Among the clachan's "extraordinary" customs was its annual election of a mayor with power to settle all disputes among its two hundred households.[25]

The social cohesiveness promoted by clachans and rundale may have been perceived by the authorities as "irregular," but few doubted its strength, and the threat that strength posed. An observer in Galway in the 1820s noted that the system "tends to encourage such strong attachments, generally strengthened through intermarriage . . . This is frequently the source of much disturbance at fairs and any public meeting."[26]

The rundale–clachan lifestyle was also inimical to the interests of the landlords, allowing almost unlimited subdivision of a family's plot. The landlord George Hill, writing in 1845 about his estate in Gweedore, County Donegal, complained that rundale "was a complete bar to any improvement" of the land, for any farmer who began work in his fields early would only see the fruits of his labors devoured by his neighbors' cows. The divisions between the many separate plots required by rundale consumed an inordinate amount of land—25 percent, by one estimate—and there were numerous disagreements and disputes over the reapportionment of land.[27]

Avoiding and resolving such disputes were among the prime functions of Irish peasant society. Indeed, at the very heart of the struggle for control of the Irish countryside lay the question of who should settle such disagreements—a clachan's "mayor" or elders, the landlord, a magistrate, or secret societies acting in the name of the community. And every bit as illuminating as the question of how land disputes were to be resolved was the question of how they were to be avoided. For it was toward that end that the peasants of Ireland developed an elaborate series of festive rituals that sought to repair the frayed ends of the communal social fabric— and to test the intentions of those in a position to unravel it.

Mummery and the Peasant Calendar

Peasant life in eighteenth- and nineteenth-century Ireland was certainly poor, nasty, brutish, and short, to steal a phrase from Hobbes, but there were certain days that rose above the drudgery. These festive "great days" included St. Brigid's Day, February 1, the traditional start of the farmer's year; Easter;

May 1, or Beltane, the first day of the peasants' summer; Midsummer's Day, celebrated either June 23 or June 28; Lughnasa, the harvest festival that morphed into Garland Sunday and Black Crom's Sunday, on either the last Sunday of July or the first Sunday of August; Samhain, the first day of winter, on November 1; Christmas; and New Year's.

These were days not only for celebration and togetherness, but for testing and reaffirming the collective and interdependent nature of peasant life. In a world without insurance policies, people needed to be able to count on one another for help—to bring in the harvest, cut turf for fuel, or help find a missing cow. Phelim McGuire, a Leitrim resident who lived through the famine, recalled decades later that the sharing of work played an important role in the community: "A man would give another a day's labor at a set job such as building or roofing a house that had to be finished quickly. He would then be paid back at some time with similar work."[28]

It was a small, tight-knit world—the neighbors turned to for help were often relatives. In his classic study of a rural Irish community in the 1930s, Conrad Arensberg noted that even that far into the twentieth century, failure to fulfill the obligations of cooperation could bring punitive action on the part of the aggrieved.[29] In this world, a favor unreturned amounted to not just insurance fraud, but a betrayal of blood ties. Reciprocity was a key to keeping the peace with one's neighbors and kinsmen.

Keeping the peace with the landlords was even more important—no small issue in a country where many of the landlords were the descendants of foreign conquerors who discriminated against the natives. The key here was a sort of grand bargain—as long as landlords granted the peasants enough land to live off of, the peasants recognized their right to own the land, no matter how inequitable the relationship. As one historian of nineteenth-century Ireland put it, peasant recognition "of the legitimacy of unequal relationships implies the existence of obligations on the part of the powerful to those who are less so."[30]

A crisis was the worst time to learn of a neighbor's withdrawal from the system of mutual support, or a landlord's abandonment of his traditional obligations to his tenants, so a series of festive rituals were used to test everyone in the neighborhood several times a year. The rituals varied from place to place, but in their essential elements, there was a remarkable continuity. They involved small bands moving in procession from house to house, bestowing a favor in the form of a performance, and demanding food, drink, or money in return.

The performers were often men masquerading as women, or dressed in straw costumes, brightly colored clothing, or white shirts or smocks. At times they simply turned their clothes inside out. Often they were disguised in blackface or whiteface. They received a treat at the end of the performance, and the household's obligations to its neighbors were symbolically acknowledged and reaffirmed.

The means were festive, but the purpose was serious, so there was an edge to many of the performances. A failure to admit the performers, and thus affirm one's commitment to the community, could sometimes result in retribution. And the props often carried an implicit threat. In the spring of 1842, a Capt. Fitzmaurice of Balla, County Mayo, was visited by a group of "Mayboys" in white shirts, some carrying swords. They wanted a drink—a simple affirmation of the captain's adherence to the rules of the countryside— but Fitzmaurice failed the test miserably. Feeling threatened, he tried to seize the swords, and the whole mess ended up in court.[31]

This was the trick or treat of Halloween writ large, a tradition carried on by young adults with a serious stake in the future of the community they were someday to inherit. On the eve of St. Brigid's Day (once called Imbolc), the February 1 start of the farming season, groups of young people called "Biddies" or "biddy boys" carried a likeness of the saint from house to house, levying tribute in the form of food and money. In the south and the west, the Biddies were young musicians dressed in women's clothing, white shirts, and hats of straw. Led by a captain, they would entertain at homes.[32] On Easter, in County Wexford, groups of four to six "Tobies" paraded, dressing "as fantastically as they could in scraps of drapery of all descriptions," demanding eggs from households and performing a song.

May Day featured processions to the houses of the gentry, where the entertainers performed for money. In Armagh, the figure of a "May Baby" was placed on a pole and marched to a gentleman's house, where a sexual pantomime was performed. The entertainers, some dressed in straw, were generally rewarded with drinking money. In Wexford, two dozen young men and women in bright clothing would perform a comedy that featured a man dressed as a woman. In Roscommon and Galway, the Mayboys would visit homes, offering rhymes with a specific warning about the size of the donation they expected: "If it is but of the small, it won't agree with the boys at all."

On Midsummer's night, celebrated on June 23 (St. John's Eve) or June 28 (the eve of Saints Peter and Paul), there were processions to collect fuel for a community bonfire, and woe to homeowners who failed to contribute—such a breach of the communal spirit might result in the theft of turf.[33] On the eve of Samhain—Halloween—a more elaborate ritual was held. In Cork, a figure in a white shirt would lead a procession of youths blowing horns as they stopped at farmhouses, reciting verse in exchange for tribute. In Fermanagh, "strawboys" with blackened faces or masks would barge into homes, playing music, dancing with the single girls, and snatching food. Others used the occasion to settle scores—especially with families who kept eligible daughters out of circulation. In County Waterford, we find a kind of trick-or-treating familiar to Americans.[34]

Strawboys would also crash weddings, where their captain would dance with the bride while his companions were treated to food and drink. Glassie describes the dance as "the last request the community of bachelors would make of the woman who was being taken from them."[35] Thus it was in a sense contractual—given in exchange for the community's blessing.

By far the most extensive collection of festivities centered on Christmas and New Year's. In Kilkenny, during the two weeks before Christmas, musicians in blackface would perform for drinks at every home in the district, in a custom known as "calling the waits." Similar practices were reported in Cavan and Longford.[36]

On December 26, St. Stephen's Day, it was a widespread custom for groups of wren boys to parade from house to house with a bird they had captured and killed (sometimes a toy bird was substituted). The wren boys were often masked and sometimes dressed as women. In Munster, the leader, or "captain," dressed in mock military fashion. The wren boys would chant an ode to the wren in exchange for a drink. Should a homeowner be reluctant to contribute, the boys might threaten to bury the bird before his door, ensuring bad luck for the household. In Ulster border counties like Cavan and Leitrim, the wren boys' performance was more complex, taking on the character of play. As such it was heavily influenced by mummery, an import from England and Scotland.[37]

The folk drama of the mummers was the most elaborate festive ritual of the year. The play was mostly closely associated with Ulster and its periphery, though it was also performed in Dublin, Waterford, and Mayo. The mummers made their appearances around Christmas, and the performances often ran through early January.

In some ways, the play was akin to the other processions of the peasant calendar, featuring bands of costumed peasants visiting homes and receiving a treat in exchange for a performance. But the mummers performance was at once more structured and more dynamic. Some elements remained constant—a sword fight between two combatants ending in the death and resurrection of one. But the number of performers could vary, as could the intensity of their performance. And in sectarian Ulster, the outcome of the combat could change with the audience—St. George might triumph before a Protestant family, St. Patrick before a Catholic one.

The play required far more organization than the outings of the biddy boys and wren boys. Mummers would begin practicing around Halloween, drilled in their lines by a captain.[38] Performers dressed according to their role—some in straw, some in blackface, some as women. Occasionally they took on the appearance of a paramilitary troop, with garish uniforms and outsized wooden swords. The general practice was for mummers to visit all the homes in a locale, their approach often signaled by the blowing of horns or beating of drums. A captain would knock on the door of a home, asking permission to enter. Once inside he would read a few lines of rhyme to introduce the next character, who would do the same. Among the characters would be two "champions" armed with wooden swords who would quarrel and fight.

In Antrim, it was frequently St. George who killed the Turkish Knight. In Catholic areas of Ulster such as Donegal and south Fermanagh, it was often Prince George who did combat with Prince Patrick—the saints transformed into symbols of sovereignty. Either might be killed, but just as important as the dead man's identity was what happened next—his resurrection by a "doctor," who would say, "Rise up, dead man, and fight again." The slain would be resurrected, the play would end in amity between the combatants, a collection of food or money would be made to pay the "doctor," and the performers might sing a few songs at the request of the audience. On the way out, the mummers often filched any food that was lying about.

Despite its happy ending, there was no mistaking the frightening aspects of the play. It featured threats, a sword fight and a killing, followed by a collection of money and, sometimes, the theft of food. The players had often been drinking. As Glassie points out, the action took place not on a stage, removed from the audience, but in a home, before the hearth, within a few feet of the audience, with a character called "the fool" shooing the curious with an inflated pig's bladder on a stick. Some of the most violent lines are directed toward that audience, as in the character Little Devil Doubt's threat to "sweep you all to your grave." When Little Devil Doubt didn't get any money, dramatic violence could become real, which is why a "captain" was needed to keep order.

"If there was any thing done to any occupant—or in the premises around the man's house—well, the captain would see to that: that the injury would be repaired," one mummer said. "And as well that that man—if he found out during the night or that day that he had done anything, transgressed in any one way—he may get a hidin'. And he may get a hiding that he'd lie in bed for a week after."[39]

Another aspect of the play that straddled the fine line between the humorous and the unsettling was that while all the performers were male, they sometimes filled female roles, wearing women's clothing. Women characters usually had a central role in only two areas—Antrim, where an old woman, the mother of the vanquished combatant, would call for a doctor; and the west Ulster borderlands. In Fermanagh, Miss Funny or Biddy Funny often made the collection for the doctor; and in Leitrim and Donegal, a Mary Ann made an appearance as an assistant to the fool.[40]

The mummers play contained layers of meaning. On a symbolic level, it has been called a death and revival drama designed to encourage the regeneration of fields in the depths of the long Irish winter, a time when peasant anxieties were at their height.[41] December was a time when many agricultural laborers were truly landless, the conacre fields they depended on for food having reverted to their owners for the month.

In fact, all the ritual parades may have been linked to peasant agricultural anxieties. The folklorist Alan Gailey writes that the processions occurred at seasonal high points such as the start of the farmer's year on St. Brigid's Day and the May 1 start of summer: "Scholars have seen in this seasonal connection an ultimate ritual significance for the different ceremonies, claiming that the original concern of the performers must have been for the well-being of their fields and folds. . . . As if the mimed human life-cycle would assist nature in the unfolding of the seasons."

The theme of death and revival may explain the ubiquity of straw clothing in the ritual processions, according to Gailey, who suggests that use of fresh straw from a recent harvest is a way to encourage nature at a dead time of year. Coming as it did in the period around New Year's, the play underlined the death of the old year and the birth of the new one. Gailey believed the festive rituals went back to the early Christian period, and probably further.[42]

Joe McGowan of north Sligo, a modern mummer who writes about Irish folkways, argues that the mummer/wren boy tradition predates Christianity, even if some elements were later imported: "Its roots embedded in pagan rituals, when sacrifice was deemed necessary to appease the gods, the tradition is ancient and timeless."[43] Where the blood of children and cattle were once offered, now it was the wren or a combatant in the mummers play. The congruities between hunting the wren and mumming may be one of the reasons the latter caught on in Ireland. Certainly the theme of death and resurrection resonated among Christians of all denominations.

Depending on the tenor of the times, the play could be used to mock sectarian divisions or reinforce them. The folklorist Glassie has noted that pitting St. George against St. Patrick in a duel to the death brought religious and political tensions to the surface, then dissipated them in laughter at outrageous costumes and nonsensical banter.[44] Cromwell, one of the most feared and hated figures in Irish history, was often mocked with a long and very silly copper nose. On the other hand, when communal tensions were high, the notion of resurrection and renewed combat—Prince Patrick slain by Prince George, only to be raised from the dead, with contributions from the Irish people, to fight again—could impart a subversive political subtext to many of the mummers plays performed in Catholic areas of Ulster.

In other, more Catholic parts of Ireland—County Wexford, for example—the play assumed an openly subversive nature, including an eloquent if fictional damnation of English rule by the Irish patriot Daniel O'Connell:

So now your cause and Penal laws, I'll expel by exhortation.
Those notorious tithes I'll lay aside or in blood I'll steep the nation.
Your tyranny won't frighten me, nor your hellish emigration,
Your infernal ends, they stood your friends—if I live I'll free the nation.[45]

But the mummers play was far more than an expression of peasant anxiety or political mockery. Though at times it seemed to emphasize the differences between England and Ireland, as when Prince Patrick and Prince George engaged in mortal combat, on another level it served to draw together the community. On the simplest level, the goal was to collect the means to throw a party. All the households visited by the mummers would be invited. In Ulster, this might be the only social event of the year at which Catholics and Protestants would mix, according to Glassie. And it afforded the usually young, unmarried mummers an opportunity to court women—a way of knitting together families, and thus communities.

The play also served as a bridge between neighboring locales. Because each squad of mummers had its own territory, it was important to prevent encroachment by neighboring bands. This was best accomplished by reciprocal invitations to the mummers balls. "They would keep on havin' parties," one old Fermanagh mummer recalled. "One would be linked with the other, do you see. They were kind of associated."[46]

On a deeper level, the mummers play was positive reinforcement of the norms of a communal agricultural society where neighbors had to rely on one another. In his study of a community in the west of Ireland, Hugh

Brody points to a connection between parties or feasts and socioeconomic cooperation.[47] In the case of the mummers, those who contributed to the performers received in return not only a bit of folk drama, but also entry to a party the rest of the community would attend. As Glassie writes in *All Silver and No Brass*, his study of south Fermanagh mummers, "Miss Funny's collection was no cheap shot at capital gains. It was a joint venture in community strength, a momentarily sealed social contract."

Likewise, the gift of eggs at Easter was "a social transaction," and the fuel donated to the community bonfire on Midsummer's night reaffirmed one's "commitment to friends and neighbors." The gifts of the "great days" constituted "a formal statement of alliance." More broadly, Glassie views rural Irish hospitality toward one's neighbors as a contract of mutual support, and community as "a social arrangement for mutual aid."[48]

Alliance with one's friends and neighbors implied allegiance to the unwritten yet ironclad rules of economic cooperation—the contract that was so crucial to peasant solidarity in pre-famine Ireland. The solemn nature of the covenant was underlined by a feature common to many of the festive rituals—overtones of human or animal sacrifice.

A killing, for example, defined the mummers play: the wren boys sacrificed a bird. One May Eve, rabbits were once burned, and in Dublin, horse heads were tossed into bonfires. Elsewhere, cattle were driven through the bonfires of May Eve and Midsummer's Eve, and people jumped over them as well. "Leaping through the fire symbolized human sacrifice," wrote James Bonwick, historian of Irish paganism.[49]

Animal sacrifice became explicit in certain periods in autumn. Sheep and geese were killed on the Feast of St. Michael, September 29. And the shedding of animal blood was ritualized in the period leading up to St. Martin's Day, also known as Old Halloween, on November 11. Ellen Cullen of Barraghmore in Leitrim told the Irish Folklore Commission, "Before St. Martin's Day (a few days before) a fowl was killed by cutting off its head, letting the blood spill. The main thing was the spilling of the blood. The blood was then spilled in the four corners of the kitchen. This spilling of blood brought a blessing on the stock for years." The tradition endured past the midpoint of the twentieth century, frightening the wits out of a young Joe McGowan when he saw an elderly neighbor spatter the whitewashed walls of her County Sligo home with the blood of a sacrificed bird.[50]

Holiday customs, imbued with bloody, centuries-old symbolism, helped to cement the unwritten rules of the countryside; and precisely for that reason they were viewed as a threat by those charged with enforcing formal, written, English law. In the barony of Farney in south County Monaghan, where the Blackstaff clachan was broken up in 1798, the old custom of mid-summer bonfires on St. John's Eve was suppressed in the 1830s. In 1845, the mayor of Cork cracked down on wren boy activity there, banning "the hunting of the little bird on St. Stephen's Day by all the idle fellows of the country."[51] It may be no coincidence that the ban on house-to-house solicitations by "idle fellows" came in the first hard winter of the famine. An alarmed observer in County Cork felt the need to inform the British authorities in Dublin Castle about the paramilitary posturing of wren boys "marching and counter-marching to a fife and a drum" under the leadership of a captain in an old cavalry uniform with a green cockade.[52]

Sir William Wilde recalled in the years immediately after the famine the official campaign against some forms of popular culture in the years previous. "The ire of the authorities was chiefly directed against cakes [the peasants' balls and suppers] and dances," he wrote in 1851. "When information was obtained with respect to one of them, thither the magistrate, with his posse comitatus, repaired, broke into the assembly, dispersed the merry-makers, spilled the whisky, danced on the fiddle, and carried off to the nearest blackhole, or guard-room, the owners of the house." Wilde recounted an 1830 case in County Roscommon in which a justice of the peace was convicted and exiled for life for opening fire on a crowd of revelers he had chased from a peasant dance.[53]

The authorities suppressed wren boy processions, midsummer bonfires, and mummers balls not only because they were occasions for riotous revelry, but also because they were the glue that helped hold together an alternative law of the land—one created by the peasantry, not Parliament. When English law was broken, there was recourse to the courts. But when informal "fireside law" governing land use was broken, peasants often turned for redress to gunmen who, like the mummers, dressed in straw, white shirts, and women's garments.

For if the appearance of mummers, wren boys, strawboys, and similar groups was a function of seasonal anxiety about the Irish peasant's "fields and folds," the appearance of secret societies like the Molly Maguires, whose members dressed in exactly the same garments, was a function of similar fears about their tenure on those fields. Groups like the mummers helped foster the reciprocity that was one pillar of peasant existence, while groups like the Molly Maguires upheld the other pillar—the right to subsistence. In a very real sense, then, the secret societies were merely the flip side of festive groups such as the mummers. The masks of the mummers were the benevolent face of an alternative social order. The darker side of that alternative order surfaced only when positive measures like the festive processions failed to ensure that favors were reciprocated among the peasantry, and that landlords granted the peasantry the land it needed to subsist. That's when the secret society enforcers stepped in, dressed like mummers but carrying guns instead of wooden swords.

3   The Secret Societies

> It appears that in Ireland, crime is generally, somehow or other, the crime
> of the community, whereas in England it is the crime of an individual.
> —Edward Golding, Monaghan magistrate

It was the day before Halloween, and the season of vengeance was nigh. In the wee hours of October 30, 1816, after a secret meeting in the Catholic church in Stonetown, a large group of men approached Wildgoose Lodge, a remote farmhouse in County Louth. They numbered about a hundred and came from all over the Ulster borderlands—Louth, Monaghan, Armagh, Cavan, and Meath.

The men tried to rush the door, but they were repulsed by the inhabitants, a family called Lynch. What happened next would horrify generations to come. Someone bound the door, while another touched an ember to a corner of the thatched roof. As the fire on the roof grew, so did the desperation of the people trapped inside, who included two servants and baby.

"I am just the servant girl," one cried out. "I have no call to be in the house. Let me out."

"You did not take warning in time" was the answer from outside. Still, the plea provoked a debate among the attackers. But any hope of mercy for the two servant girls and the baby died when someone declared, "The nits should be burned & destroyed as well as the louse."

Eight people roasted to death in Wildgoose Lodge that night.[1]

As with any Irish atrocity, there was a history to this one. More than six months earlier, on April 10, "the Wednesday night before Easter," as one witness put it, members of an agrarian secret society had raided Wildgoose Lodge for arms. The Lynches put up a struggle, and the head of the family, Edward, took the rare step of reporting the attack and prosecuting those responsible. Three of them were condemned to death.

Unfortunately for Edward Lynch, he made his stand in precisely the wrong place, at precisely the wrong time. Secret society activity was undergoing a resurgence in south Ulster in 1816, the same year that landlords successfully pressed for legislation to ease farm evictions. Delegates from all over Ulster gathered that year just a few miles from Wildgoose Lodge, in Carrickmacross, County Monaghan, to resurrect an old underground network, the Defenders, under a new name, the Ribbonmen.[2]

The crackdown that followed the burning of Wildgoose Lodge resulted in the hanging of eighteen men, twelve of whom were gibbeted—their bodies left to rot in public view, as an example. While their fate failed to stop the spread of the Ribbonmen, it did make a lasting impression on William Carleton, who wrote a short story based on the case that was freighted with gothic horror: "Those who took an active part in the murder stood for some time about the conflagration, and as it threw its red light upon their fierce faces and rough persons, soiled as they now were with smoke and black streaks of ashes, the scene seemed to change to hell, the murderers to spirits of the damned rejoicing over the arrival and torture of some guilty soul."[3]

The modern poet Seamus Heaney, in an imagined conversation with Carleton that touched on the case, offered a different view of the Ribbonmen, one that can only be labeled nostalgic:

'The angry role was never my vocation,'
I said. 'I come from County Derry
Where the last marching bands of Ribbonmen
On Patrick's Day still played their "Hymn to Mary."'[4]

Descriptions of the secret societies of rural Ireland could vary widely even when they came from the same source. In the 1880s, the author R. Shelton Mackenzie offered a sympathetic portrait of John Cussen, alias "Captain Rock," a man identified as the leader a violent Whiteboy organization: "His birth was respectable, his education good, his fortune had been ample, his mind was affluent in varied and vigorous resources; he had formerly won favor and fame from the world's opinion."[5]

Thirty years earlier, another of Mackenzie's books offered a contrasting portrait of the Ribbonman William Gorman. Gorman was in the dock, listening to testimony linking him to another arson atrocity, one that killed eighteen people: "A savage joy flashed over his face; his eyes were lighted up with a fire as lurid as that which he had kindled in the habitation of his enemies . . . when the groans of his victims were described, his teeth, which were unusually prominent, were bared to the gums; and, though he had drained the cup of vengeance to the dregs, still he seemed to smack his lips, and to lick the blood with which his injures had been redressed!"[6]

Depending on the context, the secret societies were seen as either blood-thirsty and demonic or peaceful and devout. It would be trite—and inaccurate—to say that the truth falls somewhere between these descriptions. In fact, it encompasses all of them. There was always a duality to the secret societies of Ireland—they could be as benevolent, and as brutal, as any agency that enforces the law, which is often how they viewed their role. The mummers and various secret societies were early examples of this good cop/bad cop sort of complicity, but there have been plenty of others examples of violent Irish movements with legal or benevolent sides. In the anthracite region of Pennsylvania, the Hibernians and Molly Maguires were flip sides of the same coin, as were, more recently, the perfectly legal Sinn Féin political party and the outlawed Irish Republican Army.

Organized agrarian violence in Ireland dates to at least 1711–13, when a movement of poor cottiers called the Houghers maimed cattle in Connacht. Fifty years later, in Ulster, Presbyterians farmers and weavers formed the Hearts of Oak to fight burdensome taxation, and in the early 1770s, a similar movement, the Hearts of Steel, rose up against high rents and the eviction of tenant farmers.[7]

These movements rose and fell over the course of a few short years. But in the 1760s, oath-bound conspiracies became an ongoing phenomenon among the Catholic peasantry. Some were purely local affairs that defy generalization, but there were two broad categories—the Whiteboys on the one hand, and the Defenders and Ribbonmen on the other.

Generally speaking, the loose-knit, largely apolitical Whiteboys tended to be concentrated in southern Ireland, where they were mostly concerned with issues related to the land and rural life. The more tightly organized Defenders and their successors, the Ribbonmen, were more concentrated in Ulster and its periphery, where they busied themselves in sectarian battles, labor activity, nationalist politics, and tenant rights.

It is important not to be too bound by semantics. "Whiteboy" became an overarching term for agrarian rebels in the latter half of the eighteenth century, and many nineteenth-century observers used "Ribbonmen" as a generic term for all members of violent peasant societies, perhaps because the Ribbonmen tried hard to absorb local peasant rings. Ribbonmen became entangled in the land issue, and some groups commonly categorized as Whiteboys—for example, the followers of Capt. Rock who troubled Munster in the 1820s—were deeply sectarian. Grievances overlapped.

Of the two broader categories, the Whiteboys were the more closely associated with the cycle of the peasant calendar and festive groups such as mummers, strawboys, and wren boys. The name Whiteboy is best understood as a category, rather than a specific organization, for the Whiteboys went under a bewildering array of local names—Rockites, Blackfeet, Whitefeet, Terry Alts, and, in their earliest days, "the fairies." Sometimes they claimed allegiance to a mythical woman—Joanna Meskill, Lady Clare, or Queen Sive.

The Whiteboys first surfaced in the early 1760s in the Munster counties of Limerick, Tipperary, Waterford, and Cork. Landlords were evicting tenant farmers and enclosing commons so they could graze cattle—a response to London's decision in the late 1750s to allow the sale of Irish beef and butter in Britain. For the next century, the agrarian secret societies targeted not so much the landlord system but market-oriented changes in that system.[8]

"Those who have been most earnest and anxious for the improvement of their estates have come most frequently under the ban" of the secret societies, wrote an observer of Tipperary in 1840. "Whilst the carefree, spendthrift good-for-nothing landlord who hunts, and shoots, and drinks, and runs in debt, who even exacts the most exorbitant rents from his tenants, provided only he does not interfere with their time-honored customs of subdividing land, squatting, con-acre, and reckless marriage, may live in peace."[9]

These "good-for-nothing" landlords were left alone because they posed no threat to peasant occupation of the land. For Whiteboys, the worst crime in the world was taking land from a tenant farmer, for the loss of a field could mean starvation. As the market economy spread, so did Whiteboy groups determined to uphold a traditional, or "moral" economy. Access to land was the oldest law of the land, and it clashed head-on with English rule. As one member of Parliament put it in 1825, "Though the English Laws have been introduced among them, yet many of their own ancient laws continue to exist in the shape of habits: their dispositions and their practices are in a state of complete contrast with the theory of Law, as regards tenure of land."[10]

Nothing could underline the divide between Irish custom and English law more than the frequency with which observers described the secret societies as "midnight legislators," even while denouncing their lawlessness. In fact, the Whiteboys' rules constituted an alternative social order so comprehensive that one lord lieutenant of Ireland called them "a complete system of legislation."[11] The Whiteboys at different times and to varying degrees sought to regulate nearly the whole of rural life—from land tenure to marriage to mutual aid to the tithes levied for Protestant ministers and the fees charged by Catholic priests. They also punished a wife-beater on at least one occasion. Whiteboys in Kilkenny in the 1760s kidnapped the daughters of rich farmers and then forced them into marriage, a practice that continued into the 1830s.

A central purpose of many Whiteboy groups was enforcing the contract of mutual support that was Irish peasant society. In east Munster they compelled farmers to donate food to needy neighbors. The followers of Capt. Rock warned farmers in north Kerry in January 1822 to sell their potatoes "to the neighbors at home." Likewise, dairy farmers near Tipperary were warned a few months later not to send milk to market until it had been supplied to neighbors who needed it "at a reasonable price." In his landmark study of the Rockite rebellion, James S. Donnelly, Jr., labeled this phenomenon "localism"—the notion that poor inhabitants of any particular locale had "a superior if not exclusive claim . . . to the land, employment, and food available" there. The warnings perfectly reflected what happens when hard times and a market economy clash with a deeply held belief that a community is, or should be, a social arrangement for mutual aid.[12]

That notion of community is one reason the disturbances occurred in industrial as well as agricultural settings. In the Castlecomer coal field on the border of Kilkenny and Queen's Counties, where many mine workers also tilled small plots of land, there were reports that the Whitefeet had nine thousand sworn members in the early 1830s, when they battled farm evictions and changes in the mines.[13]

The Whiteboys could be brutal, and there was a clear seasonal pattern to that brutality. Crimes such as murder, threatening notices, and attacks on houses peaked in the winter, then ebbed during the summer. A tabulation of Whiteboy crimes in the province of Munster for 1833 shows a high of sixty-five in January and a low of eight in July.[14]

In a study of assassinations in Tipperary in the years leading up to the famine, Michael Beames found that most occurred from October to January, and he cited a rough correlation with rural holidays: "There are clear linkages between Whiteboyism, the cycle of the peasant economy, and rural custom."[15]

Whiteboys stressed those links in the disguises they adopted. In addition to the white shirts that gave them their name, the Whiteboys dressed in straw clothing and women's garments, and often blackened or whitened their faces. In doing so, they donned not only the costumes of the mummers and strawboys, but also their mantle as defenders of a collective society. The disguises hid identities, to be sure, but they were meant to reveal as much as they concealed: for peasants concerned with enforcement of the law of the land, they were a badge of legitimacy. The timing of White-boy violence—pegged closely to the most important days of the peasant calendar—also signaled that the murderers, like the mummers, were acting on behalf of the community.

In the rare instance where secret societies battled each other, the division extended to the festive groups. The 1806–11 war in the province of Munster between the Caravats, a peasant Whiteboy group, and the middle-class Shanavests extended to rival teams of mummers and wren boys.[16]

The organizational structure of the Whiteboys in many ways mirrored the festive groups and other elements of the communal society. Whiteboys may have lacked a central structure for an entire province, but like local bands of mummers, they had their own specific territory and enjoyed recip-rocal relations with neighboring bands. This proved important, allowing a Whiteboy group from one area to call on assassins from another when a killing was planned. One provision of a Whitefeet oath gave evidence of this reciprocity: "I Sware I will go 10 miles on foot and 15 miles on horse back in five minutes' warning." The use of strangers made it more difficult for authorities to catch the killers.[17]

Marching Whiteboys were headed by a "captain" and were often accom-panied by musicians and horn-blowers, much as the mummers as Mayboys were. However, there is evidence of a more sophisticated command struc-ture among some Whiteboy groupings. The Whitefeet of Queen's County were said to be run by a committee in the early 1830s. A magistrate re-ported that "there is what they call a head committee, composed of seven members, who sit and discuss all matters"—much like those clachan lead-ers, the "head of quarters" who divvied up land and resolved disputes. The Whitefeet leaders decided who was eligible for membership and adminis-tered the oath binding new members to secrecy.

The name "Whiteboy" gives a clue to the identity of these members. In Ireland, boys were not male children, but unmarried adult males, or a man in all-male company—hence, the terms "strawboys" and "wren boys." Not-ing that the Devon Commission reported in the mid-1840s that "the im-mediate perpetrators of agrarian outrages are generally the sons and the labourers or servants of farmers, or as they are generally called, 'farmer's boys,'" John William Knott argued that the "boys" were especially active in secret societies because they were protecting their future rights to the land. And the historian R. F. Foster has suggested that the nocturnal collec-tive violence of unmarried men was linked to machismo and sexual frus-tration.[18] That helps explain why peasants considered the abduction of unmarried women to be "a kind of Whiteboy offense," as one contemporary observer put it. "A party of men go by night to the house of the woman, who is generally a farmer's daughter, with a small fortune, and somewhat above the rank of the intended husband . . . and lodge her in some hiding place with the man who intends that she should be his wife," wrote G. C. Lewis in 1836. "Sometimes the parties are married forthwith, sometimes a communication is made to the father that the man is willing to marry the girl, if the fortune is paid." Usually, the father felt compelled to sanction the wedding and provide the dowry.[19]

Mummers and strawboys promoted the social contract (and sought wives in the process) through positive measures, but were known to exact vengeance from those who refused to reaffirm a commitment to the community (and allow their daughters into the courting pool). It was easy for Whiteboys to invert the playful blackmail of the mummers and the amorous antics of the strawboys for the same purpose. James O'Neill, who studied the link between popular culture and the Whiteboys of Tipperary, suggested that the secret societies probably fulfilled functions that were similar to those of "spontaneous communal groups such as the Wren Boys or May Boys, who generally acted as guardians of a widely accepted standard of proper and improper behavior."[20]

The progression from wren boy to Whiteboy (or Ribbonman) seemed obvious to a least one mid-nineteenth-century observer. "It really was a sort of melo-dramatic exhibition," wrote Sir William Wilde. "Those who wore cut paper round their hat, as wren-boys, when they grew up to be young men decorated themselves with ribbons and white shirts to act as Mayboys—and, as mummers, painted their faces white and went through the Christmas pantomime with old rusty swords. These were the mechanics, stage-managers, wardrobe keepers, scene-shifters and 'property manufacturers' of the Roscommon Ribbonmen." He cited the sense of frolic and adventure in marching by moonlight to the sound of fiddles or bagpipes, armed with an old gun or rusting halberd.[21]

His description could have applied almost anywhere from the Ulster borderlands south, and well beyond. For the phenomenon of peasants and proto-industrial workers protesting social and economic change in festive guises such as women's clothing was not limited to Ireland—there were a number of such episodes in Britain and France during the early 1800s.

Among the most famous of these primitive rebels were the Luddites, weavers in the English Midlands who between 1811 and 1813 smashed the new machines that were costing them their jobs. Led by a mythical "Ned

Ludd," "General Ludd," or "Lady Ludd," they dressed and acted remarkably like mummers: "They were nearly all disguised, some having their faces blackened and others wearing masks to conceal their features effectively. Many of them were dressed in carter's smock frocks, others had their coats turned inside out, some had their checked shirts over their clothes, and a few actually dressed themselves partly in women's apparel." The Luddites, like the mummers, were known to move about the countryside at night in small bands, seeking gifts from the gentry and well-off farmers.[22]

Less than twenty years later, England was again convulsed by a group of machine-breakers, this time agricultural workers newly displaced by mechanical threshers. Again, their leader, "Captain Swing," was mythical, and the rioters dressed in frocks and blackened their faces as they paraded from farm to farm, demanding money, food, and beer, ordering farmers to increase wages, and smashing farm machinery.[23]

At about the same time as the Swing riots in England, French peasants in the Pyrenees launched the "War of the Demoiselles," dressed as the young women from whom they took their name. "Masked or with blackened faces, almost all wearing shirts or white skirts, and all armed with guns, hatchets, or hoes," they marched in formation, headed by a "captain" in a military costume. The Demoiselles demanded food from households and staged mock trials, all as part of a protest against an 1827 law that restricted their communal rights of access to state and private forests. Historian Peter Sahlins argues that the Demoiselles were rooted in the custom and costumes of Carnival, which, like the mummers play, "was a drama enacted by the peasants themselves that symbolically ordered relations within communities and between communities and the wider society."[24]

Finally, there were the Rebecca riots and the "Scotch Cattle" disorders in Wales in the first half of the nineteenth century. The Rebeccas convulsed rural western Wales between 1839 and 1843, violently protesting a range of grievances—originally, the construction of toll roads, but later monthly pay for industrial workers, the hoarding of grain by farmers, and the taking of a farm against the wishes of the community. Again, we have men dressing up as women. Again, the protesters perambulated the countryside, making door-to-door collections like the mummers. Again, there was a link to festive custom—the Rebecca riots occurred in areas where there had been a revival in the 1830s of a sort of charivari called the "ceffyl pren," which involved riding an individual or his effigy out of town on a rail or wooden horse. This sort of rough justice was accompanied by rough music—the beating of drums, the firing of guns—and always occurred at night, with participants blackening their faces and dressing in women's clothes as they enacted a mock trial of the victim. It had its roots in Christmas games.[25]

The "Scotch Cattle" were local bands of disguised Welsh coal miners who reciprocated with each other in a brutal campaign to buoy wages and punish strikebreakers. "Every herd of 'Scotch Cattle' had a bull as leader, selected for his strength and violence," a Welsh historian wrote. "The band of, say, Merthyr, was directed to punish a delinquent at Tredegar; one at Tredegar to visit Hirwain. Each man was armed, face blackened, and the skin and horns of a cow worn, and, with great bellowings, they would assail a house, smash the furniture, and burn down the premises."[26]

What all these outbreaks have in common is that they occurred at a time of economic transition that displaced traditional rights and customs, and to some degree the participants expropriated the format of familiar festive customs.

In the outbreaks that most resemble the Whiteboy disturbances of Ireland—the Rebecca riots and the War of the Demoiselles—participants and the authorities who tried to suppress them literally spoke different languages: Welsh and English in the Rebecca riots, Spanish (or a Spanish-influenced dialect) and French in the case of the Demoiselles. Such situations give the indigenous language rich potential as a means of subversion. E. P. Thompson, the great historian of the English working class, posits a link between the rough music used to ritually enforce a community's rules, and local dialect, because rituals like the ceffyl pren of Wales were part of an orally transmitted culture.[27]

As a market economy swept across Ireland from the mid-eighteenth century onward, disturbances similar to the Rebecca riots occurred in those areas where the waves of economic change crashed upon the rocks of Gaelic culture. Beginning in 1765, the government tried to combat the disturbances with a series of laws that came to be known as "Whiteboy Acts." They banned, among other things, the swearing of illegal oaths, posting threatening notices, appearing armed in disguise, and assembling at night "to the terror of his majesty's subjects."[28]

The Whiteboy Acts may have created a new incentive for rural insurgents to disguise themselves as festive groups, but the confusion predated the laws. As economic change gave rise to the Irish secret societies, it became increasingly difficult to tell the difference between a strawboy or a mummer and a Whiteboy. One of the first Whiteboy leaders hanged in the disturbances that swept Waterford and Tipperary in the early 1760s declared before his execution, "I acted among them as Captain, such as the

Mayboys have." In Clonmel, mummers were mistaken for Whiteboys in 1774—and in the next century an observer there noted that the typical secret society leader "performed his whole part as if he were Tom-fool to a corps of Christmas mummers." When young men in east Limerick took a Whiteboy oath in 1818, they did so dressed as wren boys on St. Stephen's Day, the day of the traditional wren procession.[29]

The link between mummers and secret societies in the Roscommon of the 1820s occasioned the comparison by Sir Wilde noted above. In County Cavan in the 1830s, a Ribbonman turned informer who was sworn in to the secret society on January 1 told of membership renewals every three months, around those days associated with festive processions of the Biddies, the Mayboys, and the strawboys—that is, "within a day or two" of February 1, May 1, and November 1.[30]

There were reports of "Molly Maguires" attacking wedding parties in west Donegal, and of "mummers" in the same area becoming embroiled in agrarian troubles as late as 1897—two incidents that only make sense if Mollies and mummers are different names for the same phenomenon.[31] If you were to plot these locations on a map of Ireland, you would end up with a line running from the southeast to the northwest, and dates that give a hint of when the market economy was altering the structure of peasant society. The coordinates conform with the observation that innovation in Ireland—in this case the market economy—has repeatedly spread from the east and south to the north and west.[32]

One way to cut through some of the confusion between festive groups such as mummers and agrarian insurgents like the Whiteboys is to view them as slightly different manifestations of peasant anxiety. When Irish peasants, worried about the regeneration of their crops, donned women's clothing, straw costumes, white shirts, and blackface for a benevolent ritual emphasizing death and rebirth, they were mummers. When, worried about marriage prospects, they wore the same outfits at Halloween to court women and punish farmers who withheld daughters from the courting pool, they were strawboys. And when those same peasants, facing eviction and starvation, adopted identical disguises for deadly vengeance on the landlords, they were Whiteboys, sometimes referred to in the 1800s as Ribbonmen.

Defenders and Ribbonmen

The Defenders and Ribbonmen were the second major type of secret society in pre-famine Ireland. While the latter term was often expanded to include any type of conspiratorial activity in the nineteenth century, it originally had a more specific meaning. In contrast to the Whiteboys of the south, these two northern groups had a stronger sectarian and political focus. In the south, where land was the issue, the Whiteboys targeted Catholic and Protestant landlords alike. In the north, the flight of the earls had ensured that there were fewer Catholic landlords, so it was much easier for a secret society to maintain religious solidarity.[33]

Defenders and Ribbonmen were militantly Catholic and nationalist. They were more tightly organized than the Whiteboys, with parish committees reporting to county delegates, who in turn acted in concert, developing a system of passwords for communication. The elements of peasant folk drama that played so important a role in the symbolism of the Whiteboys were usually more muted among the Defenders and Ribbonmen.

One contemporary account traced the troubles that gave rise to the Defenders to a drunken brawl near the small town of Markethill in County Armagh on July 4, 1784—the first Independence Day following the end of the American Revolution.[34] Events across the Atlantic had been influencing the north of Ireland since 1717, when large numbers of Presbyterians began immigrating to the colonies, partly in response to an invitation from James Logan, the secretary of the Commonwealth of Pennsylvania. Logan had been born to Scottish parents in Ulster, and fearing Indian unrest in Pennsylvania, which was dominated by Quaker pacifists, he later recalled that he "thought it might be prudent to plant a settlement of such men as those who formerly had defended Londonderry and Inniskillen as a frontier in case of any disturbance." The Scots–Irish responded so enthusiastically that between 1700 and 1776 an estimated two hundred thousand people left Ulster for America, cutting the province's Protestant population by a third. The emigration peaked in the years just before the American Revolution, when thirty thousand Ulster Presbyterians left for the colonies.[35]

The exodus caused considerable consternation among the Protestants who remained behind, especially in the Ulster borderlands, where emigration upset the delicate balance between the descendants of settlers and natives. By the late 1720s, enthusiasm for emigration was likened to a "contagious distemper" that threatened the economy. "The worst is that it affects only protestants, and reigns chiefly in the north, which is the seat of our linen manufacture," wrote one government official.[36]

The coming of the American Revolution halted the outflow but raised new problems. In March 1778, it was announced that France had entered the war on the side of the colonies, and a month later, John Paul Jones sailed into Belfast Lough and vanquished the *Drake*, a British sloop. With the government facing severe financial problems, the Protestant citizenry of Ireland took the island's defense into their own hands by forming the Volunteers, an unauthorized militia of up to eighteen thousand that was eventually, and only grudgingly, accepted by government officials in Dublin Castle.[37]

The official doubts about the Volunteers stemmed in part from their links to the "Patriot" wing of the Irish Parliament, which sought greater independence from London and more power for the middle classes, from which the Volunteers were largely recruited. Catholic membership in the Volunteers was another source of tension, especially in the Ulster border-lands, because it gave Catholics access to arms, which was still illegal, and thus raised fears among those lower-class Protestants excluded from the Volunteers that it would tip the balance of powers in that region. The Volunteers' political demands grew more radical in 1782, when at a convention in Dungannon, Tyrone, they adopted a series of resolutions that demanded legislative independence. The following year, in another convention at Dungannon, Volunteer delegates debated Catholic suffrage.[38]

The debate came amid renewed immigration to America following the end of the war there. Five thousand left from ports in Ulster and Dublin in 1783, and the number doubled the following year. Most were Presbyterians from Ulster, raising fears in the government that emigration would weaken the Protestant Ascendancy and the linen industry.[39] Certainly in a divided border county like Armagh, the long outflow of Protestants can only have exacerbated economic competition between Catholics and Protestants. And tensions were only made worse when, on June 5, 1784, a Volunteer unit at Loughall, Armagh, invited Catholics to join its ranks.

This, then, was the backdrop for the outbreak of violence that began in Markethill less than a month later: lower-class Protestants, their numbers depleted by emigration, faced a challenge to their economic and political supremacy from Catholics who appeared to be on the brink of expanded civil rights.

In the wake of the July 4 brawl, the story goes, a "Captain Whiskey" assumed command of a new Protestant secret society, the Peep O'Day Boys, at a meeting in the barn of a women identified only as "widow M'P—n" (a McParlan from the vicinity of Markethill would, oddly enough, play a leading role in the saga of the Pennsylvania Molly Maguires).[40] Wherever the Peep O'Day Boys were founded and whatever the precise catalyst, they began raiding Catholic homesteads in the area, and Catholics responded by forming their own secret society, the appropriately named Defenders.

The Defenders, composed largely of artisans, publicans, and laborers, spread quickly through the Ulster borderlands and into the south. There the organization merged with the revolutionary republicanism of the United Irishmen, who had been influenced by the French Revolution.[41]

The Defenders played a key role in resistance to a militia draft launched in 1793 after Britain went to war with revolutionary France. The Defenders had good reason to oppose the draft—Ulster's Protestant sheriffs tended to conscript Catholics first, and government officials admitted that the militia was designed more to police Ireland than defend it. After rumors circulated that conscription was meant to punish those who had supported the Catholic Emancipation Act of 1793, widespread antidraft riots left 230 dead—five times the number killed in the previous fifty years of agrarian disturbances. In discussing the 1793 riots, the great historian of the era, William Lecky, described the Defenders as the means by which "the great mass of poorer Roman Catholics passed into the ranks of disaffection."[42]

Miners were at the forefront of the disturbances in the coal districts of Leinster. Along the border between Kilkenny and Queen's County, miners intimidated the constables who were trying to enroll names for the draft. More ominously, they threatened to flood the mines. In the coal town of Castlecomer, a crowd freed a prisoner from detention. The disaffection spread to issues other than the draft, including rent, tithes, and taxes. Crowds in Castlecomer cried out for the overthrow of the government.[43]

Vicious fighting also broke out in the Ulster borderlands, with up to thirty-five rioters killed and ten soldiers wounded in clashes at Manorhamilton in Leitrim. Another nineteen rioters were reported killed at Boyle, in the same county. Widespread disturbances broke out in the Defender strongholds of Cavan, Monaghan, and Armagh, with homes raided and Protestants driven off. In Roscommon and Sligo, "almost the whole of the lower orders of Roman Catholics" were reported to be "in a state of insurrection."

In Mayo, a thousand peasants armed with pikes fought a pitched battle with soldiers that left thirty-six dead. Antidraft rioters shouted pro-French slogans and threatened Catholic priests who urged compliance with the law.[44]

The level of violence presaged both the rebellion that swept Ireland in 1798 and the antidraft disturbances of the American Civil War, to which Irish immigrants contributed mightily. To some degree, the 1793 outbreaks reflected an identity crisis. The government was trying to force Catholics to join a new military establishment designed to hold the island for Protestant England against a France that was seen by both Defenders and the newly radicalized United Irishmen as the salvation of Ireland.

By the summer of 1796, the United Irish movement had effected an uneasy alliance with the Defenders. The alliance proved the United movement's greatest strength in planning for an uprising—it brought in thousands of peasants ready for action—and its greatest weakness in executing that plan. When rebellion did finally break out in May 1798, in response to heavy-handed British effort to repress the United Irish, sectarian tensions hobbled what was in effect a series of poorly coordinated local risings. In County Wexford, the United Irish were mowed down at Vinegar Hill, their pockets filled with barley and their heads filled with visions of independence.

"Terraced thousands died, shaking scythes at cannon," Heaney wrote. "They buried us without shroud or coffin / And in August the barley grew up out of the grave."[45] Fleeing rebels massacred Protestant civilians and advancing Redcoats slaughtered wounded Irishmen. News of the atrocities blew like a cold wind between Protestant United men and their Defender allies in Ulster, where uprisings in Antrim and Down were drowned in a welter of blood.

The final chapter in the rebellion began in Killala, County Mayo, where a thousand French troops under General Joseph Humbert landed on August 22 at the behest of United Irish representatives in Paris. Thousands of peasants, many of them Defenders, rallied to the French. After some initial rebel successes, the British under Lord Cornwallis tightened a noose around Humbert's forces as they marched east in an effort to link up with rebels in the Midlands.

The rebel army spent its last night at Cloone, in County Leitrim, on September 7. The next day, the Englishman Cornwallis caught up with the Frenchman Humbert in neighboring Longford, in a tiny village called Ballinamuck.

The village traced its name to that old defensive earthwork, the Black Pig's Dyke, for, according to legend, a local man had stopped the pig from rooting up the earth there by striking it in the head with a stone. Where the pig came to a halt was known in Gaelic as "Beal Atha na Muice," or "the mouth of the ford of the pig." Eighteen centuries later, the last great battle of the Gaelic speakers took place there, in the valley of the Black Pig. The harried rebel army came to a halt in Ballinamuck, looking for a defensive position. They made their stand on the hill of Shanmullah. After a brief engagement, the French were permitted to surrender, but their peasant allies were given no quarter. The Irish were cut to pieces as they tried to flee, their bodies scattered across the bogs and fields of Ballinamuck. With the subsequent mopping up of Killala, the rebellion was over, at a cost of thirty thousand lives.[46] But something more potent than barley would spring from the graves of Ballinamuck.

The Ribbonmen

In the wake of 1798, the Defenders were suppressed, yet like the slain combatants of the mummers play, they rose to fight again—this time as "Ribbonmen." They took their name from the strips of cloth they tied to their garments as a badge of solidarity, and perhaps as a kind of supernatural protection. Sir William Wilde described the Roscommon Ribbonmen of the 1820s as "adorned with ribbons of as many colours as could be procured, tied upon their hats or arms, like the Spanish contrabandista."

Kyla Madden, a professor of Irish history, points out that the practice of wearing ribbons had long been associated with various festivals of Irish rural life, and particularly with the feast of Brigid, when the saint was believed to endow with special healing powers the white ribbons, or "brats," worn in her honor. She suggests that all across the Ulster borderlands, from Galway to Armagh, "the belief that the *brat* had protective powers might explain why rural protestors and 'midnight legislators' often adorned themselves with ribbons."[47]

The similarities between the Defenders and Ribbonmen illustrate a great deal about the nature of the latter. The revival had begun before the Napoleonic wars ended, in precisely those areas where the Defenders had been strongest—the Ulster borderlands, and later, Dublin. Both groups were active in the same areas of Ulster, Leinster, and Connacht. The Ribbonmen fought the Orange Order, a direct descendant of the Peep O'Day Boys. Daniel O'Connell, describing the differences between Ribbonmen and Whiteboys in 1825, said, "The Catholics of the north are, I believe, more organized into Ribbonmen, and the Ribbonmen do not, if I may so say, choose to fritter away their strength in those driftless acts of outrage which the peasantry in the south do."[48]

Joseph Lee captured something of their essence when he described the Ribbonmen as "integral to the life of the community."[49] These were not marginal men or outlaws on the run, but hardheaded community leaders who constituted a sort of government in exile, albeit a local government in an internal exile. They fought for their alternative vision of Ireland with death notices, assassinations and the occasional spectacular atrocity like Wildgoose Lodge. They cared little for English law as they upheld the older order of the Irish countryside.

The Ribbon Societies, like the Defenders, drew their membership from tradesmen in towns and cities as well as rural residents. Local lodges of up to forty men were divided into three units of about a dozen oath-bound members headed by a committeeman. The three committeemen were in turn headed by a "body master," often a local publican whose premises served as meeting place—and informal courtroom. The four would form a committee that acted, in the words of one observer, as "a sort of Parochial tribunal, that adjudicate in all Cases of Complaint and Quarrel among the members of the Body, and also issue their Orders to the Ribandmen in their Parishes which they are bound to obey." Parish units sent delegates to a countywide body, which in turn sent representatives to provincial bodies that set the rules and appointed a national "Board of Erin." There were hand signals and passwords, changed every three months, to help Ribbonmen from different areas recognize one another.[50]

The sign for October 1846 involved placing the thumb of the right hand on the right breast of the waistcoat. The countersign was the thumb of the left hand to the left breast of waistcoat. The passwords consisted of the following exchange: "What do you think of the change?" "What change do you mean, sir?" "The split in the association."[51]

While there had been local activity before 1816, the old Defender network was formally revived in that year, when delegates from the northern counties met in Carrickmacross, in south Monaghan, amid mounting sectarian tension there. Called the Board of Erin, it was led by John Rice of Carrickmacross.

A separate Ribbon network evolved in Dublin, under the leadership of Richard Jones, a native of the Barony of Farney, of which Carrickmacross is the main town. The two groups were reconciled in 1838, when Rice stepped down from his position. Jones was arrested in Dublin the following year in a case that effectively ended the Dublin group's activity.[52]

Offshoots of Ribbonism took root wherever the Irish emigrated in large numbers—Scotland, England, Wales, and the United States. In the face of pressure from the authorities and opposition from the Catholic Church, the Ribbon Societies adopted a variety of names—the Society of St. Patrick and the Northern Union in Ulster, the Irish Sons of Freedom in Dublin, the Hibernia Sick and Funeral Society in Britain, and the Hibernia Society in the United States.[53]

The similarities between the Defenders and the Ribbonmen tell us much, but their differences are just as illuminating, for they shed light on the many contradictions of the latter. The Ribbonmen were members of a secret society that paraded openly, a rebel movement that never staged a national revolt, an exclusively Catholic organization that was damned by the church, a benevolent group capable of stunning malevolence. These paradoxes reflect a movement in transition from the Defender style of revolutionary secret society to a more open political movement, a change necessitated by the wide variety of the Ribbon Societies' activities.

The Ribbonmen at various times functioned as a local defense force against the Orange Order, a mutual aid society, a primitive trade union, a vehicle for ordinary criminal activity like illegal distilling, and a political campaign organization. An observer summed up this bewildering variety of functions in an 1877 description of the Ribbon Society: "In Ulster it professed to be a defensive or retaliatory league against Orangeism. In Munster it was a combination against tithe-proctors. In Connaught it was an organization against rack-rentings and evictions. In Leinster it often was mere trade-unionism."[54]

It was as a counterweight to the Orange Order that the northern Society of Ribbonmen was perhaps best known. Clashes between the two groups tended to occur in the summer, during Ulster's "marching season," when Protestant parades often led to violence. One such battle occurred in south County Down on July 12, 1849, the anniversary of the Protestant victory at the Battle of the Boyne. As an Orange procession made its way through a Catholic district near Castlewellan, the marchers clashed with Ribbonmen at Dolly's Brea. An estimated thirty Catholics were killed when the Orangemen, joined by police and troops, opened fire on the Ribbonmen.[55]

The clashes were not limited to Ireland. Near Newcastle in England, where Orangemen and Ribbonmen had emigrated to work in the coal and iron industries, a July 12, 1856, battle on the banks of the Tyne River was reported to have left "a considerable number killed and wounded on both sides." New York City was troubled by vicious rioting between Orangemen and the neo-Ribbon Ancient Order of Hibernians in the early 1870s.[56]

As a mutual aid society, the Ribbonmen helped provide funds for the care of sick members and the funerals of dead ones, as the name of the British organization indicates. Funerals of members sometimes occasioned mass public displays—five hundred Ribbonmen turned out when a leader was buried in Fermanagh in 1837, and thousands marched in military formation at a funeral in Leitrim the following year. Mutual aid could evolve into labor activity, especially in proto-industrial settings like Ireland's canal system. Ribbonmen set prevailing wages for repair work on the Royal Canal following a bad storm in 1839, through what one army officer in Longford described as "a system of general intimidation, carried out to the most alarming degree."[57]

But the lines between mutual defense and a protection racket could become blurred, as noted by the Dublin Ribbon leader Richard Jones, when he accused his northern rivals of maintaining a separate organization so they could "rob your fellow countrymen with impunity." In County Longford in May 1839, the chief constable of Ballymahon feared violence because a local Ribbon leader had undertaken to collect payments to the local landlord associated with market day, which the local peasantry adamantly opposed.[58]

Instances like this, in which Ribbonmen acted like the Sicilian Mafia in enforcing the landlord's will on the peasantry, were notably rare in the second quarter of the nineteenth century, and with good reason. Political, economic, and demographic trends were conspiring to force the Ribbonmen of the Ulster borderlands to take a deeper interest in the land question. It was this development, more than any other, that set the stage for the Molly Maguires.

4   Land and Politics

Almost every civil war, rebellion, insurrection and disturbance in Ireland, from the time of the Tudors downwards, arose more or less directly from questions connected with the possession of lands.

—Philip H. Bagenal

Nonviolent movements for social change in Ireland have a long history of turning bloody in the face of repression. The United Irish reformers of the early 1790s, suppressed in 1794, became the United Irish revolutionaries of 1798. And in the late 1960s, the Northern Ireland Civil Rights Association, in combating institutional discrimination against Catholics, triggered a hard-line Protestant backlash that led to the Troubles. Much the same thing happened in the two decades leading up to the famine, when peaceful campaigns for Catholic rights and the repeal of the union between Britain and Ireland had a dire effect on landlord–tenant relations.

The effort by Daniel "The Liberator" O'Connell, a Dublin lawyer and Kerry landlord, to emancipate Catholics from the last of the Penal Laws—to allow them the full right to hold civil offices and have political representation—was launched with the formation of the Catholic Association in 1823. Its mobilization of the Irish masses, supported by the clergy, stood as the most viable challenge to the established order since the Rebellion of 1798.

O'Connell, who opposed violence, secret societies, and trade unions, would seem an unlikely impetus for the land war that ensued. But even with the aid of the Catholic Church and a disciplined organization that reached down to the parish level, he could not completely control the forces he had helped unleash. Protestant landlords who had long rewarded the political deference of Catholic tenants with fair dealing were angered by the flexing of Catholic political muscle. Many retaliated with evictions.

In County Cavan, for example, Sir George Hodson ejected large numbers of his Catholic tenants in the 1820s, and Rev. Marcus Beresford, a prominent member of the Orange Order, did the same in the late 1830s and early 1840s. Both relet the holding to Protestant tenants they considered politically reliable.[1]

In adjacent County Leitrim, politics played a similar role in the decay of landlord–tenant relations. That much was made clear by the almost comical testimony of Thomas Kingston Little, agent for Sir Morgan Crofton, in Mohill on July 17, 1844, before the Devon Commission, which was examining the state of the Irish countryside:

Q. Have any tenants been removed from the estate and had land taken from them, from causes not arising out of their incapacity to pay rent, such as political and religious grounds?

A. Oh, no! We know nothing of that kind; I never knew any case of that kind . . .

Q. You have already stated that there were no ejectments of tenants on account of political or religious differences; have there been any ejectments, or unusual proceedings, on account of any voting for the election of the board of guardians?

A. There was, prior to my being appointed as agent [in September 1842]. The tenants upon the townland of Drumnalt behaved very badly. They had an abatement [of rent], and the abatement was withdrawn.

Q. What do you mean by "behaving badly"?

A. They voted contrary to Sir Morgan Crofton's wishes.[2]

Even when tenants were not evicted for supporting O'Connell, his campaign for Catholic rights (and his later effort to repeal the union between Britain and Ireland) undermined their tenure on the land. An observer in Leitrim in 1845 noted that "since the great political struggle" for Catholic emancipation, "when the landlords were beaten throughout Ireland at the general election, and their tenants polled almost to a man against them," the landlords had generally refused to offer tenants the security of leases. The trend was particularly clear in Leitrim, he noted, and the Devon Commission made the same point about Cavan.[3]

In essence, O'Connell's campaigns helped to upend the grand bargain of the Irish countryside—many Catholic tenants were no longer willing to acquiesce to an unequal relationship with their Protestant landlords, and many of those landlords no longer felt any obligation to rent the tenants the land they needed in order to live. All of this had little direct impact on

O'Connell and his middle-class supporters in towns and cities. But it was a disaster for peasants.

There were other powerful reasons for evictions, the shortening or elimination of leases, and the general decay of protections for the peasantry. At the same time that the political situation was dividing landlords and tenants, economic and demographic conditions were changing drastically. The effect was to undermine Ulster custom, the unwritten rules of the countryside that had long defined landlord–tenant relations in the Ulster borderlands. Ulster custom, or tenant right as it was sometimes called, varied from place to place, but to a certain degree it served as a sort of social safety net for tenants. Originally it aided the Protestants who settled the north after the flight of the earls, but its extension to Catholic tenants demonstrated the degree to which Ulster custom benefited landlords as well.

In overwhelmingly Catholic parts of County Monaghan, for example, outgoing tenant farmers had the right to "sell" improvements they had made to a successor, but the profits from the sale were used to pay off any remaining debt to the landlord before the tenant could claim his share.[4] Elsewhere, tenant right meant that rents were kept below market levels.[5] This informal system depended on a paternalistic relationship between landlord and tenant, and as long as the custom was upheld there was little need for gunmen in women's clothing to uphold traditional rights. The Ribbonmen could largely confine their activities to the sectarian struggle.

But by the latter half of the 1820s, economic, social, and political changes had begun to transform rural Ulster into a place where the traditional social order no longer worked to the benefit of landlords. The changes had begun by the late 1700s as landlords raised rents and consolidated their estates, a reflection of their increasing integration into the British market system. Transportation improvements allowed farmers to meet the growing demand for foodstuffs from an industrializing England.[6]

What this meant for farmers and agricultural laborers was explored by the historian Kevin O'Neill in his study of the pre-famine economic and social conditions in Killeshandra, a County Cavan parish on the border with Leitrim that he described as typical of south Ulster. It was also an early stronghold of the Molly Maguires.

O'Neill pointed out that it took decades after the arrival of market forces in the late 1700s for them to become central to the economy of the region— decades in which those affected protested violently against changes that threatened their livelihoods and their way of life.[7]

As the consolidation of farms dried up the supply of small rental holdings, longtime tenants found themselves turned out of their fields. The alternatives were daywork on larger farms, seasonal migration for work to other parts of the British Isles, the production of illegal whiskey, or emigration. By the 1830s the number of the landless had risen markedly in rural Cavan, and by 1841 they constituted a majority.[8]

All this was happening as a market-driven increase in productivity led to a rise in the population of rural Cavan—it is estimated that the number of young adults seeking farms peaked immediately before the famine. In families that still held land, the traditional subdivision of the fields among children had all but disappeared by 1841. That forced younger siblings to fend for themselves, and the eldest son who would inherit the farm to undergo a prolonged adolescence—an ideal condition for the growth of festive groups like the mummers, composed largely of unmarried young adults.

The rising population had exceeded the demand for labor as early as the 1820s, resulting in falling living standards for farm workers. Competition for fields triggered increased tension between Catholics and Protestants, as did rising rents from 1826 until the famine, for the landlords were largely Protestant. This was accompanied by a dramatic decline in the linen industry that further hurt those laborers who depended on weaving to supplement their income. South Ulster counties such as Cavan and Monaghan were transformed, in the words of one historian, into "rural slums," with many inhabitants too poorly clothed to attend church on Sunday.[9]

These economic conditions had a profound affect on Ulster custom. Competition for land sent tenant-right payments soaring through most of the 1830s, but poor market and crop conditions had the reverse effect in the years 1839–41. On the brink of the famine, the collapse of tenant-right payments effectively made the safety net of Ulster custom worthless.

As politics, demographics, and economics wreaked havoc on the traditional structure of rural Ireland, the issue of electoral retaliation was pointedly raised by Maria Edgeworth, the Longford novelist whose most famous work, *Castle Rackrent*, dealt with a brutal landlord. "Landlords, if you begin this recriminatory system on or after elections, where will it end?" she asked in 1835.[10] The question was rhetorical, but the answer leads us back to Ballinamuck, the battlefield that Edgeworth had toured with her father in 1798.

It was there, just months after Edgeworth posed her question, that a new battle erupted in the spring of 1835. With evictions mounting as the land issue became entwined with the politics, the secret societies began to weigh in, violently, in defense of tenants who had defied their landlords at the polls. Their stand at Ballinamuck made it the symbolic if not the actual birthplace of Molly Maguire.

Molly was a character as elusive as she was dangerous, and the false trails about her origins are legion. But let us follow the path to Ballinamuck, and to another locale long linked to the rise of the Mollies, the barony of Farney in Monaghan, for the journey reveals much about the conditions that gave birth to the last of Ireland's great peasant conspiracies against the landlords, and of the propaganda that both sides employed in that struggle.

The story that Ballinamuck was the birthplace of the Mollies seems to have been spread by the Mollies themselves; the notion that the movement was born in Farney was spread by one of the nineteenth century's greatest propagandists for the landlords of Ireland. The stories have much in common, but their greatest similarity is that not one shred of evidence can be found in the contemporary records to support the idea that outbreaks in either place were the work of a group calling itself the Molly Maguires.

Ballinamuck

Thomas Campbell Foster, a *Times* of London reporter who traveled the Ulster borderlands in 1845, reported that, "in this neighborhood [Cavan], the commencement of 'Molly Maguireism' is traced to Ballynamuck in the County of Longford . . . a whole village was destroyed, and the population ejected . . . the tenants who replaced them were all either shot, or they fled from fear."[11] Foster, writing a decade after the Ballinamuck disturbances, was not alone in linking the secret society to the village. Local folklore, too, drew a connection between the troubles there and the Mollies.[12]

The conflict had its roots in the crisis over Catholic liberation that first erupted in Waterford in 1826, when tenants defied their landlords to vote for an O'Connell candidate. From 1830 to 1837, six elections in Longford were contested by the Conservatives on the one side and O'Connell supporters and their allies on the other. John Barnes, a relatively evenhanded magistrate assigned to the area around Ballinamuck, blamed agrarian violence there on the frequent elections, with "the priests taking one side, and the landlords taking another, each party pulling the tenantry according to their wishes."[13]

After their party suffered a loss in the 1832 election, Conservative Longford landlords decided they needed to enlarge their electoral base by increasing the number of Protestant tenants on their estates. Lord Lorton, who owned a heavily subdivided estate in Ballinamuck, was among the most active in this effort. Through his land agent, Thomas Courtenay, Lorton began a policy of consolidating holdings, dispossessing the Catholic tenants, and replacing them with Protestants.

The process was well under way by the spring of 1834, and culminated in May 1835, when, with leases expiring, Lorton launched what he described as a "pretty general clearance of the miserable people." While keeping some Catholic tenants, he brought in eight Protestant families as well.

The move, Magistrate Barnes reported, created a "general impression among the people and the priests that Lorton wished to Protestantize his estate—the fact that all who were ejected were Catholics and all new tenants were Protestants confirmed this impression."[14] Barnes concluded that a number of the evictions were politically motivated.

The results were grimly predictable, given Irish history. In 1793, the perception that the Militia Act was being used to punish Catholics for their political gains had triggered widespread violence by the Defenders. Forty years later, the politically inspired evictions in Longford had the same effect with their descendants, the Ribbonmen.

In May 1835, a Catholic, Peter Hart, was killed for voting Conservative. The next month, John Brock, one of the first of the new Protestant tenants, was shot and killed in a field behind his home.

Brock's replacement, James Diamond, suffered a series of attacks; eight Ribbonmen were convicted and banished for seven years in one of them. In all, four of the new Protestant tenants were killed, two were severely beaten, and three had their cattle killed. "Nothing can equal the outrages which are both daily and nightly being committed in the county," a local newspaper reported.[15]

The entry of secret societies also added a new level of volatility to polling places, which became notoriously violent carnivals throughout the country during the 1830s and 1840s. In a typical Irish election, thousands of people would turn out for days of balloting, with crowds of nonvoters often intimidating those who did have the franchise. Threatening letters and violence were used to sway voters before elections and to punish them afterward.[16]

During an election in County Longford in December 1836, groups of armed Ribbonmen appeared at the homes of voters, warning them not to cast ballots for the Tory candidate, Charles Fox. The violence was so common that it became unremarkable. In the 1836 Longford election, an official in Ballymahon reported to Dublin Castle on the day of the vote that "there has been a great deal of rioting today, but nothing of importance has occurred." After the Liberal candidate won the election, warning letters signed "Capt. Rock" were used to enforce a boycott on those who had voted Conservative.[17]

The continuing campaign of terror and the difficulty in prosecuting those responsible led Lorton to take a desperate step. In 1837 he told his agent, Courtenay, that unless convictions were forthcoming, he was to clear "all the ground that has fallen out of lease" and rent it to "new tenants, for whom good houses are to be built." Still not satisfied when the leases for Ballinamuck and the land around it expired in February of the following year, Lorton instituted eviction proceedings. "My feelings had been very much wounded and excited by the determined manner in which they picked off every Protestant they could," he said of the Catholics tenantry.

Barnes reported in April of that year that "47 notices were served upon the tenants of Lord Lorton, in and near they village of Ballynamuck . . . It is much to be feared that turning out so many persons (all Roman Catholics) will sooner or later have an effect on the peace of that district."[18]

Over the next year, Ribbonmen conducted nocturnal raids on homes, posted warning letters across the county, and fired warning shots. In January 1839, Bernard Higgins was killed near Ballinamuck after he had seized a cow for overdue rent.

But the destruction of the village, when it finally came that spring, was almost anticlimactic. Lorton had offered the tenants cash payments and the use of any timber from their homes if they demolished the structures themselves, and more than forty grudgingly accepted. When Courtenay, accompanied by 100 policemen and 260 soldiers, arrived in Ballinamuck to complete the work in April, they tore down just five homes.[19]

By that time, thousands of people had been ejected by Lorton and other Conservative landlords in the county. The repercussions did indeed "have an effect on the peace" of that district, as Barnes had predicted. In June, a man and his son were beaten near Ballinamuck because they worked for a Protestant. In July, the home of James Grimes near Ballinamuck was robbed by two men, one with his face blackened. Elsewhere in the county, gunmen were turning up in odd disguises. Less than three weeks after the evictions, a man dressed as a woman fired a shot on the farm of John Reilly, who had recently purchased two acres of land near Granard.[20] If the copies of reward notices forwarded to Dublin Castle are any indication, the walls of Longford town, Drumlish, and Granard were covered with broadsheets offering money for information during this period.

The blackened faces and women's clothing signaled that the struggle was over land—a point underlined by the proximity of some attacks to holidays. Brock was killed on June 24, 1835—suspiciously close to the Midsummer night celebrations, which were traditionally held on June 23 and June 28 in Longford. Another Protestant tenant, Arthur Cathcart, was fired at on December 29, 1835. On January 2, 1838, a gunman with a blackened cape and another wearing a straw cape entered a home near Drumlish, just south of Ballinamuck.[21]

Though they were in some cases dressing as women, the peasant guerrillas of Longford were not, at this point, fighting under the auspices of "Molly Maguire." Not a single mention of that name shows up in the extensive County Longford files of agrarian crimes reported to Dublin Castle for the years 1835–39. Instead, the mythical character whose signature appeared on the warning notices of that period was "Captain Rock."

It is true that folklore later attributed the murder of Brock and others to the "Molly Maguires," and that the word in Cavan about a decade later was that the Ballinamuck land war was the commencement of "Molly Maguireism." But those references are best understood in a symbolic sense, denoting Ballinamuck as the birthplace of a new departure for the Ribbonmen—a land war fought by men in the guise of mummers. Only in retrospect was the site of the last great battle of the 1798 insurrection—and the first great battle of a new land war—designated as the birthplace of the Molly Maguires. As a symbol and as propaganda, Ballinamuck was simply too perfect for the Mollies to pass up.

Farney

Another location long associated with the birth of the Molly Maguires is that of the Shirley estate in the barony of Farney in south Monaghan. There, as in Ballinamuck, a land war was fought on two levels—in streets and fields, and in hearts and minds. In some ways, the picture in Farney was similar to that of Ballinamuck, with O'Connell's movement undermining the traditional structure of landlord–tenant relations. There is much more information on the struggle that finally erupted in south Monaghan in 1843, thanks to the detailed though far from reliable memoir of the agent on the Shirley estate, W. Steuart Trench. He was the era's prime propagandist for the landlords, and there are strong reasons to doubt that anyone at the time called the peasant guerrillas he faced in Farney "Molly Maguires."

Of one thing we can be sure—Farney had long been a battleground. It was there, in the fourth century, that the men of Connacht were said to have routed the forces of Ulster in a seven-day battle to avenge the slaying of Conn of the Hundred Battles by fifty men disguised as women. Hugh Roe MacMahon led cattle raids in the barony in the late 1500s, Mountjoy "spoiled all of Farney" in 1600, and Defenders battled troops at Carrickmacross, Farney's main town, in 1793.[22]

By the early 1800s, Farney was a center of two symbiotic trends—Ribbon activity and sectarian conflict. The barony's overwhelming Catholic majority was reported to be boycotting Protestant merchants in 1813, and in the following year the campaign escalated with threatening notes and attacks on individuals and property. Protestants feared a secret society was trying to drive them from the area.[23]

In 1816, as we have seen, delegates from across Ulster met at Carrickmacross to reconstitute the old Defender network, and that same year, Ribbonmen burned Wildgoose Lodge, just a few miles from the town. This, then, was the sectarian thatch into which O'Connell's civil rights movement dropped like a firebrand in the 1826 election, making Monaghan a national sensation. Four candidates were vying for the county's two seats in Parliament—Charles Powell Leslie, an incumbent who served as colonel of the Monaghan Militia and opposed Catholic emancipation; Henry R. Westenra, an incumbent and the son-in-law of Lord Rossmore, a staunch supporter of emancipation; Evelyn J. Shirley, an English Liberal and largely absentee landlord; and Walter Tyler, who was not considered viable.

Branding Leslie a bigot, O'Connell decided to intervene in the election, and the Catholic Association and the clergy urged voters to cast their two ballots for Westenra and Shirley—a position complicated by a pact between Shirley and Leslie that they would ask their supporters to cast their second ballot for each other. Westenra could win only if those who voted for Shirley also defied him by voting against his ally, Leslie. And, indeed, voters from the Shirley estate said they would "give one vote for their landlord, and the other they would give for their religion and their country."[24]

The campaign was heated, and O'Connell sent an aide to campaign for Westenra. A daylong riot during the balloting left three dead and several injured. And when it was over, the voters had turned out Leslie for Westenra, infuriating Shirley, despite his own victory.

As in Longford a decade later, Monaghan landlords began evicting Catholic tenants who had defied them at the ballot box. Among the leaders of the eviction campaign was Shirley, who also raised rents by a third, ruining a favorable reputation among his tenants. "Up to this time, Mr. Shirley was a good landlord, and admitted tenant-right to the fullest extent on the property," recalled the local Catholic priest, Rev. Thomas Smollen. "But after that election he never showed the same friendly feelings to the people."[25]

Trench, the estate manager for Shirley in the 1840s, described the divisive effect of elections in terms remarkably similar to those of Barnes, the Ballinamuck magistrate, though Trench's sympathies were clearly with the landlords. "I know of nothing more detrimental to the peace and prosperity of a district, than an election of members of Parliament, conducted as such elections generally are in Ireland," Trench wrote in his memoirs. "The priest on the one side urges vehemently the constitutional rights of the tenant; and the landlord on the other is indignant that all the influence he might naturally expect from his position, education and wealth should, from this difference in creed, be rudely forced from his hands under the sanction of what he must admit is the tenant's constitutional right."[26]

The eviction campaign by landlords indignant at their loss of influence set the stage for the next act of the drama. In the fall of 1828, one O'Connell's chief supporters in the north, the Belfast journalist Jack Lawless, arrived in Carrickmacross to announce a nonviolent "invasion of Ulster" by supporters of emancipation. His plan for a march by fifty thousand supporters was designed to drum up support for the "Catholic rent," a defense fund for tenants who had voted against the landlords. One of the towns on Lawless's route was the largely Presbyterian Ballybay. As thousands of armed Orangemen gathered there to counter the march, infantry, lancers, and the entire county police force were dispatched to Carrickmacross to prevent a collision between the two sides. The show of force persuaded Lawless to take a different route, but clashes occurred nonetheless; at least one Catholic was killed, and several were wounded.

The "invasion" proceeded on its way, to Armagh and to Omagh, leading Protestants there to form one of the two hundred Brunswick Clubs that had sprung up in opposition to O'Connell by 1828. With aristocratic leaders and a heavy leavening of clergymen and lawyers, the anti-Catholic Brunswick clubs attracted many who had shied away from the Orange Society. One more poisonous sectarian plant had evolved in the hothouse of Ulster politics.[27]

Religious controversies continued in Farney throughout the next decade, as Catholics campaigned against the tithes they were required to pay to support the Anglican Church of Ireland. A riot left several injured in Magheracloone in February 1832 when magistrates and dragoons tried to collect the money. Protestant proselytizing by Shirley's estate agent, Sandy Mitchell, and another employee, Capt. Richard Bowden, only added to the suspicions of the Catholic tenants and their clergy. Shirley, an Anglican, found himself embroiled in a bitter dispute with the local Catholic hierarchy in the mid-1830s, after he insisted that the Bible be read at a school he had opened for children on his estate. One tenant who aided in the founding of an alternative school was reportedly evicted, though he was not in arrears. After a conservative Monaghan newspaper, the *Northern Standard*,

ran an editorial by Bowden that accused the local priest of "ignorant bigotry," it was successfully sued.[28]

By the late 1830s, the constant drumbeat of sectarian troubles had made
Farney perhaps the most important Ribbon center in Ireland. The leaders
of the movement's two main factions were, as we have seen, John Rice, a
Carrickmacross farmer, and Richard Jones, a Dublin haymarket clerk and
native of Farney.[29]

Given the level of bitterness on the Shirley estate, it should come as no
surprise that when Mitchell, the estate agent, died of a heart attack in the
spring of 1843, the tenants celebrated with bonfires on the hilltops. Mitchell had been a magistrate as well as a land agent—a common combination
that placed the law firmly in the hands of the landlord. He was remembered as a man who maintained a network of spies among the tenants and
who leveraged marriages with the threat of eviction—the sort of interference sure to enrage festive groups like the strawboys, who were deeply
concerned with the issue of marriage.[30]

Mitchell's replacement was Trench, an Anglo-Irishmen who had some
experience with Ribbonmen in Tipperary. Upon arrival in March, the new
estate agent perceived a wild, Irish-speaking peasantry that was either at
his feet or at his throat. "The Celt in all his purity had been allowed to increase and multiply. Irish was the language at the time chiefly spoken by
the people," he wrote in his memoirs decades later. "Though the people
were most docile and easily led, and generally obedient to their superiors,
yet when once assembled in masses or roused by any common cause, their
old national temperament seemed suddenly to rise to the surface, and they
became capable of the most frenzied excitement."[31]

The bonfires that accompanied Mitchell's death hinted at the old connection between festive custom and disorder. The local authorities had some
limited success in the 1830s when they tried to suppress the Midsummer's
Eve fires, which, it was believed, "tended to create riots in the country."
Mummers, too, were known to march the streets of Carrickmacross, with
the Prince George character killing his rival combatant, the Turkey Champion, in their age-old duel.[32]

The barony was a crowded one. Subdivision of land had so flourished
that the 44,107 inhabitants of Farney were crowded onto 67,333 acres. The
version of tenant right they practiced proved highly favorable to the landlord. "It was then the common practice on the estate, when a tenant became insolvent," Trench recalled, "that he should come to the office of the
estate and consent to his interest in the farm as yearly tenant being sold to
some other tenant, approved by the landlord or his agent, and that the

proceeds should be applied to clear his rent and pay his numerous debts." The purchase money frequently amounted to ten or twelve pounds per acre, and creditors would show up on the day of the defaulter's goodwill sale, a schedule of debts would be drawn up, and the landlord would be paid first.[33]

Trench's employer was precisely the sort most feared by peasants. Shirley was a transplanted English Protestant determined to improve his estate by consolidating it, and to improve his tenants by educating them, and if possible converting them. His efforts typified the attempts by many south Ulster landlords to integrate their estates into the British market economy. He showed little sympathy to those tenants squeezed by the process and consistently voted with the Conservatives in Parliament.[34]

As Trench emerged from a meeting with his new employer and chief clerk in Carrickmacross to discuss the situation on Friday, March 31, 1843, they were confronted by a crowd of tenants complaining that "we are pressed and ground down, and we must have a removal of our grievances." The peasants said they would pay no rent until the rates were reduced, and Shirley replied that they would have their answer on Monday. The vast gulf between what the landlord said and what the tenants heard—a split that mirrored so many others—became apparent as word spread that on Monday the tenants' grievances would be resolved and the amount of their rent reduction announced.

The next day, an alarmed Shirley had a placard posted that proclaimed "his opinion that the present distress has not been caused, so far as the Shirley tenantry are concerned, by high rents; and that, therefore . . . he does not feel bound to make, at present, either a temporary or permanent reduction in the rent." He would not attend any meeting on Monday, the placard said, and the tenants were admonished to stay at home.

The placard went up on Saturday and was torn down on Sunday. On Monday a crowd that Trench estimated at ten thousand gathered in Carrickmacross as Shirley held a council of war with the agent for the neighboring estate of the Marquis of Bath. They agreed to stand firm against any reduction and sent the hapless Trench to announce the news to the swarming crowd. He was promptly mobbed, beaten, dragged through the streets, and nearly strangled before being deposited on the front step of the landlord's manor, minus most of his clothes and all of his dignity.

Thus began the affair soon to be a cause célèbre throughout Ireland. The day that Trench was humiliated, Shirley requested a company of infantry and a troop of dragoons. The soldiers were dispatched and paraded through Carrickmacross in a show of force. O'Connell arrived on April 25, telling a crowd of twenty thousand that though tyranny flourished in Farney "to a lamentable excess," Ribbonism was not the answer.[35]

Amid all the street theatrics, both military and political, another drama was unfolding in the countryside, where Trench's rent collectors were running into extreme difficulty. Men, women, and children dogged their steps, hurling stones. After the arrest of fourteen tenants, warning notices went up threatening bailiffs, and the tenants began keeping watch on their movements. In May, a group of men dressed in women's clothing, with their faces blackened, assaulted a man serving a legal notice on a tenant in default. The costumes they wore were those of the Whiteboys and mummers, but Trench tells us that they had adopted a new name.

"They established a system of what they called 'Molly Maguires,'" Trench wrote. "These 'Molly Maguires' were generally stout, active young men dressed up in women's clothes, with faces blackened, or otherwise disguised; sometimes they wore crape over their countenances, sometimes smeared themselves in the most fantastic manner with burnt cork about their eyes, mouths and cheeks." These Mollies, he wrote, "carried pistols under their petticoats," and waged such a remorseless war against the landlord's employees that soon none were willing to serve legal papers or round up the cattle of tenants delinquent in their rent.

Trench recalled that it was decided at a council of war that the Molly Maguires must be put down. The climax came when a magistrate, accompanied by a Shirley bailiff and eighteen soldiers, attempted to post a blanket notice of eviction at a church. A stone-throwing mob confronted the troop, which opened fire, killing one man and wounding several others. The landlord's party retreated, and while the inquest that followed raised doubts about the decision to open fire, no criminal charges were brought.[36] In the wake of what became known as the Battle of Magheracloone, Trench convinced his employer to take a more conciliatory approach, which he says defused the situation.

For all of Trench's references to "Molly Maguires" in the memoir he wrote decades later, the term appears in not a single one of the contemporary reports forwarded to Dublin Castle on the agrarian agitation in Farney in 1843. There are descriptions of "Rockite notices" and of men with blackened faces in the thick file of Monaghan Outrage Papers for that year, but Mollies don't add to the bulk—they are never mentioned. And in extensive testimony given just a year later to the Devon Commission, which was investigating conditions in the Irish countryside, Trench went into some detail about the events of 1843 but never once mentioned "Molly Maguires." Indeed, in two days of testimony before the Devon Commission in

Carrickmacross in April 1844, not a single witness spoke the name.[37] For that matter, no contemporary mention of "Molly Maguires" has been found in connection with agrarian crime anywhere before late 1844.

When his memoir, *Realities of Irish Life*, was published decades later in 1868, Trench was criticized for his gross exaggerations, which included illustrations of the peasantry as "gorillas, always flourishing shillelaghs, and grinning horribly." The landlords, meanwhile, were portrayed as demigods, "formed by nature to be the masters and guides and managers of such a silly, helpless people." Indeed, one critic called Trench's work, "one the most misleading books on Ireland published in many years." The *New York Times* called it "semi-sensational," and mocked the author's portrayal of himself as "a man of unflinching nerve, of great physical endurance, unfailing in resource, generous to a fault, prompt in action and always doing just the right thing at just the right time." The local Catholic priest, Rev. Smollen, pointed out that while Trench was saved from the mob by another priest, Fr. Keelaghan, "Mr. Trench gives him no place in his Realities."[38]

Given the harsh contemporary criticism of the book's accuracy, and absent any mention of the Mollies elsewhere before 1844, it seems likely that in writing more than two decades after the events in question Trench committed a bit of literary and historical fraud, embroidering his account with a name that had grown infamous by the 1860s, but which was still unheard of in 1843.

Even local landlords contradicted Trench on the nature of the conspiracy he faced. Trench acknowledged that Ribbonmen were active on the Shirley estate, but claimed "that the Ribbon Confederacy . . . had nothing whatever to do" with the outrages in the spring of 1843, which he viewed as isolated and spontaneous, "a sudden rising of the people, by no means previously planned or premeditated."[39]

Lord Rossmore, a Monaghan estate owner with a bit more knowledge of the county than Trench, took a starkly different view. "A similar event having taken place last autumn upon a neighboring estates in the adjacent county seems to lead to the inference that this has not been an isolated movement, taken up at the instant; neither is it connected with any sectarian feeling," Rossmore wrote to Dublin Castle on April 4, 1843. Instead, he pointed to other factors—falling farm prices, "a superabounding population," and the "introduction of a fresh agent to the Shirley property" who lacked his predecessor's influence: Trench.

In May of 1843, another writer informed Dublin Castle that "a regular conspiracy had been organized on the Farney estate"—hardly the spontaneous uprising that Trench saw.[40] The agent's notion that there were two vast yet unrelated peasant movements at work on the Shirley estate—an isolated uprising of Mollies on the one hand, and long-standing Ribbon activity on the other—stretches credibility. Sectarianism and political divisions had laid the groundwork for discontent, but the appearance of armed men disguised as mummers clearly indicated that, in south Monaghan, land had become the main issue on the eve of the famine.

If Trench's hindsight was suspect, his foresight was undeniable. In the summer of 1844, as the Devon Commission was wrapping up its fact-finding, he offered the following prediction: "I strongly feel that matters are not likely to continue as they are. I cannot shut my eyes to the fact that, though the people are being educated, they are suffering severe want. They are growing in intelligence and in numbers, and in a knowledge of their strength, as well as of their wretchedness . . . I think there is a danger, if the humbler classes continue much longer to acquire knowledge and to want food, that a long-threatened convulsion may be the consequence."[41]

Summer had barely ended before the first pangs of that convulsion were felt, not in Monaghan but along the Cavan–Leitrim border. There, "the humbler classes" were giving birth to Molly Maguire, though she would not be named for months.

5 The Molly Maguires

In Cavan-town, where we sat down,
Our Irish hearts to inspire,
There's bould recruits and undaunted yout's,
An' they'r led by Mollie Maguire!

—Molly Maguire ballad

Molly Maguire made her debut in the historic record in the same cold, dark season that the mummers typically made their entrance. On December 10, 1844, the *Freeman's Journal* in Dublin reported on the appearance of a group that "called themselves the 'Molly Maguires,' a fantastic name, but they assembled at night, and committed outrages of every kind."

About a week earlier, on December 2, magistrates had held a special meeting at the Ballyconnell Courthouse in County Cavan to complain of "armed bodies of men marching by night, breaking open houses, dragging certain inmates out into the open air, compelling them on their knees by the terror of guns presented to their breasts to take unlawful oaths, searching for firearms and when found carrying them off." The outbreak was seen as an assault on the legal system, "putting a stop to the regular course of justice" by making it impossible to execute court decrees.[1]

At issue was the very question of who ruled the countryside—the magistrates and constables, or "armed and organized bodies of Whiteboys." The raids on homes for arms, the assaults, and the threats became so serious that Capt. John MacLeod, a special magistrate from Fermanagh, was dispatched to Ballinamore, Leitrim, to deal with the outbreak.[2] A military detachment and thirty-six extra constables were sent as well.

The disturbances caused profound worry not only among the authorities, but also among Catholic reformers. On December 22, Thomas Steele, a top aide to O'Connell, wrote the Emancipator from Leitrim that the Catholic clergy and supporters of the repeal movement were doing their best to counter the influence of the new organization: "I have strong reason to hope that the poor, wretched duped and deluded 'Molly Maguires' will, as a party, soon cease to have an existence."[3]

His hope proved premature, as police reports make clear. In one, Robert Anderson of Killeshandra in County Cavan complained that on the night of January 20, 1845, he was attending a wake at the home of Patrick Murphy near Carrigallen, less than two miles across the Leitrim County line, when the shout went up to "clear the way for 'Molly Maguire.'"

"Clear the way" echoed the line used for the entrance of characters in the mummers play, and sure enough, when "Molly" stepped through the door, she was wearing an amalgam of mummers or wren boys costumes. Her white shirt, petticoat, and hat were of the sort worn by the Miss Funny or Mary Anne character, the blackened neck and face were typical of the Fool, and the hay hoop around her waist was a nod to Jack Straw.

But Molly was no lady, and there was nothing playful about the violence that ensued at the Murphy home in the townland of Drumbreanlis. Anderson and John Montgomery, the only Protestants at the wake, were among four men viciously beaten, apparently as part of "preconcerted plan," according to a police report. The motive was listed as sectarian: "A party feud is the supposed cause of the outrage."[4]

In fact, the curtain had risen on this performance months before Molly made her actual entrance. The troubles that erupted in late 1844 had been percolating since early autumn along the Cavan–Leitrim border. Conditions there were desperate a year before the potato crop failed—a priest testified before the Devon Commission in 1844 that the small tenants could not be worse off. At a time when one Leitrim farmer told the commission that at least ten to twelve acres were the minimum needed to support a family, nearly 51 percent of all farms in the county covered just one to five acres. Things weren't much better in Cavan, where 42 percent of all farms fell into the one-to-five-acre category. (By contrast, in more prosperous County Antrim, 29 percent of farms were of the smallest size.)[5]

Given the untenable nature of the small holdings, it should come as no surprise that the Devon Commission found that "ejectment proceedings," the first step in eviction, were very common in Cavan, and that lawsuits against tenants for debt to the landlord, which could lead to imprisonment, were used extensively in Leitrim.[6]

As hard as these economic steps were for the peasantry, noneconomic evictions especially rankled Ribbonmen determined to protect Catholics from sectarian depredations. In Cavan, the majority of tenants who were removed from estates immediately before the famine appear to have been ejected on political or religious grounds.[7]

Matters came to a head with the close of the 1844 harvest. Starting in late September, sporadic trouble broke out in a triangle running from Ballinamore in Leitrim to Swalinbar and Belturbet in Cavan. On September 26 a "Rockite" notice was posted in Leganamer, Leitrim; the next night a home was attacked just over the county line in Clarbally, Cavan.[8] The attacks may have been pegged to the Feast of St. Michael on September 29, when farmers traditionally killed an animal and gave portions of meat to the poor of the neighborhood—and when the hunting season traditionally began.[9]

The violence grew markedly more widespread and intense in the short season of ritual bloodletting between Halloween and "oul Halloween," or St. Martin's Day, November 11. On November 3 in Cavan, threatening notices signed "Captain Smart" were posted at the homes of Peter Kiernan of Killywillin and John Rainbird of Newton, who had both taken holdings from which the former tenant had been evicted.[10] A report on agrarian crimes in Leitrim between November 1, 1844, and February 21, 1845, shows that the first reported incident in the Mohill district was on November 4, in the Carrick-on-Shannon district on November 8, and in the Ballinamore district on November 9.

Thereafter, trouble followed every few days. In the Ballinamore district, for example, the following incidents were reported for the month:

Nov. 12: Assault on Thomas Guckian.
Nov. 17: Attack on home of John Gallagher and others.
Nov. 18: Threatening notice posted at home of John and Solomon Campbell.
Nov. 20: Arthur Nelson's home raided for weapons.
Nov. 21: Peter and William Cannon forced to take unlawful oaths.
Nov. 22: Robert Ferguson's pile of turf set on fire.
Nov. 24: Homes attacked in Drumreilly parish.
Nov. 28: Henry Menmaugh and others threatened by armed man.
Nov. 28: Pat McLoughlin's home raided.[11]

By the end of the year, Leitrim ranked fourth among Ireland's thirty-two counties in the number of agrarian crimes, with seventy-two, behind perennially troubled Tipperary, which had 254; Roscommon, with 93; and Limerick, with 73. And unlike in neighboring Roscommon, where just nine agrarian crimes were recorded from September through December, the outrages were on the rise in Leitrim, where 41 were reported in the last four months of the year. By far the biggest category was threatening notices.[12]

The sheer volume of incidents made it impossible for the perpetrators to peg them to major holidays. In fact, quite the opposite occurred. After a steady drumbeat of attacks in December, the trouble mysteriously abated around New Year's. There were no incidents between December 31 and January 13 in the Ballinamore district, December 29 and January 17 in the Mohill district, and December 25 and January 20 in the Carrick-on-Shannon district.[13] This would have been precisely the same period in which mummer and wren boy groups were perambulating the countryside at night in disguises identical to those of the Mollies.

At the end of January, with the mumming season behind them, the Mollies resumed their violent campaign. First there were minor incidents, like the January 20 beating of four men at the wake in Drumbreanlis. Then, on January 29, came the most spectacular Molly crime to date. Two gunmen, waiting at the gate to a manor, Garadice Lodge in Leitrim, assassinated Capt. MacLeod, the special magistrate from Fermanagh who had been dispatched to Ballinamore to deal with the outbreak.

The killing came two days before the eve of Brigid, but perhaps as interesting as the timing was the locale—the manor sat beside Garadice Lough, not far from Magh Slécht, the old stomping ground of that bloody idol Crom Cruach. Thus the first Molly Maguire killing took place within a couple of miles of the site in Ireland most closely linked to human sacrifice, a couple of days before a holiday with deep pagan roots. In part, the killing was an act of propaganda, designed to make people take notice, and if the timing and locale sent a message to the peasantry that was lost on landlords, so much the better. The message the landlords received was loud and clear anyway.

"You will readily perceive that this is no ordinary murder, that it has been committed with a degree of audacity which is quite astonishing," wrote William Sydney Clements, the future Lord Leitrim, who was himself killed by secret society gunmen thirty-three years later.[14] The local aristocrats were not the only ones to take notice. The MacLeod killing inspired Anthony Trollope, then working as a postal clerk in Ireland, to write the first of his many novels. He finished *The Macdermots of Ballycloran* in July 1845, six months after Capt. MacLeod was slain. The book centered on the killing of a Leitrim magistrate, Capt. Ussher, at the gates of an estate.[15]

The official report on the McLeod killing left the motive open to debate—it found that some attributed the killing to his refusal to grant bail "to certain individuals," while others said it stemmed from a ruling at a court session in Bawnboy, Cavan. But there was no real doubt about who was behind the killing. Newspapers immediately linked the crime to the Mollies, and within months the secret society was crowing about it in a ballad, "A New Song on Molly Maguire," that shed light on the motive:

> There was McCloud so big and Proud I think it fit to mention
> to put men in jail and take no bail it was his whole intention
> till liberty as you may see some persons did inspire
> to lay him down the dirty hound they say it was Molly Maguire.[16]

Magistrates' reports and the folklore of the region name different suspects in the case, but they agree that the gunmen fled to America.[17]

In mid-May, Molly assassins claimed another victim. James Gallagher, an agent for Col. Enery, a Cavan landlord and magistrate, was walking near his employer's home outside Ballyconnell when he was blasted with a blunderbuss at such close range that his clothes were left smoldering. After briefly chasing his assailants, he collapsed and died.

The killing took place on the evening of May 14, just days before Whitsuntide, which as Lady Wilde reminds us was always considered to be "a fatal and unlucky time," one associated with violent death.[18] The event proved fatal and unlucky for a number of individuals beyond the unfortunate Mr. Gallagher. Within days the victim's aged mother and shocked wife died, his daughter lost her mind, and two policemen were arrested as the gunmen in the case based on the word of an informer.[19]

The informer, John Brady, told the authorities that the Mollies decided at a meeting at Denis McDonnell's pub in Ballyconnell to kill Gallagher because he was "too hard on the tenants." According to Brady, the assignment was given to two members of the revenue police, Sweeney and McDermott, who carried out the killing disguised in "colored clothes," presumably the bright tatterdemalion of the mummers. Sweeney and McDermott were arrested but eventually released—revenue policemen, the bane of illegal whiskey distillers, made awfully convenient patsies. Nearly five years after the killing, a new batch of suspects were rounded up, including an alleged triggerman named Michael Reilly, aka "Mickey the Rat."[20]

Whomever the individuals involved, there's little doubt about the organization. The Mollies bragged about the killing in "A New Song on Molly Maguire," the same ballad that celebrated the MacLeod murder:

> And Galagher to that you all know he was another villin
> To execute his masters plan he always was quite willing

To distrain every poor man it was his whole desire
Till he was laid flat by a . . . a Son of Molly Maguire.

Five weeks after Gallagher was slain, Molly assassins resumed their campaign against local magistrates. On Sunday, June 22, a day removed from the traditional bonfires of Midsummer's Eve, George Bell Booth of Drumcarbin was gunned down in Crossdoney, Cavan, on his way home from church. The killing was clearly pegged to the peasant calendar, but there may have been other considerations—the victim had been a leader of the Orange Order in Cavan, and tensions between Catholics and Protestants were particularly high that month. A thirteen-year ban on sectarian parading had expired on June 1, when Parliament failed to renew the Party Procession Act of 1832, clearing the way for Orangemen to reassert their local strength with a traditional march on the July 12 anniversary of the Battle of the Boyne.[21]

The Bell Booth killing matched the MacLeod murder in the sensation it created. "A murder at noonday in the Phoenix Park of one of his Excellency's household would be in no respect more extraordinary or daring," a Church of Ireland minister, Rev. J. C. Martin of Killeshandra, wrote the lord lieutenant of Ireland the next day.[22]

And as in the case of MacLeod, the killing quickly became grist for Molly death threats and ballads:

There is one Bell, a child of hell
An' a Magistrate in Station,
Let Lots be drew an' see which av you
Will tumble him to damnation![23]

The near-fatal shooting of another borderlands magistrate on Halloween 1845 in Fermanagh raised the specter of a concerted campaign of terror against local law enforcement officials. Folliot W. Barton was ambushed as he rode home to Pettigo, Fermanagh, from dining with his cousin, Col. Hugh Barton, a leader of the local Orangemen. There were immediate suspicions that the Mollies were involved. "It was a deep and well laid plot of Molly Maguireism," the local newspaper reported, and the Ribbon Detection Society, a private organization that raised money to pay for investigators and informants, helped to pay for a Dublin police detective to investigate the case. Col. Barton complained on November 3 that the magistrates of the county lived "in constant fear of assassination."[24]

But almost as quickly, rumors began to spread about the victim's romantic dalliances, and that a Protestant was behind the shooting. Within hours of the attack, the local police inspector, W. Foot, wrote Dublin Castle that the incident did not appear to be connected to the "confederacy" that existed elsewhere in Fermanagh.[25]

The investigation bogged down as local magistrates inexplicably ordered the constabulary not to cooperate with the Dublin police detective brought in to investigate. Despite testimony that one of the accused had threatened to leave the victim "as low as M'Leod," the trial ended in quick acquittals, amid accusations of perjury by prosecution witnesses and intimidation by men with blackened faces.[26] Given the inconclusive trial and the lack of any evidence that the Mollies themselves ever claimed responsibility for the Barton shooting, it cannot definitively be chalked up to the secret society.

But there can be no doubt that the organization was targeting magistrates. Two years to the day after the Barton shooting, after Sunday Mass on October 31, "a large assemblage" of Ribbonmen gathered at Pat McManus's pub in Kinawley to draw up a hit list of landlords and law enforcement officials in Cavan and Fermanagh, an informer reported. Among those marked for death were the local magnate, Lord Erne, and several magistrates—Capt. Johnstone of Swalinbar, Col. Enery of Ballyconnell (Gallagher's employer), and a Capt. Phillips, who lived near Belturbet.[27]

Who were these Mollies, who plotted holiday mayhem and then celebrated the deeds in song? A rough profile of the group began to emerge in the month after the Booth slaying, when two men shed invaluable light on the structure and goals of the organization. One did so in a confession, the other in a manifesto.

The Organization

In July 1845, in the last fading light of peasant, Gaelic Ireland, John Brady of Templeport, in western County Cavan, found himself in jail in Cavan town, with plenty of time to think. He pondered a misspent past—"I was brought into this business by foolery and whisky"—and a dark future—he had been convicted of handing a landlord named Burk a warning notice to reduce his rent.

In fact, the future was to be far darker than Brady could possibly imagine. This year's "hungry July," that bleak month when the last of the potatoes ran out before the new harvest, would stretch into hungry August and hungry September and hungry October, on and on, as the potato crop failed.

The great famine eventually sent nearly 2.5 million Irishmen into exile or the grave. But Brady reached a decision about his future more than a month before the first reports of rotting potatoes hit the Dublin newspapers. He decided to tell the authorities about the inner workings of the secret society he had joined at John Maguire's pub in Bawnboy, Tullyhaw.

"I belong to the society called the Molly Maguires," Brady said in a confession dated July 24:

> It is the same as the Ribbon business—it is now about two years since I was sworn in . . . They did not meet often for fear of being detected—we did not commit any outrage until latterly—in winter last, we began to be more active and to meet oftener, and it was then that we got the name of the Molly Maguires—the object they had in mind was to get rid of any one in the county that was severe or hard on the tenants—or on Catholics, on account of their religion—there is a committee in every parish and when anyone was objected to, his name was put round and a meeting was then called to see what should be done to him—when anything was agreed to be done, a person was appointed from another district and a sum of money was made to enable him to go to America or elsewhere if it was thought dangerous for him to remain at home—this sum varied for 5 to 10 pounds—but never more. If a man was appointed to do any particular duty it would be dangerous for him to refuse.[28]

In the same month that Brady was regaling the constabulary and magistrates with the origins, structure, and procedures of the Molly Maguires, another member of the secret society who lived just over the county line in Leitrim was offering the authorities a detailed look at the group's goals.

Philip O'Reilly's extraordinary manifesto, printed as a broadsheet under the name *Molly Maguire*, quickly landed in the hands of the magistrate for Ballinamore. Forwarded to Dublin Castle in July 1845, it is worth quoting in full:

> ADDRESS OF "MOLLY MAGUIRE," TO HER CHILDREN.
>   My Dear Children,
>   With a heart full of sorrow I am obliged to give you this public warning, from the numerous shabby acts that is daily committing by paltry and vile miscreants, and those acts are left on my Dear Children, who are as innocent of them as those unborn, and I hope I have given you better instruction, than to disgrace myself and Milesian Name, now in my old days. I have, thank God, learned you to bear

with christian patience your many privations more than any other children on the face of the earth; but in the end I have a set of men called *Landlords*, having less regard for you than for their dogs, not caring if you had enough of Dry Potatoes to Eat, or a bag to cover you at night, that a heap of manure and a Pig was your only property, and a drink of water your only beverage. I have lived to see you, so reduced and it is now too plain, there is no redress, for even after all the fuss about the *Land Commission*, it now turns out to be the greatest delusion was ever attempted on any people. I am my dear little ones, old enough to see Lord Stanley's Humbug Bill* about old ditches, it now lies with yourselves my dear children, not to starve in the midst of plenty, and to obtain that end, and to obtain your fond Mother's Blessing, may I beg of you my Dear Children, to observe the following rules, viz.—

1 KEEP STRICTLY TO THE LAND QUESTION, BY ALLOWING no landlord, more than fair value for his teneur.

2 NO RENT TO BE PAID UNTIL HARVEST.

3 NO EVEN THEN WITHOUT AN ABATEMENT, WHERE THE land is too high.

4 NO UNDERMINING OF TENANTS, NOR BAILIFF'S FEES TO be paid.

5 NO TURNING OUT OF TENANTS, UNLESS TWO YEARS RENT due before ejectment served.

6 ASSIST TO THE UTMOST OF YOUR POWER THE GOOD LANDLORD, in getting his Rents.

7 CHERISH AND RESPECT THE GOOD LANDLORD, AND GOOD agent.

8 KEEP FROM TRAVELING BY NIGHT.

9 TAKE NO ARMS, BY DAY, OR BY NIGHT, FROM ANY MAN, as from such acts a deal of misfortune springs, having, I trust you have, more arms than you will ever have need for.

10 AVAIL [*sic*] COMING IN CONTACT WITH EITHER THE MILITARY, or police, they are only doing what they cannot help.

11 FOR MY SAKE, THEN, NO DISTINCTION TO ANY MAN ON account of his religion, his acts alone you are to look to.

---

* The bill would have created a process by which tenants could have gained permission to make certain improvements to their holdings, over the objections of their landlord. It did not address evictions, and never became law. See E. D. Steele, *Irish Land and British Politics: Tenant Right and Nationality, 1865–1870* (Cambridge: Cambridge University Press, 1974), 16–17.

12 LET BYGONES BE BYGONES Except in the most glaring case; but
watch for the time to come

My Dear Children—I have laid down the above Rules for you
guidance, and by strictly observing, you will have the well wishes of
every good man, except the heartless LANDLORDS, and by it you will
be known as true sons of mine; but the wretch that will violate this,
my parental command, inflicts on him a salutatory chastisement, but
above all, my dear little ones, the LANDLORDS that will treat those Rules
of mine with contempt, it grieves me to the heart to bid you commit
mortal sin, but my patience is nearly worn out; but before you do so,
for God's sake, and my sake, and take no life, or limb, without first
giving the victim their written warnings, should they be not regarded,
let him that loves the danger perish in it, but I hope none will be so
obstinate for all the Military or Police under Her Majesty will not
save the tip of the wretch, that will have no feeling for my Starving
Children, Attend my Dear Little Ones, to these Rules of mine and the
Lord will prosper you cause, which is the prayer of your affectionate
Mother,

"MOLLY MAGUIRE,"
Maguire's Grove, Parish of Cloone.[29]

The document is the most comprehensive statement yet found of the
objectives and strategy of the Molly Maguires by one of their own. As much
a warning to Mollies as it was to landlords, the document points to divisions in the organization about what its focus should be. The first seven
points make clear that in O'Reilly's view, the name Molly Maguire could
properly be invoked only in the struggle over land, and that that, rather than
the sectarian conflict, was the real issue in the Ulster borderlands at the
dawn of the famine. The religious tensions that had for so long topped
the Ribbon Society's agenda had been eclipsed, as #11 points out. In fact,
the broadside's cryptic criticism of "the numerous shabby acts" by "paltry
and vile miscreants" could be read as a reference to those responsible for
the Booth assassination the month before, for whom the main struggle remained sectarian.

Taken together, Brady's confession and O'Reilly's manifesto make clear
that the Molly Maguires were, at least in core areas like Cavan and Leitrim,
members of an organized conspiracy whose growing focus on land issues
was underlined by the use of disguises borrowed from festive groups like
the mummers. Despite their Whiteboy trappings, the Mollies were in es-

sence Ribbonmen who had adopted a new name, a new agenda, and a new set of symbols, while keeping their old organizational structure.

In addition to Brady's word on the Mollies' evolution from Ribbonmen, we have the statement of George Kells of Ballyconnell, Cavan, an informer who claimed perfect knowledge of "many of the ill-disposed designated by the name 'Mollie Maguire' but more properly known by the appellation 'Ribbonmen.'" Others agreed. "What is the Molly Maguireism which has disturbed this county?" Foster of the *Times* wrote from Cavan in 1845. "It is the same as 'Ribandism,' say the magistrates." An informer from Leitrim described the organizational structure of the Mollies in terms identical to that of the Society of Ribbonmen, with delegates from the northern counties meeting regularly with their counterparts in Liverpool, Manchester, and Glasgow.[30]

From early on, it was clear that the Mollies drew the bulk of their membership from the same pool of unmarried young male farm laborers that the mummers and wren boys drew from. "I find that the outrages which at present disturb the district are committed by farmers' servant boys, no landholder or person of any responsibility taking part in them," a Leitrim magistrate reported in February 1845. "And I am quite confident when the spring work commences and when the farmers must of necessity look after his laborers, outrages will cease and night walking will be given up."

The following month the same magistrate, William Lynas of Ballinamore, reported on the arrest and jailing of a group that raided the home of George Johnston of Aroody, near Fenagh. "We succeeded in lodging fortytwo persons in the brideswell of this town," he wrote. "All of them are persons of the very worst character and not one over 20 years of age."

Later that year, James Cavanagh, bailiff for Digby March, a Leitrim landlord, complained in a deposition that on September 27 an armed party that included young men in women's clothes forced him to surrender eviction papers he was trying to serve. He identified the men as "servant boys to James McLennon of Cavan."[31]

As the historian John William Knott noted, the reason that farmer's sons and servant boys were so active in agrarian secret societies was that they were protecting their future rights to the land.[32] Thus it should come as no surprise that the Mollies sometimes became involved in the sort of family conflict that was common in an era when eldest sons could not take control of a farm until their father ceded it to them. A threatening notice sent to John McElhenny of Inishkeel in west Donegal warned him in February 1846 to "get the affair between yourself and your son settled in a short time. Don't sleep on it or you will have a party of the Molly McGuire some night about your house."[33]

The relationship between the Mollies and farmers was complex. In some cases it was sharply antagonistic, as one might expect, given the heavy representation of farm laborers in the organization. But among small farmers who stood to benefit from the Mollies' anti-rent campaign, there was a degree of at least grudging acceptance. Two reports to Dublin just three days apart underlined this dichotomy.

"It seems to me as if most of the small farmers in this part of the country are more or less interested in the present system of intimidation that prevails here, and wish to encourage it under the expectation that a reduction of rents will follow from it," Nicholas Kelly, another Ballinamore magistrate, wrote on June 16, 1845. On June 19, a Carrigallen magistrate reported that there had been no outrages in his neighborhood for over a week, and suggested a reason: "Several farmers in the vicinity have formed themselves into a protective association, four of them sit up each night to protect the person and property of the remainder. Similar associations have been formed in the County of Cavan bordering Leitrim."[34]

There is much to suggest that in addition to dividing bigger farmers from laborers, the Mollies' new departure led to a regional split within the Ribbon Society itself. The official history of the Ancient Order of Hibernians in the United States contends that the Molly Maguires of Ireland seceded from the Ribbonmen, and Michael Davitt, the Land League leader of the 1870s, agreed that they "grew out of and became a rival to the Ribbon society."[35]

Contemporary evidence supports the notion. In early December 1846, after a respected Catholic road contractor, George McClean, was killed near Crossmaglen, County Armagh, the constabulary found an interesting note on Neal Kelly, who was picked up as a suspect. "Dear John," it read. "I write these few lines to you to let me know the reason why you did not appear at Crossmaglen on the day you appointed. Well, then when you do not wish to appear in the county of Armagh, we will make a split of the counties." The local magistrate, M. Singleton, concluded that the letter had been written in November, and that McClean's murder was connected to a split in the Ribbon Society involving counties Monaghan, Louth, and Armagh.[36]

Certainly, the behavior of secret society members in those three eastern counties differed from their counterparts in the western borderlands. Monaghan, Louth, and Armagh were relatively quiescent during 1846, unlike neighboring Cavan, but these three eastern counties were the scene of a major outbreak of agrarian crime immediately after the famine.[37] It appears that while the potato crops failed, the Ribbonmen of Monaghan, Louth, and Armagh refused to go along with the Mollies' new focus on land.

One explanation is that the western strongholds of the Mollies—Cavan, Leitrim, and Roscommon—experienced greater population growth in the first four decades of the nineteenth century, creating greater pressure for access to land. They certainly experienced a greater death rate during the famine years of 1845–51—at least 50 deaths per 1,000 people—than did the eastern counties of Armagh (20.1), Louth (14.6), and Monaghan (36).[38] Also, the proximity of market towns and ports like Newry and Dundalk meant that by the time of the famine, the latter three counties were more fully integrated into the British economy. Armagh and Monaghan also had a significant Protestant population, and only small pockets of Gaelic speakers. Generally speaking, the Molly Maguires flourished in areas where waves of economic change crashed on the rocks of Gaelic culture. In the eastern counties, there were fewer rocks.

All this is not to suggest that the sectarian struggle, long the raison d'être of the borderlands Ribbonmen, was unknown in Molly Maguire strongholds like Cavan, Leitrim, and Roscommon. On May 8, 1846, a Molly Maguire notice warned a teacher in Mohill to leave Leitrim for religious reasons: "Bernard Maginnis will take notice that I understand by good authority that he is a protestant . . . go home (to) the north and teach protestants, let me never see your face in the county Leitrim for we have enough false teachers without you."[39]

But in general, with famine settling on the countryside like a shroud, the Mollies had better things to worry about than the age-old feud between Catholic and Protestant. A survey of the Outrage Papers—the records of agrarian crime reported to the Dublin Castle—shows that for 1846, the overwhelming majority of Molly Maguire incidents concerned access to land and food. Numerous other reports of Molly activity in the years 1845–48 support that finding.

In the eastern end of south Ulster, there was just one report involving Molly Maguires in 1846, near the pockets of Gaelic speakers where counties Armagh, Down, and Louth adjoin close to the mouth of the Newry River. There, an Armagh magistrate reported on December 22, 1846, that "within a few weeks past, different letters signed 'Molly Maguire' were sent through the post office in Newry to some of the merchants, threatening them, if they should send any meal out of the country." Attached was a report from Carlingford in Louth stating "that a serious attack is intended to be made by a large party of the country people (County of Armagh side) . . . upon one or two vessels now loading with oatmeal at Newry, and bound for Scotland."[40]

In the fall of 1846 food was the central issue in Cavan. The "well-disposed citizens of Bultersbridge" in Cavan cited food thefts in a petition for a police station, complaining that John Reilly's mill had been "attacked or entered by a number of men and a quantity of grain taken away there-from." Likewise, the "merchants, traders and shopkeepers" of Ballyjames-duff wanted the military stationed there because its inhabitants were "in great dread of their houses and their stores being broken open and robbed by the numbers of idle people who congregate in the neighborhood." Farmers were said to be forming themselves into small societies for mutual protection.[41]

In addition to food raids, there was symbolic protest. In October, a magistrate at Ballyconnell, in Tullyhaw, reported that during a court session, "a body of men upwards of 400 in number marched into town in regular order, headed by a man carrying a loaf of bread on a pole," and halted in front of the courthouse.

In County Leitrim, just weeks after O'Reilly's manifesto instructed that the Mollies make no distinction "on any man on account of his religion," Turk Dickson received a warning notice from "Molly's men," damning him as "an Orange rascal," before mentioning his real sin—the taking of land from an evicted tenant.[42]

In the fall of 1846, the parish priest of Carrigallen, just over the border from Cavan, joined a call for a military garrison there, citing nightly outrages and robberies "by persons assuming the fantastical name of Molly Maguires." James Kiernan seconded the proposal, complaining that thieves were "plundering the farmers in their houses by night and on the highway coming home from markets."[43]

In Roscommon, southwest of Leitrim, the major issue was a shortage of land for conacre brought on by the conversion of acreage to grazing. The local newspaper reported in 1845 that Molly Maguires were "threading a number of needles and attaching a pin to the end of each thread, and then concealing the whole in the grass, which are then picked up and swallowed by the cattle in feeding, and immediately prove fatal to the poor animals."[44]

A large portion of a farm near Strokestown owned by John Balfe was turned up one night in spring 1845 by a party of "Maguires" who sought to compel him to rent it as conacre. After a gun battle with the constabulary, the Mollies fled, leaving thirty spades on the ground. They didn't stay away. In November, Mr. Balfe reported that Mollies turned up thirty acres.

Similar reports came in on February 3, 1846, when Mollies were said to have turned up land and fired on a constable near Drumsna, and on March 6, 1846, when they turned up four acres on the estates of Lord Mountsandford near Castlerea. On March 3, Christopher Taeffe was stopped by two gunmen and told to let out a farm in conacre.

Renting land from which a tenant had been evicted remained a serious offense. On September 14, 1846, Charles Connor, a blacksmith near Elphin, complained that the "nocturnal ruffians called the Mollies" were enforcing a boycott against his business because he had rented two acres of land that had been taken from another.[45]

The Mollies thus maintained a militant focus on access to land and food. They maintained a tight geographic focus as well, on Cavan, Leitrim, Roscommon, and Longford. During the famine era, there were only a smattering of incidents in which "Molly Maguire" was invoked in eastern counties like Armagh, Down, and Louth. Monaghan, just west of Louth, was where Trench claimed to have encountered Molly Maguires in 1843, but the name was noticeably scarce there as well. For all of 1846, despite unrest on the Shirley estate, there was not a single report to Dublin Castle mentioning Molly Maguires in the county. The absence of Molly activity there supports the notion that in 1846 the Mollies were in the process of splitting from the eastern Ribbonmen.

By contrast, Cavan, the county just to the west of Monaghan, reverberated with cries of "Molly Maguire" all through the later half of the 1840s. It was there that Brady had detailed the inner workings of Molly Maguires in 1845, the same year that Foster of the *Times* had printed of vivid portrait of "the excited and disturbed state of County Cavan."

"On walking through the town of Cavan, the walls are seen to be placarded with the proclamation of his Excellency the Lord Lieutenant, declaring the county in a state of disturbance, and to require addition police force," he wrote. "Armed police and soldiers are everywhere seen about the town. Notices, offering rewards for private information relative to the secret society commonly called 'ribandmen' or 'Molly Maguires' . . . are everywhere stuck up."[46]

Any respite the troops provided was only temporary. On May 5, 1846, John B. Graves of Alva reported that "Molly Maguireism is again appearing in many districts and within a week several robberies of dwelling houses and the serving of . . . threatening notices has been reported to me."

Leitrim, of course, was troubled from the start, and the strife only worsened. Magistrates meeting in Mohill on May 27, 1845, reported the "the alarming state of the county," particularly the Baronies of Mohill, Leitrim, and Carrigallen, and areas bordering Counties Longford, Cavan, and Fermanagh. Just three days later, a former Leitrim magistrate, G. Montgomery, complained to Dublin Castle that "the Molly Maguire system is rapidly spreading" along the eastern side of Lough Allen.[47]

In Roscommon, where conacre was such an issue, the propertied lived in fear for their lives. In October 1846, Charles Hogg, a saddler in Boyle, warned that "a dangerous system (Molly Maguire) was carried on in this and the neighboring county, Leitrim, and still continues to exist, having as its object the assassination and extermination of those who have been selected as victims of its displeasure." The following month, a notice assuming the trappings of a court order threatened death to Denis O'Conor if he kept an unpopular tenant, "in the spite of me and the rest of the community." It closed with, "Obey orders or otherwise perish, Written by the Clerk of this System, Molly Maguire."

County Longford, where the Ballinamuck land war had raged, saw Molly activity as well, but to a lesser extent than neighboring Roscommon. William Morrison of Edenmore complained of a September 27, 1846, attempt to break into his house by a party of armed men—"known in this and neighboring counties by the name Molly Maguires"—who had been driven off after an exchange of gunfire. If the Mollies were less active in Longford, they at times seemed more literate—an 1847 poster there signed "Molly Anne Maguire" described landlords and their agents as "worse than Nero, Maxentius, or Caligula."[48]

Compared to the level of unrest in Cavan and Leitrim, their neighbor to the north, Fermanagh, was relatively quiet in 1846, with few reports of Ribbon activity, and none of Molly Maguires. There had been some hints of trouble in 1845 in south Fermanagh, near the Cavan border—the Mollies were reported in August to be planning the murder of a Protestant minister, Rev. John Sweney of Cleenish.[49]

But for the most part, secret society violence in Fermanagh in the early years of the famine remained at the level of barroom plotting. Perhaps that was because Fermanagh, like the counties of the eastern borderlands, had escaped the high population growth of 1800–1840, and its highest death rate during the famine, at 39 per 1,000, was far closer to Monaghan's than it was to that of Cavan (51.8) or Leitrim (50.2). Like the eastern counties, Fermanagh had a mixed, largely English-speaking population that was already well integrated into the market economy. Lastly, Fermanagh landlords like the 3rd Earl of Enniskillen, whose estate bordered western Cavan, took an active part in suppressing secret society activity through the Ribbon Detection Society.[50]

North of Leitrim and west of Fermanagh, County Donegal would become a locus of Molly Maguire activity after the famine, but sparse economic development and low population growth in the decades leading up to that catastrophe helped spare it some of the worst distress. Still, there were scattered reports of Molly activity in the mid-1840s. James Cassidy of Ballyshannon incurred the wrath of the secret society by taking over another's farm. After he received several threatening letters signed "Molly Maguire," five stacks of wheat and a stack of oats on his farm were destroyed on November 27, 1846.[51]

Of course, one of the problems with anonymous threats is that anyone can make them. Some Molly notices in fringe areas like Donegal and Monaghan may not have been authorized by the organization. What is certain is that in their core areas, the Mollies showed a remarkable willingness to move beyond mere threats by taking on the authorities with aggressive shows of force.

The gunfights with the Roscommon constabulary over conacre were no exceptions: the Mollies showed so little fear of the police that O'Reilly felt the need to address the issue in point #10 of his manifesto. The month before it appeared in Leitrim, Mollies there had clashed violently with the police, as a Dublin newspaper reported: "An affray took place at Mohill, on Thursday night, between the Police and a party of 'Molly Maguires.' According to our informant, the parties fired on each other. One of the peasantry was shot through the heart, and others were wounded. The Molly Maguires retreated, but soon returned, with a reinforcement, rescued the body of their deceased companion and compelled the police to fly.'"[52]

In addition to defying the landlords and the law, the Mollies were also willing to take on the third pillar of rural authority—the Catholic Church. In 1845, the priests of Roscommon were said to have been "duly cautioned" by the Mollies as rumors flew that the clerics had consulted the Vatican about the possibility of excommunicating members of the secret society. The *Athlone Sentinel* reported on January 23, 1846, that Mollies had demolished the pews of a Catholic church in that county.[53]

Members of the Catholic lay community also energetically opposed the Mollies. As we have seen, O'Connell's right-hand man, Thomas Steele, was mobilizing Catholic repeal activists to counter the secret society almost from the start. "I organized in Leitrim and Cavan bodies of volunteer pacificators, whom I appointed Repeal Wardens," he wrote in January 1845. "Who, under the sanctified guidance of the Catholic clergy, exercised rigid surveillance in their respective districts over all those, who, under the instigation of evil advisors, or under the impulse of their own folly, may be disposed to violate the law, and consequently mar the hopes for Ireland."[54] In early June, Steele issued a statement "to the Molly Maguires of the Counties of Leitrim, Cavan, etc." condemning them as "miscreant traitors to Ireland," "midnight villains," and "traitorous wretches."[55]

The condemnations may have had some effect. Within weeks of the latest denunciation by Steele, the resident magistrate in Ballinamore, Leitrim, reported nascent battle lines forming between the Mollies and a hitherto unheard of group: "I am glad to find that there is now a split among the party here. They are divided into two sections, one called the Mollys, and the others, Molsheens. They have had already some skirmishing, but I trust it will soon grow into a regular quarrel, and when that occurs we shall soon get finally under the whole system."[56]

But for all their willingness to mix it up on the local level, the Mollies remained wary of revolutionary action on the national level. Thomas D'Arcy McGee, a representative of Young Ireland, the nationalist movement that split with O'Connell over the use of physical force, claimed to have contacted the secret society in early August 1848. Seeking to enlist the Mollies in the Young Ireland uprising in much the same way that the United Irish had enlisted the Defenders, McGee traveled to Sligo and Leitrim, where he reported meeting with a leader of the secret society.

"This Gentlemen I found wary, resolute and intelligent," McGee recalled. "He said: 'I have no doubt of what you say, but I must have certain facts to lay before our district chiefs. At present we don't know what to believe. One day we hear one thing—another, another. Bring us by this day assurances that the South is going to rise or has risen, and we will rise two thousand before the week is out.'"[57]

The unnamed leader had good reason for caution: a few days before, Young Ireland had not so much risen but stumbled—into a loud scuffle with the police at Ballingarry, a coal town in Tipperary. Some miners rallied to the cause, but the affair in late July was so trifling that it was put down by the police, not troops. The dragoons arrived only later, to scour the famished countryside for the leaders of Young Ireland, most of whom would eventually be caught and exiled. To the north, in Roscommon, other soldiers were dealing with a bigger threat, if one is to judge by the sentences. There, they were hanging Molly Maguires.

The Mahon Murder

On August 8, 1848, just days after Young Ireland collapsed in Tipperary, the military in Roscommon was making elaborate preparations for an execution. A squadron of cavalry and three companies of infantry were on hand to ensure that no rescue was attempted.

None was. The condemned man, a Roscommon shebeen keeper named James Hasty, duly ascended the gallows and denounced "that accursed system of Molly Maguireism" before being hanged for the murder of an improving Protestant landlord, Maj. Denis Mahon of Strokestown, the previous year.[58] Mahon's killing, just a few days after Halloween, was perhaps the most sensational in Ireland attributed to the Mollies.

The conflict in the townlands outside Strokestown was another example of a wave of economic change crashing onto the eroding cliffs of Celtic culture, undermining an ancient way of life. The crowded, collective peasant lifestyle persisted there into the 1830s and 1840s in classic rundale–clachan hamlets. In addition to the mummery that Sir William Wilde had described in Roscommon, the Gaelic language was still sufficiently entrenched in the rural townlands that bilingualism was considered an important qualification for the "drivers" who rode herd on the tenantry for landlords.[59]

The catalyst that brought an end to this way of life—and to Denis Mahon—was pure mismanagement of an estate. The longtime landlords, the Mahons, were actually tenants themselves, leasing their vast estate around Strokestown from the crown. By 1834, when its forty-one-year lease ran out, the estate was already in debt, and its owner, Maurice Mahon, was mentally unstable. The lease was allowed to lapse for a portion of the estate, the townland of Ballykilcline in the parish of Kilglass, and the management of that townland reverted to a sluggish bureaucracy with the grand title of Their Lords, His Majesty's Commissioners of Woods and Forests. For two years the Lords neglected to collect rents in tiny, faraway Ballykilcline, delighting the townland's hard-pressed tenants, who had theretofore been dutiful in their payments. It was not until 1836 that the Lords got around to demanding rent, which by now was three years in arrears. The sums due were well beyond the reach of most tenants.[60]

The result was a prolonged land war that wracked the townland of Ballykilcline from 1836 to 1845, as tenants fought demands for rent payments and the threat of eviction with measures ranging from a lawsuit and petitions to riots, threats, beatings, and murder. Peasant resistance was reported to be organized around two groups—a number of tenants who took legal action to defend their interests, the self-styled "Defendants"; and a more shadowy group that was linked to illegal action, the Molly Maguires.

As the historian James Robert Scally points out, the name of the former group "was too close the 'Defenders' of 1798 to have no meaning in this part of the country." Ballinamuck, the Waterloo of that uprising, lay in neighboring Longford, and was the scene of its own land war during the first half of Ballykilcline's defiance of the crown.

Scally, who wrote a detailed study of the Ballykilcline "rebellion," found convincing evidence that the Defendants group "took a kind of authority unto itself," enforcing peasant solidarity and compliance with its edicts by disciplining those who tried to reach an individual settlement with the Commissioners of Woods and Forests. George Knox, the crown's agent for the townland, identified several Defendants as the ringleaders of plots and threats, and called them "the most lawless and violent set of people in the County of Roscommon." Even considering the agent's bias, an obvious question arises about the Defendants' relationship with the Molly Maguires, for Knox reported that the Mollies also may have had something to do with beatings and threats. An intriguing suggestion that the Defendants and Molly Maguires were, in fact, one and the same came from the tenants themselves. When they had exhausted their legal avenues, several tenants, in a desperate effort to avoid eviction, sent petitions that linked leading Defendants to Molly Maguireism.

It may be, as Scally has suggested, that those tenants were merely trying to confirm dubious rumors of a Molly Maguire conspiracy in order to curry favor with authorities.[61] But the same can hardly be said for Hasty, who denounced "Molly Maguireism" as he stood on the gallows. It may be that the group used the term "Defendants" when it engaged in legal action, and "Molly Maguires" when it took part in illegal activity, which included visiting homes in Kilglass to raise money for a legal defense fund.[62]

Violence came late to the dispute. In the spring of 1844, Knox sought to serve papers on several Ballykilcline tenants who had returned to their cabins after being evicted. The process-servers met "the most determined Resistance and Opposition," Knox reported. "But for the Accidental Presence of a few Police, the Process-servers would have been murdered."

Several ringleaders of the disturbance were arrested, and on the night before their trial Knox wrote that "a brutal Murder has taken place ... on a Person considered to be an informer to the Government." The Defendants were acquitted—one of their few victories on the legal front.[63]

The triumph was short-lived. By 1847, with their lawsuit lost, their petitions ignored, and their will to fight broken by the famine, the vast majority of Ballykilcline's five-hundred-odd tenants acquiesced in a plan of assisted emigration to the United States. Fourteen Defendants and their families were the first to be evicted.

By then, however, the spirit of defiance had spread to the surrounding areas. "There is no part of this kingdom so thickly populated with Mollies as the parish of Kilglass," a small farmer, Patrick Sheaghan, complained in February 1847.[64]

Their numbers were reinforced by the rigors of hunger and the determination of many landlords to make their estates profitable, regardless the cost. On May 13, 1847, the *Freeman's Journal* shed some light on just how high the cost could be for families evicted from their holdings: "In the parish of Kilglass, the skeleton bodies of seven wretches were found inside a hedge. The dogs of the surrounding villages had the flesh almost eaten off."[65]

Among the local landlords determined to evict tenants was Maj. Denis Mahon. In 1836, the same year that the Ballykilcline struggle began, the townland's landlord, Maurice Mahon, suffered a final mental breakdown. His cousin, Maj. Mahon, laid claim to the estate, but he did not come into possession of it until 1845—the dawn of a dangerous period for anyone in the Irish countryside.

"Matters look very threatening in Roscommon," a cousin of Mahon's, Denis Kelly, wrote in August of the following year. "Last week a large assemblage paraded near Castlerea with a loaf on a pole and a placard FOOD OR BLOOD, and there was a similar assemblage at Loughrea."

Soon there was trouble even closer to home. On August 22, tenants of Mahon who had been let go from a public works project sent the landlord a dire warning in a petition. "Our families are well and truly suffering in our presence and we cannot withstand their cries for food. We have no food for them, our potatoes are rotten and we have no grain," it read. "Are we to resort to outrage? Gentlemen, we fear the peace of the country will be much disturbed if relief be not more extensively afforded to the suffering peasantry. We are not joining in anything illegal or contrary to the laws of God or the land unless pressed by HUNGER." A few weeks later, a correspondent warned Mahon that someone was using threats to collect money to hire Hugh O'Ferrall, the Dublin lawyer for the Ballykilcline Defendants, "to give your honor opposition and obstruction in collecting your rent and arrears."[66]

Mahon, too, turned to Dublin for help, hiring the estate management firm Guinness and Mahon (yet another cousin, John Ross Mahon, was a partner). In a grim review of the Mahon holdings, the firm concluded that nine acres, sown in wheat, was the minimum needed to support a tenant family, instead of the three acres, sown in potatoes, that was then the average. John Ross Mahon recommended a plan of assisted emigration similar to the Ballykilcline scheme to winnow the estate of tenants. In December 1846, amid a bleak and hungry winter, he started serving notices of eviction.[67]

The emigration plan was hampered by two developments—news of the fate of the first group of tenants that Mahon put aboard ship for passage to North America, and a bitter controversy with a local Catholic priest.

The ship carrying the initial 490 evicted tenants, the *Virginius* out of Liverpool, was rumored to have been wrecked with great loss of life, and Mahon was held responsible for their fate. Though the *Virginius* did, in fact, dock in Grosse Isle, Canada, in late May, the rumor was essentially true, for the ship was a wreck. Of the 490 Mahon tenants who had embarked on it, about a third—158—had died at sea. Of the survivors—"ghastly, yellow spectres" in the words of one Canadian official—only about a half dozen were well enough walk off on their own two legs. The "coffin ship" had become a part of Roscommon's consciousness by August 1847.[68]

At the end of that month, Maj. Mahon, recently returned to Strokestown after several months in England, ran into more trouble when he became embroiled in a dispute with the town's Catholic priest, Rev. Michael McDermott.

Mahon served as chairman of the Strokestown Relief Committee, but Fr. McDermott had filled in while the landlord was away. At an August 28 meeting of the committee, Mahon's questions about how affairs had been conducted in his absence enraged the priest, who accused the major of amusing himself by "burning houses and turning out the people to starve." Mahon's response did little to satisfy Rev. McDermott, or the starving for that matter: "That, I was obliged to assure the reverend gentleman, was not the case, and that whatever I did with regard to my property I conceived rested with myself, and that I would not allow him or any man to meddle with me in that respect."[69]

What Mahon intended to do with regard to his property was made clear in a letter to his cousin and agent, John Ross Mahon, written on November 2, 1847. Complaining of a "system of combination" against rent payments by some of his tenants, Mahon warned, "I shall evict the whole, and not one of them shall get land again."[70]

The tenants had the last word. The night that Mahon wrote the letter, he was killed in an ambush in the townland of Doorty, as he returned from a meeting of the relief committee. "The people were said to be displeased with him for two reasons," a Dublin newspaper reported. "The first was his refusal to continue the conacre system, the second was his clearing away what he deemed the surplus population."[71]

Mahon's death, like that of Mitchell in Farney, was celebrated with bonfires—it came, after all, just two days after Samhain. It wasn't just celebrated; it was emulated, in a spate of attacks on other Roscommon landlords—Lord Crofton of Mote Park, Denis Kelly of Castle Kelly, William Talbot of Mount Talbot—that spurred fears of an extensive conspiracy. Stephen J. Campbell, a famine historian who has studied the Mahon family papers and has written about the murder, concluded that it was neither sectarian, nor a spontaneous act of revenge. Rather, he said, "it appears it was a result of a conspiracy which targeted landlords as enemies of the people." The author Peter Duffy, who pored over trial testimony, found any number of hints that the crime was the work of a secret society angered by the eviction of tenants. The murder was widely believed by the community to be the work of the Molly Maguires, he said—a belief that can only have been reinforced by Hasty's scaffold confession.[72]

The Character of Molly Maguire

Who was the mythical woman for whom this conspiracy was named? The best answer, odd as it seems, may be that Molly Maguire was a character from the folk drama of the mummers and wren boys, drafted into the land war to show the peasants of the Ulster borderlands exactly who the rebels were and what they stood for. In ballads, proclamations, the way they dressed, and the legends they spread about their origins, the Mollies disseminated a very specific and uniform message—they were defenders of community, like the mummers and the rebels of 1798.

Consider the name. "Maguire" called to mind the faded Gaelic glory of the Fermanagh chieftains who once reigned over a significant portion of the Ulster borderlands. It may also have held a hidden meaning—an Irish–English dictionary dating from the mid-nineteenth century listed one Irish word for jester as "magaire,"[73] and the female mummer and wren boy characters were nothing if not jesters. Indeed, among the County Kerry wren boys, there was a character called the oinseach, or female jester.[74] But the most intriguing clue about the identity of our character is not her last name but her first, for she wasn't always "Molly." From the very start, she was sometimes referred to by one other name: Mary Anne.

William Lynas, a magistrate in Ballinamore, Leitrim, reported on February 25, 1845, that a threatening notice posted near Cashcarrigan had ended with the words "beware of Mary Ann McGuire." On October 10, 1847, Benjamin Holmes, the resident magistrate in Swalinbar, County Cavan, re-

ported that the signature "Mary Anne Maguire" had appeared on a threatening notice sent to a man who had apparently been demanding kickbacks
from laborers on public works projects. (The promised murder was explic-
itly pegged to Samhain: "Your life will not be your own many days after
the first of November.")[75] As late as 1851, a warning sent to the land agent
for Lord Leitrim was signed "Maryanne Maguire." And as we have seen, a
particularly literate poster denouncing landlords in Longford in 1847 com-
bined the two forms under the signature Molly Anne Maguire.

These variations on the name are significant because in the nineteenth
century there were other groups of peasant men using the name Mary
Anne as they roamed the Irish countryside in women's clothes—the wren
boys and the mummers. A Leitrim resident told the Irish Folklore Commission, "In the old mummers, before my time, there used to be a fellow dressed
as a woman, with a woman's skirt and apron upon him. He was called
Mary Anne."[76]

A resident of Ballyhaunis, Mayo, described an identical character in
discussing wren boys: "In bye-gone times a 'set' of wren-boys consisted of
from 10 to 20 members, all adults, laborers, tradesmen, car-drivers, etc.,
including . . . the 'Mary Anne,' a male dressed as a woman."[77] Likewise,
"Mary Ann McMonagle" turned up as a character in the mummers play in
Beltany, County Donegal.[78]

The similarities between the mummer character "Mary Ann McMonagle" and "Mary Ann Maguire" would not have been lost on Irish peasants,
for whom the latter may have sounded a bit like "Mary Ann Jester." And
there is reason to believe that the "Mary Ann" of the mummer and wren
boy performances started life as a Molly. Mummery was brought to Ulster
by English settlers from Chesire, Lancashire, Warwickshire, and Oxfordshire, where the play featured a character by the name of Molly Masket or
Mally Masket—indeed, in some parts of England, the mummers were
known collectively as "Molly's six children."[79]

It was not unusual for a mumming character to undergo a name change
when he or she crossed the Irish Sea. A character who turned up frequently
among the Warwickshire and Oxfordshire mummers—"Jack Finney" or
"John Finney"—was transformed into "Johnny Funny" or "John Funny" in
parts of Ulster. In Fermanagh, Johnny Funny underwent a gender change,
becoming the female Biddy Funny. Like Johnny, Biddy was the character who
collected money.[80]

The transformation of John Finney into Johnny Funny and Biddy Funny
gives some idea of the process by which the Molly Masket character could
be localized as Mickey Mulligan (in County Tyrone), Master Man (in

Dromore, Donegal), Mary Ann McMonagle, and, perhaps, Mary Ann and Molly Maguire.

The legends about the original Molly Maguire lend further credence to a strong link with the mummers and wren boys. According to one story, our character was the widow Maguire, an "aged woman" who became a cause célèbre when she was evicted from her farm in Ballymena, County Antrim. Another held that she was a "a crazy old woman in County Fermanagh, who imagined that she had great armies and organizations of men under her control." In the Pennsylvania of the 1870s, she was reported to be a widow in Donegal whose son was killed as he tried to stop her eviction from her shebeen.[81] What makes these stories interesting is that while neither Antrim nor Fermanagh were ever real Molly Maguire strongholds, and Donegal became one only late in the game, those three counties are among the few where women characters appeared regularly in the mummers plays.

In Antrim, the female character was called "the old woman," much like that "aged woman," the widow Maguire. She was the one who called for a doctor to resurrect her slain son. In Fermanagh, the female character was "Biddy Funny." In Donegal, there were female characters named "the Lady" and, most strikingly, "Mary Ann McMonagle."

Thus the very name and the folklore placing the original Molly Maguire in locales with female mummer characters can be seen as an effort by the Mollies to link the two traditions in the popular mind. "Molly's children" were mummers in England, but in Ireland the term acquired a far more ominous meaning.

In addition to looking and sounding like mummers, the Mollies acted like them. A County Armagh native born near Markethill, Armagh, the center of the very first Defender troubles, had this to say about their lineal descendants, the Mollies:

> Some of the people of the provinces of Ulster and Connaught resolved not to starve as long as there was any food stowed away in the public markets or warehouses or any storekeeper who might have a supply of stock on hand. They immediately organized under the name Molly McGuire. The objects were to take from those who had abundance & give to the poor who were then dying by hundredth with hunger.... Their mode of operation was to have there leader dressed up in a suit of womens clothing to represent the Irish Mother begging bread for her children under these disguises. The leader or Molly as she was called went to the storekeeper provided she knew he was pretty well off & demanded of him the amount levied on him

in the shape of meal flour and general groceries. If the things were not forwarded at the time & place designated by Molly in the limited time she prescribed she and her men immediately visited the store or house & after securing the inmates they immediately proceeded to help themselves to everything in the shape of provisions on the premises taking with them all they could possibly carry.[82]

James McParlan, a private detective, wrote this description shortly before he was assigned to infiltrate the American branch of the Mollies in Pennsylvania. His observations about the Irish Mollies were confirmed by Asenath Nicholson, an American who toured Ireland during the famine and worked to relieve the misery she saw all around her. "A class of persons, driven to madness by idleness and hunger, were prowling at night through some parts of the country, calling themselves Molly Maguires," she reported. "These go from house to house, in disguise, demanding money." If refused, they would maul the occupant with a thorny branch or the sharp teeth of a wool card. "Many of the marauders have been apprehended," Nicholson wrote. "Yet the practice did not cease, for they were encouraged by the country folk."[83]

The practice did not cease, because the levying of tribute was part and parcel of country life. The similarity of the Mollies to mummers and wren boys in both descriptions is striking. We have role-playing, with a man dressed up as a woman trying to save her dying child. We have visits to homes. We have blackmail—no longer lighthearted, amid the crisis of the famine. We have the theft of food or money. And on a larger level, we have collective action, taken for the collective good with collective approval.

The female characters associated with the mummers and the Mollies— the old woman, the crazy woman, the mother seeking to save or resurrect her child—echo Celtic mythology and Catholic theology. In Celtic myth, "the country is a woman, the spouse of the king, and before her marriage she is a hag or a woman whose mind is deranged." The early Whiteboys pledged loyalty to Queen Sieve, a one-eyed old hag.[84] And in a nation decimated by famine, "Molly," a nickname for Mary, neatly intertwined the mummers theme of death and rebirth with images the Virgin Mary, the Crucifixion, and the Resurrection.

The Mollies emphasized that theme, adding the mummers emphasis on "renewed combat" to death and resurrection. Consider the Molly Maguire ballad about the killing of Bell Booth. The narrative is a straightforward description of a killing until near the end, where it digresses into the supernatural:

One night as I lay in a shed I found a terrible rattle
The ghost of Bell came back from hell to fight me another battle.[85]

Why would the ghost of Bell come back to fight another battle? Perhaps to stress the links with the mummers play, which features a battle, a killing, and the lines "Rise up dead man and fight again."

The Mollies used the theme of rising to fight again as a way to portray themselves as the heirs of the Defenders of 1798. They employed powerful symbolism to stress this link in stories about where the movement was founded and where it was headquartered. Foster, the *Times* reporter, wrote in 1845 that the Mollies were reported to have gotten their start at Ballinamuck, adding that the parish of Cloone, in Leitrim, "is said to be the head quarters of Molly." O'Reilly's manifesto listed "Maguire's Grove, Parish of Cloone" as the address for Molly Maguire.[86]

Ballinamuck had indeed been the scene of a land war between 1835 and 1838, and in claiming birth there, the Mollies firmly rooted themselves in the issue of tenant right. But the Mollies were saying something much more when they asserted that their movement was founded in Ballinamuck, and when they used nearby Cloone as an address for Molly Maguire in warning notices, for Cloone was the last headquarters of the rebel army in 1798. Ballinamuck, where Cornwallis caught up with the rebels, was well remembered as the Golgotha of that uprising. Indeed it was so well-remembered in 1845 that Cavan Protestants, hinting darkly about the influence of secret societies, complained that a planned September 8 march by Catholics in Killeshandra was timed to commemorate the battle.[87] After much consternation, the march was called off, but the point had been made: if the Orangemen could invoke memories of one battle—the Boyne—to emphasize Catholic weakness, then their secret society adversaries could use memories of another—Ballinamuck—to emphasize Catholic strength. The Mollies were saying they had sprung from the same Ballinamuck fields that served as the graves of the Defenders. They were claiming the mantle of the 1798 rebels—and the land issue—as their own.

The same dynamic can be seen just over the county line in Ballykilcline, Roscommon. There, tenants waging a legal battle to halt their eviction styled themselves "the Defendants," a name redolent of 1798, while those waging a very illegal battle against eviction called themselves "Molly Maguires." It should come as no surprise that some tenants insisted there was no difference between the two.

There can be little doubt of the potency of Molly symbolism. In his *History of the Ancient Order of Hibernians and Ladies' Auxiliary*, John O'Dea noted how quickly the name Molly Maguire had been "admitted to popular fame." Indeed, it swept Ireland from the east coast to the west coast in a very short time at the dawn of the famine. By contrast, O'Dea reported, the Ribbonmen, from whom the Mollies apparently split, had trouble gaining acceptance for their formal name, "The St. Patrick's Fraternal Society."[88] If the name Molly Maguire was more quickly accepted by the peasants, it was because the trappings of that organization were far more in tune with peasant folkways than those of the St. Patrick's Fraternal Society.

Indeed, the Mollies were so in tune with the holiday mayhem of the previous millennium that it seems almost as if, for a brief time, the catastrophe that scoured Ireland in the 1840s had stripped away all the centuries of Christianity and left that bloody idol, Crom, standing once more at Magh Slécht in County Cavan. As if holiday human sacrifice and violent cross-dressing, sublimated in the underground stream of Irish folk drama, had been transported by it into the modern era—an ancient darkness flowing forth once last time with the Celtic twilight. The historian Thomas Pakenham, a descendant of the murdered Major Mahon, captured some of this sense in a discussion of another, and in many ways similar, disturbance—the Mau Mau rebellion by Kenya's Kikuyu tribe in the 1950s. "Was it more atavistic than nationalistic, a return to the bloody rituals of pagan Africa?" he wrote, adding, "The British discriminated against them at every level: making them outsiders in their own country. But the grievance that touched them most widely was the land."[89] Change "Africa" to "Ireland" and Pakenham could have been describing the men who killed his ancestor. And like the secret society of the Mau Mau, the Molly Maguires were crushed more by hunger than by arms.

For all their skills in the black art of murder and in the symbolism of subversion, the Mollies were in the end largely consumed by the very famine that helped fuel their struggle. Hunger proved the landlord's best weapon in the ongoing war with the peasantry, dooming the Gaelic Ireland in which the Mollies thrived. Indeed, it could be argued the blackest hearts in that tortured land beat not in the breasts of the atavistic Mollies, but in those of the rational, educated, calculating men of property and their agents. Some landlords labored mightily to help the starving, but others came to the same conclusion as that great spokesman for their class, Trench, who found the horror of the famine to be a blessing in disguise: "Nothing but the successive failure of the potato crop could have produced the emigration which will, I trust, give us room to become more civilised."[90]

Among those who gave Ireland "room to become more civilised" were ninety-nine families from Tonagh, Cavan, who were evicted in a driving rainstorm in September 1847, "set adrift in the world" as their homes were torn down, though only one family owed back rent. A Dublin newspaper reported that the occupants of five homes escaped eviction because they were suffering "the pestilence which has so effectually aided the "clearance system."

Because those seriously ill with famine-related fever could not be removed from the homes, the homes were, in effect, removed from them. The local priest said the land agent "ordered a large winnowing sheet to be secured over the beds in which the fever victims lay—fortunately, they happened to be perfectly delirious at the time—and then directed the houses to be unroofed, cautiously and slowly, because, he said, he very much disliked the bother and discomfort of a coroner's inquest." The constabulary, on hand to enforce the eviction, at least had the decency to weep.[91]

The peasantry lacked land, food, shelter, and money; the landlords, only shame.

The scene at Tonagh (where four of the fever victims died the next day) was repeated all over Ireland. Hundreds of thousands starved or perished of the fever, and hundreds of thousands more fled or were driven like cattle from the rural heartland of the Molly Maguires. Some left clutching clay from St. Mogue's grave; others carried a stone in their heart from too long a sacrifice. Those who could made their way to the great emigration port of Liverpool, or boarded ships in Newry, Belfast, or Derry, entering a pipeline to the New World that had been laid by the Scots–Irish more than a century before.

For many, that pipeline ended in eastern Pennsylvania.

Part III

6　Brotherly Love

The Schuylkill region seems to have been marked by nature for individual enterprise.

—North American Review

In short, if you wish to enjoy God's bounty,
Go anywhere except to Schuylkill County.

—Nineteenth-century miner's ballad

On the surface, the three bands of brothers had much in common. The Bannans, the Gowens, and the Mohans all had roots in Ulster. They all arrived in Schuylkill County, Pennsylvania, in the years before the Civil War, forged links to the growing coal industry, and became leaders of their respective communities. Members of all three families were deeply involved in local education. Far more important, members of all three families served as highly effective propagandists for their disparate social and economic interests, for nearly everything that the three families had in common divided them as well.

First there was the past in Ulster. The patriarchs of the Bannans and Gowens were members of the Church of Ireland, the former from near Belfast, the latter from County Tyrone, while the Mohans were Catholics from Fermanagh.[1] Then there was the matter of March 17—the birthday of the patriarchs of both the Gowen and Bannan families. One of the Bannans came to loathe St. Patrick's Day, precisely because it was a cause for Irish Catholic celebration. Even among coreligionists like the Bannans and Gowens, there could be sharp divisions—for example, the first of the Gowens to come to this country sent his sons to a Catholic school.

But the sharpest differences between the three families involved not the past but the future, for in antebellum Schuylkill County the future was coal, and members of each family came to embody radically different and mutually exclusive visions of the industry's future. Benjamin Bannan, a newspaper publisher, fervently believed that the region's mineral resources could best be exploited by individual entrepreneurs who competed with the aid of a cooperative workforce. Franklin Gowen, the president of the Philadelphia and Reading Railroad, came to believe that he had to monopolize the industry—by crushing both the independent mine operators Bannan idealized, and the labor movement the Mohans supported—in order to stabilize coal production. The mine workers of the Mohan family believed that their interests differed markedly from those of the coal operators, and relied on various forms of collective action to safeguard those interests.

This is not to suggest that the three families were warring clans. On the contrary, they lived and worked in nearby towns—the Gowens and Bannans in Pottsville, the Mohans in the Minersville area—and at various times their paths crossed, for the families were involved in politics and civic affairs. Benjamin Bannan and Charles Mohan served together on a committee for Irish famine relief. The Civil War drew together some members of the families: John Mohan served alongside John Bannan as privates in Co. E of the 55th Pennsylvania Volunteers, and Michael Mohan served under George Washington Gowen in Co. C of the 48th Pennsylvania Volunteers.[2]

But even as the war drew some members of the three families together, the overall force of the conflict was centrifugal. The patriarch of the Gowen clan was such a died-in-the-wool Democrat that the conflict seemed to him a Republican plot; Benjamin Bannan was so rock-ribbed a Republican that he used the wartime expansion of government powers to conspire against his Democratic opponents. Those opponents included not only Franklin Gowen, but also an entire community of Irish Catholic miners that included some of the Mohans.

The Civil War widened the fault lines among the families, but before and after the war, members of each family played important roles in transferring the long-running conflict of their ancestral homeland to the heart of Pennsylvania's anthracite region. At center stage for most of the conflict was Benjamin Bannan. His father, for whom he was named, was born in 1770 near Belfast. The elder Bannan followed the trail to the Philadelphia area blazed by other Ulstermen earlier in the century, settling near Molatton in Berks County, where he worked as a farmer and schoolteacher. He died in 1816 and was buried in the Episcopal cemetery in Douglasville.

His influence on his sons—Abraham, John, and Benjamin—is clear; all three were involved in education to varying degrees. Abraham was a schoolteacher in his native Union Township, Berks County, before study-ing law and moving north to practice in Orwigsburg, then the seat of Schuylkill County.

John, who was born in 1796, served in the War of 1812, then joined his brother Abraham in Orwigsburg. There, he was instrumental in founding a school, the Orwigsburg Academy, and became a lawyer, like his brother. John had the more distinguished of the two careers. He specialized in prop-erty law at a time when rights to coal lands were becoming a valuable com-modity, and in the process acquired several valuable tracts. He served three terms as county solicitor between 1825 and 1856, and was also a prosecu-tor, trying the earliest Whiteboy-style murder case in Schuylkill County. John also seems to have been active in the militia—he was sometimes re-ferred to as "Colonel," a rank not likely to have been achieved by a teenager in the War of 1812. In short, John Bannan personified the synthesis of law, business, and military in Schuylkill County.

The youngest brother, Benjamin, also taught school briefly and later served for fourteen years as president of the Pottsville school board. He found his true calling, journalism, after apprenticing as a printer for a Berks County newspaper owned by George Getz, a former congressman. After six years, he was ready to strike out on his own, and, joining his brothers in Schuylkill County, he purchased a defunct newspaper, the *Miners' Journal*, at age twenty-one in 1829. It may be no coincidence that he purchased the news-paper and its list of 250 subscribers from the county sheriff at a time when John Bannan was the county solicitor.[3]

The young publisher's timing could not have been better, for the Schuylkill County coal industry was going through a period of explosive growth. Port Carbon, the terminus of the new Schuylkill Canal near Potts-ville, had just one family in 1829, when Bannan arrived in Schuylkill County; within a year it had 926 residents. The number of buildings in Pottsville it-self grew by 600 percent between 1826 and 1829. In the fifteen years after 1829, Pottsville's population doubled.[4] A large portion of the new residents were immigrants, many of them Irish Catholics.

In addition to Benjamin Bannan's varied business and civic interests—he sold policies for the Spring Garden Insurance Company, peddled garden seeds and books, ran a bindery, and helped create an institute to train teachers—the young publisher was also active in immigration issues. In 1833, Bannan served on Pottsville's Naturalization Committee, conferring citizenship on the growing numbers of foreigners finding work in Schuylkill County's coal mines. With him on the committee were several Irishmen—William Haggerty, John Curry, and James Cleary—who would go on to play

prominent roles in the Hibernia Benevolent Institution, the county's leading fraternal organization for Irish immigrants.[5]

Bannan's interest in immigration was natural for the son of a naturalized Ulsterman, but it was also at least partly commercial. Some of his
book advertisements were directed at the largely immigrant Catholic
population, and by the 1840s he was an agent for those who wanted to
pay the passage to America for friends and relatives in Ireland, or who
wanted to send money home.[6] The swelling ranks of Irish Catholic workers
in Schuylkill County meant not only labor for the mines, but also money in
Bannan's pocket.

The money Bannan made from immigrants didn't stop him from gradually developing a hatred for Irish Catholics as virulent as any in his father's native Belfast. But Bannan's was no simpleminded sectarianism. He
came to hate the Irish Catholic mine workers of the anthracite region because of the challenge they posed to his worldview. Bannan, like many
mine operators in the Schuylkill coal field, espoused a virtual theology
that linked free enterprise by small businessmen to industrial efficiency,
economic growth, the Protestant work ethic, and the future of American
democracy, as embodied first by the Whigs and later by the Republicans.[7]
Add equal measures of temperance, abolitionism, and evangelical fervor
and you have the antithesis of everything that the typical Irish immigrant
to the county held dear. The recognition that Bannan himself had helped
populate the coal region with a people whose worldview so utterly contradicted his own may only have further embittered him.

That a deep antipathy toward Irish Catholics was not the inevitable
product of an Ulster Protestant heritage is aptly demonstrated by the life
of James Gowen, the patriarch of the second family. Gowen was born on
March 17, 1790, twenty years to the day after the elder Bannan. He was
raised in Newtownstewart, County Tyrone, and attended the Academy of
Strabane, then worked as a teacher for a time before immigrating to Philadelphia in 1811. There he played a leading role in the Hibernian Society for
the Relief of Emigrants from Ireland, which helped many a Catholic and
was not related to the neo-Ribbon Hibernia Benevolent Institution. Though
an ardent Episcopalian, he strongly supported religious tolerance, and even
sent his two oldest sons to a Catholic school in Emmetsburg, Maryland.
His support for the Democratic Party during the Civil War was so strong
that some neighbors suspected him of treason. But there can be no doubt
of the degree to which Gowen embraced his new country—he named the
third of his five sons Franklin Benjamin Gowen and the last George Washington Gowen.[8]

Franklin and George were close. The former, born in 1836, was apprenticed to a Lancaster merchant after attending an elite school in nearby Lititz. He frequently visited George, who also attended the school, until in 1852 he moved to Shamokin, a coal town in Northumberland County, to manage an iron furnace for the merchant. By 1858 he and a partner, J. G. Turner, were operating a colliery at Mount Laffee. Franklin brought in his brother George to work as company bookkeeper, but the mine failed the following year, and the older Gowen began to study law. He was admitted to the county bar in 1860 and became active in Democratic politics.

The Civil War divided the family to some degree. Despite his father's deep suspicions about the conflict, George Gowen enlisted in the 48th Pennsylvania Volunteers, and rose to colonel before being killed just days before Lee surrendered at Appomattox. Franklin, running as a Democrat, was elected district attorney of Schuylkill County in 1862, at the very dawn of the Molly Maguire troubles, taking office within days of the murder of James Bergen. In the words of his biographer, Marvin W. Schlegel, "Gowen seemed to show a lack of interest" in the Bergen killing and similar crimes attributed to the Mollies. "No one was convicted for any of them, or even so much as arrested," he wrote. "A partial explanation lay in the fact that the Irish were solidly Democratic, and the party could not afford to offend them."

Drafted in 1863, a year of violent opposition to conscription both in Schuylkill County and New York City, Gowen, by then a husband and father, used an option open to few of the Democratic miners who had elected him—he paid for a substitute to take his place. The following year he resigned to focus on a lucrative private practice. By the end of the war he was representing the Reading Railroad, a company he would eventually use to establish a monopoly on coal production in the southern anthracite fields.[9] In doing so he destroyed both Bannan's ideal of an industry run by independent entrepreneurs and the hopes of Irish Catholic miners that collective action could gain them a fair share of the profits of their labor.

Which brings us to our third family, the Mohans of the Minersville area. The information available on the Mohans is less complete than that on the Bannans and Gowens—the most extensive glimpse comes in *Biographical and Portrait Cyclopedia of Schuylkill County* published in 1893. It describes how Charles Mohan, a native of Fermanagh, came to the United States in 1823 and built a log cabin near the current site of St. Vincent's Church on Sunbury Street in Minersville. Mohan found work in the collieries and eventually became a mine boss, marrying Arretta Reed and fathering ten children, among them John, Terrance, and Charles. Mohan was

born around 1800, and seems to have operated a very successful inn, probably the same one that his son later operated. In an era when porter and
politics went hand in hand, Mohan was elected to Minersville Town Council in 1843. Four years later he was appointed to a countywide committee
coordinating relief efforts for the starving of his homeland. In the 1850 census he listed his occupation as miner and owned real estate worth $2,000, a
sum well above that listed by the typical Irish mine worker. He appears to
have died between 1857 and 1860; his wife, Aretta, is listed as the head of the
household, an innkeeper worth $7,000, in the 1860 census. Their son John
went on to play a prominent role in the business and civil affairs of Minersville, serving on the school board and as a director of the First National Bank.

In addition to a wife and several children, it seems that Charles had at
least one and possibly several brothers in the Minersville area. Another en-
trepreneurial Mohan, Michael, was elected to Minersville borough council
in 1850. Born around 1810, he was a successful shoemaker with real estate
valued at $4,000 in 1850.[10] As was the case with Charles, Michael's last
name was sometimes spelled "Mochan" or "Mahan." And when Michael
died sometime in the 1850s, some of his children were taken in by Charles's
widow, Arretta.

One of Michael's sons, Hugh, left behind a brief glimpse of the world
these younger Mohans inhabited. In an autobiographical sketch published
in California in 1880, Hugh described his early years: "Born in Minersville,
Penn., March 9th, 1848; educated in public schools of that town; worked in
coal mines; spent a while learning the machinist trade; moved to Columbia
County in 1865; was elected Secretary of the Workingmen's Union;
returned to Pottsville; was appointed a school teacher; and was elected
Secretary of Democratic Committee, and acted as reporter on the Standard . . .
was elected State Secretary of the Emerald Beneficial Association, and served
two terms almost; was Orator of the Day in Easton on St. Patrick's Day; also
in Minersville."[11] In short, young Hugh Mohan's life in the anthracite region
was grounded in the coal mines, the labor movement, Democratic politics,
and Irish fraternal organizations.

In addition to Charles and Michael, there was a third Fermanagh-born
Mohan in town in the 1840s. A Luke Mochan was listed as a Minersville
subscriber to I. Daniel Rupp's *History of Northampton, Lehigh, Monroe, Car-
bon, and Schuylkill Counties*, published in 1845. He didn't stay long. By 1850
Luke "Mahan" was raising a family in Coal Township, Northumberland
County. But something—perhaps the deaths of two brothers in Minersville—
drew him back to the West Branch. In 1860 Luke was spelling his name
Mohan, working as a miner, and living in Foster Township, northwest of

Minersville, with his wife, Isabella, and their five children—Isabella, Thomas, Mary, Bridget, Ellen, and Philip. Ten years later, he was living even closer to Minersville, in Forestville. He had immigrated in 1836, applied for citizenship in 1838, and finally gotten it about five years later.[12]

While it is not certain that Luke was a brother of the Minersville Mohans, both he and Michael were born in Fermanagh just a few years apart and had sons named Philip, which hints at not only a connection, but also the possibility of a fourth brother. Though he does not turn up in Schuylkill County census records for 1840 or 1850, a Philip Mohan was active in politics, or at least one celebrated political brawl, in a village near Minersville in 1848. He vanished from the region after serving a prison sentence, possibly relocating to neighboring Berks County, where a forty-year-old Philip Mohan was working as a railroad watchman in Upper Bern Township, just over the county line, in 1870.

Of the four contemporary Mohans—Charles, Michael, Philip, and Luke—the first two were by far the most successful and assimilated, with thriving businesses in the growing town of Minersville. Philip decamped, leaving Luke and his growing family in the hills outside town. There, the only work was in the dark and treacherous mines, where the Old World echoed far more loudly than it did in the streets of Minersville.

Luke's sons confronted the dangers of that world through two forms of collective action. The eldest, Thomas, was active in both industrial unionism and an Irish fraternal organization, much like Hugh Mohan of Minserville. Thomas ran for secretary of the Schuylkill County miners' union in 1874, and, shortly after the union was crushed in the summer of 1876, he became bodymaster of the Forestville Hibernians, taking over for a man charged with Molly Maguire activity. Four years later, his younger brother, Philip, was involved in efforts to revive the union. Spies from the Pinkerton Agency dutifully forwarded to Franklin Gowen reports on the activities of both Forestville Mohans. And a chance encounter with one of the Minersville Mohans nearly sank the most famous of those spies.[13]

The profound differences over the future of the anthracite industry that Benjamin Bannan, Franklin Gowen, and members of the Mohan clan came to embody were explored to an extraordinary degree by a committee of the Pennsylvania Senate in the first half of the 1830s. Supporters of small-scale entrepreneurs on the one hand, and large corporations on the other, held a robust debate that at times offered an eerily accurate picture of what was to come. And while the perspective of Irish mine workers was all but ignored in this debate, the one instance in which it surfaced was enough to chill anyone with even a passing knowledge of landlord–tenant relations in Ireland.

The debate came on the heels of an economic explosion that transformed the Pottsville region in the late 1820s, just as Benjamin Bannan arrived to take over the *Miners' Journal*. It was largely fueled by an influx of speculators and entrepreneurs seeking a quick buck in Schuylkill County, which was still free of the coal monopolies that controlled neighboring counties to the north.

Pottsville is located in the southernmost of four anthracite fields that stretch from Dauphin County in the southwest to Susquehanna County in the northeast. The Southern Coal Field also includes the West Branch region and Tamaqua in Schuylkill County and Lansford and Jim Thorpe (once Mauch Chunk) in Carbon County. The Western Middle Coal Field, just over Broad Mountain, stretches from Trevorton in the west past Mahanoy City in the east. Because most of its coal, like that of the Southern Field, was shipped to Philadelphia, the two were generally lumped together as the Schuylkill coal field. The Eastern Middle Coal Field is centered around Hazleton in Luzerne County, but includes Banks Township in Carbon County. It was often referred to as the Lehigh field, and most of its coal went to New York. The same was true of Wyoming coal from the Northern Field, which encompasses Wilkes-Barre, Pittston, and Scranton in Luzerne and Lackawanna Counties. The Lehigh and Wyoming coal fields were controlled by monopolies from early on.

By contrast, in the early years of the Schuylkill coal trade, the mine operators were, for the most part, individuals and partnerships, rather than big companies. Two factors prevented the quick emergence of a monopoly such as existed in the nearby Lehigh coal field, where the Lehigh Coal and Navigation Company under Josiah White and Erskine Hazard had been granted the right to mine, trade in, and transport coal.[14]

The first factor was that the Schuylkill Navigation Company, which ran the Schuylkill Canal and thus controlled the only transportation outlet for the county's coal, was incorporated without mining privileges. The second and by far the more important factor was the geology of Schuylkill County, where major coal deposits lay close to the surface.

"The Schuylkill region seems to have been marked by nature for individual enterprise," the *North American Review* noted in 1836. Pamphlets spoke of coal seams breaking to the surface of streambeds and mountainsides. It was said that less than fifty dollars was needed to open a mine.[15]

This accident of geology had important economic and social consequences. The ease with which many entrepreneurs entered the mining industry in Schuylkill County ensured cutthroat competition by under-capitalized operators desperate to recoup their investment and pay off creditors.

The historian Grace Palladino, who has examined West Branch labor unrest during the Civil War, argues that the cost of the competition included unsafe mines, habitual cash shortages, and declining working conditions. It was the mine workers and their families, she said, who "shouldered the heaviest burdens of this anarchistic trade."[16]

In examining Schuylkill County's dismal mine-safety record, the author Anthony F. C. Wallace also found that early investors in coal lands sought to maximize the return on those investments by maximizing coal production. Likewise, those who operated the mines were not especially interested in the safety of their employees or the mine itself, Wallace found, because efforts to improve safety meant more expenditures and less coal.[17]

But most members of the coal establishment—the mine operators and the landowners from whom they leased the mines—viewed the peculiar circumstances of the Schuylkill region as a blessing rather than a curse. The county's geology encouraged individual enterprise, and its exploiters viewed themselves as the bulwark of a Jeffersonian democracy based not on small farms, but on small businesses. In this view, of which Bannan was the prime spokesman, there was a harmony of interests between employer and employee, for one could not flourish without the other. The debate on the merits of incorporated coal companies versus individual businessmen came to a head when a Pennsylvania State Senate committee undertook an investigation of the anthracite trade in 1833.

The entrepreneurs' argument was summed up early in the committee's report, released in 1834: "So long as the wealth, the enterprise, the intelligence, and the patriotism of our citizens cannot be concentrated in the few, but are equally distributed among the many, and equality of rights continues to form a fundamental principle of our government, it must remain as their common heritage, constituting a large portion of the present wealth of the State, and her principal strength in after ages."[18]

Spokesmen for the individual operators warned the committee that corporations would have a dire effect on the coal industry, the region, and the Commonwealth. They said the corporations would glut the market, strive for monopoly, influence the votes of their large work forces, and transfer the profits of the region's mineral wealth to faraway (and possibly foreign) capitalists.

The most dire warnings evoked images of a colony ruled by tyrants distant and arbitrary. "The effect of incorporated companies upon the general prosperity of the country may be compared to the dominion of despotism and tyranny, usurping the rights and trampling upon the liberties of the people," wrote Volney Palmer, a Pottsville coal operator. "As a population or community of slaves differs from that of freemen, so does a population or community growing up under such companies differ from that created by individual operators."[19]

Col. Jacob Krebs, a member of Senate committee who represented Schuylkill County, voiced some concerns that were especially frightful to the growing number of Irish immigrants in the coal fields. Under incorporated coal companies, Krebs said, "the miners, workmen and managers and superintendents are mere tenants at will from day to day, and know not the moment they may receive orders from the board of directors to leave the district." He continued: "The operation of the incorporated coal companies with non-resident stockholders upon the improvement of the coal region is similar to that charged upon the Irish absentee landlord— they impoverish the country by expending the revenues drawn from it in distant places."[20]

Supporters of the incorporated companies pointed out that they provided not only greater job opportunities, but also more reliable employment, though at lower wages than the independents. The result, they said, was a more orderly industry and a more stable society. William Milnes, the agent for the North American Coal Company, contended, for example, that miners employed by corporations "are more domestic and more settled." Mine workers with families preferred to work for the corporations, even at lower wages, he wrote, pointing to men in his employ who could have made two dollars per week more elsewhere, "because they can have regular and constant employ."[21] What Charles Mohan, Sr., a mine worker and family man, thought of all this can only been guessed—the Senate was assiduous in seeking the views of coal executives, but didn't bother to consult their employees, who often found their ability to switch jobs compromised by debts to the company store.

Benjamin Bannan was the only member of the three Ulster families to take a direct role in the debate. (Franklin Gowen, that later champion of coal corporations, had not even been born yet.) Bannan used the pages of the *Miners' Journal* to argue that the coal corporations were doomed to fail, with disastrous consequences for everyone. "Creditors and stockholders will be brethren in affliction," Bannan wrote on February 24, 1834. "The capital of the company will vanish and be converted into denuded and gutted hills, rocky ridges and sterile plains, rendered dangerous by the pit falls, drifts, shafts and piles of earth and stones now called 'permanent improvements.'"

It was a prescient view, given the fate of the region under Gowen's Philadelphia and Reading Railroad, which finally did achieve a monopoly decades later. For all their eloquence and prescience, the advocates of individual enterprise won the debate but lost the war. Little was done to limit the spread of corporations, and they continued to make important inroads in the Schuylkill coal field over the next decade. For Irish mine workers, what emerged from the debate was a nightmare vision of the future that looked very much like their past, with the prospect that they would be reduced to their former status as tenant farmers, subject to eviction at any time, ruled by distant powers bent on expropriating the region's wealth.

Already by the mid-1830s, mine workers were beginning to see a long slide in their standard of living, with increasing competition depressing the price of coal and wages.[22] In 1837, Krebs's fears about distant capitalists were incorporated in the form of the New York–based Forest Improvement Company, which was chartered to open mines, build rail links to them, and underwrite capital expenditures. While supposedly barred from actual mining operations, the corporation quickly dominated the coal industry in the Swatara and West Branch districts, north and west of Minersville. The principal of the company, Charles Heckscher, an immigrant German merchant from New York with close links to the financier Moses Taylor, first used various partners and managers to operate the mines on the company's land. But by 1860, Heckscher and his nephews, Eugene Borda and Richard Heckscher, themselves operated five of the biggest collieries in the region.

Smaller operators complained that the company constituted a "monopoly highly injurious to the individual enterprises of the citizens of the County." Bannan's *Miners' Journal* warned individual mine owners to be careful "how they aid a coal company . . . gaining a strong foothold in our region."[23] But gain a foothold it did, and the stability that the Forest Improvement Company brought to the West Branch of the Schuylkill helped stamp it with a peculiarly Irish character. With fifteen thousand acres, the company dwarfed the holdings of other coal speculators and operators. With steady work and hundreds of openings for unskilled labor, the Heckscher collieries were a magnet for Irishmen seeking to establish themselves in the New World.

As Palladino writes, Irish immigrants "tended to be employed by centralized, well-organized companies that needed to attract large numbers of men to their often geographically isolated, and largely undeveloped, mining towns. Thus Irish immigrants . . . comprised the bulk of the work force in newer coal districts like Cass Township, Schuylkill County, Hazleton in Luzerne County, or Jeansville in Carbon County."[24] The remoteness of these locations, and the fact that they were sparsely occupied, made them among the few rural areas of the United States where Irish immigrants settled in concentrated numbers and retained a strong ethnic identity.

In the years before the famine, many of these immigrants came from Ulster, as one of Bannan's advertisements as a shipping agent makes clear: "The subscriber has now made arrangements to bring passengers direct from Londonderry to Philadelphia in good sailing vessels sailing from that port twice every month." Nearly half of the Bank of Ireland branches to which Bannan offered to remit money for passage to America were in the eight counties of Ulster.[25]

A more comprehensive picture of pre-famine emigration from Ireland to the coal fields emerges from Rupp's *History of Northampton, Lehigh, Monroe, Carbon, and Schuylkill Counties*, which lists the residences and birthplaces of many subscribers. Of the seventy-six Irish immigrants in Schuylkill County whose places of birth are listed, coal-producing County Kilkenny leads with twelve, Cavan follows with nine, and Donegal and Galway tie for third place with five each. Of the total, nearly 45 percent come from Ulster, and 38 percent hail from those counties in the province and its periphery where there was at least some Molly Maguire activity— Donegal, Fermanagh, Cavan, Armagh, Louth, Monaghan, Leitrim, Longford, and Roscommon.

In adjacent Carbon County, an even higher proportion—nearly 77 percent of the total—came from Ulster. Of the 108 Irish subscribers in Carbon County whose birthplaces are listed, twenty-five hailed from Donegal, twenty-three from Cavan, fifteen from Londonderry, nine from Monaghan, and six from Antrim. Almost half—48 percent—came from counties where the Mollies were active. In both Schuylkill and Carbon Counties, the Molly stronghold of Cavan was the second biggest source of Irish immigrants listed.[26]

The large numbers of Ulstermen in both counties is all the more remarkable because there were few coal mines in the province, outside of Ballycastle in Antrim and Coalisland in Tyrone.

The explanation lies in the shipping links between Ulster and Philadelphia that had been forged more than a century before by James Logan, the Armagh-born secretary of Penn's colony. Fearful of Indian unrest in the early 1700s, Logan had invited over his fellow Scots–Irish for their experience in handling restless natives, and their brutal treatment of Indians on the Pennsylvania frontier set the standard as they pioneered westward migration.[27] More than a century after the Scots–Irish first began arriving the pipeline from Ulster to Pennsylvania was still open, but it was increasingly filled with Catholics rather than Presbyterians.

The new immigrants carried their own legacy from the deadly competition for land in the north of Ireland—a tradition of collective action that soon became evident, in two related forms. The first was the creation of a neo-Ribbon group, the Hibernians. The second was union activity. When the two forms eventually merged, the result was the American branch of the Molly Maguires.

7   The Hibernians

You must love without dissimulation, hating evil, cleaving to good. Love
one another with brotherly love.

                      —Charter of the Ancient Order of Hibernians

In the 1830s, the anthracite region became home to one more band of
brothers with roots in Ulster, a group that Benjamin Bannan and Franklin
Gowen would fight, and at least one Mohan would join. In the same year
that Col. Krebs warned that corporations would reduce Schuylkill County
to the status of an Irish tenant farm, Irish immigrants there formed a neo-
Ribbon society.

The organization that came to be known as the Ancient Order of Hibernians, or AOH, was incorporated in 1833 as Pottsville's Hibernia Benevolent
Institution, often referred to as the Hibernian Benevolent Society or simply
the Hibernian Society. A St. Patrick's Society had been active in Pottsville
even earlier, parading on March 17, 1832, "decorated with the usual em-
blematic costume," the *Miners' Journal* reported, suggesting that this was not
the society's first outing.[1] In 1836 the Schuylkill County Hibernians united
with other former Ribbonmen in New York City. The new, national group
marked its birth with a charter from a Ribbon Society in Ireland.[2]

The decision to merge and affiliate with a parent Ribbon body in the
British Isles came against a backdrop of changing economic conditions in
the coal region and growing nativism in New York and throughout the nation. In the fall of 1834, the inventor Samuel B. Morse published a series of
letters claiming that the Catholic Church—and Catholic emigration—were
being used by European monarchies to subvert democracy in America.
That same year, Rev. Lyman Beecher called from the pulpit for "decisive action" against ascendant Catholicism in Boston, and a nativist mob obliged
him the next day by burning a Catholic convent and school. Unrepentant,
Beecher a year later published "A Plea for the West" suggesting that Catho-

lic schools constituted a conspiracy against America's children. And in 1836, Maria Monk's "Awful Disclosures of the Hotel Dieu Nunnery of Montreal" became a runaway best seller with its spurious tales of sexual depravity among nuns.

The polemics were soon followed by political action. In June 1835, the Native American Democratic Association was founded in New York City on an anti-Catholic and anti-immigration platform. It won 39 percent of the vote in city elections that November—largely because the Whigs failed to field a slate—and ran Morse as its candidate for mayor in the spring of 1836. Now facing Whig opposition, he won a mere 6 percent of the vote.[3]

This, then, was the context in which a neo-Ribbon organization was chartered in the United States, on May 4, 1836. Just as the Defenders sprang up as a response to raids by Protestant Peep O'Day Boys in Ulster, and the Molly Maguires were born amid changing economic and political conditions in the Ulster borderlands, so the Hibernians were born as New York's Irish community came under attack from nativists, and Schuylkill County's Irish mine workers were squeezed by industrial pressures.

It is possible that the new organization served at least one other purpose—to help fugitives from Ireland's land wars. In an 1888 article about the Buckshots, as the early Mollies of Carbon County were called, the *New York Times* reported, "The Buckshots were a secret society formed more than thirty years ago, the original object of which was to provide protection and asylum in this country to fugitives from Ireland who had escaped from the old country after killing some obnoxious landlord or constable."[4]

In the anthracite region, as in New York, the new organization served as a focus of Irish American political activity. It was firmly wedded to the Democratic Party, part of an ethnic allegiance that dated as far back as the support and sympathy United Irish émigrés received from Jefferson's adherents.[5]

A charter for the Hibernian Society was brought to the United States from the governing body of one of the two Ribbon groupings in the British Isles by a Ribbonman working on a ship that sailed regularly between Britain and the United States. It offered "full instruction with our authority to establish branches of our society in America."

Qualifications for membership were simple: "All members must be Roman Catholics, and Irish or of Irish descent, and of good moral character, and none of your members shall join in any secret societies contrary to the laws of the Catholic Church, and at all times your motto shall be: Friendship, unity and Christian charity." It continued: "You must love without dissimulation, hating evil, cleaving to good. Love one another with brotherly love."

It was, in short, to be a fraternal and mutual aid society of Irish Catholic immigrants. After a special admonition to "aid and protect" Irishwomen of all creeds, the parent body granted the American organization full autonomy, within the limits of Catholic doctrine: "You are at liberty to make such laws as will guide your workings and for the welfare of our old Society; but such laws must be at all times according to the teachings of the Holy Catholic Church, and the obligation that we send you, and all your workings, must be submitted to any Catholic priest, when called for."

The charter closed with one final instruction: "Send a copy to our late friend that you spoke of and who is now working in Pennsylvania." It was signed by Patrick McGuire, County Fermanagh; Patrick McKenna, County Monaghan; Patrick Reilly, County Meath; John Farrell, County Meath; James McManus, County Antrim; Patrick Dunn, County Tyrone; Daniel Gallagher, Glasgow; John Reilly, County Cavan; John Derkin, County Mayo; Patrick Boyle, County Sligo; Thomas O'Rorke, County Leitrim; John McMahon, County Longford; Patrick Hammill, Westmeath; John Murphy, Liverpool.[6]

A few facts can be gleaned from the document.

The residences of its signatories, who constituted the parent group's governing body, or "Board of Erin," show that the American organization chose to affiliate with the Northern Union, a Ribbon group based in Ulster and its borderlands, where religious or sectarian communalism lent it a bit more vitality than its Dublin-based rival, the Irish Sons of Freedom.[7]

The charter's insistence that no member "join any secret society contrary to the laws of the Catholic Church" highlights the odd position of the Ribbon and Hibernian Societies in embracing a church that had repeatedly condemned secret societies. The prohibition may have referred to membership in Masonic groups, or it may have served as cover for the Hibernians, allowing them to claim that they could not possibly be members of a secret society, because their charter specifically forbade it.*

---

* That sort of duplicity was not unknown as Hibernians tried to reconcile themselves with a disapproving church. A Catholic priest in Philadelphia reported the following deathbed confession of a former Ribbonman and Hibernian in the 1880s: "I joined them [the Ancient Order of Hibernians] about 40 years ago, in Ireland, under the name of Ribbonmen, and have belonged to them ever since. It is the same society, under a different name, with the name changed, at various times, in order to avoid the condemnation of the church. I have been going to the Sacraments, about every three months, and according to the rules of the Society, we took our oath for three months, which ran out on a Saturday, at 12 o'clock. This was done in order to enable us, if questioned by the

Last but not least, there is Board of Erin's insistence that a copy of the charter be passed on to our "late friend" who was working in Pennsylvania. The man's identity is not disclosed, but he must have been highly influential—the American organization had its headquarters in Schuylkill County for a number of years before 1853.

John O'Dea, the historian of the American branch of the Ancient Order of Hibernians, wrote that the society's secret signs and passwords were sent from the Board of Erin in Ireland "to the President of the Divisions in Schuylkill County, being then transmitted by messenger to the other Divisions."[8] Divisions were the local chapters, each headed by a "body master."

We may never know the exact identity of the first president of the Hibernian Society, but he was one of a group of Irish émigrés centered on Pottsville who played leading roles in Democratic politics between 1836 and 1848. In that year, the Hibernia Benevolent Institution of Pottsville listed the following officers: president, Patrick Fogarty; vice president, Bernard Riley; secretary, Peter Mudey; treasurer, Michael Daly.

It was an eminently respectable and upwardly mobile group. Fogarty was a merchant and civic activist who sat on a commission that helped plan the growth of Pottsville.[9] "Riley," actually Reilly, was an immigrant who became a successful railroad contractor; Reilly Township was named for him. (An unrelated James Bernard Reilly played a role in the Molly troubles of the 1870s, when he was a lawyer, prosecutor, and congressman.)[10] Mudey was a schoolteacher turned publican who was active in Democratic politics.[11]

Other members of the Irish American community who seemed to play a big role in Hibernian activities included James Cleary of Pottsville, a tavern owner and militia captain; Edward O'Connor, the proprietor of the Pottsville House; John Maginnis of Pottsville and Edward Colehan of Port Carbon, both mine operators, the former from Monaghan and the latter from Galway; Thomas Brady, a doctor; John C. Neville, a one-armed immigrant lawyer; William B. Hull, a Port Carbon barkeep; and the Irish nationalist William Haggerty.

These men were all listed as officers of the Hibernians' annual St. Patrick's Day dinners at various times between 1836 and 1848. (The close connection between leadership of the society and the March 17 dinner is

---

priest, in the confessional, to say that we did not belong to any secret society. The oath, which was of the most solemn kind, was renewed within 24 hours." See letter by Rev. Thomas Barry, Church of the Visitation, Archbishop Wood Collection, Philadelphia Archdiocesan Archives.

evidenced by the lineup for 1848, one of the few for which we know the officers of the Hibernia Benevolent Institution. Its president, Fogarty, and vice president, Reilly, were the chairman and secretary of the St. Patrick's Day banquet that year.)[12]

Around 1838, according to O'Dea, the organization began to be called the Ancient Order of Hibernians in New York, though to the public its members were known as "St. Patrick's Boys."[13] In Schuylkill County, it continued to go by the names Hibernia Benevolent Institution or Hibernian Benevolent Society, through the 1850s and possibly as late as 1870, when it gained a charter from the state and formally adopted the name Ancient Order of Hibernians.

The society was a secret one, and the only clues to its membership and activities are infrequent mentions in newspapers, especially in the latter half of March, when reports on the Hibernians' annual St. Patrick's Day banquet were published. The newspaper reports show that those who led the banquet were active during the remainder of the year concerning the same issues as the Hibernian Society's Ribbon parent in Ireland—politics, embryonic trade unionism, the Irish national struggle, and mutual aid.

On March 17, 1838, the year that the St. Patrick's Fraternal Society changed its name to the Hibernians, two events attracted the interest of the *Miners' Journal* in Pottsville: a funeral and a banquet. The funeral was for James Kinsley, sixty-five, late of Killegney, County Wexford. "Mr. Kinsley," the newspaper reported, "was a captain of a company in the Rebellion of 1798, and took an active part in behalf of his oppressed countrymen. He was wounded in the battle of Roscommon, in which engagement he bravely fought for twelve successive hours without moving from his position. In 1819, he left his country for the United States, where he has ever since been known as an excellent citizen and an honest man. His remains were accompanied to the tomb, on Monday last, by the St. Patrick's Society, in full regalia, numbering nearly two hundred, and an immense concourse of people."

Hugh and James Kinsley, a Port Carbon merchant and coal operator, had played active roles in the St. Patrick's Day banquet in 1836, the first for which there is any mention in Pottsville. The St. Patrick's Society that paid homage to the dead hero of '98 on March 17, 1838, was almost certainly the same organization that was listed under a different name when it held a banquet in Pottsville that night to commemorate St. Patrick's Day.

The *Miners' Journal* reported that "the Anniversary of Ireland's Patron Saint was celebrated by the Hibernia Benevolent Institution of Pottsville, with a large concourse of invited guests and citizens, in a splendid manner at the Town Hall." Glasses were lifted to the "martyrs of '98" and to Daniel O'Connell, "the champion of Ireland." The organizers of the dinner included two prominent Democrats, O'Connor and Colehan.[14]

The composition of the group was one reflection of the political influence of Schuylkill County's growing Irish community. Another was a contest for the allegiance of Irish voters by the *Miners' Journal*, a publication with Whig loyalties, and the *Pottsville Emporium*, a paper founded by Democrats in 1838 as a counterweight to Bannan and edited by Strange Palmer. The *Emporium* began the rivalry by running a column signed "Erin" that put an Irish slant on the political questions of the day. The *Miners' Journal* responded with a column signed "Emmett."

When Emmett alleged in 1840 that Martin Van Buren harbored prejudice against the Catholic Church, forty-two leading Schuylkill County Irishmen signed a statement condemning "the fervour of political rancour" and "those who perpetuate the unhappy demons of religious discord." The letter insisted that both political parties treat members of the county's Irish community as "American citizens, and not as Irishmen," but it is worth noting that the statement was issued only after Bannan attempted to lure Irish American voters away from the Democratic Party to the Whigs. Members of the Hibernian Society played a key role in the statement—twenty-four of forty-two signatories appeared at the society's St. Patrick's Day banquet between 1838 and 1844.[15]

The annual St. Patrick's Day festivities that the society sponsored underlined its growing clout. As early as 1840, the "St. Patrick's Society" mustered 230 members for its March 17 parade. Two of the parade's five leaders—Cleary and Thomas Quin—were members of the Schuylkill County Democratic Committee. The Hibernian banquet that evening was hosted by O'Connor and attended by numerous members of the Democratic committee. Also on hand were two Catholic priests—a sign the new organization had not yet run afoul of the Church.[16]

The parade doubled in size the following year, with five hundred delegates turning out, including contingents from Port Carbon and Minersville. In 1842, the number in the procession rose to nearly eight hundred.[17]

The society and its members were becoming a force to be reckoned with, and in more than just local politics. Two interrelated events in 1842 demonstrated the Schuylkill County Hibernians' growing influence. One was a bitter international debate over Irish American attitudes toward slavery. The other was a strike by 1,500 West Branch miners.

The slavery debate grew out of the formation at O'Connor's hotel on February 15, 1841, of the Pottsville Repeal Association, a branch of a national organization formed to support Daniel O'Connell's campaign to overturn the union between Britain and Ireland. Hibernians played a leading role in the group. Among the leaders of the Repeal Association were Haggerty, Cleary, Colehan, Neville, Brady, Fogarty, George Dougherty, and James Downey—all prominent in the Hibernians' banquet at O'Connor's in March.[18]

By July, the Pottsville Repeal Association had 204 members, and in February 1842, Haggerty served as a vice president of the National Repeal Convention at the old State House in Philadelphia, where a heated debate arose on a proposal to repudiate O'Connell's vociferous opposition to American slavery. The proposal was rejected but the issue would not go way.[19]

Support for the repeal movement suffered a serious blow not long after the national convention, amid growing publicity about an Irish resolution condemning slavery in the United States. It was signed by O'Connell, Rev. Theobald Mathew (the Catholic leader of the Irish temperance movement), and tens of thousands of others in Ireland. "Irishmen and Irishwomen! Treat the colored people as your equals—as brethren," the resolution exhorted.

The call to embrace abolition and treat blacks as brethren was anathema to the Irish Catholic Democrats of Schuylkill County, whose party condoned slavery. A March meeting in Pottsville of the "friends of Ireland," led by Hibernian Democrats O'Connor and Haggerty, condemned the O'Connell resolution in the strongest terms. Echoing the 1840 statement by forty-two leading Irishmen in the Erin versus Emmett controversy, the meeting proclaimed "that we do not form a distinct class of the community, but consider ourselves in every respect as citizens of this great and glorious republic—that we look upon every attempt to address us otherwise than as citizens upon the subject of the abolition of negro slavery or on any other subject, as base and iniquitous."[20] Few things, it seems, aroused the fury of Schuylkill County's Irish leaders more than that which posed a threat to their community's allegiance to the Democratic Party.

The Pottsville meeting announced its opinion that the signatures of O'Connell and Mathew were forgeries and claimed that slavery in the United States was the fault of Great Britain.[21] Thereafter, mention of the Pottsville Repeal Association faded in local newspapers; the *Pottsville Emporium*, a Democratic newspaper, noted on August 5, 1843, that "the violent and denunciatory course of O'Connell towards this country has had the effect to dampen the ardor of Repealers."

But even as enthusiasm for the cause faded in Schuylkill County, the Pottsville proclamation critical of O'Connell began to generate international controversy when it was picked up by New York newspapers and disseminated far and wide. An English-language newspaper in Paris, *Galignani's Messenger*, reprinted portions of it, marveling at "the Pottsville paddies, who evidently deem themselves of no small consequence in those parts."[22]

The *Dublin Monitor* viewed the proclamation with "grief, indignation and astonishment," and asked, "Have you, Messrs. O'Connor, Haggerty and Co.—your names tell you to be Irish—so soon forgotten the rod held over you at home? Have you so soon sided with the oppressor?" The *Monitor* mocked the notion that O'Connell's signature was a forgery: "There is no *real* doubt of the genuineness of the address, either at home or with you. You, gentlemen of Pottsville, *know* it—you *feel* it to be genuine; but the pro-slavery spirit has caught some of Ireland's sons in America in its grasp."[23]

The fiery response to the Pottsville proclamation led to one last broadside by the anthracite Irish, from the hand of Brady, a Democratic politician who had served as vice president of the Schuylkill County Hibernians' St. Patrick's Day banquet the year before. In the debate over slavery, "there was no vulgar epithet too opprobrious" for the abolitionists to heap on the Irish of Pottsville, Brady complained. Where O'Connell's proclamation urged Irishmen to join the abolition cause, Brady, rather disingenuously, saw a call for miscegenation. Abolitionists, he argued, were attempting to provoke a civil war: "They seek to cause revolution; to ensanguine a country once hallowed by the blood of freemen, now with the blood of civil strife."[24]

The heated rhetoric that O'Connor and Haggerty generated may have had something to do with a yawning gulf in perceptions about their standing to challenge an international figure like O'Connell. The Pottsville men viewed the town as the national headquarters of the Hibernian Society, and themselves as leaders of the American Irish. Newspapers in Dublin and Paris saw them as self-important nobodies from a remote town in the hinterlands.

Thomas Davis, a native or Ireland long resident in Rhode Island, offered some socioeconomic context for Irish American tolerance of slavery at an abolition meeting in Dublin's Royal Exchange. "The Africans in America are hewers of wood and drawers of water," he said. "The Irish come out to labor likewise, and thus the two classes come into juxtaposition; and I know not that I have seen bitterer hatred manifested than by the Irish toward the Africans."[25]

Even as Davis and Brady waged this debate, another issue was coming to the fore in the hills outside Pottsville. It would bring Hibernian leaders and rank-and-file Irish mine workers into a fierce confrontation with the local power structure. And the denouement would involve blacklisting, labor competition, and racial violence.

Labor Unrest

On May 17, the Philadelphia and Reading Railroad began service between the anthracite region and its coal wharves in the Port Richmond section of Philadelphia. Less than two months later, on July 7, West Branch mine workers met in Minersville and decided to strike.

The two events were by no means coincidental.

"The immediate effect" of the Reading's completion, says an 1881 history of Schuylkill County, was a "rivalry between the canal and railroad companies for the coal traffic." As the competitors slashed rates for the transportation of coal, mining companies cut prices, glutting the market. Low prices meant low wages and only partial employment for the mine workers, who were "reduced to great suffering."[26]

At a time when a minimum of $6.00 a week was needed to sustain a worker, weekly wages fell to $5.25 for miners and $4.20 for mine laborers. Even that paltry sum was often paid in company scrip or "store orders" that forced employees to patronize company stores whose limited merchandise was matched only by their high prices.[27]

"The possession of the order alone, without any money, may leave them in a miserable situation," the *Pottsville Emporium* wrote of the miners:

A wife or child may be very sick, and the storekeeper has no medicine. A physician may be required, who cannot be paid in store goods, and cannot be expected to attend without being paid for his services ... There may be actual wants which the storekeeper cannot supply. He may have no flour, no meat, no butter, and if he has he may refuse to let the workman have either of them on the order, for these are cash articles. But there is no choice. The poor man must take what there is, at such prices as the merchant shall dictate. In many instances these prices are exorbitant and outrageous and even where this is not the case, there is always room for suspicion that the workingman has been unjustly dealt with. This result of all this has been that the poor man, laboring hard for weeks and months, has found himself at the end of the year, not only, without a cent, but actually in debt to his employer to a large amount.[28]

For some Irish immigrants, the company store doubtless recalled the hated practice of landlords in Ireland who required their tenants to have their oats ground at the landlord's mill at exorbitant prices.[29] Some coal operators had cash flow problems so dire that mine workers who were owed a large sum in back wages were said to have been refused twelve cents in cash to buy medicine for a sick child, and two dollars to buy a coffin for a dead one.[30]

By early July, the mine workers of the West Branch were fed up. At least 1,500, "principally natives of Ireland," according to the *Miners' Journal*, walked off the job, demanding an end to the company store system.

It began peaceably enough on Thursday, July 7, with a procession through the streets of Minersville by 1,000 strikers, "preceded by music." The mine workers were addressed by several speakers who exhorted them to act moderately but firmly, "to commit no act which could possibly tend to breach the peace." On Friday, 2,300 men gathered in the town for more speeches. A tentative settlement was reached, but it collapsed the next day and things started to turn ugly.

On Saturday, July 9, several hundred miners armed with clubs marched down a railroad track from the West Branch to the county seat, Pottsville. They drove a few workers from their jobs, and then headed off to nearby Mount Carbon, where they sent more workers home. The strikers' unexpected arrival in the county seat gave rise to the coal establishment's enduring nightmare—wild miners stomping out of the hills to wreak havoc in the heart of Pottsville.

That evening, alarmed residents of Minersville asked for help, and two companies of local militia were dispatched. They arrived to find the town quiet, but Pottsville authorities called up two other militia companies, just in case.

On Monday, authorities in Pottsville received word of another march to the town by up to a thousand men gathered at Mount Laffee, just north of the county seat. The sheriff and burgess met the marchers at the borough limits and asked all those carrying sticks or clubs to cast them aside. When the marchers complied, they were permitted to enter Pottsville, where they were addressed by District Attorney Francis Hughes, a prominent Democrat, and several others. The meeting, which was "characterized by moderation and decorum throughout," ended with the formation of a committee to take up the miners' grievances with the coal operators, the *Pottsville Emporium* reported. The committee included several leading Irish Democrats who were active in the Hibernian Society—Brady, O'Connor, and Colehan, himself a mine operator.

The grievances were simply stated:

We protest therefore against the order system, firstly because by it we lose one-third if not one-half of our hard earnings, secondly because we are obliged to deal in places where we do not wish to deal; thirdly because we cannot get such goods as we want and we are obliged to take such as we do not want, fourthly because such goods as will command prices from other persons we cannot get at all; fifthly because it is an immoral mode of doing business; sixthly, and most especially, because it takes from us the only pleasure enjoyed by the workingman, of spending his earnings where and in what manner he pleases.[31]

The plea failed to sway the coal companies or their chief spokesman, Bannan, for the strike and the intervention of the committee challenged his cherished belief that the coal industry comprised independent, fair-minded businessmen and sturdy, independent workingmen who could work out their differences on an individual basis because their economic interests were perfectly aligned.

"Combinations or general turnout have never been known to result beneficially to the workingmen of any district in which they have taken place," Bannan warned in print. "Our advice to the miners and laborers of this region then is, to drop all coalition—allow no one to dictate to you—consult with your employer—go to him, if you want to work, and after making your contract, go peaceably to your duties as good and well meaning citizens should; always remembering that your interests are identical, and that whatever benefits him, will also benefit you."

For Bannan, the problem was not grasping mine owners who compensated for their lack of capital by shortchanging safety and their men. It was "fiends in human shape" who had "for their own selfish and base political purposes, endeavored to excite the miners and laborers of this region against their employers, by false and malicious representations."[32]

Those fiends, Bannan made clear, were the members of the committee that had been formed to present the miners' case. He denounced them as "narrow-minded and bigoted partisans," a clear reference to Democrats like O'Connor and Brady.

Bannan's antipathy toward the Hibernian committeemen was matched by the coal operators, who refused to meet with them.[33] As the strike dragged on, events took a violent turn.

In late June a Minersville tailor named Birne, described as one of the leaders of the strike, was charged with beating a Llewellyn mine owner and several mine workers. A grand jury handed down twelve indictments in the case.[34] Threatening letters were left at several collieries whose employees continued to work, warning that they would be killed if they did not join the strike. The home of a miner who continued working at Samuel

Heilner's colliery in Cass Township was attacked by twenty or thirty people throwing stones. A mine foreman fired a shotgun into the crowd, fell-
ing two people, and then went to Llewellyn for help. When he returned
with several men, the crowd had dispersed. Barney McElroy of Minersville
was arrested the next day and charged with riot.[35]

If violence was a sign of desperation, the miners were clearly in trouble.
In the first week of August, the strike collapsed and its leaders were blacklisted, Bannan noted with satisfaction. "Many of those who had good situations cannot now find employment," the *Miners' Journal* reported. "Nearly
all the ringleaders who have not been arrested have absconded—and we
are pleased to learn that the operators generally manifest a disposition not
to employ any who took a prominent part in the late difficulties."[36]

While Bannan and the coal operators gloated over their victory, Hibernian leaders organized relief measures for those left destitute by the suppression of the strike. Serving on the relief committee with Brady and
Colahan was a young Pat Dormer, who thirty years later would play a small
but crucial role in the Molly Maguire story. The group also petitioned for
pardons for those convicted of strike-related crimes and launched an unsuccessful campaign to have the state legislature outlaw the cause of the
strike—payment in company scrip redeemable only at company stores.[37]

There was one last ugly note to be struck. Hundreds of Irish miners,
out of work because of the strike, had made their way to Philadelphia,
where simmering economic, sectarian, and racial tensions were just beginning to boil over in late July. The city was in the throes of an economic
slump, and a mass protest meeting of the unemployed was planned for
Monday, August 1. For many Irish Catholics, the issue of unemployment
was intertwined with that of race, for they viewed freed blacks as competitors in the labor market. Old sectarian tensions were also at work—
Irish Catholics were said to be making clubs in late July, in preparation
for an early August battle with Protestants. It was hinted that some of
those making clubs were strangers to the city—perhaps the West Branch
Irishmen.

The pot boiled over on August 1. As the unemployed prepared to march
outside the old State House—Independence Hall—word spread of a riot
involving another procession in Moyamensing, just south of the city limits. There, black immigrants who were parading under a temperance banner to commemorate the abolition of slavery in their native West Indies
were confronted by a group of young white men. A riot ensued. When
word of it reached Independence Hall—the site of that heated debate on
slavery at the Repeal Convention just six months earlier—many of the

unemployed quickly forgot about their own procession. They hastened south, where they were reported to have "joined most cordially in the ferocious attack on the colored people."

Fierce fighting lasted for three days, with a black church and temperance hall burned, at least sixteen people hospitalized, several killed, and hundreds of blacks forced to flee the city. The Irish, primed for a sectarian brawl, were in the forefront of it all, even finding time for the long-planned green–orange battle on August 1 or August 2. "Some hundreds" of anthracite miners from the Pottsville region, in Philadelphia as a result of the strike, were singled out as having been "actively engaged" in the racial violence.[38]

The actions of the unemployed miners cannot be fully understood outside the context of the abolition debate. As Pottsville Hibernian leaders like Brady were taking up the cudgels against abolition and the blacklisting of miners, their blacklisted followers in Philadelphia were wielding clubs against freed blacks commemorating the abolition of slavery in the West Indies.

Richard Allen, the Dublin correspondent of *The Liberator*, summed it up on September 19 when he wrote of "how annoyed, how disgusted" he was that Irishmen had taken a leading role in the Philadelphia riots, and of the "sickening feeling" that he had when he read Brady's letter from Pottsville. "The truth is, our countrymen are enthusiastic in their *right* or *wrong*," he wrote. "If enlisted on the wrong side, they are a terrible engine of oppression. The wrong path once taken, they know no bounds. Their natural enthusiasm perverted makes them a terrible foe."[39]

Slavery would remain at the top of the nation's agenda for the next two decades, and the events of 1842 conditioned the response of many anthracite Irishmen to the crisis that erupted in 1861. Likewise, the grievances that caused the strike of 1842 would remain—a familiar pattern in the coal fields. Chained to the company store system, miners were gouged above ground and mutilated below it.

The relentless toll of mine accidents is suggested by an item in the *Pottsville Emporium* on August 10, 1844: "We are again called upon to chronicle another awful accident and loss of life in the mines—indeed the hearts sickens at the frequent repetition of these distressing scenes.... The last accident to which we refer above occurred on Friday night of last week, in the mines of Messers. Milnes and Spencer on the West Norwegian, about 2½ miles from Pottsville—the same place at which but a few days since, a poor fellow, Patrick Devaney, was ground to death in a coal breaker." Three miners on the night shift—Henry Fox, Jonathan Nixon, and John Ricket—

had been assigned a particularly dangerous task: drilling through to a nearby abandoned shaft that had filled with water, so that it could be drained. They succeeded all too well. "The water burst upon them with such tremendous force as to fill the mine in the course of 10 minutes," the *Emporium* reported. "It is supposed that the men were dashed down the gangway and instantaneously killed."

The newspapers of the day offered a steady stream of such short, grim stories about sudden death in the mines. And there was another, equally dire danger that generally went unreported: the slow accumulation of inhaled coal dust that caused black lung, or "miner's asthma."

In all that follows, it is important not to forget this constant drumbeat of death. In normal times, it was mere background music. But when mine disasters claimed handfuls of men at a time, the beat grew deafening. It would eventually subside, but it never, ever went away. The role of lax mine safety in fomenting violence is made clear by an anonymous death threat delivered to one West Branch mine superintendent: "It's better one damned bugger should die than a whole crew."[40]

Poor working conditions were a fixed part of the scene, like poor pay and company stores. The latter issues, festering since 1842, erupted anew after seven years. The catalyst, once again, was the Reading Railroad. In 1849, after seven years of competition, the Reading reached an accord with the Schuylkill Navigation Company that set coal tonnage quotas and rates. Competition between the railroad and the canal had led to the strike of 1842; collusion would have the same effect in 1849.

On March 9, coal operators concerned about the cost of transportation and the influence of commodities speculators met in Pottsville to impose a moratorium on the shipment of coal until prices stabilized. The suspension lasted from March 19 until May 2. It played right into the hands of a new union movement headed by John Bates, an English Chartist who had emigrated to St. Clair, north of Pottsville. When the operators prepared to resume operations on May 2, the miners struck, demanding higher pay.

An English miner on the West Branch explained the origins and success of the strike in a letter to a friend at home:

All the miners and laborers have been standing out for more wages a fortnight, all over the country, or nearly all, and a good turn out we had. The miners wanted nine dollars a week, the inside laborers five dollars and a half a week. All the coal masters had turned out for more price on the coal, against the merchants of Philadelphia and New York six weeks and would not let their coal go down to the city. As soon as they were agreed, we stood out, and we got all we asked.... We have also made an end of store orders; all our payments are to be made in cash. The masters did not like it, but the men were all determined and now we believe the Union will go on. The masters formed a Union last summer, something like a secret order, and that was the cause of the strike. So we followed their footsteps and we shall form a society called the "Association of Miners and Laborers of Schuylkill County."[41]

There is no evidence that members of the Hibernian Society played any important role in the new union. It was composed of committees at each mine, overseen by a Central Committee that had veto power over local labor settlements.

Bannan spoke for the many of the operators when he declared that "it would be better to let our colliers *rot*, and our region become a *wilderness*, than such tyranny should be engrafted on the business of this region by a few restless spirits."[42] He had little to worry about. Bates's union collapsed within a year, and the mine operators were once more free to slash wages and pay out the pittance in store orders.

While the Irish of the West Branch region were finding their efforts to establish a lasting labor movement frustrated, they could at least point to advances on another front—politics. There, the Hibernian Society was achieving a measure of success in resisting corporate power.

Politics

A Philadelphian who could not attend the Hibernians' 1848 St. Patrick's Day banquet in Pottsville offered a telling glimpse of the group's political clout. Addressing "Messrs. Patrick Fogarty, Michael Cochran, John Maginnis, Edward Colehan, Edward O'Connor and George S. Hookey, committee of arrangement of the Pottsville Hibernia Benevolent Institution," J. Silver wrote, "Without your aid at the polls, the laboring producers of our country would have been eaten up, as in Ireland, and their honest earning filched from them by corporate aristocracies . . . whose armies besiege our Legislatures and monopolize legislation."[43]

The anticorporate note—the idea that big business was illicitly using the legislature to stack the deck against honest workingmen—would be struck again and again for the next 150 years by anthracite Irishmen connected to the Hibernians. And Silver's letter reflected more than mere hyperbole—Cochran, Colehan, and O'Connor all served as vice presidents of a Democratic mass meeting in Pottsville that year, as did several guests at the March 17, 1848, banquet.

The Hibernians' entry into politics was by no means easy or welcome, even in the Democratic Party. When Mudey ran for a state legislature seat in 1840, challenging the endorsed Democratic candidate, he was denounced as a "usurper" and "tool of the Whigs" in a pamphlet circulated among German Democrats. Signed "Many Democrats," it pointed out that Mudey was "an Irishmen by birth, a Catholic by profession."[44]

In 1843, Strange Palmer's son, Robert, complained in the *Pottsville Emporium* of a "determination to support none but Irish candidates and Catholic candidates."[45] In 1844, the political "grasping" of the Schuylkill Irish was condemned by another Pottsville newspaper, Francis Wynkoop's *Anthracite Gazette*. "If we designate them the Roman Catholic Party, they must look to their own political acts for the reason," Wynkoop wrote. "It is no fault of Americans that this title is applied to them. By their secret combination—by their political scheming—by the language of their acknowledged journals, they have courted the appellation. . . . They are unlike the other naturalized citizens of the country in many respects. In the first place, they are bound together, united, consolidated—in the next they are continually struggling, jostling and grasping for office."[46]

Wynkoop was not alone in seeing Irish Democrats as a political threat—the *Miners' Journal* blamed bloc voting by the Irish for the defeat of Whig presidential candidate Henry Clay in Schuylkill County in 1844.[47] The "secret combination" Wynkoop condemned was almost certainly the Hibernian Society. The Irish brought to the Schuylkill County political scene an unprecedented degree of savvy and ethnic solidarity—likely due in part to experience with Ribbon agitation in Ulster.[48] Of seven regulars at the Hibernian banquets whose place of birth can be traced, three—James Downey of Fermanagh, John Maginnis of Monaghan, and John Gaynor of Cavan—came from south Ulster. Downey and Maginnis were members of the Schuylkill County Democratic Committee. Two other politically active Hibernian regulars, William B. Hull and John Curry, came to Port Carbon from the Ulster coal town of Ballycastle, a stronghold of the Ribbon Society and of the United Irishmen before that. Hull served as president of the Hibernian's first St. Patrick's Day banquet, in 1836.[49]

The Hibernians' political activity and their role in the 1842 strike and slavery debate demonstrate that by the time the potato famine began in 1845, a neo-Ribbon movement was already flourishing among the anthracite region's Irish Catholics. Its leaders—a doctor, coal operators, publicans, and politicians—were respected members of the community. Centered in Pottsville, with chapters in the canal town of Port Carbon and the West Branch coal center of Minersville, the Hibernian Society wielded influence that extended well beyond local Democratic politics to the state, national, and international scenes, as evidenced by Haggerty's role in the National Repeal Convention and the furor over the Pottsville proclamation on emancipation.

By 1845, Hibernian leaders had demonstrated a deep interest in Democratic politics, a firm commitment to labor activity on behalf of Irish mine workers, and an acute fear of the emancipation of slaves. The society needed only a huge influx of Irish immigrants to give it real muscle. When it came as a result of the famine, that influx forever altered the nature of the society, moving its center of gravity from the county seat of Pottsville to the Irish coal patches in the hills. It was there, in the hills, that Pottsville's Hibernian leaders soon found themselves involved in a sensational murder case involving an Irish mine worker charged in a Whiteboy-style execution.

8

Another Ulster

Altho' I'm in a foreign land,
From the cause I'll ne'er retire,
May heaven smile on every chil'
That belongs to Molly Maguire!

—Molly Maguire ballad

The murder of John Reese was more than an echo from the Old World. It was a harbinger for the new one.

In the summer of 1846, Reese, a Welshman, shot and killed an Irish neighbor, Thomas Collahan, in Delaware Mines, a heavily Irish patch near St. Clair. When Reese was acquitted on grounds of self-defense, his former neighbors were not pleased. They were even less pleased when, following his release, Reese insisted that he and his family visit his brother before leaving the county for good. Their route took them back through Delaware Mines, and Reese made the mistake of stopping to chat with some of his former neighbors.

The last house he visited was that of a Mrs. Brennan, who asked the wan, drawn Reese if it was really him. When he replied that it was, she signaled to a man who was standing nearby with a pick. The man's face had been whitened—a familiar motif in Whiteboy crimes—and he was disguised in borrowed clothes. When the Reese party moved off, the white-faced man rushed after them and swung his pick, hitting Reese in the head. As Reese's sister cried for help, onlookers laughed and clapped while the attacker escaped. The date was December 30, and for the Irish of Delaware Mines, justice had been served.

Reese died at his brother's house early the next morning, and a former neighbor and Irish immigrant, Martin Shay, was charged with his murder on January 2. Defense witnesses swore that Shay was working in a mine a mile away at the time of the killing. They said he was too mild-mannered

a man to commit murder. They pointed to other suspects. But the prosecutors, who included John Bannan and the noted Democrat Francis W. Hughes,
pointed out that Shay had time to leave the mine and return. They insinu-
ated that the killing was the work of a conspiracy and that Shay, who seemed
to have no other motive, was the appointed executioner. The jury, which included not a single Irishman (another harbinger), returned a guilty verdict
and Shay was sentenced to death.[1]

Shortly thereafter, a concerted and remarkably successful effort to ob-
tain a pardon for Shay was begun by Peter F. Mudey, the secretary of the
Hibernia Benevolent Institution of Pottsville; Edward O'Connor, another
Hibernian leader; and Strange Palmer, who in addition to editing the local
Democratic paper, the *Emporium*, happened to be a judge.

In January 1848, the three led a meeting in Pottsville that passed a
resolution urging that the death penalty be replaced by "the more humane
and equally efficient punishment of imprisonment for life." Gov. Francis
Shunk, a Democrat, pardoned Shay after Hughes, the prosecutor, found in
a review of the case that there was "strong doubt of the defendant's guilt."
The statement says as much about Hughes's indebtedness to Irish Democratic votes as it does about Shay's guilt or innocence, and the governor's
critics gleefully seized on the issue of the pardon.[2]

As Anthony F. C. Wallace points out, the case was remarkable, from
beginning to end, as an example of the rough, alternative justice of the
Irish countryside being transferred to the hills of Pennsylvania. A killer set
free by the judicial system is executed on behalf of—indeed in front of—
the community, in classic secret society style: by a man in whiteface, near a
holiday. The community provides his defense through alibis, and when that
fails, members of a neo-Ribbon group rally the community to obtain a pardon through political pressure.

There is nothing to indicate that the Hibernian Society had any
role in planning the killing, which has never been considered a Molly
Maguire murder. But the Mollies were in some ways more than an
organization—they were a mind-set as well. If, as Karl Marx noted in
1859, Ireland produced agrarian secret societies the way a woodland
sprouts mushrooms, that stemmed from a conviction that the system was
rotten, that the law was a stacked deck, and that conspiratorial violence
was justified as a means to balance the scales of justice. If nothing else,
the Reese murder case showed how that mind-set had been transplanted
to Pennsylvania.

Peasant Culture in the Coal Fields

In fact, the Shay case was but a particularly vivid demonstration of the degree to which Irish folkways in general were sinking roots into the hills of Schuylkill County. The trend did not go unnoticed. "The manners, customs and mode of thought of the Irish people" had been transplanted wholesale to the anthracite region, a long-standing resident noted a few decades after the famine.[3] It was a trend that accelerated with the arrival of each new refugee from Ireland.

And there were plenty of new arrivals. In the sixteen years from the start of the great famine to the opening of the Civil War, Schuylkill County's Irish population soared. In 1840, the county had 29,053 residents. By 1850, that had doubled, to 60,713, 15 percent of whom were Irish. In 1860, there were 89,510 residents, a quarter of them Irish.[4]

Famine immigrants arrived in the anthracite region by a variety of routes. Shipping lines had long connected Philadelphia with Ulster ports; many pre-famine immigrants, once they had established themselves in the anthracite region, brought over their relatives, paying the cost of their passage—$24 in 1842—to shipping agents such as Bannan. Others came through Canada, working for a time in Nova Scotia. However they arrived in Philadelphia, immigrants could pay the Reading Railroad $2.50 for a second-class fare to Pottsville.[5]

The less fortunate—and there were thousands after 1845—could take a canal boat, walk, or work for the railroad instead of riding it. Arriving in the anthracite region, the immigrants found a ready market for their unskilled labor, especially in the growing West Branch collieries.

It has been suggested that the famine Irish, inured to hardship, were particularly suited to rough-and-tumble mining regions like the West Branch. If the food was bad and the housing poor, at least it was on offer, thanks to the Heckschers, who controlled 75 percent of the workforce in Cass Township. Cass was the ultimate company town, and that fact encouraged a collective response to industrial conditions.[6] There, the immigrants reconstructed a semblance of communal life, for the coal patches were as small and remote as the clachans many had left behind, and every bit as impoverished. Everyone knew one another; many were related. The men all worked together in a dangerous job, bonding as "butties." "The very smallness of the patch threw [residents] together on terms of intimacy," the folklorist George Korson wrote. "There was a sharing of meager worldly possessions and an expression of sympathy in times of illness or trouble."[7]

The rhythms of life and work on the West Branch, too, proved remarkably similar to that of the Irish countryside. The bulk of the work in the mines was done between March and November, much as it was on an Irish farm. An old resident of Minersville explained the colliery calendar of the 1800s to a Works Progress Administration folklorist in 1939. "During the summer months the mines worked steadily, but about the third week of November the canal would freeze, and there would be little or no activity at the mines," recalled Albert MacClay. "Shortly after the 17th of March, the railroads would again begin to send cars in and work would be resumed."[8]

Many of the Old World folk patterns persisted in the New World for generations after the famine, and in some cases became permanent fixtures. Halloween, which was brought to the United States by Irish immigrants, is one of the best examples. In the anthracite region, groups of young men and boys from the collieries visited homes in the neighborhood and put on a performance, much like the strawboys who would crash into the kitchens of Irish country homes, repeating verse and dancing with the female inhabitants.

A Pottsville librarian, Edith Patterson, recalled in 1939 that as young girl she used to look forward to the visit of these breaker boys on Halloween, when "they appeared in the large kitchen, ready to sing and dance." The master of the house, Audenried mine superintendent Edward L. Bullock, would reward the boys with "a distribution of nickels all around" when they sang a song in his honor.[9] Coordinated performances by small bands of trick-or-treaters remained an integral element of Halloween in Cass Township well into the 1930s. The groups practiced beforehand, and then sang, danced, or recited poetry in the homes they visited.[10]

The echoes of the Old World were not limited to Halloween. On May 1, "Maying parties" of young men and women visited the countryside, and up until the twentieth century, English, Irish, Scottish, and Welsh immigrants observed Midsummer's Day much as they had in the British Isles. On June 25, there would be a "community celebration held at twilight around huge bonfires built of flour or cracker barrels placed one on top of another around a pole set in the ground and extending some distance in the air," a member of the WPA Federal Writers' Project reported after interviewing older county residents in 1939. "The barrels were filled with excelsior or other flammable material and when set on fire lit up the surrounding countryside."[11] At Christmastime, mummers visited farm homes in southern Schuylkill County, though mummery does not seem to have spread to the mining region until the era just before the Civil War, when, as we shall see, it developed strong political overtones.

In addition to holiday customs, many other Irish folkways and superstitions were transplanted to the coal fields. One of the best documented is
the Irish wake. Mourners came from far and near, without invitation, to
pay their respects to the deceased, remaining with the body all night. Food
and drink were abundant. Friends and relatives renewed acquaintances
and discussed the news of the day. "Sometimes games were indulged in to
keep people awake, and pranks perpetrated on individuals for the general
amusement of the gathering," a WPA folklorist in the anthracite region
reported. "Irish keeners or 'paid criers' were part of every community . . .
Upon entering a corpse house, one was usually greeted by one of these
professional criers who went into a heart-rending period of lamentation in
which was stressed the virtues of the deceased and his particular friendship for you. One was slightly embarrassed, especially if he did not know
the dead person so well, but this embarrassment was suddenly changed
to amazement when the wailer was seen to sit down and engage in some
humorous banter, only to arise again to greet the next visitor with a like
performance."[12]

There were also instances of the charivaris, or "rough music," that the
English historian E. P. Thompson found so common in the British Isles. In
these cases, the community noisily mocked the participants in a remarriage,
or in a marriage held to be a misalliance. Such rough music, in the form of
the "ceffyl pren," or wooden horse, was closely associated with the Rebecca
rioters in Wales in the late 1830s and early 1840s. It survived past the midpoint of the twentieth century in Ireland, where unpopular marriages were
"marked by noisy gatherings of young men" who serenaded the couple with
horns.[13]

A similar form of rough music—the "calithumpian" band—was a common feature at Schuylkill County weddings. Young people angry at not
being invited would create a din in front of the wedding house with instruments like tin horns, whistles, conch shells, drums, and crude fiddles.[14]
In 1864, five Schuylkill County Irishmen—Bartholomew Boyle, Patrick
Whalen, Michael Whalen, Peter Gallagher, and John Kelley—were convicted of riot for leading a "horse fiddle" concert for Bridget Munks on the
night before her April wedding in Ashland, just north of the West Branch
region. Munks, who ran a shebeen (she was probably a widow), succeeded
in having the defendants fined six cents apiece.[15]

Peasant superstitions—"hobgoblins, ghosts, witches, fairies, banshees
and many signs and omens"—were also transplanted wholesale to the hills
of Pennsylvania.[16] An Irish immigrant in Scranton told a reporter in 1877

that "some years ago," the friends of an Irish mine worker killed by a cave-in insisted that fairies had taken him.[17] On a moonlit night, some "in fun and some in earnest," they went to what was believed to be a fairy gathering spot, in hopes of getting the dead man back by throwing an object.* In Coal Castle, the burning mine served as a sort of holy well. And everywhere there were the informal, music-filled get-togethers that the Irish call a ceili. They were sometimes held at the end of a hard day in the mines, in a company-owned house. After the furniture was carried out and the bottles broken open, the dancing began. Fiddlers called out reels, jigs, and breakdowns as the slanting rays of the setting sun caught the coal dust kicked up by a drumbeat of dancing feet.[18]

If the old customs survived, it was in part because the old language persisted—Irish-speaking immigrants who arrived in the anthracite region in the late 1840s found priests who ministered to them in their own language, and Irish was still spoken extensively in part of the coal fields into the late 1870s.[19] As these immigrants poured into sparsely populated, developing mining areas like the West Branch, the opportunities for assimilation were limited. English, Welsh, and American-born miners dominated towns like Minersville and Llewellyn. Many of the Irish preferred communal life among their own in the rural townships, in hamlets clustered around the collieries—Coal Castle, Heckscherville, Glen Carbon, Forestville, and Branchdale.

Compounding the ethnic segregation was class stratification. A state labor report that discussed the condition of antebellum anthracite miners outlined the process, pointing out that periodic overproduction led to inadequate wages and privation: "As the mass of the working class sank ... deeper into poverty, hopelessness and degradation, the line dividing them from the employing class, and their better paid and provided confidential servants such as superintendents, store keepers, clerks, etc., was widened day by day, until they were completely separated in feeling, habits of thoughts, purposes, interest and sympathy, as if they were separate people in races and civilization."[20]

Thus, Irish labor helped transform Schuylkill County into a flourishing bastion of American free enterprise, even as the laborers' lifestyle, language, religion, and customs turned the hills outside Minersville into some-

* The belief that the dead had been abducted by fairies, and could be recovered from them, featured prominently in the Bridget Cleary murder case in Tipperary in 1895. See Angela Bourke, *The Burning of Bridget Cleary* (New York: Viking, 2000), 13, 18, 42–43.

thing entirely different—a small slice of rural Ireland with a culture and a consciousness all its own. This contradiction may have existed elsewhere in the nation, but in few places was it quite so profound as on the West Branch. There, the boomtown ethos of the coal operators clashed head-on with the premodern mentality of their employees, who were for the most part peasants with picks and shovels, many of them Irish speakers who would never have emigrated had the alternative been something other than slow death in a dank hovel.[21]

To help resolve some of the tensions between Ireland's agricultural past and America's industrial present, the immigrants on the West Branch decided to carve out their own political fiefdom. The new entity was called Cass Township.

A Place of Their Own

Until 1848, the vast bulk of the West Branch mining region lay in Branch Township, to the north, south, and west of Minersville. Irish Democrats dominated the northern part of the township, which included Coal Castle, Heckscherville, and Forestville. They seceded in 1848. The Democratic Party nominated the diplomat Lewis Cass as its presidential candidate that year, and the township was named in his honor—an unmistakable sign of its political proclivities.[22]

The split from Branch Township, like a much bigger secession in 1861, was not accomplished without bloodshed. In February 1848, an election-day riot broke out at a polling place in Llewellyn, Branch Township. The *Miners' Journal* reported that "the disturbance was engendered by the feeling of animosity existing between Irish Catholics and native Americans, the former voting a ticket composed exclusively of Irishmen, and the latter of Americans. There seemed to be a predetermination by the former to overawe the latter in the exercise of their elective privilege."[23]

In an incident that had all the earmarks of an election-day brawl in Ireland, a club-wielding crowd beat seventeen people. Even the Democratic *Pottsville Emporium* was appalled, referring to the incident at the tavern of Philip Kehres as "unprovoked, brutal and murderous." A dozen men were indicted for riot, nine were convicted, and two identified as leaders were sentenced to thirty days of hard labor.[24]

The names connected with the incident offer a glimpse of the leadership of the West Branch Irish community. Edward Connelly of Branchdale and Francis Gallagher of Forestville, two bar owners and civic leaders, were arrested then freed after it became clear that they had not taken part in the violence.

Two other men were convicted of leading the riot—Philip Mohan and "Big John Kelly." The former was most likely a member of the prominent and politically active Mohan clan, which played a continuing role in the Cass Township secession: the final settlement between Branch and Cass was concluded at the home of John Mohan, in 1861.[25]

The second leader, John Kelly, quickly became prominent in the affairs of the new township. He was born in Ireland around 1812, and arrived in Branch Township with his wife, Ann, sometime between 1837 and 1840. A decade later, Kelly listed his occupation as laborer in the 1850 census, but he was clearly a man on the move.[26] That same year he gained a license to sell liquor, and he served, along with Richard Heckscher of the Forest Improvement Company, as one of Cass Township's representatives on the county committee that arranged the Fourth of July celebration in Pottsville.[27]

Kelly was elected a Cass Township supervisor in March 1853, and just two weeks later was granted a license for a tavern in Primrose, between Minersville and Forestville. The tavern served as something of a community center, eventually becoming a polling place for the South Cass precinct.[28]

There are also hints that Kelly may have been involved in Hibernian affairs. On March 17, 1854, a John Kelly rose from his chair at the Pottsville banquet of the Young Men's Hibernia Benevolent Association and lifted his glass to "the daughters of the Emerald isle—celebrated throughout the world for their virtue, integrity and industry."[29] The name is a common one, but the John Kelly most likely to have joined other county Democrats like Meyer Strouse at the Middle Ward Hotel that year was the up-and-coming Cass Township politician, bar owner, and civic leader. Kelly was listed as an innkeeper worth $500 in the 1860 census. He died of natural causes at age forty-seven in October of that year.[30]

Kelly's story demonstrates the possibilities that the creation of Cass Township opened to immigrants, who were swiftly elected to positions like constable, auditor, and school board member. Up in northern end of the township, Patrick O'Connor of Coal Castle, a native of County Limerick, had a career remarkably similar to Kelly's. Like Kelly, he was working as an immigrant mine laborer in 1850. In 1853, the same year that Kelly became a Cass supervisor, O'Connor was elected auditor. Like Kelly, he subsequently gained a license for a tavern that became a polling place. And finally, like Kelly, O'Connor did not live to see the Civil War, dying in 1858 at about age forty-six. The two were buried in the same cemetery—St. Vincent's in Minersville, a stone's throw from the inn that Charles Mohan ran before he, too, died in the late 1850s.[31] Kelly and O'Connor typified the new sort of civic leaders who were emerging in the hills—hungry immigrants, fresh from the pits, who managed to improve their hard lot through the Democratic Party, barroom politics, and a certain dexterity with their fists.

In Kelly's case especially, the portrait that emerges is that of the classic Ribbonman—a hardheaded publican and community leader. He bears something of a resemblance to a prominent figure in folklore about the origin of the Pennsylvania Molly Maguires. In his book *Lament for the Molly Maguires*, Arthur Lewis discusses an oral tradition that the Mollies got their start in a Cass Township tavern run by one Jeremiah Reilly in the late 1840s, during a period of sectarian riots in the villages surrounding Pottsville. Reilly was described as a former Ribbonman who led an assault on a bar in Yorkville, just outside Pottsville, because some of its English and Welsh regulars had assaulted a priest who was passing by after celebrating Mass in Cass Township.[32]

The tradition cannot be verified. Census records for 1850 show no Jeremiah Reilly in Cass Township, and he does not turn up in lists of local bar owners, as do John Kelly and Patrick O'Connor. In fact, he does not turn up anywhere in contemporary references to Cass Township.

But there are a lot of intriguing similarities between the real-life Kelly and the legendary Reilly: both were two-fisted Cass Irishmen who served as civic leaders. Both not only owned bars, but also were involved in a riot at a bar outside Pottsville owned by a member of another ethnic group. And there is documentary evidence to suggest that a few years after his death, Kelly's bar did in fact play a central role in the birth of the Pennsylvania Mollies. It may well be that stories about Kelly were transmuted over the generations into folklore about "Reilly."

The stories of Kelly and Reilly make clear that there were a series of riots in the villages around Pottsville in 1848. Like the polling-place donnybrook in Llewellyn, the trigger was politics. When the general election rolled around in November, a brawl broke out in Middleport after Patrick Reddington, late of County Roscommon, threatened some voters as they prepared to cast their ballots. Several people were severely beaten; Reddington and five others were later convicted of riot.[33]

At Mount Carbon that same day, Irish employees of the Reading Railroad challenged Whig voters to a fight. Several people were badly beaten, though it appears no charges were filed—much to the displeasure of the *Miners' Journal*.[34]

The following year offered clear evidence that the growing clout of the county's newest immigrants extended beyond election-day head bashing.

The Irish, allied with German farmers and some English and Welsh miners, helped the Democratic Party regain control of Schuylkill County from the Whigs in 1849.[35]

The political differences between the two parties were profound. Whigs placed a strong emphasis on moral crusades, supporting enforcement of Sabbath laws and prohibition on alcohol sales, insisting that rum and beer shops had turned Schuylkill County into a "crime and pauper factory" and that "nothing short of a prohibitory law can ever reach the root of evil, or effectually cure the moral leprosy" of drunkenness.[36] The Whigs also supported tougher rules for naturalization, proposing a waiting period of twenty-one years before an immigrant could become a citizen.

The Democrats opposed limitations on immigration, fought new regulations on Sunday sales and drinking, and greeted famine immigrants with open arms. The *Pottsville Emporium* announced in 1847 that "the Democratic party welcomes these 'oppressed and starving poor' [from Ireland] whether Roman Catholics or Protestants, to the shores of our beloved country, where they need no longer be oppressed—where they need no longer endure the pangs of starvation."[37]

Having learned a lesson in 1849, Bannan, the Whigs' chief spokesman in Schuylkill County, courted the Irish vote in the elections of 1852 by attempting to tar Democratic candidates such as Franklin Pierce as anti-Catholic or anti-immigrant. He also argued that Democratic support for free trade strengthened the English economy at the expense of Ireland. Those arguments carried little weight among Irish Democrats, and Pierce carried the county, defeating Winfield Scott. Bannan, disgusted, swore publicly to never again seek Catholic support.[38]

The election offers one measure of the impact of Irish political enclaves like Cass Township. The percentage of the Irish Catholics in the township in 1850 has been estimated at up to 65 percent. In 1852, the Democrats won 66 percent of the votes cast in Cass.[39]

Backlash

As Irish Catholic political power grew in Schuylkill County, so did opposition to it. The leader of the anti-Catholic crusade was Benjamin Bannan; its chief organ was his newspaper. Irish Catholics posed a fundamental challenge to Bannan's vision of Schuylkill County as a bastion of free enterprise where independent mine operators lived in harmony with their upwardly mobile employees.[40]

Most of the Irish mine laborers of the West Branch were far from upwardly mobile—they had little chance for advancement, thanks to their lack of experience and the discrimination of English, Welsh, and Scottish foremen. They did not live in harmony with small, independent mine owners, because the mines were owned by a huge corporation, the Forest Improvement Company. Nothing about Cass Township or its inhabitants fit Bannan's worldview, and he grew to hate them for it.[41]

When Bannan railed against the drunkenness of Irish Catholic miners, he pointed to the number of shebeens in Cass Township. When he damned the Catholic Church for its role in politics, he pointed to Cass Township. When he blasted voter fraud by Democrats, he cited Cass Township.[42] In fact, as the careers of John Kelly and Patrick O'Connor prove, the most reliable path to upward mobility in Cass Township was through Democratic Party politics and the ownership of a tavern, and Bannan abhorred the former only slightly more than the latter.

The very name of Cass Township was repugnant to the Whig newspaper publisher, for it honored a leading Democrat whom Bannan regularly disparaged in the pages of his newspaper.[43] In the wake of the 1852 election, Bannan launched a venomous nativist campaign, accusing the Irish of not respecting the Sabbath, opposing the public school system, and blocking passage of a temperance law. He urged that Catholics be banished from the Whig Party, contending that their priests politically controlled them.

The lack of upward mobility among the Irish Catholic mine workers certainly played an important role in Bannan's thinking, and in many ways his attitude mirrored the old sectarian animosities of his father's Belfast. But his fury at growing Irish Catholic political strength may well have been linked to the realization that as a shipping and remittance agent, he had helped to bring so many of these Catholic Democrats to Schuylkill County over the previous two decades. At times Bannan sounded like he was desperately trying to convince himself that the damage Catholic immigration had done to the Whig cause in Schuylkill County was not irreversible.

"You are the *minority,*" Bannan warned Catholics amid an 1853 debate over the use of tax dollars for Catholic schools. "You are in the power of the Protestants, *and must ever remain so,* as long as you remain in this country."[44] Bannan's campaign was not purely nativist, for it was open to Protestant immigrants who had their own grudges against Irish Catholics. As waves of Irish immigrants replaced workers in the mines of England, Scotland, and Wales, miners from those lands flocked to the burgeoning Schuylkill coal fields.

The *Pottsville Emporium* reported at the height of the famine that "during the past week a considerable accession was made to our mining population by the arrival of emigrants from Scotland. They allege that the poverty-stricken laborers from Ireland flood their country and so reduce the wages that they must emigrate or suffer privation greater than they have yet endured. They announce more acoming."[45]

These English, Scottish, and Welsh miners, displaced from jobs in their native lands by famine immigrants, soon found themselves working beside other Irish émigrés in the anthracite region. Ethnic tensions were further exacerbated when these more experienced miners, inculcated with the values of the industrial revolution, were quickly appointed to supervisory positions.

In late March 1855, for example, a Scottish boss at the Brook and Breury colliery in Branchdale, John Beveridge, was beaten within an inch of his life in a midnight attack on his home, supposedly because he refused to employ several Irishmen. The attack took place at a time of heightened sectarian and labor–management tensions. Just days before, Bannan had raised the notion in the *Miners' Journal* that all Protestants should vote against Catholic candidates. And workers at the Forest Improvement Company's mines in Branchdale were on strike at the time.

In response to the attack on Beveridge, three militia companies from Pottsville marched on Branchdale and, in a series of surprise 4:00 A.M. raids, arrested twenty-eight suspects, although just four men had participated in the beating. The sweeping nature of the arrests ensured that many strikers were rounded up, too.[46] As they marched the Irishmen back to Pottsville, the militia units added insult to injury with the music they played—"The Boyne Water," an Orange anthem from Ulster that celebrated the defeat of Catholic Ireland.

When the *Anthracite Gazette* of Pottsville suggested that the tune was inappropriately sectarian, Bannan rushed to the defense of the militia, accusing Irish Catholics of introducing their old prejudices to the county as he pointed out that "The Boyne Water" happened to be one of the militia's favorite tunes. While the controversy raged in the pages of the county's newspapers, the sheriff who called out the militia denied a report that he had asked that the tune not be played.[47]

Most of the Branchdale defendants were freed—there was no evidence against them. But among those who landed in Schuylkill County court in the first court session after March were a couple of men who would become noted Molly leaders—Pat Hester and Pat Dormer.[48] The details of the cases remain murky, but Hester was living near Branchdale when the militia marched in, and Dormer had been active in labor issues since the aftermath of the 1842 strike.

In the weeks after the Branchdale affair, labor trouble became entangled with ethnic strife. In mid-April, the owner of a strikebound colliery on the Yoe Tract near Pottsville fired every employee who would not return to work—Irish to a man—and replaced them with English and German workers. When the inevitable retaliation came, three blocks of houses went up in flames and a number of strikebreakers were threatened. The militia was called out again and staged its customary 4:00 A.M. raids, this time commanded by the mine owner himself. As at Branchdale, a number of men were arrested. And as at Branchdale, most were released for lack of evidence.[49]

The scene was repeated in mid-May, with a strike at the Gordon, Bedell and Co. colliery at Woodville near Tremont, where nonstrikers were beaten and driven from their homes. An overeager local militia unit swung into action, accompanied by "martial music," only to be disappointed by the news that the sheriff had no need of their assistance. That did not stop the mine owners from hiring a squad of twelve militiamen as guards, turning the armed forces of the state into a private army for the protection of corporate property. The Miners' Journal felt the move was perfectly justified— Bannan had just advised Tremont residents facing violence by "Irish ruffians" to take the law into their own hands.[50]

To Irish Catholics, it seemed that the game was rigged. Efforts to advance their economic interests through collective action like strikes were inevitably met by religious bigotry, economic oppression, and government coercion, all of it endorsed by the local newspaper.

Bannan's anti-Catholic crusade came not only during a sensitive period in anthracite industrial relations, but at a volatile time in American politics. Whig support for the Kansas–Nebraska Act in March 1854 sounded the death knell of that party, for it repealed the Missouri Compromise, which banned the extension of slavery into those territories. Northern Whigs who opposed slavery fled the party in droves—many, like Bannan, into the waiting arms of the anti-immigrant and anti-slavery Know Nothings.[51]

By 1855, Bannan was urging voters to support the nativists in all ten state and local contests in Schuylkill County. He provided extensive coverage of Know Nothing political meetings in Pottsville, including one where it was resolved that "self preservation compels us to extend the term of Naturalization in the future, to protect those precious rights and privileges (of American citizenship) from the insidious attacks of the Jesuits of Europe."[52]

When the Know Nothings were defeated in October of that year, Bannan blamed alcohol and Catholicism. But the nativist party had already run aground on the same reef that sank the Whigs, slavery. The trouble began at a national convention in June 1855, when Know Nothings from the South succeeded in pushing through a resolution that endorsed the status quo on slavery, which left open the possibility that the "peculiar institution" would spread to territories. Northern delegates walked out in protest. The walkout was repeated in February 1856, when Millard Fillmore was nominated as the Know Nothing candidate for president. Northern nativists bolted the party and formed a new one, the North Americans, and sought an alliance with the emerging Republican Party.

The Republicans nominated John Fremont as their presidential candidates; the Democrats, James Buchanan of Pennsylvania. Bannan moved with the North Americans into an alliance with the Republicans—and into stronger opposition to slavery. Claiming a common ground between the two parties, he contended that the Republicans, like the North Americans, not only opposed slavery, but also the "growth of the Papal power in this country."

Buchanan's victory led to the demise of the Know Nothings and helped push Bannan even further into the Republican camp, where he would remain, despite the party's rejection of nativism. Bannan's anti-Catholic diatribes would never completely disappear, but they never again matched the stridency of the Know Nothing era.[53]

The anti-immigrant backlash that Bannan spearheaded may well have borne some strange fruit, though. For it is a curious fact that just as Bannan's culture war against the Irish Catholics of the anthracite region was reaching a climax, a particularly political form of mummery emerged in the coal towns. There is reason to think that the two developments were related.

The Fantasticals

On December 25, 1855, an odd sight greeted residents of Pottsville. A group of rowdies from nearby Port Carbon, the last stop on the Schuylkill Canal, were marching through town like demented militiamen in a display of mock patriotism.

"On Christmas day, amid the pelting of a pitiless storm, some twenty individuals belonging to Port Carbon, entered and paraded through the streets of our borough," the *Miners' Journal* reported:

They were arrayed in every imaginable burlesque costume, and wore tiles apparently manufactured from damaged hardware, and discarded hats reduced to a shocking bad state. The captain wielded with herculean grasp a long wooden scimitar, and manoevered his men with a military skill to the music of a well soaked fife and drum, operated by well soaked performers. A member of the company bore upon a fragile stick a piece of not the whitest muslin we ever saw, upon which was inscribed "Santa Anna Life guard—O, git out." The Falstaffian army created much amusement, and if the weather had been pleasant, the array on the part of the Guards would, we presume, have been more formidable, in point of numbers.[54]

The spectacle, like many others in Schuylkill County in the mid-1800s, would at first seem incomprehensible. But placed in the context of the day, everything about it makes sense. For 1855 was not only the year in which Bannan's anti-Catholic crusade climaxed, but the year in which the militia of Schuylkill County had broken mine strikes and humiliated Irish Catholics by playing an Orange anthem. The "well soaked" fantasticals appeared to be mocking not only Bannan's calls for sobriety, but also mine operators' calls for troops and the militia's choice of music.

Holiday customs in the region had long contained elements of mummery. As far back as 1829, residents in the farming area of southern Schuylkill County were parading from house to house in disguise, firing volleys on New Year's Eve. Gunplay was noted in mining districts as well, and it sometimes led to trouble. In 1851 a young man named Alexander Cowan accidentally shot himself as he and others fired guns outside the Potts colliery. In Minersville, drunken German mummers appeared on the streets in fancy costumes on Shrove Tuesday, cutting "quite a ridiculous figure" as they kept up the Fastnacht festivities of their native land.[55]

After the arrival of Irish famine refugees, however, Schuylkill County mummery developed political overtones. The change was related to developments in Philadelphia, where English and Swedish settlers had been disguising themselves in women's clothes, blackface and masks at Christmastime for generations. According to one account, the first parade of mummers was held during the War of 1812 by Jackson's Rangers, a sort of home guard of boys too young to serve. On New Year's Day they paraded on horseback from home to home, reciting a rhyme.[56]

Despite an official ban on masquerades, mummery was well entrenched in Philadelphia by 1820, and it flourished in the years that followed amid a fresh influx of arrivals from the British Isles; nineteenth-century mummery in the city had a distinctly immigrant flavor.[57] And in the two decades before the potato famine, opposition to the state's militia system began to influence the masked home-visiting and firing of guns that had long been the hallmark of Philadelphia mummery.

The opposition stemmed from an 1822 reorganization of the Commonwealth's militia. Under the new law, all men between the ages of twenty-one and forty-five were required to muster regularly for drill on pain of a fifty-cent fine.[58] There was a vast gulf between these units and some volunteer militia companies that amounted to clubs for the scions of Philadelphia's leading families. For these upper-class volunteers—today's First Troop Philadelphia City Calvary is a surviving example—musters were a social event of the first order, allowing members to show off their smart uniforms.

In some ways, the volunteer militia units were mirror images of the mummers. They paraded regularly, in a festive atmosphere, accompanied by musicians. Their annual cycle of public displays—at Christmas, Washington's birthday in February, Muster Day in May, the Fourth of July, and an October 22 reenactment of the Battle of Red Bank near Camden, New Jersey—in some ways mimicked the old festive calendar of the Irish countryside, whose highlights fell in December, February, May, late June, and October. But the purposes for which the militia and the mummers marched could not have been more different. The disciplined parades of the volunteer militia symbolized social order, not the rowdy social inversion of the mummers. Instead of bringing the community together, the militias tended to emphasize social divisions with uniforms that ostentatiously displayed the wearers' wealth.[59]

No wonder the volunteers were so resented by the working class, for whom muster day, or "battalion day," merely meant a lot of pointless parading and a day's lost wages. Tradesmen, who were known to stage raucous, militant "strike parades" when they staged walkouts for higher wages, knew exactly how to react: they rebelled through the age-old weapon of mockery.*

In 1825, the 84th Regiment, an infantry unit drawn from the city's working-class Northern Liberties neighborhood, elected as its colonel John Pluck, a bowlegged hunchback who had long been the object of ridicule. Pluck became something of a celebrity, and joined in the spirit during a militia parade by sporting an enormous woman's bonnet, a huge sword, and spurs half a yard long.

---

* Historian Susan G. Davis points out that in antebellum Pennsylvania "turnout" was an interchangeable word for a strike and a parade: "Thus, striking and parading were closely connected concepts and activities." *Parades and Power*, 133.

Soon, workers were showing up drunk for militia drill, in tattered clothing that spoofed the military's penchant for uniforms, wearing black-face and wielding weapons that ranged from brooms to dead fish. Styled "fantasticals," they were accompanied by callithumpian bands that produced their usual cacophony with "conch-shells, old cracked instruments, stones, shingles, tin-horns, speaking trumpets, here and there a bassoon, old kettles, pot-lids, dozens of cow-bells strung upon poles and iron hoops." All in all, it made for some very rough music, but that was the point. The fantasticals, Susan G. Davis says, were poking fun at the "brilliantly dressed, well-disciplined, obedient network of young men from good families" who served in volunteer units.

Opposition to the militia system became a plank in the Democratic Party's platform, and Democratic politicians in Philadelphia played a leading role in the fantasticals' chicanery. The use of blackface, rooted in the British Isles tradition of mummery, took on a new meaning with the race riots that periodically wracked the city.

The racial component of the fantastical tradition was underlined as it spread beyond muster day to celebrations of the Fourth of July and Christmas. Over time, Davis writes, Yuletide mummers "borrowed parodies of military dress and style and grafted them on to older seasonal folk dramas. Fantasticals and callithumpians performed in Christmas streets; their burlesques retained anti-militia, anti-authority resonances." They also maintained an element of racism—one fantastical group named itself the "Crows" after Jim Crow.[60] And the fantasticals could be a violent. Roaring from tavern to tavern, they were known to beat any barkeep who refused them a free drink. More than one New Year's fantastical procession ended in a killing.[61]

The fantasticals' brand of anti-militia mummery, with its overtones of class anger, violence, and racism, spread far beyond Philadelphia. By the early 1830s fantasticals were turning up in Albany, a major canal center, and New York City. In the latter, they became especially prevalent around Thanksgiving, and were mostly Irish and working class.[62]

In Easton, Pennsylvania, a canal hub on the Delaware that linked Philadelphia to the anthracite region, working-class fantasticals decked out in false whiskers marched on January 1, 1834, under the command of a mythical "Col. Sheffler," blowing tin horns and banging on old pots, their faces masked or painted. One banner bore the motto "Success to the malicious system."[63]

As Joseph J. Holmes noted in his study of the state militia's decline, public ridicule was probably more damaging to Pennsylvania's compulsory military system than were any of its other many problems, which included short-ages of men, officers, equipment, and training. "Institutions cannot nor-mally withstand being scoffed at and mocked by the public," he noted. If mockery was the weapon that finally did in mandatory militia service, it was the mummers who wielded it to the most devastating effect. The Pennsylvania state legislature finally abandoned the compulsory militia in April 1858, but not before the fantasticals had reached Schuylkill County.[64]

The groundwork for them had been well laid. By 1853, muster days had become a drunken farce in the county—the *Miners' Journal* ran its report on the annual militia drill under the dateline "Military Broken Head Quar-ters, May 23." The accompanying story was filled with so many snide refer-ences to alcohol that one reader felt compelled to respond. "A great deal of drunkenness and disorderly conduct did prevail, more than I have seen before," wrote "a Citizen." "Several Captains marched the men under their command home sooner than they would have done, had a different state of affairs prevailed among the congregation of 'rowdies' which seemed to pour in from every direction."[65]

Just two years after "rowdies" disrupted Schuylkill County's militia drill, they put in another appearance, as the fantasticals of the "Santa Anna Life Guard" marched through Pottsville on Christmas Day, 1855. The name "Santa Anna" referred to the Mexican general defeated by Tex-ans in their bid for independence, and demonstrates the fantasticals' pre-dilection for naming their formations after vanquished enemies of the United States. The slogan "O, git out" that appeared with it neatly summa-rized the views of many laboring men on the use of the militia in labor disturbances.[66]

The fantasticals appeared again, two years later, in Cressona, by the Schuylkill south of Pottsville. "The day succeeding Christmas was rather more lively out-doors," the *Miners' Journal* reported:

The prominent feature of the day was a burlesque, by some of the "fast men" of the place. With but few exceptions the horses looked as though a peck of oats would be an extremely welcome luxury. The riders were not very warlike, but everybody thought they were "funny." By means of paint and outré clothing, most of them were beyond recognition. The regimentals embraced all sorts of style and kinds of colors. The hats were of very origi-nal shapes. In some cases, the head, "the palace of the soul," was sur-mounted by a steeple, hideous enough to be the residence of a Hindoo Idol. The music consisted of the voice of the lieutenant, tin horns and ten penny whistles.[67]

The ethnic background of the fantasticals who marched in Port Carbon and Cressona is not made clear by the *Miners' Journal*. However, it's worth noting that this form of mummery, which appeared a few dozen miles away in Easton as early as 1834, did not show up in Schuylkill County until more than two decades later, after there had been a massive influx of Irish immigrants to the coal fields. In Philadelphia and New York, the fantasticals had close connections to the immigrant and Irish communities. It is probably no accident that Schuylkill County's first reported troupe of fantasticals, with their working-class, Democratic, and racial overtones, surfaced in the canal town of Port Carbon.

The town was home to a significant number of Irish boatmen who regularly journeyed to and from the fantasticals' birthplace, Philadelphia. Port Carbon was an early center of the heavily Democratic Hibernian Society, a direct descendant of the Defenders who had led opposition to a militia draft in Ireland. Hibernian leaders had made their racial views clear in the O'Connell abolition controversy. Furthermore, the canals of Ireland had long been Ribbon strongholds, and it seems likely that Hibernian boatmen in Port Carbon were well versed in the subversive subtext of mummery.

Cressona, where the fantasticals put in their next appearance, was also a major transportation center with direct links to Philadelphia—it was home to the shops and roundhouse of the Mine Hill and Schuylkill Haven Railroad, and later the Philadelphia and Reading Railroad. The year the fantasticals appeared there was, like 1855, one in which the militia had broken a mine strike, this one at the Heckscher collieries in Cass Township.[68]

Davis has suggested that street performances like those of the mummer fantasticals were rites of solidarity that immigrants used to create images of an alternative social order. The year of their first recorded march in Schuylkill County just happened to be the one in which Port Carbon's Irish most needed an alternative to nativist hectoring about sobriety, piety, and productivity. The callithumpian tunes that the fantasticals played on their fife and drums served as a cultural counterpoint to the "The Boyne Waters" played by the militia.

The clash may have been cultural, but sometimes real blood flowed when Irish American mummers brought the noisy customs of the Old Country to the doorsteps of their native-born neighbors in the anthracite region. On December 31, 1876, nine-year-old John Boyle was among "a lot of mischievous boys, dressed in fantastic costume" who were going door to door in Mount Pleasant, in the manner of Irish mummers. The boys "by their noise disturbed and annoyed" the inhabitants of one house, and when they refused to leave (probably because they'd been denied a treat), things turned ugly. Alfred D. Minnick, a young company store clerk who was visiting the home, tried to frighten the boys with a pistol, and it went off, killing young Boyle. No charges were brought against Minnick. It's not known exactly how Boyle was dressed, but some young Schuylkill County fantasticals were known to don women's clothing, like the mummers and Mollies of Ireland.[69]

Changing of the Guard

Just as the fantasticals were emerging in Schuylkill County, the name Molly Maguire began to appear in print there. In 1857, Bannan complained in the *Miners' Journal* about the heavily political nature of speeches at the Hibernians' annual St. Patrick's Day banquet, and of a heavily political Irish American secret society called the Molly Maguires. His failure to realize that the two groups were one in the same says as much about the changing nature of the Hibernians as it does about Bannan's estrangement from the county's Irish American community.

Regular mention of the Hibernian Society dried up in the *Miners' Journal* just as Irish immigration hit flood tide in 1848—probably in reaction to that influx. But we do know that the period 1845–55 was one of explosive rank-and-file growth for the Hibernians in the hard coal fields, and one of decline for its longtime Pottsville leadership. Within a decade of the onset of the famine, the society had made "rapid progress" throughout the anthracite region, spreading to Luzerne, Lehigh, Columbia, Lackawanna, Northumberland, and Carbon Counties, the official history of the order says.[70]

The Hibernians worked hard to relieve the suffering that was filling their ranks. In February 1847, the secretary of the Hibernia Benevolent Institution of Pottsville, the publican and schoolteacher Peter F. Mudey, called a special meeting of the society, "to take into consideration the propriety of contributing a sum of money . . . to aid the sufferers in Ireland."

That same month a public meeting had been held in Pottsville to create a relief fund for famine victims. Appointed to the fund's standing committee were several men prominent in the Hibernians' annual March 17 banquet that year, including Neville, O'Connor, and Brady. Also serving on the committee was one who most assuredly did not attend the banquet—Benjamin Bannan. Charles Mohan represented the town of Minersville.[71]

On March 27, the *Pottsville Emporium* reported that Michael Daly had contributed $500 to the relief fund from the "Hibernia Benevolent Society, Pottsville." But the effort to alleviate the horrors of hunger proved every bit as futile as a campaign to aid the abortive Young Ireland rising a year later, an event that sparked a new wave of Irish nationalist activity in Schuylkill County. A meeting was held in Pottsville on August 17, 1848, less than two weeks after Young Ireland's stillborn rising in Tipperary. The anthracite Irish, not realizing the rising was already over, collected $405 for arms. At a meeting chaired by Hibernian banquet regulars Colehan, Patrick Fogarty, and the newcomer Bernard Reilly, a railroad contractor born in County Cavan, a letter was read from William Haslet Mitchel, the brother of imprisoned Young Ireland leader John Mitchel. It made an impression—within two weeks the Mitchel Guards, a nascent militia unit, and a Mitchel Club had been formed in Pottsville, with Neville as president of the latter.[72]

The newer immigrants now joining the society in large numbers were far poorer than the coal operators, professional men, and Pottsville politicians who had led it in the pre-famine era. The transfer of the society's national headquarters from Schuylkill County to New York City around 1853, coupled with the growing numbers of poor Irish immigrants in the remote coal townships where jobs were plentiful, diluted the influence of longtime Pottsville leaders such as Brady. Mudey, the secretary of the society, had moved to Philadelphia and taken a job as a dry goods salesman in 1849. The Hibernians, who for years had been holding banquets at Mudey's tavern, Town Hall in Pottsville, where forced to find a new venue.

One sign of a new generation of Hibernian leadership was the emergence in 1854 of the Young Men's Hibernia Benevolent Association of Schuylkill County. The first banquet of this branch of the society attracted several men who had been involved in the effort to aid Young Ireland in 1848, including John Neville, Thomas Farrell, and John Maginnis. Also on hand was John Kelly.[73]

The exact process by which the Pottsville elite lost control of the society is unknown, but both the Hibernians and the Ribbonmen before them were notoriously riven with factions. At some point a bodymaster from Branchdale, Mount Laffee, or Glen Carbon may simply have amassed enough votes from the men with dirt under their fingernails to oust the professionals from Pottsville.

A nineteenth-century *New York Times* report about the origins of the Molly Maguires said that while the organization was founded to provide asylum for fugitive Ribbonmen, the order "gradually passed into the hands of men of desperate character, both fugitives from Ireland and naturalized citizens of the coal regions, and they utilized it for purposes of their own."

The article focused on the Buckshots, as the Mollies of Carbon County were originally known. It made a few points worth noting about the behavior of the secret society before the Civil War. The first is that it did not engage in premeditated murder (though some beating victims died after being "given the raps," the killing was not intentional). The second was that "the raps" were, in effect, a means of policing the communal ethos of the Irish. Members of the community who refused to buy a raffle ticket or contribute to whatever cause the Buckshots were collecting for left themselves vulnerable to a beating. Outsiders, at least in the 1850s, were generally left alone.[74]

Whatever the evolution of the organization, what can be said for certain is that the changing of the guard was complete by 1867, when a former Forestville resident, Barney Dolan, was elected the organization's leader in Schuylkill County. His predecessor is unknown, but two developments suggest that the tipping point may have come a decade earlier.

The first is that the Hibernian Society was growing more overtly partisan. In 1857, Bannan complained that a harangue by the Democrat Francis Hughes had made the Hibernian Society's March 17 banquet "political in complexion." In his complaint, the first of its kind, Bannan suggested that the St. Patrick's Day festivities were degenerating amid "party matters and philippics."[75]

The changing character of the Hibernian Society was also reflected in a nickname for the group that began to gain currency in the latter half of the 1850s—"the Molly Maguires." The name appeared in print for the first time in the anthracite region in October 1857. "'The Molly Maguires—A new and exclusively Catholic secret organization . . . has recently spring up in our Eastern cities," the *Miners' Journal* reported in autumn 1857:

> It was originally started as an offset to "Know-Nothingism," but since the decline of that order has been found so useful in controlling the Native Democracy, with whom the Maguires are politically associated, that it is kept up with increased zeal. The fundamental principle of the new organization is to "taboo" every political aspirant that is not of the Romish faith, unless they will aid and assist the members. Under its practical working, every Locofoco convention is in effect so "packed" beforehand, and so admirably managed by the secret drill of its members, that the Native Democrats are

thrust to the wall with no hope of political preferment. So powerful has it already become, that it is even said to control in a measure the action of the dignitaries of the government in their appointments to office.

Bannan went on to cite clerical opposition to the organization in a Philadelphia parish, St. Philip de Neri:

[The Rev. Cantwell] understood from good authority, that certain persons of his church had regularly enrolled themselves as members of a secret political organization, and as such, were not fit to belong to this church. If he succeeded in ascertaining their names, he would certainly excommunicate them from membership; for such societies, in a country like this, are not only entirely useless, but calculated to bring reproach upon the religion which the members profess, and to array the native-born population in opposition to the church. He felt assured that the members of the "Molly Maguire" have adopted a course that must eventually bring disgrace upon them, and he could see nothing but disaster as the result of their secret political labors.

In a separate item, the newspaper linked the Mollies to election fraud in Philadelphia.[76]

The priest at St. Philip de Neri had good cause for concern—nativist rioters had targeted the church in 1844 amid rumors of an arms cache there.[77] Those bloody July riots may have been the reason that some parishioners felt a need to affiliate with a neo-Ribbon organization.

Just one week after printing Fr. Cantwell's condemnation, Bannan published a speech by Lemuel Todd, chairman of the American Republican State Committee, that cited "the advances of that foreign priestly influence, which, through the aid of the 'Molly Maguire' and other like associations, aims to, and in some districts, does actually control the nominations of the Democratic party."

The original *Miners' Journal* article wasn't based on the paper's own reporting—it was essentially a rehash of an article that appeared in the *Philadelphia Sunday Transcript*. Other newspapers picked up the *Transcript* article, and their rewrites offered details that Bannan skipped. The *Chicago Journal*, for example, made it clear that "Molly Maguire" was merely a nickname for the new order, or how it "was known in street parlance." Its description underlined the organization's likeness to the Hibernian order: "It is bound by oaths, is strictly organized with presiding and subordinate officers, pass-words, signs, grips, degrees, etc."[78] The emphasis in all these accounts is entirely on the political activity of an Irish Catholic secret society (either vehemently opposed by the clergy or utterly controlled by it), with nary a mention of violence.

The currency of "Molly Maguires" as a moniker for Hibernians is interesting, for there were any number of secret Irish societies from which to choose a nickname—Ribbonmen, Whitefeet, Rockites, Caravets, Terry Alts. But Molly Maguires was the most logical choice because the Hibernians had gained their 1836 charter from the Northern Union grouping of Ribbonmen. Famine immigrants who had watched the metamorphosis of Northern Union Ribbonmen into "Mollies" in the Ulster borderlands would naturally have used that nickname for the American offshoot of the secret society.

The name surfaced amid the Panic of 1857, which brought labor unrest, unemployment, and widespread hunger to the anthracite region. Irish mine workers struck the Heckscher collieries in Branchdale in the spring of that year, seeking the dismissal of the inside boss because he was an Englishmen. "The Irish think there are too many Englishmen, Scotchmen & Welshmen at the mines & are affrayed to loose the control," the mine's superintendent, Eugene Borda, wrote to Charlemagne Tower, his lawyer, who just happened to be the district attorney. "I am informed just now [that the workers] are threatening to burn the breakers and have threatened the engineer at the pumping engine who is affrayed to remain at his work. I want you to call upon the Sheriff and get a strong force to protect our works."[79]

By autumn, amid the worsening economic situation, Borda was more concerned with getting his mine workers fed than with getting them arrested. He appealed to the Heckschers for help. "Hunger knows no law and it begins to tell dreadfully in many parts of [Schuylkill] County," he wrote. "Men have had but little work this summer and are idle now with nothing coming and positively starving." With unemployment and food prices at unparalleled heights, Borda argued strenuously against an order to lay off the workforce: "We are in a powder keg, and a spark will be enough to bring ruin all around. You must not therefore tell me discharge hands and do not pay them, it cannot be done without increasing risks. The operators must come together in faith [and] distribute food in the shape of bread."[80] A decade after fleeing the potato famine, the Irish mine workers of Cass Township were once more looking starvation in the face.

The explosion Borda feared did not come, but the following year brought little relief. Mine workers in Ashland went on strike for higher wages in

May 1858, complaining that they could not even afford the tools of their trade, like blasting powder. Spurred on in part by canal boatmen who were involved in a labor dispute of their own, the Ashland miners tried to make the strike general, marching throughout the region to shut down other collieries. Some on the West Branch joined in.

As Schuylkill County mine strikes went, this was a fairly peaceful one. There were no shootings and no beatings. The strikers resolved "not to get drunk, bellow, make threats, give insults, stop those who want to work from doing so, annoy persons," or break the law, and they mostly stuck to it, with the exception of some stone-throwing at a Mount Laffee mine and some anonymous threats—all of which got them exactly nowhere with the anthracite establishment.

The *Miners' Journal* offered the strikers a stark choice: "work or starve." Then a full regiment of state militia was brought in to break the strike and arrest its leaders on conspiracy charges. The mustering of the militia against avowedly peaceful miners constituted such an overreaction that even the *Miners' Journal* mocked it.

District Attorney Charlemagne Tower, a coal operator, nonetheless obtained conspiracy convictions against at least two leaders of the strike for "endeavoring in an unlawful manner to raise wages."[81] The use of troops and criminal charges to break a peaceful strike would soon have dire consequences for the industry, for it taught mine workers that to succeed, strikes would have to be run from the shadows, by men ready to use violence.

Watching all these events with close interest was another coal operator, Franklin Gowen. He and a partner leased a Mount Laffee colliery at the beginning of 1858. The mine failed the following, and Gowen embarked on the study a law, a path that would soon make him the county prosecutor.[82]

As the decade drew to a close, immigration had effectively transformed certain mining regions of Schuylkill County into another—and for mine workers, more dangerous—version of Ireland. This proved especially true in Cass Township, where by 1860 up to 78 percent of mine laborers and 70 percent of miners were Irish natives.

To a remarkable degree, life on the West Branch had come to resemble that which the immigrants had left behind. Just a decade after the failure of the potato crops had decimated the townlands, those who fled it were again living a rural, communal existence among their own, the old language and customs largely intact. They faced the familiar threats of dire poverty and starvation, thanks to callous absentee mine owners who had effectively turned the anthracite region into an internal colony. As in Ireland, the agents of those owners relied on military force to put down those who attempted to advance their economic interests by collective action.

Irish Catholic immigrants also faced a vicious strain of religious bigotry fostered by the chief spokesman for the coal establishment, Benjamin Bannan, which echoed the Orange taunts of his father's Ulster. And to round it all out, there was a neo-Ribbon society nicknamed the Molly Maguires to whom these immigrants could turn for succor and support in the face of these hard times.

In fact, by the end of the 1850s, the only aspect of West Branch society that differed significantly from that of the Ulster borderlands was the political strength of the Irish Catholic community. Though the anthracite region was riven by deep economic, social, and religious fault lines, even the poorest Irish immigrants could obtain the right to vote. It was a right they exercised early and perhaps often, to their clear advantage. But for all their growing electoral clout throughout the region, on the West Branch the Irish lost an entire cadre of seasoned political leaders in the years leading up to the Civil War—John Kelly and Patrick O'Connor in Cass Township, and Charles and Michael Mohan in Minersville.

With the coming of the Civil War, the Protestant, Republican mining establishment would try to use the wartime expansion of federal power in an effort to curtail the voting rights of their longtime enemies, the Irish Catholic Democrats who worked the mines. This time, there would indeed be an explosion—perhaps because so many of the community leaders who could have stopped it were gone.

The outlines of the struggle to come were foreshadowed to an eerie degree by the street theater and formal drama of the 1850s. For the upper classes, there was *Mars in Mahantango*, an anonymous play printed on Bannan's presses in 1852. Its theme was the marriage of Schuylkill County's military leadership to its mining establishment (Mahantango Street, named for a local creek, was one of the more desirable addresses in Pottsville). In the romantic comedy, Brigadier General Maxwell of the county militia weds Caradori, the daughter of "a wealthy coal operator," rescuing her from her father's financial ruin.[83] For the lower classes, there was the mocking street theater of the fantasticals, which emerged in 1855 as a drunken, cacophonous call to arms just as Bannan's Kulturkampf against Irish Catholics was reaching its climax. And for the nativists, there was an uglier form of folk drama, as the Hibernians discovered when they gathered for the annual St. Patrick's Day procession on March 17, 1857. "In the morning, an effigy of St. Patrick, his neck decorated with a string of potatoes, was discovered hanging from a telegraph wire at center and Market streets," the *Miners' Journal* reported on March 21. "About 8 o'clock it was removed, by order of the chief burgess."

It was almost as if every side in the coming drama needed to rehearse their roles before assuming them in earnest—anti-militia mummers marching through the streets in paramilitary array, the military wooing and saving the coal establishment, and last but by no means least, Protestants slipping a noose around the neck of the Hibernians' patron saint.

9 **Resurrection**

Things fall apart; the centre cannot hold;
Mere anarchy is loosed upon the world
> —William Butler Yeats, "The Second Coming"

The Union fell apart with the roar of Confederate cannon at Fort Sumter in April 1861, but, for a time, the center held in Schuylkill County. With the coming of war, the county's political leaders temporarily put aside their bitter differences. Die-hard Democrats like Francis Hughes and Bernard Reilly joined staunch Republicans on a committee to support the families of the men who rallied to the nation's colors.[1]

It was a smart move for the Democrats, for many of their own were among the volunteers. Democrats and Republicans, Catholics and Protestants, miners and professional men alike marched off to war in a display of unity that impressed even a bigot like Bannan. Pointing to militia units with large numbers of Irishmen, such as the Columbian Infantry of Glen Carbon and the Schuylkill Guards of Minersville, he noted that "our adopted citizens . . . are not unmindful of the duty they owe the government now in this hour of danger, when it is threatened with destruction. Throughout the whole North, the same spirit of patriotism pervades the English, French, Germans, Scotch, Irish and Welsh citizens. They seem to have banished all differences."

Of the 285 West Branch men who rushed off to serve in the first weeks of the war, more than a third—ninety-nine of them—bore distinctly Irish names. Among them were James Bergen of Coal Castle and Philip Mohan of Minersville, who enlisted for three months on April 20, 1861, then reupped that summer.[2]

The sense of ethnic and social unity cited did not last long—the loss of so many workers created a labor shortage that undermined the coal establishment's near-total control of the region. "It is believed that miners will be scarce in the different mining regions this year, so many having enlisted for the war," Bannan wrote in March 1862. "But we would advise all to avoid the foolish and unprofitable turnouts as much as possible."[3]

His advice went unheeded—the Irish mine workers of the West Branch, who were near starvation just five years before, were not about to abandon the advantage that the labor shortage had given them. Indeed, that shortage became the determining factor in the outcome of labor disputes for the next three years.

One sign that labor problems had not ended with the outbreak of fighting was a Whiteboy-style warning to a Heckscher superintendent posted in Foster Township just a few months after the war began: "Mr. Snow—If you don't leave the neighborhood of Glen Carbon inside of Monday, September 23, 1861, remark the consequences—if written words nor writing will do, we will try what virtue there is in cold lead . . . —Captain Rock Esq."[4]

But even as they employed the old methods of the Irish countryside, the West Branch mine workers were moving toward a more sophisticated means of advancing their economic interests, with the formation of a regional labor organization that used selective strikes as a central strategy. The union was based on committees at each mine, which in turn sent several representatives to a larger body that coordinated policy. In later years, at least, the organization was sophisticated enough to have a strike fund. It was described as a secret society, and appears to have been an outgrowth of the Hibernian Society.[5]

The movement began among workers at the Forest Improvement Company mines, possibly as early as 1860, and was called the Union Benevolent Society. The name bears more than a passing resemblance to the Hibernian Benevolent Society, and in a few short years the labor group was being equated with the Molly Maguires. A "disinterested observer" wrote in the *Miners' Journal* in early 1864 that the Union Benevolent Society was merely a disguise for the Mollies, and that members sought to "prevent emigration from one colliery to another, to restrict the energy and industry of the respectable foreigner who refused to cooperate; to secure labor for themselves; to regulate the cost of labor; to dictate the price of mining; and to control the operations of each colliery."[6]

The description echoed one by Bannan in February 1863. "Leagued together in a secret association known as the 'Molly Maguire,' these men have dictated what bosses shall be discharged or employed," he wrote. "At Heckscherville, a man from Luzerne was discharged at their dictation, without the man being aware of what he had done to earn their enmity."[7]

In his 1907 history of American coal miners, Andrew Roy suggested that a union organized by employees of the Forest Improvement Company paved the way for the creation of local organizations elsewhere in the anthracite region during the Civil War.[8] Many men who would go on to become notorious Molly Maguires were living and working on the West Branch in the first half of the 1860s. Foremost among these was Barney Dolan, later the leader of the Schuylkill County AOH, who resided in Forestville in 1860 with his brother Patrick. There is good reason to believe that Barney Dolan was in the front ranks of those challenging the Heckscher hegemony. Pat Hester, who became a Hibernian bodymaster in Northumberland County, was living in Reilly Township in 1860—as we've seen, he was charged with assault after a Branchdale mine boss was badly beaten in a midnight attack on his home in 1855. Michael "Muff" Lawler, who became the Shenandoah bodymaster, and Patrick Tully, who gained notoriety as a Molly in Centralia in Columbia County, were both in Glen Carbon the 1860s.[9]

As the Capt. Rock notice from Glen Carbon suggests, the emerging labor organization on the West Branch wedded many elements of a traditional Ribbon society to the more advanced form of industrial unionism. Anonymous threats were joined with a new willingness to confront mine operators in the open when no crime was being contemplated.

The peculiar duality of the union was probably influenced by the labor struggles that had preceded it, especially the strike of 1858. By using a regiment of militia against peaceful strikers, and conspiracy charges against high-profile strike leaders in that year, the authorities guaranteed that any successful labor movement would have to be both conspiratorial, to shield its leadership, and paramilitary, to counter the militia. Because of the labor shortage, the Heckschers could not simply replace strikers—the military was their only recourse.

Richard Heckscher of Forestville, the nephew of the West Branch coal baron, recalled how the company's Civil War labor troubles got started:

> The beginning of these serious troubles date back to the spring of 1862 when the ringleaders in these outrages formed a fiendable combination forcing all the hands in all our collieries to join in the same, or else compelled them to leave their places. As soon as this combination was completed a committee was chosen, consisting of several men from each colliery who assumed at once not only to regulate matters concerning their own association but to control regularly our whole works, dictate to us what wages we should pay for certain work and who should be engaged and who should be discharged, etc.[10]

By May 1862, the miners were ready to act. On Monday, May 5, 1,500 workers went on strike at the Heckscherville, Thomaston, Forestville, and Swatara collieries, all of which were linked to the Forest Improvement Company. Among the strikers' demands were a ten-cent-per-wagonload pay increase for miners and a twenty-five-cents-per-day increase for laborers. The strikers also protested high prices in company stores.[11]

The *Philadelphia Inquirer* noted the ramifications of the strike for the war effort—anthracite was used to fuel navy warships blockading the Confederacy: "The affair is much more important that at first appears, from the fact that the supply of coal to the government will be stopped; and that, if the strikers succeed in their demands, all the operators in that region may be compelled to pay higher rates then the government contracts will allow."[12]

On Tuesday, the miners raised the stakes by stopping the pumps that prevented the mines from flooding. The sheriff appeared at Heckscherville with a small force the next day and got the pumps working again, but was chased away by the strikers. He appealed to Curtin for help, and the governor responded by dispatching a state militia unit—150 men from the Gray Reserves of Philadelphia, a volunteer unit comprising the "social, political and economic elite of Philadelphia society."[13]

An armed clash was feared, for newspapers were reporting that the strikers had nearly as many guns as did the militiamen. "It is possible the strikers may resist the starting of the pumps, and that a collision may ensue," the *Inquirer* warned. "[The miners] are well supplied with arms if disposed to use them."

The Gray Reserves arrived in Minersville Wednesday night and in a show of force—essentially a bit of state-sanctioned street theater—they marched out to Forestville, where they spent a night disturbed only by the accidental discharge of a militiaman's rifle. On Thursday, the Grays paraded to Heckscherville, where at 2:00 A.M. five hundred strikers had driven off twenty-five militiamen guarding the pumps that kept the mines from flooding.

Despite a front-page *Inquirer* headline about "The War at the Coal Mines," the much-dreaded clash between strikers and soldiers was averted. Even as militia reinforcements were dispatched, a settlement was mediated by Capt. Charles S. Smith of the militia and R. A. Wilder, superintendent of the Mine Hill and Schuylkill Haven Railroad, who had a strong interest in ensuring a resumption of coal shipments. Under the terms of the deal, the miners won the raises they sought in exchange for promising to respect property in any future strike.

With a settlement in hand, the upper-crust volunteers of the Gray Reserves departed, to loud derision. Like the fantasticals, the West Branch strikers considered them a "laughing stock," the *New York Times* reported, and a history of the unit complained that the returning militiamen had to endure "the taunts and jest of a considerable part of the community."[14]

The affair over, the Heckscherville strikers blamed the trouble on miners from Swatara.[15] It wouldn't be the last time that a strike was blamed on troublemakers from another mine, and it contrasts with the view of a Swatara mine superintendent, Charles Hewitt, who left one of the most detailed descriptions of the unrest:

> The first commencement of our difficulties with the hands was in spring of 1862, when after a 10-day strike of our hands, for what we deemed an unfair and disproportionate advance in wages, an armed mob of some 300 rioters coming from the direction of Mr. Heckscher's collieries, evidently by prearrangement with our men, stopped by force our large pumping engine at the South Tuckerville Slope, blew off the steam, raked out the fires and notified the boss and engineer that whoever lit the fires again until the men's permission had been obtained would be subject to the penalty of death.

Hewitt reported that he "resisted the unreasonable demands of our men for several days longer" but eventually yielded, fearing that his mine would drown with the pumps stopped. He complained that the workers "had formed a 'union' of a most formidable character."[16] Had he held out a little longer, the result might have been different. A day after the first militia contingent reached Minersville, reinforcements arrived, bringing the total number of soldiers in the area to eight hundred.[17]

With the dispute settled, Bannan did his best to downplay it, telling readers that "strikes are very common in the coal regions." He allowed that the miners had a right to strike, but criticized them for stopping the pumps. He chided the sheriff for letting the situation get out of control and the *Inquirer* for sensationalism. "So ends this 'Terrible Riot' in the Schuylkill Coal Region, which has been magnified by some of the city journals into a second siege of Yorktown, and which has been used by stockjobbers in the city to further their own speculative purposes," he wrote.[18]

But coal speculators were not the only ones who used the strike for their own ends. Schuylkill coal operators found in labor unrest a pretext to increase prices, and Bannan himself soon turned the strike into a stick with which to beat his political opponents. His special targets were those Democrats who in 1860 had supported the unsuccessful presidential candidacy of John C. Breckenridge, a supporter of slavery who went on to become a Confederate general. "We have been creditably informed that some scurvy Breckenridge politicians were at the bottom of the recent turnout on the West Branch which threatened the destruction of property," he wrote a week after the settlement.[19]

As labor unrest spread to other Schuylkill County mines and factories, Bannan grew more strident. "If unlawful combinations urged on by un-scrupulous politicians continue to interfere with the miners so that the supply of coal for government purposes is threatened, we would not be surprised to see a military force sent here, and to see the mines taken possession of by the government," he wrote. "Stopping the government's supply of fuel is an indirect way of aiding the Rebellion, and a serious mat-ter, and if the miserable, God-forsaken politicians and demagogues here who create difficulty among the men and incite them to unlawful acts are caught, they will be severely punished. In our opinion, they should be hung."[20]

The brief sense of common purpose that Schuylkill County had enjoyed following the commencement of the war had frayed badly by the summer of 1862. Labor militancy was increasingly seen as treasonable in Republican circles; in Democratic ones, it became hard to distinguish the fervent Lin-coln supporter from the mean-spirited mine boss. Political and economic roles overlapped, sometimes with fatal results.

On June 14, 1862, an unpopular mine foreman, Frank Langdon, was killed in Audenried, on the Schuylkill–Carbon County line, after attending a meeting to plan a patriotic celebration for July 4. The meeting took place at a tavern, and several drinkers expressed antigovernment sentiments. Langdon was attacked with sticks and stones as he walked home alone af-ter the meeting, and he died the following day. Historians have cited the killing of Langdon as the first by the Pennsylvania Mollies, but it was clearly a drunken crime of opportunity, not cold, calculated murder. Sticks and stones were not the weapons of choice for Molly assassins.[21]

Another barroom killing a couple of weeks later hinted at the tensions created within the Irish community by the use of the military in the strike. On June 29, 1862, two foursomes were drinking in Edward Connelly's tav-ern in Branchdale. One was a group of locals, David, Daniel, and William Kelly, along with Lawrence Flynn. The second group had names every bit as Irish—James Hogan, James Connor, John Carr, and John Welsh—but they weren't from Reilly Township. A James Connor and a John Welsh, pos-sibly the same John Welsh who became an important labor leader after the war, were living in Forestville, just down the road from Branchdale in Cass, during that period. Sheriff's records indicate the two later traveled identical distances to the ensuing trial. A Thomas Hogan was living in Foster Township, just to the north of Cass in 1860.

Words seem to have passed between the two groups inside the bar, for they soon met outside. Perhaps someone had spilled a drink on someone else, but it is also possible that the recent strike was the issue—David Kelly was a labor committeeman, and Connors and Carr were both members of Minersville militia units. While Connors squared off with David Kelly, Daniel Kelly went after Hogan. Knives gave the locals an edge: Hogan was killed and Connors was wounded. The attackers were all acquitted. The pattern here—labor militants attacking local residents who had served in the army, and getting away with it—would recur throughout the war.[22]

The violence that boiled over that summer was the result of a volatile mix of labor economics and politics, for 1862 was an election year. In Bannan's mind, labor unrest and the election were linked. Strikes arose not because miners had legitimate grievances, but because treacherous Democrats were manipulating secret combinations for traitorous political purposes. The military was the only answer. And he was about to be handed a military solution far more elegant than occupation of the mines. It involved conscription—the return of the compulsory militia system that the mummers had helped kill just a few years before.

The Politics of Conscription

On July 17, 1862, Congress created the first national military draft in U.S. history, through a back door called the Militia Act. Seventy years before, an identically named law had touched off widespread Defender disturbances in Ireland, but there were few immediate repercussions to the new U.S. law. That was probably because of its innocuous wording: the act authorized the secretary of war to draft the militiamen of states that had not upgraded their military organizations.[23] In fact, the law led directly to conscription and the appointment of draft commissioners in counties throughout the United States. To aid them in their task, Secretary of War Edwin Stanton issued an August 8 order suspending the writ of habeas corpus—just as the English had done in Ireland seventy years before.

Republicans were quick to take advantage of this unprecedented expansion of federal powers for their own partisan purposes—this was, after all, an election year. Historian Mark E. Neely, Jr., writes that the arrests of thousands of Democratic politicians and editors following the suspension of habeas corpus was viewed as the work of "small-minded, vindictive and narrowly partisan local office-holders."[24] Which brings us to a certain Schuylkill County newspaper publisher—one who realized the Union Army could hold far more troublesome Irish miners than any prison.

"I had chosen Benjamin Bannan... as [draft] commissioner for that county, not only for his high character and admitted ability, but because of his intimate knowledge of all the political ramifications of the Commonwealth, including the Molly Maguires." What makes that statement in the memoirs of Pennsylvania Draft Commissioner Alexander McClure so interesting is not only the emphasis on Bannan's political acumen, but the specific mention of it in relation to the Molly Maguires. At the time of Bannan's appointment in the summer of 1862, "the Molly Maguires" was no more than a nickname for a politically active group of Irish Catholic Democrats, the Hibernians. For staunch Republicans like Bannan and McClure, taking into consideration the Molly Maguires meant setting an unfairly high draft quota for Cass Township, a stronghold of Irish Catholic Democrats. "Of course, such a township would not have an excess of volunteers in the service, and an unusually large quota was officially returned to Commissioner Bannan, with directions to fill the same with conscripts," McClure wrote in his memoirs.[25]

Bannan knew well that the coal areas of the county had produced more than their share of soldiers—in fact, he attributed the West Branch strike precisely to the labor shortage created by the number of Union Army volunteers from that region.[26] But in the summer of 1862, the 285 West Branch residents who had rushed to their nation's defense in April 1861 no longer mattered. What mattered, crucially, was an upcoming election—one that would decide the composition of Congress. Republicans feared that a Democratic victory would undermine the war effort, and Bannan was convinced that the war needed to be fought on the home front, by whatever means necessary.

"The Democrats are quietly acting to prevent all their voters from going [to war]... We may lose the congressional district if the draft is not made and the men got off before the election," he wrote Gov. Andrew G. Curtin. "The larger portion required from the county will come from the Democratic districts... While we are fighting the enemy in the field, it is equally important that some attention should be paid to the affairs at home and see that the Administration is not voted down in the next Congress."[27] Here, then, was a man who truly understood all the political ramifications, a man who could be counted on to turn Irish miners who voted Democratic into Union Army soldiers who, most crucially, were not really capable of voting at all. And with luck Bannan would do it in time for the upcoming election.

The Schuylkill County draft commissioner was not alone in this. McClure stressed in his memoirs that his choice of draft commissioners had "disarmed all apprehension as to any partisan aims in the execution of the draft." His actions and the correspondence of his appointees prove otherwise. R. Lyle White of Meadville, the Crawford County draft commissioner, wrote Gov. Curtin that the draft "could not fail to have a healthful political effect."[28] The reason was simple—Republicans like Bannan were convinced that Democratic leaders were urging their voters to stay home and vote, rather than join an army that denied them the franchise. They assumed that Republicans were more likely to volunteer for the Union Army, giving Democrats a political advantage on the home front.

A. Myers of Clarion, Pennsylvania, explained the politics of conscription and the consequences of denying soldiers the vote in a September 12, 1862, letter to Gov. Curtin:

> There's another reason why the draft should soon be made and the persons drafted sent to the rendezvous. Which is this—Those who have gone are nearly all from the Republican and loyal Democratic ranks. And the draft would now come off sections which have withheld their support for the war. If we are to lose the soldier vote that went some time ago, the Breckenridge ticket ought to lose the vote now. By drafting and putting the men in camps out of their districts, this can be done. I believe the soldier ought to vote but the wisdom of our supreme bench says not. Our loss on this account endangers our success.[29]

Ezra B. Chase, the Democratic district attorney of Luzerne County, was detained in the wave of arrests that followed the August 8 suspension of habeas corpus, allegedly because he had urged members of his party to stay out of uniform. The police chief of Wilkes-Barre said Chase had advised Democrats "not to go to the war but to stay at home and go to the polls, and that they could more readily settle the present difficulties of our country, by electing men . . . who would bring the Southern Confederacy back into the Union without any fighting."[30]

At stake in the fall election were not only seats in Congress, but also a local position that was crucial to the coal industry during periods of labor unrest—district attorney of Schuylkill County. Throughout the strikes of the 1840s and 1850s, district attorneys like the Republican Charlemagne

Tower had been at the beck and call of mine owners. Now the Democrats were fielding a highly credible candidate—Franklin Benjamin Gowen.

Like many Irish Catholics in the coal fields, Gowen was, as we have seen, a son of Ulster, though a Protestant one. As the 1862 election approached, even Bannan, the Republican chairman, had to admit that Gowen was a man "of ability"—he'd been appointed secretary of the May meeting of the county bar association that Bannan's brother John had chaired—even if he was "without experience and in bad company."[31]

The "bad company" was Francis W. Hughes, the county's Democratic leader. Hughes was the last spicy ingredient in the steaming stew of Bannan's suspicions about Schuylkill County Democrats. At forty-five, Hughes was at the pinnacle of his political career. He had been elected to the Pennsylvania State Senate at age twenty-six and gone on to serve as attorney general of Pennsylvania and secretary of the Commonwealth. He had built a successful career as a criminal and corporate attorney, and was careful to court the main constituencies of his party. Though of Welsh extraction, he was a regular visitor at the Hibernian St. Patrick's Day banquets in Pottsville. In 1860, as a delegate to the Democratic national convention, he had supported Breckenridge, but when war broke out he condemned both secessionists and abolitionists, and worked to support the families of militiamen who went to fight. In 1862, he presided over the Pennsylvania Democratic convention, which resolved to fight the Confederacy, restore "the Union as it was," and preserve "the Constitution as it is." Hughes was then selected to direct the Democrats' 1862 election campaign in Pennsylvania.

But in 1862 Hughes had a problem that no amount of eloquence or political acumen could explain away—his family. The *Miners' Journal* gleefully pointed out that Hughes's brother, Isaac, lived in New Bern, North Carolina, where Schuylkill County's 48th Regiment was fighting even as Republicans and Democrats debated in Pottsville. Worse still, Hughes's nephew and former law partner, John Hughes, had returned to New Bern and enlisted in the Confederate Army just a few months after running for Congress as a Democrat in Schuylkill and Northumberland Counties in 1860.

Francis Hughes countered that another nephew, Francis P. Dewees, had joined a Pennsylvania regiment on April 17, 1861. Critics scoffed, saying that Dewees had done so reluctantly, and left the army when his three-month enlistment was up.

But the most damaging revelation was yet to come. On September 27, Bannan's newspaper reported that Hughes had written a resolution in the early months of 1861 that urged Pennsylvania to consider seceding from the Union. Attempting to limit the damage, Hughes released the text of the resolution, which he had never introduced. He succeeded only in heightening the furor, for the document suggested that Pennsylvania become "the great manufacturing workshop" of the Confederacy.

The Commonwealth resounded with cries of treason.[32] For Bannan, the ardent Republican and newly appointed draft commissioner, the picture was now complete: Irish Democrats on the West Branch were avoiding military service and interrupting the supply of coal because secret combinations were being politically manipulated by traitors like Francis W. Hughes.

Bannan doubtless felt that he was merely evening the score with his political manipulation of the draft. He had no idea that he was about to trigger an earthquake.

Draft Resistance

The first big tremors came in October, in Cass Township. There had been some resistance earlier to draft enrollers, when deputy U.S. marshals were driven away by violence in August, the *New York Times* reported, noting that "the trouble is in the same locality where the miners recently had a difficulty with the operators."[33]

But "that blew over," Bannan reported, and an incomplete list was compiled. In early October, more serious difficulties arose with a break-in at the home of Heckscherville's Catholic priest. A housekeeper was beaten and money stolen. Suspicion fell—or was deftly placed—on Cass Township's two draft enrollers, William Ziegler and Casper Hughes. The parish rolls for St. Kieran's would, after all, have nicely filled out Bannan's incomplete draft list.

Ziegler was forced to flee his Heckscherville home for nearby New Castle. As a crowd of men marched out of Heckscherville crying for "the heart's blood of Ziegler," the county sheriff rushed to New Castle with seventy militiamen from Pottsville. Two men were arrested but later released, and order was restored with the help of Catholic priests. The sheriff's failure to take a firmer hand outraged Bannan, who blamed the disturbances on antiwar Democrats and concluded his newspaper account of the affair with a heartfelt if by now familiar wish: "If a few of the Breckenridge leaders in this county were hung, it would be a blessing to the community."[34]

Elsewhere in that same edition, he reiterated the details of Democratic leader Hughes's links with the South and, connecting the draft to the upcoming election, issued a dire warning to Democrats:

Every man who attempts to vote illegally at the election on Tuesday next will be placed on the Draft.

Every person who has sworn that he is not naturalized, and attempts to vote, will be placed on the Draft.

A list of these persons has been prepared and will be at the polls for inspection.

His warning had little impact on the voting, for the governor had ignored Bannan's advice and delayed the draft until after the election. The Cass Township residents whom Bannan had wanted to ship off to the war gave Gowen and Democratic congressional candidate Meyer Strouse their most lopsided margins of victory. Both won in the North Cass precinct by a stunning 229 votes to 22. In the South Cass precinct, the margin was big, but not ten-to-one: 307 to 109 for Strouse, 307 to 111 for Gowen.

Bannan complained that in Cass a "reign of terror, inaugurated by unscrupulous partizans," had kept Union voters from the polls, and driven Protestants from the township. There were also "serious discrepancies" between voter rolls and draft rolls for the township, he warned.[35]

On October 16, the names for the draft were selected. The results were everything the Cass Township Irish feared. "A disproportionate number of Irishmen were being called," said a longtime local newspaperman and historian, Jim Haas. "Employers, too, were using conscription to get rid of Irish 'trouble-makers' by taking them out of the mines and putting them in the army."[36] A tense week passed as Schuylkill County awaited the day when the draftees would be shipped off. On Tuesday, October 21, the earthquake struck. In an apparent display of paramilitary muscle, hundreds—possibly thousands—of armed men marched from colliery to colliery in Cass Township, calling the workers out on strike to protest the draft. Parading with music, the marchers in some ways resembled the anti-militia fantasticals of just a few years before: "ranged in line, headed by drum, fife and flag, and carrying clubs, loaded rifles and shot-guns."

This time, of course, no one was laughing. "The disturbance in the coal fields, relative to the draft, is more in the form of a conspiracy than a riot," the *Philadelphia Inquirer* reported. "The disaffected have sent committees to almost every colliery, and the league cannot probably be dissolved by any military force."[37]

A chief complaint of the strikers was that the enrollment lists were riddled with errors. "The deputy marshals, in some instances, are said to have taken the tax duplicates, and enrolled both living and dead men," according to the *Inquirer.* "Four dead men are drafted in one township." The newspaper said there was reason to believe that some of the complaints were well-founded.[38]

Another fear was competition in the labor market from freed slaves. This had been a source of tension since 1842, when unemployed miners had battled free blacks in Philadelphia; President Lincoln's emancipation policy, which had just been announced on September 22, served to further heighten the concern. After all, the wartime labor shortage had just allowed mine workers to win a wage increase.

All in all, there appeared little room for compromise. "It was open, defiant rebellion," McClure wrote in his memoirs. "The miners threaten to offer the government of the state the alternatives of not drafting or remaining entirely unsupplied with coal from the region," the *Inquirer* reported. "It is estimated that at least 3,000 men are engaged in the affair. The rioters are nearly all armed with bludgeons, guns, pieces of iron, swords and every other variety of weapon. It will require at least two regiments and a battery to quell the tumult."[39] Typically, the strike was blamed on instigators from elsewhere—in this case, Luzerne County.

On October 22, Gov. Curtin sent an urgent telegraph to Secretary of War Edwin Stanton in Washington. "The draft is being resisted in several counties of the state. In Schuylkill County, I am just informed that 1,000 armed men are assembled and will not suffer the train to move the drafted men" to Harrisburg.[40] At Tremont, just west of Cass Township, hundreds of armed men stopped a train as it was about to leave with some drafted men. "They ordered the men to get out, and said those who wanted to go, could; but those who did not want to go might remain, and that they would protect them," the *Miners' Journal* reported. It pinpointed Cass as the center of the disturbances.[41]

At the War Department, Stanton took a hard line, authorizing Curtin to use all military force available in Pennsylvania to put down the uprising. On October 23, Curtin reported to Stanton that "notwithstanding the usual exaggerations, I think the organization to resist the draft in Schuylkill, Luzerne, and Carbon Counties is very formidable. There are several thousands in arms." He requested one thousand regular troops to deal with the disturbances.[42]

While McClure and Curtin were still weighing their options in Harrisburg, the Catholic Church joined the effort to restore calm to the region. On Wednesday, October 22, a priest from Tremont spoke to a large crowd at New Mines in Reilly Township, urging support for the Union and compliance with the law. The next day, Bishop James Frederic Wood of Philadelphia met with local priests in Pottsville, instructing them to preach against resistance to authority in their Sunday sermons.[43]

But Gov. Curtin grew only more alarmed. "We all think the resistance to the draft is the first appearance of a conspiracy," he wrote Stanton. "We know there are 5,000 men in league in three counties, and all work is interrupted by them." Curtin reiterated his request for one thousand federal troops, but only two militia regiments were available. As they descended on Pottsville, some in Harrisburg were already contemplating another way out of the problem.[44]

The retreat from the hard line was led by McClure, who considered it "an imperious necessity to avoid a conflict with the Molly Maguires." An open clash might have drawn attention to the manner in which he and Bannan had manipulated the draft for Cass Township, so McClure took the unusual step of going over the head of the secretary of war. With Curtin's approval he sent a coded message to President Lincoln that pointed out the perils of a military response and asked for a quick response.

McClure stayed up until 2:00 A.M. awaiting an answer from the White House. None arrived, but as he went to breakfast the next day in his Harrisburg hotel, he ran into Col. Edward D. Townsend, acting adjutant general of the Union Army.

Townsend beckoned him over and relayed a message: "He said the president had instructed him to inform me that he was desirous, of course, to see the law executed, or at least to appear to have been executed, to which he added, 'I think McClure will understand.'"

McClure did indeed. He summoned Bannan to an emergency meeting with the governor that very afternoon. The Schuylkill County draft commissioner had only recently urged the hanging of his political opponents, but now he told Curtin that he, too, was "most desirous of a peaceful solution to the problem." It seems his hands were, after all, as dirty as McClure's.

McClure came up with the answer—affidavits showing that Cass was exempt from the draft because its quota had been filled by volunteers who joined military units in nearby towns like Minersville and Glen Carbon.[45] It was a simple solution, because scores of Cass Township men had done just that. In fact, more than a year after the militia draft, in November 1863, John P. Hobart, a former conscription official for Schuylkill County, admitted that Cass Township had an excess of forty-two volunteers over its quota for conscripts in the 1862 draft.[46]

The miners had kept lookouts posted along the railroads Thursday and Friday to warn of the approach of any troop trains, but with the government's capitulation, the crisis was clearly winding down. On Saturday, October 25, Curtin informed Stanton that "the riots in Schuylkill County have ceased for the present." He didn't explain why.

It had taken armed miners in the streets and the intervention of the president of the United States to get Bannan to abandon his attempt to dragoon Irish Democrats. By trying to use the military as the answer to a political problem, he had forced his political opponents to field an army of their own, though the Cass strikers probably had more in common with the anti-militia fantasticals than with a truly organized military force. Indeed, this is the moment where one can almost—almost—see the mummers who helped end mandatory militia service in 1858 being transformed into the Molly Maguires who defeated the militia conscription of 1862. As Davis put it, "The militant strike parade . . . belonged to the milieu of Christmas revelry and militia burlesques."[47]

The draft disturbances raise two intriguing questions—were there really thousands of armed men prepared to resist conscription, and, if so, who organized them?

Just four years before the marching mine workers stopped a train and offered militia conscripts their freedom, another "paramilitary" band—the fantasticals—had mocked the militia system at Christmastime. Those who took to the streets in 1862 could draw on distant memories of the 1790s militia disturbances in Ireland, but with the fantasticals fresh in their minds, they may have seen their actions less as overt rebellion than as an elaborate form of street theater designed to cow the authorities—just as Ireland's Molly Maguires may have viewed their costumed demands for food during the famine as simply a more forceful form of the mummers house-to-house collections. If that was the case, the Cass Township performance proved remarkably effective, though the exact identity of the leading actors remains somewhat elusive.

Richard Heckscher of Forestville, the nephew of the Cass Township coal baron, felt that the connection between draft resistance and the West Branch labor committees, which the New York Times had hinted at in August, was so obvious that it bore no elaboration. His statement to that effect came in early 1864, right around the time that the Union Benevolent Society was being publicly described as a front for the Molly Maguires.[48]

Amid the 1862 disturbances, the Miners' Journal blamed the trouble, like the May strike, on Democratic leaders—"political demagogues" who had "poisoned the mind of the men." Bannan placed the headquarters of the antidraft movement at "the house of man named Kelly on the Primrose Hill," where one celebrating rioter was said to have accidentally shot himself in the head. He was almost certainly referring to the Primrose barroom of the recently deceased Cass Township supervisor, John Kelly. The following year, the home of Kelly's widow, Ann Kelly, served as the polling place for the South Cass precinct.[49]

The *Philadelphia Inquirer* also reported the accidental shooting, but said it took place "as the ringleaders were assembled at Coalcastle." It added that Heckscherville, "where the services of the Pennsylvania Militia were required some time since, on the occasion of a strike for higher wages," appeared to be the headquarters of "the disaffected." It hinted at a shadowy organization "which has been steadily and stubbornly resisting the due and proper execution of the laws" in the West Branch region.[50]

It seems clear from these three descriptions that the mobilization of hundreds of mine workers for the May strike and the October draft resistance were carried out by the same conspiratorial group. The descriptions of that group by Heckscher, Bannan, and the *Inquirer* are all consistent with the Hibernian Society, which had a history of secrecy, political involvement, and labor activity on the West Branch.

Furthermore, the Hibernians were the direct descendants of the Defenders, who had led popular opposition to the Militia Act in Ireland in the 1790s. The antidraft agitation in the two countries bore a number of marked similarities. What McClure called "open, defiant rebellion" had been labeled by Irish authorities seventy years earlier a "state of complete insurrection."

In both cases, the trouble arouse from Irish Catholic suspicions that the draft was being used by a Protestant ascendancy to punish them for legitimate political gains. In both cases, disturbances were organized by a secret society with roots in the north of Ireland, mobilizing hundreds of men in a paramilitary array to confront the authorities. And in both cases, mine workers were at the forefront, warning off those attempting to complete the enrollment. In Queen's and Kilkenny Counties, the birthplace of many West Branch miners, draft resisters had threatened to flood the mines, much as the Forest Improvement Company strikers had in the spring of 1862. Finally, the end result was nearly the same, with authorities backing down or compromising in the face of determined resistance—though in Ireland, that process involved considerable bloodshed.

The action in the streets marked a new departure for the Hibernian Society. In January 1862, a statewide Hibernian convention in Philadelphia had called for "the immediate consolidation of the order," and delegates had adopted resolutions "relating to the defense of liberty in America."[51] The draft resisters on the West Branch certainly would have felt their actions fell into that category.

For more than twenty-five years, the Schuylkill County Hibernian Society had led a peaceful existence as a law-abiding fraternal organization with political ambitions, but Bannan and McClure had helped turn the coal region into another Ulster. It was time to return to the old ways. And indeed, within weeks of the draft disturbances, an old rallying cry would be heard on the lips of West Branch miners amid a new wave of strikes: "Molly Maguire."

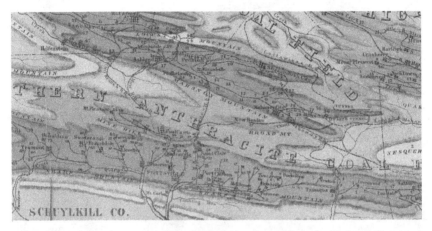

A detail from Samuel Harries Daddow's 1866 map showing much of Schuylkill County and, to the left of Pottsville, the West Branch region. Heckscherville, not labeled, is between Mt. Pleasant and Coal Castle.

Two views of Heckscherville from the December 26, 1863, edition of *Frank Leslie's Illustrated*. The village was a center of labor unrest for much of that year.

The November 5, 1863, murder of George K. Smith, the first mine official to be killed by the Molly Maguires, as shown in Allan Pinkerton's 1877 account, *The Mollie Maguires and the Detectives*.

The October 17, 1868, murder of Alexander W. Rea, the last mine official to be killed by the Mollies during the Civil War era, from the Pinkerton book.

The Mohan Hotel, from an 1889 map of Minersville, Pa. The Mohans were prominent in the political and civic affairs of the West Branch region.

The *Miners' Journal* Building in Pottsville, Pa., from the *1875 County Atlas of Schuylkill*. The newspaper's longtime publisher, Benjamin Bannan, was a harsh critic of Irish Catholics, Democrats, and labor unions.

At left, Frank Wenrich's meat market in Mahanoy City, Pa., from an atlas published in 1875, the year he was implicated in the Wiggans Patch vigilante killings. Note the eye on his sign, an odd symbol for a butcher shop, but a near-perfect match for the logo of San Francisco's famed vigilance committee—and that of the Pinkerton Detective Agency.

10

"Brave Sons of Molly"

Says Mollie to her darlin' sons,
"What tyrant shall we tumble?"

—Molly Maguire ballad

On the night of December 5, 1862, a group of men seized the engine house at the two Wolf Creek collieries of Geo. H. Potts and Co., just north of Minersville in Cass Township, and raked out the fires. They also posted a number of threatening notes, illustrated with coffins and the skull and crossbones. The notes, or "coffin notices," were signed "Brave sons of Molly."

The following day, the collieries' 400 employees went on strike. A settlement was reached on December 10, but only 150 of the men were rehired.[1]

Wolf Creek was not the only operation affected by labor unrest. A coffin notice was also posted December 5 at the Swatara mine run by Charles Hewitt in neighboring Reilly Township.[2] And at about the same time the Wolf Creek men were going on strike, miners fired guns during a "riotous demonstration" at the two slopes of William Goyne's Phoenix colliery, a short distance away at Phoenix Park in Branch Township.

Trouble flared anew on Saturday, December 13, when two hundred armed men, supposedly strangers to the area, arrived at the Phoenix colliery and forced engineers at the two slopes to put out the fires in the engine boilers. They then ransacked a company store, beat two clerks, and warned that they would kill every man there if the store were reopened or the fires relit without their permission. The rioters "boasted largely of an organization called the 'Molly Maguires' to which they belonged, and asserted that it was powerful enough to control the whole coal region," the *Miners' Journal* reported.

Labor unrest was on the rise throughout the West Branch region. Bannan blamed "a movement originating in Cass Township, where a secret association termed the "Molly Maguires" exists, the members of which boast that they can have everything their own way, and that they do not care for the law or its representatives." According to Bannan, the group claimed that at short notice it could rally three thousand men to violently enforce strikes that dictated wage rates.[3] His description strongly suggests that the "Brave sons of Molly" were the same men behind the anti-conscription movement.

There were other echoes of the draft disturbances—on December 27, the *Miners' Journal* announced that Charlemagne Tower had been appointed provost marshal to enforce the draft in Schuylkill County. As December drew to close, the name "Molly Maguire," synonymous with a politically oriented secret society since 1857, was being increasingly associated with the kind of labor issues that Hibernians had been involved with since the strike of 1842. On December 20, the *Miners' Journal* spoofed the Mollies with a tale about an Irish immigrant named Mollie Muggins who botched a meal she was cooking for some miners by making it too spicy. It was the last time the name "Molly" would be taken so lightly in the anthracite region.

The joking ended on January 2, 1863, when James Bergen was shot dead in his Coal Castle home. The killing of this onetime member of the militia came a week after Christmas, the day when Schuylkill County's fantasticals had appeared in the streets to mock militiamen. It was committed by a small band of men who visited the Bergen home and opened fire when they were denied a request for ale. In Ireland and in Philadelphia, small bands of mummers, wren boys, and fantasticals sometimes took vengeance when homeowners and barkeeps rebuffed their requests for money, food, or drink. The sequence of events in Coal Castle—request, refusal, revenge—resonates in the mummer tradition. So does the gunplay.

"Shooting in" the New Year was so much a part of mummer festivities in eastern Pennsylvania that to this day the formal name of the group that parades through Philadelphia each January 1 is "the New Years Shooters and Mummers Association." Given that the firing of guns was a staple of New Year's celebrations in Schuylkill County, and that Irishmen bent on vengeance there tended to kill their victims right around the same holiday, the difference between a Molly Maguire and a mummer was, to some degree, reduced to the direction in which his weapon was aimed.

The Coal Castle assassins cheered for Jefferson Davis as they fled, suggesting that the killing of the former Union Army soldier was linked to the antidraft agitation. In his history of the New York City draft riots, Iver Bernstein points out that Irish draft resisters there cheered for Davis as well in the summer of 1863, but he suggests that the cheers conveyed not so much sympathy for the Confederacy as antagonism toward the Republican

Party. He cites a clear precedent in the conscription disturbances in Ireland seventy years before: "The most striking historical analogue to this use of pro-Confederate cheering as a rallying point for anti-Republican sentiment was pro-French sloganeering during the violent popular resistance to the Militia Act in Ireland in the summer of 1793."[4] The same may apply to the events in Coal Castle.

James Bergen's body had been in the ground only a few days when a neighbor, James O'Connor, and "Curry" of nearby Glen Carbon, a former comrade of "Yellow Boy," were shot and wounded while they walked together. The January shootings occurred in North Cass, a precinct that had handed District Attorney Franklin Gowen a ten-to-one margin of victory three months earlier. Gowen's biographer, Marvin Schlegel, suggests that the prosecutor's lack of interest in the pursuing the cases stemmed from concern about alienating Irish Democrats.[5]

"Cass Township in this county is probably one of the most lawless spots in the country," roared the *Miners' Journal* in reporting the attacks. "The civil authorities are powerless there."[6] The authorities' impotence was aptly demonstrated by continued trouble at the Wolf Creek collieries, where the arrest of several union activists illuminates the shadowy relationship between the labor committees and the Mollies.

The biggest stumbling block to labor peace in the winter of 1862–63 was "dead work"—the driving of gangways and preparation of the coal breasts for the resumption of full-scale mining in the spring. Coal operators traditionally laid off much of their work force and reduced the wages of those who remained. This time around, the miners resisted.

On February 11, 1863, coffin notices signed "Molly Maguire" again went up at the Wolf Creek collieries of Geo. H Potts and Co. Without any apparent cause, a new strike promptly ensued. When no settlement had been reached within five days, W. G. Audenried, an officer of the company, arrived from Philadelphia to investigate. He met with a committee of five men representing the miners, including Darby McManimy and Martin Corrigan.

The committee demanded an increase in pay and the rehiring of all the laid-off workers. Audenried conceded the pay raise and the committee yielded on rehiring all the men. "So ended the conference, and apparently the whole difficulty—to the entire satisfaction of all parties concerned," the *Miners' Journal* reported on March 14. "But, in the meantime, there were other spirits moving, which started fresh complaints, and ruined the whole plan of settlement."

The "other spirits" came in the person of Thomas Keefe, a stranger to Wolf Creek who arrived the day before the settlement, ordering the pumping engineers to cease work. He repeated the message at the company store—much as the Molly Maguires at Phoenix Park had done. When Audenried questioned his authority to issue orders, Keefe replied in the cryptic tones of Ribbonism that he had been ordered to appear at a meeting "over the mountain" and had come on this errand for fear of his life. Audenried considered having him arrested, but was too busy with labor negotiations to attend to it.

On Thursday, with a settlement reached and the miners poised to go back to work, new coffin notices went up at the mine. They threatened anyone who reentered the pits until certain superintendents had been fired. The offending bosses were themselves warned to quit the premises, and informed that if they tore down the notices, as they had done others, the penalty would be "instant death."

The union men who had negotiated the settlement then set out to Forestville, to see who had posted the latest notices, "whether their own men or some other persons," the *Miners' Journal* reported. Along the way, in Minersville, who should they run into but the very folks who had posted the notices? They were union men, out to stiffen the spines of the Wolf Creek brethren.

"These men said 'Why don't you discharge your bosses as we have done ours,'" the *Miners' Journal* reported. The Wolf Creek boys took the hint and returned to the mine with a new ultimatum. Written by Corrigan and delivered by him and McManimy on Friday, a letter demanded the dismissal of the bosses on the grounds that they had torn down the coffin notices and wrongfully discharged a workman.

The union's defense of threatening notes signed by "Molly Maguire" bespoke a close link with the secret society; Audenried, who had had quite enough by this point, arranged for the arrest on conspiracy charges of Corrigan, McManimy, and Keefe.[7] The *Miners' Journal* had no doubt about who was behind the Wolf Creek trouble: "Leagued together in a secret association known as the 'Molly Maguires,' these men have dictated to their employers what bosses shall be discharged or employed . . . these things cannot longer be tolerated."[8]

The outcome of the March trial of the three accused conspirators offered Bannan and the coal operators little consolation. In his charge to the jury, the judge recommended the acquittal of Corrigan and McManimy, but suggested complicity on the part of Keefe. The jury returned a not guilty verdict after three hours of deliberation.[9]

The Wolf Creek case offers a glimpse of the complicated dynamics of the chaotic West Branch labor scene. Clearly there were labor committees at each colliery that negotiated with management. Equally clear is that these committees were not completely autonomous. There were "other spirits" at work—a shadowy organization that called strikes and enforced regional conformity in labor settlements using traditional Ribbon methods. Those methods were violence or the threat of violence, delivered anonymously under the auspices of "Molly Maguire"—a nickname for the Hibernian Society.

The coffin notices make clear that the name Molly Maguire was embraced, adopted, and defended by the union, and was not simply invented by Bannan.

More than a decade after these notices were posted, a Pinkerton spy—in a report on an 1875 meeting of eighteen Hibernian bodymasters, or local chapter leaders, at the Town Hall in Pottsville—offered a glimpse of the means by which such warning notices were approved. "After adjournment, John Reagan of St. Clair gave Frank McAndrew, B.M. [bodymaster] of Shenandoah, a threatening notice to post in front of the long chute at Turkey Run colliery. The notice was to the following effect," the spy reported. "'To the Union men now in the Union. I would have you take your tools out of this place. This is my first notice, but if I have to come back again it will be a different requisition.' The above notice was put up by two men (M.M.'s) belonging to the Shenandoah division by the orders of Frank McAndrews and was intended to intimidate the Cornishmen working at Turkey Run so that they would quit work and thereby have an opening for Reagan and his brother to get a job for the balance of the winter."[10] Aside from highlighting one of the Hibernian Society's more prosaic activities—finding work for its members—the report makes it clear that a Molly coffin notice had to be approved by a Hibernian bodymaster.

This is not to say that all coffin notices were the work of the Mollies—anonymous warnings are easily counterfeited. A notice posted at Richard Kear's Gap colliery in Cass Township in 1864 had this odd ending: "Sind by the real boys this time—so you beter loock out." Because it had been signed by "the real boys" this time, it appears that an unauthorized notice had been posted earlier.[11]

Anonymous coffin notices weren't the only form of labor–management communication, and bosses weren't the only targets. When violence wasn't being threatened, the colliery committees handled correspondence in a very straightforward manner.

In a letter dated March 3, 1863, the Heckscherville committee informed Charles Heckscher that "we have come to the following agreement that there will be no work in the different collieries from this date until the Heckscherville Colliery starts by some other person than Thomas Verner." Verner, who had a reputation for not paying his men promptly, had bought out the previous operator of the mine, Heckscher nephew Eugene Borda, who earned the gratitude of his workers by defying orders to lay them off in the hard and hungry autumn of 1857. (The question of who operated the mine was thus, a least potentially, a matter of survival.) The curious coincidence that Verner had the very same name as the first grand master of the Orange Order may have aggravated his situation.

Eight days after that letter, the committee sent another to Heckscher: "The men from all your works held a mass meeting this day and came to agreement to stop the carts from hauling fuel to the pumping engines to-morrow."[12] There were no threats of violence here—and no mention of Molly Maguire.

By March 14, labor unrest had stopped all work at five large West Branch collieries, including Heckscherville and Wolf Creek. The issue was the union's demand that that the miners name their own bosses, and the collieries linked to the Forest Improvement Company were a particular target. The *Miners' Journal* reported that "the proprietors are determined that [the mines] may fill up and rot down before they permit a mob to control any of their operations any longer."[13] That convinced the Heckscherville strikers to allow the pumps to be restarted—each day the mines filled with water would keep them closed for up to ten—but Verner was driven away by death threats when he tried to take possession of the Borda mine.[14] But by March 28, as the strike spread, "regulators" stopped the pumps in Thomaston and Heckscherville, though Wolf Creek restarted after an agreement that the workers could strike only over wages, the *Miners' Journal* reported.

At the Otto colliery in Reilly Township, Supt. David Muir had a close call with a large body of strikers who marched in from Cass when he re-opened the mine. He described the unfolding threat in a series of notes to Peter Heckscher:

New Mines, April 1, 1863:

I am sorry to hear the men intend making an attempt to stop the white ash colliery and to punish the men that was at work today. We are very poorly situated for want of anything to defend ourselves with. I hope you will try to send us assistance from Pottsville or Minersville as soon as possible. I will keep a vigilant lookout and do all in my power to prevent anything from being done, but you know the state of this place at present. Therefore

I insist that you use your endeavor to send us assistance as soon as possible.

New Mines, undated:

The mob of upwards of 100 men has been here. They passed past my house and I am afraid they will commit some outrage. It looks awful and no protection here.

Minersville, April 2, 1863:

I sent a pencil note to you this morning stating that the mob had made its appearance at the Otto and that there was about 100 men, but when I wrote the note I had not seen the whole of them—there must have been upwards of 200. They went first to the Red Ash slope and then to the White Ash breaker and fired a few shots, fortunately there was no one there. I had about 35 men—all that could be mustered—last night and we all left about 3/4 of an hour before they came so you can see that we were very fortunate in not being captured. They went from the breaker to Dewartville . . . and commenced calling at each of the men's houses that were at work yesterday. There was a number of shots fired, but I have not heard whether there was anyone shot or not. They were making a general call at every house (in the Stone Row) where anyone had worked yesterday. There are a number of the men who has escaped and I have seen them here, but I cannot say whether they all escaped or not. Dear sir, in my opinion, it is impossible to work the colliery, unless there is sufficient protection got for the men.

P.S.: Since writing the other day my daughter has come into Minersville and she informs me that the mob was in my house and searched every corner for me. They left my house and went to my son-in-law's but did not succeed in finding him as he was from home. My daughter likewise informs me that David Jones was very badly beaten on the head by the mob but did not hear of any other being hurt by them.

New Mines, April 3, 1863:

I write to inform you that all is quiet at this place at present. The pumping engines are still at work. It was fortunate for me being from home yesterday when the mob came to my house. They swore it was good for me for if they had catched me I would not be anymore.[15]

The continuing West Branch labor unrest was driving the coal establishment to distraction and gaining national attention, with newspapers up and down the East Coast weighing in on the issue as coal prices climbed.

In New York, higher ferry fares between Manhattan and Brooklyn were blamed on strike-related spikes in the cost of anthracite, though the Union Ferry Company neglected to reduce fares once coal prices fell. Complaining in April that "the high price of coal" had become a bitter joke used to justify "all sort of extortion," the *Times* dispatched a reporter to the anthracite valleys of Pennsylvania to find out what was behind all the labor unrest. The resulting story described the miners' union responsible for the strikes as a well-organized secret society that had appeared about six months before—in other words, right after the draft disturbances.

The union, or "association," had a strike fund and a clear economic policy of using scattered strikes to reduce the amount of coal produced, keeping prices and wages high. The *Times* found that "the strikes among the coal mines are an index of prosperity—of high wages, not of low; of independence, not of want." The reason was simple: When wages were low, the miners couldn't afford to strike.

And in a direct slap at Bannan's contention that the strikes were some kind of Copperhead conspiracy, the *Times* reporter noted that he hadn't heard a word of sympathy for the South. "There may be Copperheads in the mining region," he wrote. "But if so, they are remarkably quiet."

Reports of labor outrages were also overblown, he found, noting that strikes were, for the most part, "not of a lawless or violent character." There was, the article said, one exception to this rule—Heckscherville: "The miners at that place are a lawless set of ruffians, and have long been the terror of their immediate neighbors, and the pest of the whole mining region."

It was an assessment that would not have been disputed by David Muir of the Otto mines in Reilly Township, Elizabeth Bergen of Coal Castle, or Benjamin Bannan. In fact it seems likely that the *Times* reporter had talked to Bannan, for his description of the Heckscherville miners reads like something right out of the *Miners' Journal*: "The 'Molly McGuires,' as the Hoecksherville miners are called, are a lawless whisky-drinking set of outlaws whom even the priest has lost control over, and who, like the rebels of the South, can only be brought to their senses by brute force." Despite some invective about "mercurial Irishmen," the article noted that these whiskey-swilling outlaws were also dutifully pumping the water from the mines (though they had the cheek to send the Heckschers a bill for their labors).

By the end of his visit to the anthracite region, the *Times* reporter had clearly been won over to the miners' point of view: "Those who are disposed to grumble about 'the high price of coal,' should pay one visit to the mines, descend into a few of those dark, damp and dangerous collieries, behold the grim faces of the men who earn their bread in those unhealthy subterranean caverns, and they would emerge with the settled conviction that the men who will pass such a life for the sake of a living, are entitled to all they can get, even though they struck for higher wages every other day in the year."[16]

The *Times* wasn't the only big-city newspaper to sympathize with the miners. The *Boston Pilot*, an Irish American newspaper edited by Patrick Donahue, launched a blistering attack that spring on the "murderous mines, gross dishonesty and absolute selfishness" of the Schuylkill County operators. Citing as a source a friend who had often traveled to Schuylkill County, the Pilot denied that the workers were the "debauched, drunken set of rioters" described by the *Miners' Journal*, which it dismissed as a Know Nothing rag.

"How many mines in Schuylkill County are ventilated with a just regard for human life?" asked Donahue. "Let the fact that over 100 men are burned to death and blown to pieces by 'fire-damp' explosions in those mines answer the question. How many mines in the region are safe in their equipment of ropes, chains, windlasses, propping, slope railroads and engines? If the government mining engineers of Wales had authority over these mines, they would close them all at once, and have the owners sentenced to penal servitude for years."

Donahue also highlighted the inequities of the company store system, pointing out that when miners were burned at work, they had to buy their own balm at company stores with inflated prices. He summed up the miners' situation succinctly: "The mines in which they work are murderous, the payment they get is due bills backed by extortion, and the compassion they get for injuries is a hard bargain." The strikes would continue, he warned, until legislation was passed to make the mines safe and the operators honest.[17]

Bannan, speaking for the coal establishment, offered a far different solution—troops: "As the government is deeply interested in procuring the large quantities of coal she requires, at reasonable rates, we would advise the operators in Cass township, and wherever outrages on property are attempted, to apply for a national force to protect their collieries under the provost marshal of the district—and if necessary, declare martial law."[18]

The *Times* article a few weeks later alluded to this call for federal intervention, even as it dismissed it: "Some of the citizens of Pottsville are in favor of the General Government taking hold of the matter, which they say she has a right to do in view of the interest she has in supplying the market with coal; but it is not likely, as it is certainly not necessary."[19]

Federal intervention may not have been necessary, but that didn't mean it wouldn't happen. The provost marshal of the district, whom Bannan had called on to declare martial law, was Charlemagne Tower, the coal operator and former district attorney. He could be counted on to assure the government the "reasonable rates" that the *Miners' Journal* had demanded. And at the height of the 1863 West Branch strikes, Congress handed him the means to do just that.

11

Mars in Mahantango

You may have Pottsville laid in ashes and a thousand barbarities committed.

—Gen. Darius Couch, 1863

On March 3, 1863, Congress approved an unprecedented expansion of federal power with two laws that were to have dire consequences in the anthracite region. The first was the Habeas Corpus Act, which ratified the Lincoln administration's suspension of the writ the previous summer. It was a necessary precursor to the second measure: the Enlistment Act.

Like the Militia Act of 1862, its predecessor the year before, the Enlistment Act sounded innocent enough. In fact, it authorized a new, federal three-year draft. And like the Militia Act, the fundamentally unfair manner in which it was enforced in the coal region aroused violent opposition. The suspension of habeas corpus left authorities free to deal with that opposition by the harshest means available, including the taking of hostages. The man named by the U.S. provost marshal to enforce the draft in the 10th Congressional District, which included Schuylkill County, was Charlemagne Tower, who was appointed to a similar state post in December 1862.

An attorney, a coal speculator, and a former Schuylkill County district attorney, Tower was a confirmed Republican. As a young man at Harvard, he was a close friend of Charles Sumner, the abolitionist senator from Massachusetts whose 1856 beating at the hands of Rep. Preston Brooks of South Carolina foreshadowed the bloody conflict to come. Tower had already served in the war, as commander of an eighty-man militia unit, the Tower Guard, which served for three months and had seen action at Williamsport, Maryland.[1]

Tower came to the post determined to suppress any repetition of the 1862 draft troubles, when women had thrown hot water at the enrollers. "Nothing but a sufficient military force, vigorously directed to crush opposition, will prevent the re-enacting of last year's scenes and riots," he wrote Secretary of War Stanton in May. "I propose, if women or anybody else interfere, to arrest them at once and dispose of them . . . If the opposers become too numerous and threatening for me to arrest them, I shall propose to have martial law declared in this county and the general commanding this department come in with sufficient military force to put down the turbulent."[2]

Tower wanted to use federal conscription in 1863 to finish the work Bannan had started the year before, but his plan to treat those who had evaded the militia draft as deserters ran into opposition from the War Department. Thwarted in his plan to specifically target the 1862 draft evaders, Tower switched his focus to immigrants. Citing the high number of foreigners in the region, Tower, like Bannan, stressed the need for a large draft.[3] And like Bannan, Tower was deeply suspicious not only of "turbulent miners" in the West Branch, but also of their political leaders in Pottsville.

When the Schuylkill County commissioners ordered the captains of two volunteer companies in Pottsville to return two hundred muskets, Tower wrote to Gov. Curtin that two of the three commissioners and the county sheriff were opposed to the war. "We are left to surmise what connection there may be between this recall of the muskets and a preparation to resist the enrollment and the draft," he wrote.[4]

Tower's fears were fed by reports from those helping him with the draft enrollment. W. K. Jones reported from Tamaqua on June 14 that Irish miners in the village of Newkirk had opened fire when he tried to help J. F. Werner enroll the men there. "The Irish are so leagued as to make it necessary to coerce them," he wrote. In case Tower wanted to make an example of those who resisted, Jones provided him with four names, including that of Columbus McGee.[5] McGee was subsequently drafted—his name appears on an 1865 list of "deserting drafted men" in the 10th District. He was identified as a Molly Maguire years later at trials implicating him in the 1862 Audenried stoning death of the mine boss Frank Langdon.

Based on reports like Jones's, Tower warned Col. James D. Bomford, the assistant acting provost marshal for Pennsylvania, that opponents of the draft were organized and armed, and meeting twice a week. "I see no method of making these enrollments except to march through the subdistricts with a military force," he wrote. Tower already had fifty troops, but he asked Bomford for at least two hundred more, along with two pieces of artillery.[6]

The new commissioner's zeal was such that his superior, the provost marshal general, felt the need to warn him against going too far. "Vigorous measures are what I urge on you, and for that purpose I have sent you a military force that seems adequate for all the wants that have yet shown themselves," Col. James B. Fry wrote. "I want you to use it vigorously, but use it to put down opposition, and not create it, and to be sure that all against whom you adopt vigorous measures are clearly in the wrong."[7]

Fry's fears about Tower's methods were well-justified, for the means by which Tower conducted and enforced the draft ensured he did indeed create opposition to it—several of his deputies had already landed in legal trouble for their high-handed tactics with draft evaders real and imagined.[8] Undeterred, Tower decided to simply use payrolls from the mines as a way to get the names he needed—a method he knew would result in flawed lists.

Tower outlined the plan in a June 13 letter that sought the assistance of a Tamaqua man in the enrollment for two wards there: "*Quietly* get from every coal operator and other large employer in the two wards the names of all the men who work for them, their age, color, birth place, and whether married or not, and former military service, as well as present residency, and hand the lists to you or me . . . Of course, the lists are to be made as nearly as can be right."[9]

Conspicuously absent from Tower's criteria was one crucial consideration— citizenship. Canvassing might have been out of the question in light of the disturbances the year before, but in relying chiefly on mine payrolls, Tower included many immigrants who had not yet been naturalized, and were thus exempt from military service. By making mine officials his assistants in enforcing the draft, he also risked exacerbating the already tense relations between employers and their employees, a danger he fully recognized. "The coal operators . . . would in most cases aid us by giving lists of their men, but if they do this voluntarily, they are in danger of having their breakers burned and machinery destroyed and being themselves killed," Tower wrote. "If we appear at their office doors with force and demand the lists, they will give them, and furnish additional information to use, such as we need; and those who intend to resist will be overawed."[10]

But Tower did not consider the fifty-seven soldiers already posted to Pottsville sufficient for the job. He wanted at least another one hundred men. Any doubt that the collieries linked to Heckscher's Forest Improvement Company would voluntarily cooperate with the enrollment were laid to rest following a meeting with several company officials who lived in Cass Township. "I have just been assured, this evening, that I shall need to march armed men into at least four sub-districts in Schuylkill County in order to complete the enrollments there," he wrote.[11]

The reinforcements Tower wanted arrived on July 3, the day the Battle of Gettysburg ended in a decisive Union victory. Two companies of the Invalid Guard, a unit of wounded veterans unfit for frontline duty, augmented by eighty soldiers from Philadelphia, brought Tower's total troop strength in Pottsville to nearly three hundred.[12]

The reinforcements were welcome, for events in July only heightened the coal establishment's siege mentality. The invasion of Pennsylvania by Lee's Army of Northern Virginia in late June spurred the *Miners' Journal* to warn that the Confederates intended to seize Harrisburg, then lay waste to the collieries of the anthracite region.[13]

And the bloody draft riots that erupted in New York City that July led Tower to worry that a Fifth Column based in the West Branch region would march on Pottsville. Miners stomping out of the townships to ravish the county seat had been a fear dating back to 1842. Tower asked Abraham Ernst, the superintendent of the Phoenix Colliery in Branch Township, to warn of any marches on Pottsville from the hostiles of his neighborhood.

The New York riots had an even more immediate impact, for the government transferred nearly half the troops in Schuylkill County to Philadelphia, fearing a similar outbreak there. Tower complained to Fry on July 18 that he was losing 137 soldiers: "I have here now only the two companies of the Invalid Corps in charge of Maj. Dayton. I think it is my duty to say this force is far from adequate. The miners at several collieries in Schuylkill county have already stopped work and are drilling everyday, preparatory to resistance or some hostile movement. They are within four to eight miles from this town [Pottsville], and I have been told, by men whom I can believe, of threats . . . that they will march in and burn up the town."

He added that Supt. Wilder of the Mine Hill and Schuylkill Haven Railroad Company, who helped mediate the May 1862 strike, had assured him "that there is a complete organization, embracing Schuylkill, Luzerne and Carbon counties" of ten thousand well-armed men who were prepared to assemble with twelve hours notice to resist the draft. Tower asked for "at least 2,000 men and two batteries of mountain howitzers" and said he wanted preparations made to declare martial law.[14] In response, Bomford ordered Tower to go slow and to avoid any trouble until the draft was completed in Philadelphia and reinforcements could be sent.[15]

Tower's concerns were passed up the line, duly embroidered. Gen. William D. Whipple in Philadelphia reported to Fry on July 23 that in Cass Township alone, up to three thousand armed men were being drilled nightly by discharged militiamen, and that the rebels had two artillery pieces and were threatening to burn the homes and coal breakers of Republicans.[16]

Veterans were returning home, but the real problem was far different from the one Whipple outlined. The militiamen called up for service in 1862 were due to be mustered out, and Gen. Darius Couch, commander of the U.S. Army's Department of the Susquehanna, feared the impact of their loss on the coal fields. Infected with Tower's paranoia, Couch wrote Gov. Curtin a furious note about his decision not to extend the militia's term of service: "Order off these, you may have Pottsville laid in ashes and a thousand barbarities committed."[17]

Soon, a curious newspaper story emerged that pegged the number of organized draft resisters around Pottsville at well above the ten thousand previously reported. The *Guardian* of Paterson, New Jersey, reported that a "United States officer of high rank" had perambulated the area disguised as a Catholic priest. By hearing confessions he had supposedly determined the insurgents' true strength: fifteen thousand Mollies organized into companies and battalions, drilled by old soldiers and armed with seven hundred Springfield rifles. The name of this intrepid officer was not divulged, but the article did say he made a "tolerably accurate" enrollment by seizing the payrolls of the collieries. Tower had done exactly that, shortly before the article appeared.[18]

While Couch and the press waxed hysterical on the supposed strength of the forces arrayed against conscription, Tower proved just how unfounded those fears were by preparing a military operation in the West Branch with the troops he had. He had been "astonished with his success" in carrying through the enrollment elsewhere in the county in July, but he wasn't about to take any chances in the militant Irish strongholds of Cass and Reilly Townships. He moved into Heckscherville and Thomaston on August 10 with eight companies of infantry and sixty cavalrymen under Gen. Whipple. The results, after a year of warnings about organized resistance there, were more anticlimactic than apocalyptic. "A large body of men was present at the beginning and they were cross and very saucy even in the presence of the military, but they were too much afraid to use violence," Tower reported. "The enrolling officer succeeded in enrolling two hundred names at the two collieries of Heckscherville and Thomaston. The crowd dispersed after a while, so that he could not get all the names, some of the dwelling houses were shut up entirely, and the women in them would not answer any questions at all."

But Cass hadn't gone entirely quiescent. At dusk that evening, a sergeant of the 45th Pa. Militia made the mistake of riding alone near

Coal Castle, where men in Union blue had to watch their step. He was promptly jumped by four or five men and robbed of his revolver, sword, and money.[19]

Forestville was the troops' next target. After running into the same problems they faced in Heckscherville, the soldiers simply detained the clerks of four collieries and brought them to Pottsville, along with the pay-books for the mines. That accomplished, their commanding officer decided to wrap up a loose end: "On the way home, in the neighborhood where the quartermaster sergeant was knocked from his horse and robbed, the military, by order of Genl. Whipple, arrested and brought in seven men to be held until the guilty parties and the sword, revolver and money taken . . . are brought forth, and as hostages for the good behavior of the vicinage, hereafter. These men were yesterday sent down by Genl. Whipple and lodged in Fort Mifflin."[20]

The seizure of hostages was common enough on both sides in the war, but Whipple's action, if not strictly illegal, was certainly a new departure. Most hostages taken by the Union Army came from the South or border states with Southern sympathies—and they were supposed to be held "as a pledge for the fulfillment of an agreement concluded between belligerents," according to the U.S. War Department's General Order No. 100, which was published in April 1863, just months before.

The seven Cass hostages were Northern civilians, seized purely as a retaliatory measure, and they had no recourse to civil proceedings, for Congress had suspended habeas corpus.[21] Thus they were confined to the dank recesses of Fort Mifflin, a notorious Philadelphia prisoner of war camp, in the marshes where the Schuylkill flows into the Delaware.

The case outraged Democrats. One Harrisburg newspaper thundered that it trampled on "the dearest and most important guaranties of the liberties of the citizen," pointed out all of the detainees should be presumed innocent, and reminded readers that five of the men were fathers. It's unclear when the seven—James Walsh, Arthur O'Neal,* Matthew Mealy, John M. Brennan, Arthur Hunt, John Ball, and John Brennan—were released, or if the stolen items were ever returned. What was clear, the newspaper said, was that the "illegal and false imprisonment" of the men risked turning rebel sympathizers into outright rebels.[22]

---

* Twenty years earlier, an Arthur O'Neal had been implicated in a Heckscherville shooting that wounded a man named either John Berger or John Bergen, as detailed in Chapter 1.

Whatever its long-term effects, in the short term the government's use of overwhelming military force and the suspension of civil law ensured not just completion of the draft enrollment, but a more compliant and productive work force in the mines. Just to be sure that his superiors didn't miss the connection, Tower wrote on August 20 that the presence of the military had "soothed the rebellious greatly and not only prevented their making any hostile demonstrations, but even moved them to do more work, and more quietly."

"The rebellious" had been so soothed, in fact, that on August 22, a delegation from Reilly Township met with Tower and Joseph Heisler, his deputy in the West Branch, to correct the enrollment for their township. The provost marshal's use of mine payrolls had left plenty of room for error.

The completion of the enrollment allowed the army to finally remove some of the state militia, now that it was clear that Pottsville would not be "laid in ashes." In fact, when the 47th Pa. Militia Regiment, which had been dragooning the West Branch, was pulled out of Minersville on August 22, the only eruption reported was one of "great rejoicing and drinking" in Cass Township.[23]

The ten thousand well-armed men supposedly organized to oppose the draft in the anthracite region were nowhere to be seen. It may be that Tower's fears were, quite literally, fantastical, and that those parading around posed no more of a military threat than did the mummers of the "Santa Anna guard" who marched in Pottsville in 1855. Indeed, the exaggerated reports of ten thousand wild Irish coal miners wreaking havoc in Schuylkill County would, by war's end, become fodder for outright mockery.

With the enrollment completed, the actual drafting of names took place with no trouble. Tower reported that it had been completed on September 23, "attended by good order throughout."[24] What protests there were against Tower's conduct of the draft came through official channels. Meyer Strouse, the Democratic congressman for Schuylkill County, wrote to President Lincoln on September 19 to complain of "gross errors in the enrollment of a number of the districts in the coal region, which if not rectified, may lead to great and serious dissatisfaction."

He pointed out that in the Democratic West Branch townships, the number of men enrolled for the draft invariably exceeded the number of voters in the 1862 election, while in Republican Pottsville, the number of men enrolled for the draft was actually less than the number who had voted the year before. In Cass, 828 men were enrolled, while only 640 had voted; in Reilly Township, the ratio was 532 to 278; but in Pottsville, only 1,022 men were enrolled while 1,475 had voted.

Tower dismissed Strouse's objections in a letter that reveals much about his conduct of the draft: "His statement as to the apparent inconsistencies and inequalities in the enrollment may or may not be true—It is certainly not worthwhile." Tower felt he was justified, for political and economic reasons, in drafting those specifically exempt from conscription:

> After the breaking out of the rebellion, the coal business revived and many more than the usual number of miners were required. This brought a rush of aliens from foreign lands. The mining districts, where not one man in 20 can read and or write, are the "Democratic districts" as Strouse calls them. These men, in those districts, were instructed by their Democratic leaders, in county meetings, and other places, not to go to the war, but to stay at home, go to the election and vote "and put down this infernal abolition government—this infernal abolition administration." In making the enroll-ment, of course, as many of these newly arrived aliens as could be got hold of were enrolled, although not entitled to vote until they were here for five years.[25]

If they were not entitled to vote, they were not subject to conscription, but Tower insisted on drafting "as many ... as could be got hold of" for purely political reasons. Bannan had drafted Democrats in Cass Township. Now Tower was drafting potential Democrats—Irish miners who not yet been naturalized, and thus remained British subjects.

His disregard for the question of citizenship drew protest from the British consul in Philadelphia, who complained that it was all but impos-sible for Her Majesty's subjects to claim exemption from the draft, "espe-cially in the mining and manufacturing districts": "The universal statement of all applicants to this Office for Consular Certificates is that the Provost Marshal of their districts throw every possible difficulty in the way of making good their claim as aliens."

In response, Tower made clear just what was meant by "every possible difficulty." The provost marshal told Gilbert, the assistant acting provost marshal for the Eastern District of Pennsylvania, that he required all those seeking alien exemption to file an affidavit. It had to be signed by two "reputable citizens" and state that the individual was an alien, and of what government he claimed to be a subject; when he had arrived in the United States, and where he had resided; that he had never declared an intention to become a U.S. citizen, and had never voted. But even that wasn't enough for Tower: he also insisted on a personal interrogation of both the applicant and the "reputable citizens" who had signed the petition. Last, but by no means least, he insisted on proof from a court that the individual had never taken out citizenship papers: "After ascertaining in this way all the applicants' places of residence during the period he has been in this country, I then require him also to procure and file with me certificates from the several courts within whose jurisdictions he had resided, that he had not while there taken out his final papers or declared his intention to become a citizen. In the case of men whose father might have naturalized him by becoming a citizen when he was underage, I require similar certificates, in regard to the father, also."

Given the frequency with which many immigrants moved, this last requirement made it all but impossible to obtain an exemption. And as to the consular certificates that proved a holder was a foreign national, Tower recommended that they be ignored completely, because they were based on mere affidavits.[26]

The result was predictable—his enrollment list was riddled with mistakes, as Tower freely admitted. But he didn't consider it a problem. "There are some errors in them, no doubt, and a good many aliens embraced, particularly in Schuylkill County," he wrote. "To amend the lists by scanning the claims of alienage would require, if thoroughly done, at least three months. I would submit that a better way is, to make the draft and exempt the aliens and others in this district as we are now exempting them at the daily hearings."

Despite his web of red tape, a few aliens, it seems, were still eluding the dragnet of the draft by proving they were aliens. And though a few slipped through the seine, Tower had a plan to ensure the net effect would be the same. "Order a little larger ration [of the draft], from this district, on that account ESPECIALLY FROM SCHUYLKILL COUNTY; then about the same result will be obtained as if the lists were previously corrected," he wrote in early December. Like Bannan, Tower placed the burden of conscription firmly on the shoulders on the mining regions where Democrats held sway.

That doubtless contributed to the opposition that finally erupted in several mining townships when it came time to serve the draft notices. Tower reported on October 19 that officers serving draft notices in Blythe Township northeast of Pottsville had been driven off by a mob. He wanted seventy-five cavalrymen to deal with the problem.[27]

On October 26 there was trouble in Blythe and Schuylkill Townships. Disturbances were also reported in the West Branch, where "it has been found impossible to serve the notices on the drafted men in

Reilly Township," Tower reported.[28] The ongoing trouble was a far cry from the sort of insurrection that Gen. Couch had feared would "lay Pottsville in ashes." Mostly what it involved was dragging unwilling men from their homes in a draft from which many should have been exempt.

Even half a century after the war, the dragooning of Schuylkill County was still fresh in the minds of those who lived through it as children. "I can vividly recall when the Government called for men to join the Union Army," wrote Philip Francis, who was a boy in the East Delaware patch just north of Pottsville during the war. "Some men would hide from the Government officers sent to bring them. I have seen them run through the fields and woods with officers after them. There was no let up until they were caught; then they must go to the front."[29]

In the face of overwhelming military force, there was little that residents of the West Branch could do in 1863 but bide their time. The dispatch of troops to trouble spots may have kept the lid on antidraft disturbances, but it had by no means ended labor unrest in the West Branch. That quickly became evident to Henry Hawthorne Dunne, an Irish Protestant from Waterford who on October 1 took over a Heckscherville colliery linked to the Forest Improvement Company. When Dunne tried to dock the wages of some miners for sending out dirt instead of coal, he was confronted by committeemen who threatened to run him off the place. Dunne had to yield "to prevent destruction of his property." A short time later, the committee forced him to rehire two mule drivers who had been fired for bad conduct.[30]

It was not long before Dunne, Tower, the Heckschers, and the rest of the coal establishment concluded that the troops sent to the anthracite region to enforce the draft could perform an even more important task—the destruction of those troublesome labor committees. The job had already begun in neighboring Carbon County.

12

Ulster's exiles it would grieve
If their beardless boy should fall.
                    —The Cattle Raid of Cooley

In 1863, portions of Carbon County proved even more troublesome to the Republican coal establishment than did Cass Township. For it was in Carbon County that the Molly Maguires made a crucial segue—from draft resistance to attacks on mine bosses. And it was there that the War Department and coal operators first concocted a plot of their own—to smash the mine unions and lower the price of coal for government contracts. When it came to conspiracy, the military–industrial complex made the Mollies look like pikers.

The center of resistance in Carbon County was Banks Township, a mining region along the Luzerne County line dominated by immigrants from Ulster, especially County Donegal.[1] There had been little real trouble in the county during the militia draft of 1862—four women were arrested after a crowd of twenty-five stoned enrolling officers in Mauch Chunk in September of that year.[2] For unlike in Cass Township and Archbald—an Irish mining village north of Scranton where the military had fired into a stone-throwing crowd, killing one and wounding others—the antidraft emphasis in Carbon County in 1862 seems to have been on political action.

In the fall of that year, up to seven hundred men gathered for an antidraft meeting between Jeansville and Hazleton, just over the Luzerne County line. The meeting was presided over by Peter Dillon, a respected Irish labor leader from Banks Township. Dillon was no friend of the Confederacy—he had volunteered in September to help raise a regiment for the Union Army—but he was unalterably opposed to the militia draft, as he made clear at the meeting. "The substance of what he said was, that the draft should be resisted," a miner later recalled. "He said that he was a drafted man himself, and as long as there was one left, we should stand loyal to one another."[3]

One of the leading concerns voiced by the miners was support for their families. "They agreed that if they did not get the pay for their families to which they were entitled, they would oppose the draft—those drafted men who wanted to go, might go, but those who wished to stay back they would help and secure them," one miner later testified.[4] The last sentence echoes almost precisely the cries of those Cass Township draft resisters who stopped the train filled with conscripted men in Tremont.

The gathering included miners of several nationalities, but this was no ordinary American political meeting. Most of the leaders were Irish, and some of the non-Irish miners were there only because they feared their absence would invite retaliation. The gathering took place in the woods, away from any homes, and guards were stationed on a nearby road.

One "captain" was appointed from each patch—Dillon among them— and each in turn selected a deputy, in much the same way the Cass miners had appointed committeemen for their labor organization. The duties of the captains were "to march along beside the men and keep them in line," a miner later testified.[5] And march they did, in Ribbon array, as soon as the meeting ended. With an American flag at their head, they lined up in two ranks and paraded to Hazleton. This was politics, but it was the politics of Irish Ribbonism, with all the tension and contradictions inherent when a secret society ventures into the public arena with mass meetings.

Some of these Irish miners may have participated in the Cass Township disturbances in October of '62—there were numerous reports that the draft resisters there came from as far away as Luzerne County. But the next real action in Carbon County didn't come until the following year. The announcement of a federal draft in March 1863 hardened opposition to conscription, and by early summer, there was talk of violent resistance.

Charles Scrimshaw, a deputy provost marshal from the mining village of Bear Meadow, described a barroom conversation during that period with three Irish miners—Frank Cull, Charles Gallagher, and James Rodgers. "If we have to do any fighting at all, we will do it at home," Cull told him. Scrimshaw was informed that those Irish miners who had volunteered for the Union Army were no longer considered Irish by their compatriots.[6] And newspapers reported that "mob orators" from Banks Township were telling deluded miners that "they must not submit to the Lincoln tyranny, that the object is to draft every Democrat, that they must stand in the doors and resist every officer connected with the draft who comes near them."[7]

Another mass meeting against conscription, held in June as work on the draft began throughout Carbon County, offers a glimpse at the rhetoric and dynamics of the movement there. Peter Dillon, the leader of the anti-draft meeting the previous fall, attended only briefly, in the company of Rev. John Laughlin, a Catholic priest who favored compliance with the draft. Dillon did not address the crowd; there were plenty of others willing to speak in his place.

George Heycock, a Jeansville miner who attended, described the scene: "Ed Winter rose to make a speech. He said, "You are aware that we came here for the purpose of resisting the draft. We will protect the Constitution as it is and the Union as it was. They think they can compel us, and draft us, and make us go and fight against the Southerners, but if we stick together as a unit, they cannot do it, for the Southerners are fighting for their rights."

Then Patrick Tunney rose to speak, specifically calling to mind Irish resistance to English rule in the 1790s: "The Irishmen never were cowards—see what they did at Bull Run, and at the time of the Rebellion in Ireland—we will not fight for Lincoln's proclamation." The meeting considered how best to deal with those did not join the antidraft movement. A group of about three men conferred quietly, and decided to appoint committees to collect the names of men who would resist the draft. "They decided that if anyone should refuse to give his name to the committees, he should be obliged to clear out in 24 hours," recalled Heycock. Intervention by Dillon's clerical companion put a quick end to the meeting. When Fr. Laughlin walked through the crowd, pretending to jot down names in a small notebook, the crowd scattered.[8]

In calling for "the Constitution as it is, and the Union as it was," the antidraft speakers were merely repeating a Democratic Party campaign slogan.[9] But clearing the region of those who would not cooperate in draft resistance was a tactic with deep roots in the Defender tradition—and one employed the previous fall in Cass Township. As the draft widened the region's political divide, the Irish reflexively moved to enforce communal solidarity.

Those in charge of the draft were already noticing the effects. As early as June 10, E. H. Rauch, the deputy provost marshal in charge of Carbon County, was reporting threats of violence in Banks Township and at the Old Mines near Summit Hill. He requested muskets and ammunition to deal with the problem.[10] Nine days later, Rauch wrote to the provost marshal for the 11th congressional district, Samuel Yohe, that he had been unable to find an enrolling officer for Banks Township, despite three attempts, because his choices for the job feared it would "seriously endanger their lives." Those difficulties led him to suggest the same problematic course that Tower had adopted in Schuylkill County, the use of mine payrolls: "Perhaps the work can be done quite accurately by first getting from the books of [coal] operators the names of men, their estimated ages, nativity."[11]

By mid-July, Rauch could report that the Banks enrollment lists would soon be nearly complete, but, expecting trouble in the actual execution of the draft, he recommended the formation of a sort of Home Guard: "The general public opinion here is strongly in favor of a substantial military organization—of citizen volunteers. The program is to organize a company for local service and all I want to know is whether we can get muskets." The idea was shelved because Pat Sharkey, the brigade inspector for the state militia, was "the most violent Copperhead in the county," Yohe reported. The provost marshal still wanted a full company of Invalid Guard to help serve draft notices.[12] When at last L. Richards, the enrolling officer for Banks, had completed a list, it was a "very imperfect one," Rauch later testified, made possible only through the cooperation of pro-government coal operators such as George K. Smith of Yorktown.[13]

That sort of cooperation, coupled with Yohe's calls for a Home Guard, led to a sharp escalation in tension between Republican draft supporters and the county's Irish and German Democrats as conscription drew closer in the late summer and fall of 1863. On August 27, a crowd of between fifty and one hundred stomped out of Banks Township and broke open the county jail in Mauch Chunk to free an Irish deserter, Patrick Cull.

John D. Davis and Benjamin Presser of Yorktown, Welsh miners and Lincoln supporters who had failed to clear out after the June antidraft meeting, were badly beaten as they walked together that fall. "They broke my skull in three places," said Davis, who did not recover for two months. "I do not know why they beat me unless it was because I did not attend the last meeting." Presser was less fortunate. Two weeks after the beating, he died.

The attacks, as in Cass Township, were not confined to Welshmen and Protestants. A group of men broke into the home of Patrick Shannon, a mine laborer from Frenchtown, between 9:00 and 10:00 P.M. on October 10, 1863. "I was badly beaten so that I was not expected to recover," Shannon said. "I was obliged to leave the place." In the melee, a pistol shot grazed his wife's head. Shannon later identified his assailants as Peter Daly, John Donahoe, John Campbell, John Donahoe, Edward Burn, John Flyn, and Peter Dillon, who "captained" the antidraft meeting the year before.

At least three others were attacked that same night—Bill Davis, a Mrs. Billingsley, and William Heycock, a shoemaker from Jeansville. Heycock offers an entirely different glimpse of Dillon. The labor leader and anti-draft activist was not one of the men who attacked him, for Heycock testi-fied that Dillon came to his house after he was beaten and helped dress a four- or five-inch cut on his head, then stayed with him the rest of the night. "I believe it was daylight when he left," Heycock later said.

Amid the mounting violence, the idea of a Home Guard was revived, this time by George K. Smith, the Yorktown coal operator. Smith was orga-nizing a volunteer company and had secured one hundred muskets and a thousand rounds of ammunition, which were stored in Mauch Chunk, Rauch recalled.[14]

And the coal operator was helping the government in other ways. When it proved impossible to deliver draft notices in Banks Township, George Ulrich, a clerk in Smith's company store, devised a stratagem. "The man that brought [the draft notices] there wanted me to take them and serve them to the men and I said, 'no,' but he might lay them on the counter and when the men came in I would tell them to look through them and see if there was anything that belonged to them."[15] The idea did not work too well. On October 22, the day the township's 139 conscripts were to report for duty, a grand total of three showed up. That same day, Yohe reported that he would need one hundred troops to serve draft notices in Banks.[16]

With the entry of armed troops, events soon spiraled out of control. The trouble began October 29, when a military force was sent out to serve draft notices, beginning at Bear Meadow, where Rauch reported great dif-ficulty in obtaining the names of individuals: "Children from 12 to 14 years of age denied any knowledge of the names of their parents, and wives denied knowing the names of their husbands."

Attempts to move on to Jeansville, just down the road, were frustrated by the vigilance of the draft resisters, who posted guards to warn of troop movements, as their Cass Township counterparts had done the year be-fore. "The route between Janesville [sic] and Bear Meadows was well pick-eted by these people, and signal guns were fired on the approach of the military," Rauch said.

Warned that a large group of draft resisters had gathered in Jeansville, Rauch sent for reinforcements—150 troops from the 10th New Jersey

Infantry in nearby Hazleton—and resolved to move into Jeansville the next morning. Rauch said that when the Invalid Guard unit entered on October 30, it found the town filled with idlers loafing on the streets in groups of between ten and fifty. "These were all dispersed by the cavalry, and not allowed to appear in the streets," he said.[17]

A newspaper account offers a somewhat different take, suggesting that it was the presence of the troops that brought residents out of their homes. The soldiers found Jeansville "perfectly quiet" on Friday, the *New York Times* reported. "But in the course of half an hour, the streets began to fill, and the mob to cluster along the sidewalks." Capt. Yates, the commanding officer, ordered the cavalry to clear the street, determined to nip in the bud what he saw as an incipient New York–style draft riot. In course of this five-minute operation, "one Buckshot was badly sabred," the *Times* reported. "He is at this time passing the last moments of his rebellious life."[18]

A fuller picture of what transpired on the streets of Jeansville emerges from an indignant letter sent to President Lincoln by E. Greenlough Scott, a young Pottsville lawyer who traveling through town that day with William Audenried, the West Branch mine boss, who verified his account. Scott painted so vivid a picture of a town terrorized by a drunken soldiery that the letter is worth quoting at length:

As we entered Jeansville, we saw, in the middle of the street, a detachment of Invalid soldiers at rest—arms stacked. A squad of cavalry was at the other end of the street, a few individual cavalrymen remaining with the infantry. Not a full grown citizen was in sight, and, but for the pale and terrified faces of the women who were bold enough to look from their window, one might well have thought the place untenanted. As we dismounted at the tavern, before which the troops rested, we saw through the window a number of people—citizens.

Astonished at this state of affairs, I addressed the officer—"Well, lieutenant, is there any difficulty here?"

"No sir, none."

"Are you stationed here then?"

"No sir, we are stationed at Hazleton. We have come here to serve notices."

"Is there any truth in what we heard—that a rebel flag was raised here?"

"Not that I know of—there's copper enough to do it. This is a damned hard hole."

"Why, how is it that the place is deserted?"

"Because we won't let them come out. When we first got here, we ordered every one of them in. Do you see those fellows in the barroom? They can't come out—we slashed four or five of them this morning."

"Slashed! What's that?"

"Why, we cut them with sabers, or the cavalry fellows did."

"Did they resist? Was there any difficulty at all?"

"No, but there might have been—you can't trust these fellows."

... After a few more remarks, without expressing an opinion of those who took such counsel of their fears, we went toward the buggy to resume our journey, when the scene to which I particularly desire to call your attention occurred.

As we were starting, my attention was suddenly directed to a cavalryman who, from where the commander of the detachment and one or two officers were standing, spurred rapidly towards a boy, who I had not observed, with the evident intention of running or cutting him down. The boy, who could not have been over 15 or 16 years of age, was standing before a house not three or four rods off and was to all appearances there from curiosity. In fact, so intent was he on staring at the unwonted spectacle of a soldier-company, that he did not perceive the soldier till the horse nearly upon him. He then turned to fly. The soldier cut at him with his drawn saber. The officers set up a shout of laughter, which of course, was chimed in with by the men.

"Run in the house," cried a few voices.

The boy made for the door, but the soldier was too close. He turned and ran toward the rear of the house. I wish you to observe, that the boy clearly evinced a disposition to comply with the advice or order, whichever it was. But, it seems, he had not done enough, for amid the laughter and hurrahs of the officer and men, the soldier pursued him into the yard, cutting at him until the boy got into the house. Whether the boy was cut or not, I do not know, but I trust he escaped through the awkwardness of the soldier, which was as great as the malignity of the officer.

As a man, I was outraged, and, as one who had once been a soldier, grieved to see conduct which the spirit of true discipline would regard with abhorrence, and soldierly honor hold in contempt.

Let it be granted that the place was as represented; that it was necessary to confine the men temporarily to dwellings, and to summarily punish the refractory. There nonetheless remains the fact that under the eyes of an officer of the United States Army, an armed man spurred on an unarmed boy and endeavored to cut him down. . . . But what could you expect from a commanding officer who, as I saw him an hour afterward, invites enlisted men to drink liquor at a public bar? . . .

Let us ask ourselves two questions:

Can we decently express surprise now if we hear that these poor people, whose condition is despair and whose leaders are their passions, with such an example before them commit acts of violence?

How will these ignorant people regard the government—as a beneficent friend, or a deadly enemy?[19]

They were trenchant questions, but they would go unanswered.

The troops searched several house for weapons and confiscated about two dozen guns, then departed. When military authorities were questioned about the unit's conduct, they disavowed all responsibility: "In regard to the outrages committed by the soldiers of the 10th New Jersey, the reports state clearly that the officers and soldiers did not act on their own responsibility, but as an auxiliary force of the provost marshal of the district, on his requisition and by his orders."[20]

The Irish of Jeansville were left to pick up the pieces in houses raided for arms, with memories of a boy chased through his yard by a saber-wielding trooper, of civilians cut down in the streets, of soldiers laughing and drinking while residents cowered behind their curtains. Some would continue to pursue a political solution—another antidraft meeting was held November 3 in front of the Treskow Hotel, where Allen Craig, of the Carbon County Democratic Committee, argued that the draft was unconstitutional "because it was a political subject."[21]

But others in Banks Township had had enough of politics—the season of vengeance was nigh. Halloween, the traditional opening of Whiteboy and strawboy activity, fell just one day after the raid on Jeansville. As attorney Scott penned his outrage to Lincoln, some Carbon County Irishmen were contemplating an outrage of another sort.

Their intended victim, the coal operator Smith, was aware of the danger, but he persisted. When Rauch and the troops returned to Yorktown on November 4 to again try to serve draft notices, Smith gave them a map that showed where the drafted men lived. "We used this map to good advantage," Rauch later recalled, "but did not inform as to where we obtained it."[22]

There was little enough need for that. While the troops were serving draft notices, they stopped at Smith's company store and were served food and refreshments by the clerk, Ulrich. And as the troops ate, Smith, the provost marshal and the captain of the company, went upstairs to talk.[23]

The coal operator had good reason to cooperate with the military—a few days before, he and other leading mine officials in the township had been warned by a committee to halt operations until the government suspended the draft. With coal production and the draft reduced to a zero-sum game, Smith, a staunch supporter of the government, had little choice but to gamble on a military solution to his problem.

It was a bad bet.

As the troops prepared to leave Yorktown on November 4, Rauch recalled, Smith's wife "strongly appealed to me to have the soldiers retained there, predicting that they would all be murdered as soon as the soldiers left." Rauch ignored the plea, though the mood was ugly. Ulrich recalled an incident the next day. "Owen Gallagher was in our store, and one of our clerks, Thomas Horn, said something to him about the draft. Gallagher said, 'Oh, to hell with your draft. There will be war at your own firesides before tomorrow.'"[24]

A few nights earlier, there had been a gathering in a swamp between Hazleton and Frenchtown. It was the sort of nocturnal meeting that had been held in Ireland for generations, on the side of windswept hills, in the back rooms of pubs. It was presided over by a "captain," alleged to be James McDonnell. The proceedings were secret. The agenda was murder.

Fifteen years later, a witness would tell a Carbon County court that those in attendance were all members of the organization that came to be known as the Ancient Order of Hibernians. "It had three names . . . it was called the Molly Maguires and the Buckshots," testified Charles Mulhearn, a convicted member serving time for murder in the Schuylkill County prison. "They were everyone Mollies or Buckshots. It was Molly Maguires or Buckshots they were at that time." Smith was their target, because "he was after the drafted men," Mulhearn testified. McDonnell told him the organization was "protecting" the draftees.

And so, on November 5, as men warned of "murder on your own doorstep by tomorrow," Smith and his wife traveled to Mauch Chunk. He returned home suffering from a severe headache, and retired to his room. A fearful Mrs. Smith asked the store clerk, Ulrich, to stand watch in the house, armed with a pistol. When two men arrived later in the evening, purportedly with an urgent message for Smith, Ulrich and Mrs. Smith grew suspicious. One of the strangers drew a revolver and fired a shot. As Ulrich struggled with the two, a mob of about twenty-five broke into the house. They were "fixed up with big coats and their faces were blackened and false whiskers," a witness recalled. Another described the mob as "disguised and blackened, and with disguising clothes." The witnesses could have been describing a New Year's fantastical parade, a Halloween strawboy procession, or a team of Whiteboy assassins. In a sense, they were describing all three.

Smith came downstairs to investigate the disturbance, and Ulrich and one of the intruders, Long John Donahue, were wounded in the ensuing melee. After the mob fled with Donahue in tow, Mrs. Smith's sister found the coal operator shot in the head, lying in his nightshirt in a dining room thick with gun smoke and blood.[25] He was the first mine official assassinated by the Molly Maguires. He would not be the last.

The day after the killing, a "reliable union man" from Audenried, which straddled the Carbon–Schuylkill County line at Banks Township, described the situation there in a letter to Charlemagne Tower: "The reign of terror is now commenced in earnest up here—yesterday a party of men came from Hazleton and notified us to stop work immediately, otherwise the breakers would be 'pulled or burned down.' They said 'the war has gone on long enough and they were determined to put a stop to it.'" In another letter on November 7, the same correspondent reported that six English and Welsh miners had fled Honey Brook and Audenried the day before, "and more are going away today."

In a November 7 report to military authorities, Tower passed along those tidbits and reported a conversation in Pottsville about the murder of Smith: "This is only the beginning of what we shall see here," he recorded the brother-in-law of Francis Hughes as saying. "There will be a complete revolution through this country before we are through."[26]

Tower could not have been happy to learn that several suspects in Smith's murder had been freed from the Mauch Chunk jail by a mob of Banks Irishmen, and that just four days after the killing, the Pennsylvania Supreme Court had ruled that the federal draft was unconstitutional. (The court later reversed itself.)[27]

Tower termed the murder of Smith a rebellion, and recommended that "the United States flag should be raised at once on the house of Smith, and a sufficient force be quartered there, to keep it flying and overawe all the rebels."[28] In fact, the federal government and the coal establishment were soon considering measures far more extensive than the mere raising of a flag. Within days of the Smith killing, a plan was forwarded to President Lincoln to break the back of draft resistance and smash the embryonic miners' unions through the use of overwhelming military force, thus lowering the cost of labor and the price the government paid for coal.

The plan was first laid out by Col. Charles Albright, former commander of the 34th Pennsylvania Militia, a Mauch Chunk resident with intimate ties to the coal industry. In a November 9 letter to Lincoln, he tied labor troubles to draft resistance, and said the men behind the troubles "were Irish, and call themselves 'Buckshots.'" "They have caused the high price of coal more than any one thing," Albright complained. "Many of them with the work they do make from one hundred to two hundred dollars a month."

The solution he offered was simple, if brutal: "A military force of several thousand men should be sent to the coal regions, martial law enforced, and summary justice dealt out to these traitors. Protections should be afforded to those willing to work, and those who will not work should be sent to work on military fortifications during the continuance of the war. It will not be safe to have them about. Nothing but thorough work will answer. I understand a committee of coal men will call upon you and make a more full explanation of the whole matter."[29]

The speed with which the government acted on the plan makes clear that Lincoln took it very seriously indeed. Within days of the letter's arrival, Gen. Darius Couch, the Union Army commander for eastern Pennsylvania, was dispatched to discuss the plan with the coal operators of Carbon County. "The operators who I saw proposed this—that if they could be assured of the protection of the general government until the work was accomplished, they would discharge the bad characters and employ new men, having eventually a body of men that could be controlled," Couch reported to Assistant Adjutant Gene. E. D. Townsend on November 13. He added that the operation would take three months, and that once begun it should not be stopped "until the work is thoroughly done, otherwise two-thirds of the anthracite region would stop sending coal to market."[30]

Couch endorsed the plan, and it was implemented. A few days later, on November 16, Rauch, the deputy provost marshal for Carbon County, gave his superior, Yohe, an overview of the situation:

An organization exists throughout the Middle Coal Field, of Irishmen, known as "Buckshots," for the avowed purpose of resisting the draft. This organization is formidable at Old Beaver Meadow Mines, Colerain, Jeanesville, Yorktown, Audenried, Frenchtown and the vicinity of Hazleton in Luzerne County. It was not possible to obtain any information from the Irish at either of these places, and we are indebted to Englishmen, Welshmen, Protestant Irish and leading citizens of American birth for the necessary information to enable us to find the drafted men. Mr. G. K. Smith, being SUSPECTED of giving me certain information as to the domicile of drafted men was murdered in the most brutal murder, in his home and in presence of his family.

The "Buckshots" are all armed, and frequently meet in secret places, two or three times weekly. At Jeanesville we searched a number of houses for arms and about 15 pieces—guns of different kinds—were found and taken to Hazleton by Capt. Hopper (I believe it is his name), the senior military officer present.

The 10th Regt. of New Jersey Infantry is now in the region, and judiciously distributed at Hazleton, Jeanesville, Treskow, Audenried, Beaver Meadow and Mauch Chunk—numbering about 500 men, exclusive of about 50 cavalry. The leading coal operators declare their determination to expel from their mines all "Buckshots" and other bad characters, which they can only do if protected by the military. The character of the "Buckshots" is not to resist officers and soldiers, but only to assassinate well disposed citizens. They are too cowardly to show fair fight. They number, in the whole region, several thousand, but they are only so many assassins.

About 45 "Buckshots" have been arrested in the vicinity of Yorktown and they are now in charge of Maj. Genl. Sigel at Reading. They expect to make more arrests of notorious characters, and expel all evil disposed men from the region.[31]

Soon, up to seventy civilians were under military arrest for resisting the draft and disloyalty—mostly Irishmen, but some Germans and native-born Americans, confined in the dank recesses of Fort Mifflin, where they were kept in the dark on any number of levels. John Donlin, an arrested miner, recalled, "I was held four months without any official knowledge of the cause of my arrest, nor did I know why I was held, until I was carried into the courtroom for trial."[32]

The prisoners included respected community leaders like Peter Dillon and gunmaker Conrad Horn, and poor miners like John Chapman, who had twenty-five cents on him when he was arrested at Yorktown on November 9. Many, but not all, of the detained Irishmen were from Donegal—Donlin, for example, had emigrated from Longford in 1853.

Wherever they were from in Ireland, those arrested in Carbon County could claim protection as British subjects if they had not been naturalized—an issue that went straight to the heart of the disloyalty charge. Donlin, for one, wrote to the British ambassador that he was "entirely innocent," adding, "I never became a citizen of the U.S. and never voted at any election held within the U.S."[33]

It did Donlin little good. When another Irishmen arrested for disloy-alty, Michael O'Donnell, made a similar appeal, Gen. Couch cut to the real issue—the government's need for cheap coal to fuel the navy ships block-ading the Confederacy. "If O'Donnell obtains his release, 44 others will ask for the same, no doubt," Couch wrote his superiors in Washington. "The interests of the country will not permit these men to go back to the mines at present. Life is safe there now: The operators are controlling their mines instead of a gang of cowardly ruffians, traitors, and murderers; coal is be-ing produced more surely and as stated to me more plentifully, the price of which will probably steadily decrease until it reaches the proper point."[34]

On the scales of military justice, the balance between national security and civil liberties would prove lopsided indeed. With habeas corpus sus-pended, the military could hold anyone it wanted, even if it had no legal basis to do so. "One thing is clear," Couch wrote to Maj. Gen. Franz Sigel, his subordinate in Reading: "That those men who have been arrested against whom no charges can be preferred should not at present be set at liberty." The problem, Couch pointed out, was that "the U.S. could not try men for offenses that are exclusively state ones"—such as the killing of Smith.[35] Another was more delicate—there was not an ounce of proof that the vast majority of those caught in the government's dragnet had committed any crime at all.

But that did little to deter the War Department, after due consideration, from proceeding with its pacification plan. For Secretary of War Stanton and General-in-Chief H. W. Halleck were "not unmindful of the great in-terests at stake and . . . disposed to lend every assistance to the operators in carrying out the proposed reforms. There are plenty of troops on the ground to protect" the coal operators in "whatever is desired." Coach suggested a meeting with the coal operators to arrive at "a uniform understanding" of the course to be adopted.[36]

The meeting with the Hazleton coal baron Aria Pardee and other lead-ing mine operators went so well that military authorities saw in the Car-bon County operation a blueprint for the suppression of militant miners throughout the entire anthracite region. "I recently met at Reading, Pa., a committee of the coal men of Lehigh Valley," Couch wrote his superiors in Washington on December 10. "Everything is working excellently in that district. Some of the worst characters having been arrested by Genl. Sigel, others have fled from the region and the operators are again getting their mines under proper control. So soon as the other two anthracite districts viz. Schuylkill and Wyoming agree to certain propositions, the bad characters will be cleared out of the country, the supply of coal increased with less number of miners—and matters will probably resume the quiet of before the war."[37]

Charles Albright, who had first proposed the pacification program, was designated to develop a case against the arrested men, in cooperation with their former employers. He was confident of convictions: "Without question I think there will be evidence enough to convict many of the defendants. . . . I shall continue my investigations and think that by the time the military commission is convened the cases will be ready for trial."[38]

In late January, as the courts-martial of the seventy civilians drew closer, it was decided that the cases be tried in Mauch Chunk, rather than Reading, for the convenience of the coal operators. And while others agreed on the strength of the government's case, Albright himself begged off on the actual prosecution of the case just days before the courts-martial opened on January 26.[39] Soon, the army began to have some doubts.

After a military commission began trying the case, the officer in charge, Col. Henry O. Ryerson of the 10th New Jersey, wrote a damning outline of the difficulties in proving the defendants had been disloyal and had resisted the March 1863 federal conscription law (several faced additional counts of harboring deserters and helping them escape). "The judge advocate informs me, since the commencement of the trial, there are but two against whom any evidence can be brought," wrote Ryerson. "He also informs me of the whole number now confined in Fort Mifflin that there are but three or four against whom he has any evidence, with the exception of those who are implicated in the murder of George K. Smith, whom this commission cannot try . . . From my own observations since the commencement of this investigation, I am satisfied that in the outset a great many arrests were injudiciously made."

The glaring holes in the prosecution's case posed an obvious problem: if the men were tried, acquitted, and freed, Ryerson wrote, it would be a triumph for opponents of the government. Allowing them to return to their houses "after a fair trial and acquittal for the want of proof against them will be very bad upon the community. . . . If sufficient evidence cannot be produced to convict them, in my judgment it will be far more injurious to the interests of the government to have them tried and acquitted, than to release them without a trial under certain conditions." Ryerson suggested that the prisoners against whom there was no evidence "be released, upon condition that they take the oath of allegiance and enter a solemn pledge to conduct themselves hereafter as good and loyal citizens."[40]

And, indeed, charges against most of the men were subsequently dropped. What is interesting, in light of Ryerson's statement that there was evidence against only two, is that his military commission nonetheless managed to convict no fewer than thirteen defendants. The legal machinations required for that feat are best illustrated by the trial of Peter Dillon.

Though the bulk of the prosecution's case was based on his actions during the antidraft meeting in the fall of 1862, Dillon stood accused of violating a law enacted six months *after* that meeting. He denied any involvement in a "combination" against the draft, and the defense moved that all references to his actions before March 1863 be stricken, confident that Dillon could not be convicted for his brief attendance at the meeting in June 1863.

That confidence proved misplaced. In denying the defense motion and convicting Dillon, the judge advocate admitted the holes in the prosecution's case. It is rare in such cases, he said, to find "direct and positive evidence of a criminal combination." "The prisoner is clearly proved to have been present at the meeting held in June 1863, the object of which was to resist the draft. The evidence shows that the prisoner was engaged as president of the meeting held in the fall of 1862."[41]

One can only wonder what was most damning—Dillon's leadership of the fall meeting, his ambiguous role in a series of beatings a year later (he was acquitted on those charges), or the testimony of J. G. Lewis Degenhardt, superintendent of the German Pennsylvania Coal Company in Treskow. "I have always been under the impression that Peter Dillon had great influence among his countrymen," Degenhardt told the military commission. "Of late the opinion has been forced on me . . . that he has used his influence in a dangerous way . . . Whenever strikes for higher wages were made, I found Peter Dillon to be prominent among the leaders; afterwards he would usually come to us and try to effect a compromise."[42]

In other words, he was a community leader who was not afraid to confront the coal operators. And it seems he was a Hibernian, if one can believe the first sentence of the first specification of the first charge against him: "That the said Peter Dillon, did, on or about the first day of August, 1863, unite, confederate and combine with Edward Winters and many other disloyal persons, whose names are unknown, and form or unite with a society or organization commonly known and called by the name of *Buck Shots*."[43]

Dillon, a widowed father of three, one of them not yet a year old, was sentenced to five years of hard labor. "The interests of the country" would not permit him to go free. He was joined by Donlin and eleven other defendants, six of them Irishmen, all convicted of disloyalty to the United States and resisting the draft. (O'Donnell was apparently among those released after signing a pledge of loyalty.)

Any hope that the sentences would deter further outbreaks was dashed before spring could fade into summer, as the federal draft of 1864 commenced. "The miners in the vicinity of Hazleton, Luzerne Co. have been rather rebellious," an army captain in Pottsville reported. "But the cavalry under command of Lt. D. I. Pislee have succeeded in keeping them straight."[44]

Given the cavalry's performance in Jeansville eight months earlier, one can well imagine what "keeping them straight" meant. And indeed, as there had been after Jeansville, there were consequences to the cavalry's dragooning of the countryside. "The detachment of cavalry in Carbon County while out serving notice on the drafted men were fired upon by about 18 bushwhackers, but no one hurt," Capt. Hullinger reported from Pottsville a month later. "It was in the mountains and the party could not be arrested."

The populace, he said, was "in great dread of the coming draft," but that hadn't stopped labor unrest. "All the railroads and coal mines have been stopped from operations by the miners and the railroad men. Since the first of this month they have struck for higher wages. They will not allow the mines to be worked nor the railroads to be used. There has not been a pound of coal shipped from this region since the first of the month. As a general thing they are very civil but very determined to have the advance in wages."[45] And so, as Dillon and his compatriots were consigned to the dismal recesses of a Philadelphia prison filled with Confederate POWs, nothing was resolved in Carbon County, where miners fought a civil war of their own, in the mountains and in the mines.

Thanks to the letters of some other Pennsylvanians who were imprisoned on similarly trumped-up charges of draft resistance in September 1864, we have a picture of the treatment of the civilian detainees in the dank "bomb-proofs" that served as cells at Fort Mifflin. "Our treatment was inhuman," wrote James McHenry. "When first taken and incarcerated in this cell, not a stool or bench to rest our weary limbs . . . Forty-four of us in one cell, without even a separate place to attend the calls of nature, it is no wonder that one of our number was soon laid in his resting place, and many others prostrated by disease."[46]

McHenry and the others were accused of taking part in the "Fishingcreek Confederacy" in Columbia County, a Democratic bastion where an assistant provost marshal, J. Stewart Robinson, was killed in the course of hunting for draft dodgers on August 1, 1864. After the killing, incredible rumors circulated that hundreds of draft resisters had holed up in a fort in the Fishingcreek Valley that was supposed to include four cannon. At the height of the Civil War, one thousand Union troops were dispatched to dragoon the area, arresting one hundred local residents in the process. Their commander, Gen. George Cadwalader, soon determined that he was engaged in a wild goose chase, but in an echo of the Carbon County case, forty-four of the detainees went before a military commission so the authorities could save face.[47]

The Columbia County case had another important element in common with the Carbon County prosecutions—it was the brainchild of Charles Albright. Months after it became clear that the Fishingcreek Confederacy was a fabrication, Albright was crowing to fellow Republicans about his role in the case, claiming that "he not only broke up the organization and secured the arrest and commitment to Fort Mifflin of about 40 of the ringleaders, among them two prominent officers of the County, but he convinced the disaffected that they had better take prompt measures to respond to the demands of the Government."[48]

Most of the thirteen defendants convicted by the Mauch Chunk military court remained in custody until just a few months before the end of the war. Among the first to be pardoned was Donlin, whose wife, according to family lore, made a personal plea to Lincoln after a remarkable trek to Washington on foot. With warring armies on either side of her, she carried their newborn baby in an old shawl, sleeping in hayricks at night. Margaret Donlin camped out in front of the White House one morning after exhausting her pleas elsewhere and all her money on food, the story goes. At 7:00 A.M., after two days without food, she encountered the gaunt president as he stepped from the executive mansion. When she told the man before her that he looked a lot like pictures she had seen of the president, he replied, "I am Mr. Lincoln." After she related her sorrowful tale, Lincoln invited her into the White House and had breakfast with her, then gave her money for a train ride home and promised to see her husband released, according to the story.

There is nothing in War Department documents about Margaret Donlin's remarkable odyssey, but it is a matter of record that Lincoln personally ordered her husband's release, well before all the others, in Pardon 12, Special Order No. 313, dated December 30, 1864. Decades later, at her ranch on the plains of Nebraska, Margaret Donlin kept a portrait of Lincoln and told any who would listen, "He was the greatest man who ever lived, and the kindest."[49] The story offers an anthracite twist on the old Irish tradition of the aggrieved camping at the doorstep of the king, going without food until a wrong had been righted.

It would take a little longer for the other wrongs to be righted: it was not until February 24, 1865, that Peter Dillon rejoined his young children, and the other men convicted in the tribunals walked out of Fort Mifflin—a damned hard hole if ever there was one.[50]

13   "A Howling Wilderness"

With the present population in Cass Township there can never be peace.
—*Miners' Journal*, February 13, 1864

Even before the Carbon County prisoners had been tried, the pacification program was being extended to the West Branch region of Schuylkill County, at the behest of the Heckschers and Charlemagne Tower, the 10th district provost marshal. The crucial difference between the crackdowns in the two counties was that in Schuylkill, there was no pretense that it had anything to do with opposition to conscription. Draft disturbances had continued there into 1864, though they were increasingly directed against those trying to raise the $300 needed to avoid military service.

On January 9, 1864, a gang of "Irish ruffians from Cass" were reported to have assaulted Dengler's Tavern in Barry Township, where a lottery was being held to raise commutation money for drafted men. In reporting the incident, the *Miners' Journal* mentioned similar assaults the night before in Minersville, which it blamed on "Buckshots" from Cass Township.[1]

The military and the coal operators were not the only ones determined to stamp out this sort of thing. The Catholic Church, long opposed to oath-bound secret societies, was more than willing to join the law-and-order counteroffensive. Bishop Wood, who had traveled to Pottsville in 1862 to urge compliance with the draft, released a pastoral letter on January 19 that specifically condemned the "Buckshots" and the "Molly Maguires," among others. The statement, read from the pulpit of every Catholic church in the anthracite region, threatened excommunication to any who joined these "unlawful and forbidden societies."[2]

While the Catholic Church wielded its spiritual influence, West Branch mine barons were exerting their economic power. Just a few days before Bishop Wood penned his pastoral letter, Tower wrote a note introducing the Heckschers to Gen. Franz Sigel of the U.S. Army's Department of the

Lehigh in eastern Pennsylvania. He described them as "the largest coal interests in this county" and said they had for a long time been "almost stopped in their business by the interference of men representing unlawful combinations"—the West Branch miners' committees.

Military arrests were needed, Tower said, because there were insufficient grounds for ordinary criminal charges: the actions of labor leaders "are in the main just short of overt and so disguised that it is difficult for civil power to reach them ... I have long been of the opinion and am now that a quicker and stronger power should grapple with them. I think the military power should be exerted against them and very strongly." He recommended that Sigel follow the course of action used in Carbon County. "I beg to suggest to you after full consultation with the Messrs. Heckscher that you should cause the ringleaders and chief conspirators to be seized by military force and taken to Fort Mifflin," Tower wrote Sigel on January 16. "The result would be salutary in the neighborhood of the arrest and it would effectuate quiet and order henceforth throughout the Schuylkill coal district. Such results have been attained in the Lehigh Dist. by arrests you were pleased to cause to be made in Audenried in Nov. last."[3]

As part of the behind-the-scenes lobbying for a crackdown, Tower had a number of leading West Branch coal operators prepare detailed affidavits in early February about their labor difficulties and the men who caused them. The complaints by Richard Heckscher of Forestville, Alonzo Snow of Glen Carbon, Henry Dunne of Heckscherville, and Charles Hewitt of Swatara were similar, and Dunne's was typical. "For the last few years unlawful combinations have existed in parts of the mining districts in Schuylkill and the adjoining coal counties and ... disturbances have frequently occurred," he wrote:

> Violence and crime have been committed with comparative immunity—for the last year, things have grown worse—the members of the unlawful combinations ... are not satisfied to work, or not work themselves, as they see proper, but they claim the right to prevent any man from working, or any colliery from being worked except on their terms under their dictation and they proceed to execute this unlawful claim of right by means of force, threats, anonymous handbills and various other means of intimidation ... members of the combination elect or appoint some of their number, "committee men" so called, through whose instrumentality they execute their purposes, threats and frequently most wicked and malicious demands.[4]

The coal operators included in the affidavits several examples of coffin notices, and Heckscher appended correspondence from David Muir, his superintendent in Branchdale who had had such a narrow escape the year before. What is remarkable about the affidavits is that they contain virtually nothing about draft resistance, the ostensible reason for the military's presence in the coal fields.

Richard Heckscher was the only one to bring up the subject, and mentioned it only in passing in a February 1 letter about the trouble caused by the committeemen: "It is unnecessary for us to say anything to you about the efforts made by these fellows and threats used to resist the draft in Cass and neighboring townships, as you in your capacity as provost marshal are fully acquainted with same."[5] Though the affidavits contained no evidence of draft resistance beyond this brief aside, the concerted push for military action bore fruit within days of their delivery. In the first week of February, two companies of the Invalid Corps were ordered to Heckscherville, where they were placed at the disposal of Tower, with Dunne providing their quarters by driving striking miners from their company houses—a move that can only have stirred up bitter memories of famine evictions.[6]

The troops' commander, Lt. Col. Carlisle Boyd, described the situation he found:

> The working of the collieries was controlled by committees who were appointed by the [workers]. These committees fixed the price of labor, the terms upon which contracts were to be taken and the persons whom the operators were to employ.
>
> They also assumed the right to fix the quantity of coal which persons having contracts might excavate per day . . .
>
> Threatening notices were being sent to operators who disregarded the regulations of the committee, also to all [employees] who worked in disobedience to their orders. Acts of personal violence were frequent.[7]

The soldiers quickly applied the strong medicine prescribed by the coal operators, arresting seventeen of forty-three men fingered by the coal operators as leaders of the labor committees.[8] In Heckscherville, Michael Conners, James Brennan, John Keaton, Patrick Close, Thomas McGuire, and James Whelan were taken into custody and sent to Reading for military trial. The *Miners' Journal* identified the six as committeemen who had been charged with "violently stopping collieries." There was no mention of draft resistance.

Not all of the army officers supervising the roundup were disinterested military professionals. Capt. Robert Ramsey of the 45th Pennsylvania Volunteers, who as an assistant adjutant general for the coal region worked closely with Tower on the West Branch arrests, was an acolyte of Benjamin Bannan who had gone to work for the *Miner's Journal* at age fourteen and quickly become a favorite of the publisher. (He would later become Bannan's business partner in the newspaper.)

Just a week after Tower promised Ramsey that he would see to it that the ringleaders of the West Branch labor committees were arrested, Ramsey's old boss was crowing in print that the detentions were a crucial step in the ethnic transformation of Cass Township. "The government has taken the difficulties which have existed in our region into hand, and is determined to put a stop to all lawless proceedings in the county," Bannan wrote. "With the present population in Cass Township there can never be peace, and the sooner it is mixed up with other elements the better."[9]

Tower was in complete agreement on the need to either rid Cass of the Irish or substantially dilute their influence. He recommended that the army remain in Heckscherville "until a better population, a proper sentiment and a continuous thriving industry shall be denizens there."[10] A Democratic paper in Pottsville had a different view: "Verily it has come to this, that a laborer who refuses to work at a rate of wages fixed by a monopolist, thereby commits a crime which subjects him to arrest by military authorities, removal from the county and imprisonment without trial. This is American freedom under Republican rule."[11]

Even staunch enemies of the Molly Maguires found the military's conduct outrageous, and had no doubts about who was ultimately responsible for the arrests. Rev. Daniel McDermott, a Catholic priest in the anthracite region who led the clerical campaign against the secret society over a decade later, pointed a finger at coal operators when he spoke about the arrests. "Land agents, operators, being of the 'better class,' obtained the ear of those having the drafts in charge," he recalled in 1877. The poor men dragooned by the military were "sent to Fort Delaware and Fortress Monroe, and left to languish in prison," he wrote. "This was done in violation of law and without the form of a trial, and was done as supposed, at the dictation of prominent land agents or operators."[12]

Who were the labor leaders rounded up at the coal operators' behest? While a number had distinctly Welsh- or English-sounding surnames—Evans, Griffith, Peters, Wren, Reeve—for the most part they were young Irish immigrants, poor men with many mouths to feed, as Fr. McDermott described.

One was identified in army records as Barney "Colan," a particularly bold committeeman who had marched up the hill to Heckscher's Woodside home and personally handed him a notice ordering him to replace the boss of the Forestville mine, Anthony Fernholz. It seems likely that an army clerk misspelled the first letter of the last name when Heckscher's original note was copied into the letterbook now in the National Archives—there was no Barney or Bernard Colan in the Cass Township census records for 1860. However, right there in Forestville, just down the hill from Woodside, there was a twenty-two-year-old Bernard Dolan, a miner supporting his widowed mother, Mary, and younger siblings. He was the same Barney Dolan who in 1868 would become the powerful leader of Schuylkill County's Hibernians. (There was nothing like challenging the county's most powerful mine operator, face to face, to increase one's standing with neo-Ribbonmen.)

The Fernholz incident is interesting for a couple of reasons. For one, Richard Heckscher did not comply with the demand. For another, he was not beaten or shot as a result—young Barney may well have done Heckscher a favor by issuing the demand in person, rather than via a coffin notice, for if anything bad had befallen Heckscher he would have been the prime suspect.

Another Forestville mine worker whose arrest Heckscher sought was Patrick Kellagher, a thirty-one-year-old father of three who had emigrated from Fermanagh in 1840. Patrick came from a politically connected family—the James Kellagher who had been elected Cass Township treasurer in 1853 was either his father or his brother.[13]

In 1860, James Whealen, one of the men arrested in Heckscherville, was a twenty-eight-year-old miner worth just thirty dollars, with a wife and four young children ranging in age in from two to eight. Thomas McGuire, another Heckscherville detainee, was thirty-four, a famine immigrant with a wife, six children, and eighteen dollars to his name. George Mealy, at age twenty-five, had a wife, a daughter not yet a year old, and thirty dollars. Philip Nash, twenty, still lived at home in 1860 with his parents and five siblings.

There were a few older men. Thomas Ryan was a forty-year-old illiterate with a wife, six children, and twenty dollars. Edward O'Bryan was the elder statesmen of the committees at age fifty. With an estate worth thirty dollars, he supported his mother and a woman of the same last name who at thirty-three could have been either wife or daughter.[14] Like the Ribbonmen described by Lee, these men were integral parts of their community. They worked hard at dangerous jobs, paid taxes, voted, and supported their families as best they could.

Even military men had trouble with the army's case against the seventeen West Branch committeemen. Brig. Gen. Orris Ferry wrote Couch a devastating critique of the arrests on March 25, saying that the charges and specifications forwarded to him were "utterly insufficient, on their face, to hold anybody to trial either before a military or civil tribunal." Ferry, a Republican and a former judge, offered a clear-eyed, independent analysis of the situation: labor unrest had led politicians to use the draft for partisan purposes, generating violence that had been blown all out of proportion by coal operators as a justification for price-gouging—and for the military suppression of the miners unions. "I think the arrest of these 17 men was a grave mistake," he wrote:

> They were arrested, it seems, because, as a committee of laborers in the mines, they undertook to fix a tariff of hours and wages of labor, to be adopted by the mines and presented to the employers. At the same time *some persons unknown* were putting up notices threatening violence to the laborers who consented to work at different rates from those proposed by the committee. There is not a particle of evidence against the persons arrested upon which any tribunal could base a judgment of guilty of any civil or military offense.
>
> The truth is, there is a vast deal of humbug about these coal-mine difficulties. Most of the mines are and always have been free from them in any shape approaching to violence. In others, the struggle between employers and employed occasionally assumes the bad shape which is frequently witnessed in other places and occupations. Politicians have striven to give these difficulties a political tone, and the occurrence of the draft has afforded a plausible pretence to this end. In this state of affairs some outbreaks of actual violence have occurred, which have been grossly exaggerated by the coal operators in order to inflate the price of that commodity, and swell their already exorbitant profits.... to strike for higher wages, to fix tariffs and prices, and to urge their observance by employers and employed, are not crimes. Crime begins when the strikes proceed to violence or threat of violence to effect their object. I think the former ought not to be noticed by the authorities, while the latter should be promptly suppressed. The laborers are an unorganized and unarmed mob, in mortal terror of the smallest detachment of federal troops.[15]

It appears that Ferry's doubts proved decisive. The index of courts-martial and military tribunals in the National Archives includes not a single name of the forty-three men whose arrests had been sought by the

West Branch coal operators. Likewise, the archive's Turner–Baker Papers on civilians detained by the military during the Civil War offer no traces of them. Whatever arrests were made did not end in trial. Perhaps the detainees were freed after signing oaths of allegiance of the sort that were made a condition of release for their counterparts in Carbon County. However dubious the government's legal case was, there is no question that the arrests and the military's presence had helped facilitate the reopening of the strikebound Heckscher mines. The real question was what to do when the troops marched out.

The issue didn't take long to surface. When, on February 15, 1864, Boyd was ordered to quit Heckscherville and return to Pottsville with his two companies, Dunne, his Cass Township host, was appalled. Dunne had been preparing to reopen his colliery, a task that would be greatly simplified by the presence of armed troops. His appeal for continued protection convinced Boyd to ignore the order. "Mr. Dunn [sic] in whose neighborhood they were stationed, made such a strong representation to me of the serious disadvantage their removal would be, and of the great assistance their mere presence at Heckscherville would be in enabling him to commence work, that I allowed them to remain," Boyd reported to his superiors.[16]

Boyd's decision was endorsed the next day by Couch and Sigel when they came to Pottsville to get a firsthand report on the situation from leading coal operators. The *Miners' Journal* intimated that their real interest was not draft resistance, but keeping down the price the government paid for coal: "Major Generals Couch and Sigel paid a flying visit to our borough on Tuesday evening last . . . to obtain such information as was necessary to enable them to act intelligently in putting a stop to the lawlessness that prevails in this region. The government is determined to have coal, and they are determined that the collieries shall be worked, so that coal can be afforded at fair prices, and a full supply obtained for the market."

Bannan then issued a frank warning to the labor activists of the West Branch: "Those committeemen, and all others who have aided and abetted in inaugurating the system of terrorism that prevails in some sections of the region, will be arrested as soon as their names are given to the military authorities, and if guilty, punished to the full extent of the law, because the civil law is powerless." He concluded by pointing out the military's arrest the week before of several Cass committeemen and the flight of several others. Those who fled "will be arrested as soon as they return," he wrote. "There will be clean work made of it this time."[17]

Bannan had made clear what he meant by "clean work" the month before, when he advocated that "Cass and parts of Riley [sic] Township

228 | PART III

should be left a howling wilderness" to prevent strikes, and its residents "should be taught the strong arm of the law, even if it becomes necessary to use the musket and the bayonet as schoolmasters." In urging "the law-abiding portion of the miners" to abandon their unions, Bannan made clear his view of workers' rights:

> Men have a right to work or not at wages offered; both parties have a right to confer on these points—these rights are not to be interfered with—these are questions the military have nothing to do with—but when men refuse to work and prevent others from working, either by threatening letters, coffin hand-bills or even verbal threats and menaces, they are violating the laws and they must give place to those who will work, and who will be protected in their rights by the military until these lawless ruffians are removed and their places supplied with peacable, law-abiding citizens.

If anyone had any doubt about what he meant by that last sentence, Bannan pointed out that a New York firm was prepared to import up to six thousand German miners "to take the place of those who refuse to work."[18]

Two companies of the 14th Regiment remained in Heckscherville until February 20, when Boyd ordered one back to Pottsville. When they weren't arresting committeemen, the soldiers spent their time guarding the collieries—Charles Hewitt, the Swatara coal operator who had filed one of the affidavits that spurred the military crackdown, was duly rewarded with ten cavalrymen.[19]

As in Carbon County, the military occupation of the coal fields resolved none of the underlying issues. "Some of our collieries are commencing work," Boyd reported on March 15. "There still, however, seems to be an undercurrent beneath the present quiet, which is manifest in the enclosed copy of a threatening notice."

The coffin notice, which had been posted on the engine house at Richard Kear's Gap colliery, was a mass of misspellings, but the message was plain:

> Short notice—this is to give you Gap men a cliar understanding that if you don't quit work after this NOTICE you may preper for your Deth.
>
> You are the damdest turncoats in the States—there is no ples fit for you bute Hell and you will soone be there.

It was signed "Molly." The continued use of such coffin notices helped thwart Bannan's and Tower's plans for the wholesale ethnic cleansing of

Cass Township. "It is difficult to induce laborers to come here, although there would be full employment for many more than are now here," Boyd reported. "There is not yet confidence in the safety of life to those who come to labor here in opposition to the regulations of the class who have hitherto been the rulers."[20]

The Heckschers may have had trouble importing the vast number of new employees they would have needed to work their mines, but the use of the military to suppress labor disturbances proved so successful that it soon spread beyond the mining industry. When employees of the Reading Railroad struck for higher wages on July 1, 1864, the government's supply of coal dwindled as quickly as the company's revenues. The solution to the twin problems was obvious to John Tucker, a Reading executive who had served as assistant secretary of war in 1862, when he was detached from the railroad to set up a military railway department. Wartime legislation had given the government the authority to seize any railroad, should "the public safety require it." The railroad dispatched Tucker to Washington, and the government announced the seizure of the railroad on July 11, the same day that military replacement crews arrived in Philadelphia to break the strike.[21]

The public safety justification for the military's intervention suffered an embarrassing blow the very day it was announced, when one of the "new hands" made a "a grand smash" near Phoenixville, narrowly missing a passenger train because he had ignored repeated signals to stop from a work crew that had pulled up a rail. "The passenger train just got past before the accident," the Miners' Journal said. "Otherwise there would have been a terrible loss of life."[22]

Despite their difficulties in keeping trains on the tracks, the military crews succeeded in their real mission, which was to slam the brakes on one of the most effective rail walkouts of the war. The strikers offered to return to work at their old wages on July 16, but the railroad was not inclined to give many their old jobs. Charles E. Smith, the president of the railroad, was so tickled with the outcome that he wrote an effusive letter to Maj. Gen. George Cadwalader, who had dispatched the military crews: "Our difficulties having terminated by the complete submission of the men, and the discharge of more than half of them, I avail myself of the opportunity to thank you for the prompt support which you rendered to me throughout—especially for our immediate compliance with my request that you should take possession of the road."[23]

Smith's glee was slightly premature, for the hard men who ran the labor committees at the Heckscher mines could always be counted on to throw a monkey wrench into the machinery of the military–coal complex. Just when the government had reason to hope that the coal would begin flowing again, the Cass Township mine workers walked off the job.[24]

If only the army had had a corps of miners, it might have duplicated its success in breaking the rail strike. But the closest thing it had to a corps of miners was the 48th Pennsylvania Volunteers of Schuylkill County, and they were otherwise occupied all that July, digging a tunnel under the Confederate lines at Petersburg, Virginia. The plan, conceived by the regiment's commander, Col. Henry J. Pleasants, a Pottsville mining engineer, was to explode a huge mine that would allow Union troops to pour through the enemy defenses. The explosion, on July 30, was indeed stupendous, but the assault failed. It was one more bit of hard luck for the 48th, a regiment whose members couldn't seem to catch a break, at the front or at home.

In February, as the army was in the midst of rounding up the West Branch labor activists, many soldiers of the 48th Regiment were back in Schuylkill County on leave. Among them was twenty-one-year-old James Shields, a native of Donegal who immigrated as a young boy to the coal town of Silver Creek, east of Pottsville. Like the Currys of Glen Carbon, he found work in the mines to support his widowed mother, and like two of the Curry boys he joined the 48th Regiment in 1861. "Proverbial for his good conduct," Shields reenlisted on January 1, 1864, at Blains Crossroads, Tennessee, like many of his comrades. And like many of his comrades, he was rewarded with a furlough home. But as the Currys had already discovered, home was a very different place.[25]

The previous summer, the county sheriff had arrived in Silver Creek with a posse to evict several tenants from their homes. It was the sort of dirty business that had often caused trouble in Ireland, and Silver Creek was no different. The sheriff and his posse were driven off, and that night a block of buildings was burned. The sheriff returned the next day, August 13, and was met by an outraged mob. This time he called in a detachment of the Pennsylvania Militia's 45th Regiment and made five arrests.[26]

By February 27 of the following year, when Pvt. Shields and his sergeant, David McAllister, visited the Silver Creek tavern run by Shields's sister-in-law, uniforms were not longer welcome, and Irishmen in the Union Army were considered traitors. Trouble began soon after the two entered the saloon, a reputed Molly hangout. A group of drinkers spilled drinks on the sergeant's uniform and called him a "bloody English bastard." When they learned he'd been wounded in the foot, one said it was a shame he hadn't lost his leg. McAllister, every bit an Irishman, had a few choice words of his own and started shoving. Shields, ever the stickler for good conduct, insisted there be no fighting in his sister-in-law's establishment. The local men left but returned few minutes later, and this time they were armed. In the ensuing brawl, James Shields was stabbed four times in the heart.

Four men—Hugh Curran, Patrick Goldey, Charles Ryan, and Peter Hagens—were arrested, but only Curran was brought to trial. Franklin Gowen, the Democratic district attorney elected the year before, won a manslaughter conviction. Despite a five-year sentence, Curran was paroled after just four months.[27] The military saw a direct link between the Shields killing and the crackdown on the West Branch. "One of the persons whom Mr. Heckscher had on his list for arrest is now in the hands of the civil authorities, having been engaged in a most brutal murder a few weeks ago in the neighborhood of Silver Creek," Col. Boyd reported from Pottsville on March 15. But none of the four men arrested in the Shields case appeared on the list drawn up by Heckscher or any other mine operator.[28]

Perhaps Boyd was mistaken, or perhaps one of the men was using an alias (Curran also went by Peter). In any case, the killing was another clear demonstration of the precarious position in which Tower's crackdown and Bannan's ravings had placed those Schuylkill County Irishmen who donned the same Union blue as the men who had turned the county into an armed camp.

There was already plenty of friction between the occupied and the occupiers—even those in sympathy with the government found themselves terrorized by Union Army soldiers. The problem was such that no less a hard-liner than Tower was moved to complain of the "lawlessness and ill treatment" that an Audenried family had to endure from the forces quartered on their property. A tavern built by George Allen "had been very much damaged" by the soldiers, he said, and "it is pretty hard case for a man to be driven out of his house by the military who are put there to protect them."[29]

Other civilians faced far rougher treatment at the hands of occupying troops. A private of the 10th New Jersey murdered Charles P. Mendom on September 25, 1863, outside a bar. The soldier, Richard S. Cooper, was subsequently sentenced to hang. In March 1864, a squad of soldiers from the 50th Pennsylvania volunteers busted up a Schuylkill Haven tavern because the owner had expressed antigovernment sentiments.[30]

Given the tensions of occupation, plus the ongoing labor troubles and ethnic friction, there was every reason to believe that the conscription of 1864 would prove as vexed as that of 1862 and 1863. Instead, the September draft in Schuylkill County that year was the first unaccompanied by widespread disturbances. The relative calm that descended on the West Branch probably had as much to do with Tower's May 1 resignation as provost marshal and the extension of suffrage to soldiers as with the region's occupation by the military.

When Pennsylvania soldiers were granted the right to cast absentee ballots in 1864, the Republican establishment lost its incentive to disenfranchise Democratic miners via the draft. And another bit of legislation that year—the federal Act to Encourage Immigration of July 4—specifically exempted from compulsory military service the very immigrants Tower loved to draft. Also helping to restore trust in the conscription process was the departure of Tower, who had been indicted in February on charges of enlisting Philadelphia minors as Schuylkill County substitutes without their parents' permission.[31]

To be sure, there were intimations of trouble in August, when "a spirit of riot" was said to be "infusing itself among the people of the some portion of the mining district."[32] But the conciliatory approach of Tower's successor, Capt. James Bowen, discouraged an overt outbreak. Bowen, an officer of the 48th Regiment, had been detailed to aid recruiting in Pottsville in early March, and worked hard to build confidence in the fairness of the conscription system when he took over from Tower.[33]

In an account of that period written shortly after the war, Bowen describes nothing less than a complete turnaround in public opinion. "In the districts where the most violent opposition was [previously] manifested, the citizens were among the first to assist in correcting their enrollment lists in 1864, and gave all information desired by the board to assist in making the draft and secure men for the army," he wrote. "This change in the sentiment of the people can be attributed to two causes: First—the presence of the military force, and Second, though not the least, the publishing of all information connected with the draft, authorized by the Provost Marshal General's Bureau, showing the people the operations and workings of the several enrollment acts."[34]

For the first time since 1862, the Irish miners of the West Branch had reason to hope that their political and economic enemies would not use the draft as a weapon against them. And for the first time since 1862, those miners did not use force to oppose conscription. By the time a new draft was under way in 1865, the Irish of Cass Township were using letters and logic, rather than marching Ribbonmen, to make their case. "Being one of a committee of the above township on enlistments, I beg leave to ask of you the following information," one Cass Irishman wrote. "We have filled all the previous calls of the president on our district by volunteers. In the last call for 500,000 men we have given 75 one-year's men and 37 three-year's men. Now that our quota is 51 men under the present call for 300,000 men, would not our 37 three-year's men leave us clear of the present call?"[35]

But the end of violent resistance to the draft presented the coal operators with a problem: it meant the withdrawal of the troops they had been using to break the miners' union. One solution was obvious: many coal operators followed the troops out of the West Branch.

Charles Hewitt was one of the first to go, selling his Swatara colliery in late spring of 1864, not long after a regiment of the Invalid Corps left the region for Washington.[36] Charles Heckscher of Forestville was next. He resigned as president of the Forest Improvement Company in January 1865, as the war—and its promise of continued military protection—ran down. The Heckschers merged the Forest Improvement Company with the New York and Schuylkill Coal Company, of which Charles Heckscher was a director and one of the largest shareholders.[37] In his place, the New York and Schuylkill appointed as superintendent of its West Branch operations a military man with the requisite experience in occupying hostile territory—Brig. Gen. William Ward Duffield. A former commanding officer of the 9th Michigan Infantry, Duffield had served as the Union Army's military commander of the state of Kentucky in the spring of 1862.[38]

Charles Heckscher's departure from Schuylkill County was marked by a curious ceremony at his home in the Woodside section of Forestville. With a Pottsville band at their head, several hundred employees of the Forest Improvement Company marched to his house, the lamps on their miners' caps flickering in the night, to pay eloquent homage to the man they had fought so bitterly over the previous three years.

"What proper meed of praise then, sir, can be bestowed on you, for the fruits of your many years of active enterprise in Schuylkill County?" asked a representative of the miners. "The once howling wilderness, which was the resort of the creeping panther and the ravenous bear, was reclaimed by you and made to blossom as the rose." As the miners made their "sorrowful farewell," proclaiming their great respect for him, the surprised coal baron composed an appropriate reply. Citing the "the regrettable difficulties which occurred between us during the recent years," Heckscher chided the miners for allowing themselves "to be overawed by the sinister suggestions and fatal advice of a designing criminal minority," then went on to praise their turnaround. "You have come to the acknowledgement of your true interest," he told the assembled crowd. "You have overawed the few bad men who for a time succeeded in overawing you and if you will firmly adhere to this manly course all will go right hereafter, and you will be blessed with prosperity and steady work."[39]

Heckscher was deluded if he truly believed the miners had suddenly recognized a common interest with the coal operators. The obsequious tone of the ceremony in Heckscher's honor would have been recognized by Evelyn John Shirley of Monaghan, once toasted as "Lord of the Soil" by the same tenants who were waging a secret society war against him.[40]

Like Shirley's peasants in Farney, many of Heckscher's miners in the West Branch were unable to confront him in the open without fear of military arrest. In public, they were at the feet of their employer. Under the cover of darkness or disguise, they were at the throat of his deputies. And those deputies could not leave quite as easily as Heckscher.

When the army withdrew as the war wound down, Henry Dunne remained in Heckscherville as superintendent for the New York and Schuylkill Coal Company. Likewise, David Muir remained as superintendent at Branchdale in Reilly Township. The ownership of the mines had changed somewhat, but the old grudges remained. As Dunne and Muir would soon discover, the War Between the States may have ended on April 9, 1865, at Appomattox Court House in Virginia, but in the hills of northeastern Pennsylvania, the struggle between Irish miners and the coal companies that all but enslaved them was just beginning to hit full stride.

14   Parting Shots

> The coal and iron police are suggestive of Ireland to anyone who has seen
> that unfortunate country while landlordism was yet in strength.
>
> —Henry George

Many in the anthracite region had hoped that the end of the war would at last bring a measure of peace, but the assassination of President Lincoln on April 14, 1865, just five days after Lee's surrender, offered a stark reminder that wars do no always end neatly, or peacefully.

In the coal fields, as in Washington, there were conspirators ready to avenge their defeat at the hands of the Union Army. The violence they wrought would be in some ways theatrical, addressed to a wider audience, much like the cry of "Sic semper tyrannis" that the actor John Wilkes Booth uttered at Ford's Theater after killing Lincoln. And as in the case of those implicated in the Booth conspiracy, the rush to punish in the coal fields would end in a mass hanging, and enduring questions about the guilt of some of the accused.

In at least one case, the violence in the coal fields was directly linked to Lincoln's death. A few days after the assassination, three miners in what the *Miners' Journal* described as "an Irish groggery at Lorberry," a New York and Schuylkill coal patch on Swatara Creek, were badly beaten for expressing sorrow at the president's death.[1]

The beatings were only the beginning. In the months after Lincoln breathed his last, all the bitterness and insanity that four years of war can conjure bubbled to the surface in Schuylkill County. In response to diminished demand for coal, mine operators slashed prices and wages, triggering a new strike. Sullen miners vented their fury on the Johnnys who came marching home and on the mine officials who didn't leave. Some workers turned to highway robbery to recoup what was lost from their weekly wages. Irishmen fought Englishmen, and one another, and the gunplay rivaled anything the Wild West had to offer.

The new labor strife began even before Lincoln died. Maj. Gen. H. W. Halleck, the army chief of staff, asked his chief quartermaster in Philadelphia on April 13 if a local strike near Ashland in Schuylkill County would "affect the price or supply of coal to the government." His wording seemed to suggest that he wanted a pretext to send in troops: "To furnish this protection it should appear that the Government has an interest in the continued working of the mines." The quartermaster, Col. W. W. McKim, refused to play along, replying that the strike, which already appeared over, would not affect prices, and advising that there was no need for the army to intervene.[2]

The walkout at the Preston Coal Company in Big Mine Run had ended, but discontent was spreading. In late April, the *Miners' Journal* reported that coal operators were planning to reduce wages. The steep cuts, 25 to 33 percent, spurred a broad strike. "Many of the men would submit to this reduction, but others refused, and consequently the stoppage has become general," the newspaper reported in early May.[3]

In Schuylkill County, there were always some who refused to submit. For most, that defiance did not lead to violence, but a minority—mostly "striplings between the ages of 18 and 21," as the *New York Times* put it—insisted on dealing with the new trouble in the old way. An Irish gang invaded a bar in Middleport and beat an Englishman within an inch of his life because he had taken a contract to sink a mineshaft. Two other Englishmen were badly beaten near Girardville, and the pumps were stopped at two collieries near Ashland.[4]

The reason for the ethnic tension was clear—mine operators were seeking to replace Irish strikers with Englishmen and Welshmen. The president of the New York and Schuylkill Coal Company laid out such a plan in late April in the starkest terms possible. "The 20 Welshmen if they come at all will be here in ten days or a fortnight . . . they supply the places of Irish who must be displaced & if our plan of emigration succeeds, this process must be repeated until we have a mixture of races, and are released from the tyranny of the Celts."[5]

The ethnic tension and labor strife were a direct result of the actions of the mine operators—Irish strikers could win only by waging an ethnic struggle, given the operators' plans to replace them with Welshmen. But to some, the issue was not the presence of discrimination, but the absence of the army. "Now that the war is over and the military withdrawn, the Thugs . . . are commencing to inaugurate again in Schuylkill County a reign of terror," Bannan complained on May 20. "We are thus placed at the mercy of bands of guerrillas who roam around the County to murder unoffending parties." The publisher called for the creation of militias to deal with lawlessness. His plea was punctuated by an arson fire toward the end of the month that destroyed the inclined plane used to chute coal from Kirk and Baum's Crow Hollow colliery.[6]

While Bannan blustered, the coal establishment was already taking quiet steps to ensure the return of troops. On May 15, the president of the New York and Schuylkill, Otto Wilson Davis, wrote to Charles E. Smith, the president of the Reading Railroad, to enlist his support for the plan. "Have urged upon the chairman of the meetings of the coal operators, (Col. Day) to call a meeting on Thursday for the purpose of getting them in a body to ask for troops in Schuylkill Co.," Davis wrote. "As your road is interested in the question I hope its influence will be used in favor of the application."[7]

Davis then traveled to Washington to lobby the War Department in person for the return of troops. His mission was successful, though his means were apparently so questionable that he was unwilling to share them with one of his top aides on the West Branch. "Am happy to inform you that the War Department has determined to send troops to Schuylkill County," he wrote to Henry Dunne. "How they were got & why must be kept still."[8]

The solution was a temporary one—Davis was lobbying the governor for a more permanent state force—but it was clear that the Heckscher operations would be a focal point of military efforts to break the strike. "The soldiers will not stay long," Davis wrote at the end of the month. "The difficulties in getting this order were great and the government will not again interfere. If they remain a month I will be surprised. Mr. Tucker told me yesterday that in the order sent by Gen. Rawlings to Gen. Hancock, the property of the NY&S Coal Co. was specially mentioned as an object of importance."[9]

On May 26, the War Department ordered the dispatch of an infantry regiment "under a discreet and reliable commander . . . to maintain order among the operatives and miners in the collieries of the New York and Schuylkill Coal Company."[10] The commander was none other than Charles Albright of Carbon County, who the year before had helped arrange the military tribunal for Peter Dillon and several other miners there, then went on to suppress the illusory Fishingcreek Confederacy. By May 29, Bannan had something far better than an ad hoc militia to break the strike—Albright and the 202nd Pennsylvania Infantry Regiment had arrived in Mauch Chunk.

The regiment's orders were simple—break any resistance by the miners to the resumption of production. Albright immediately met with a number of leading coal operators to determine the best way to carry out that mission.

"The operators are apprehensive of considerable trouble unless the turbulent spirits are overawed by the presence of soldiers," he reported on May 30.[11] In fact, the "turbulent" were to be more than "overawed." They were to be fired from their jobs and driven from their company-owned homes. Because this was to be the last intervention by federal troops, the New York and Schuylkill wanted to make a clean sweep, even if it cut into profits. "We may want to work even at a loss while the soldiers are there so as to get rid of some of our worst men," Davis wrote.[12] Albright was more than happy to help in any way possible. He assured the president of the New York and Schuylkill, "It is my desire to do the very best I can for the large interests that are at stake in the coal region." Accordingly, the coal operators were allowed to help determine the positioning of troops.

"After inquiring about the condition of matters about Heckscherville, I found that the presence there of one company of your men had a very salutary influence," Davis wrote Albright on June 10. "We wish very much that one half of them could be quartered on the south side of Mine Hill near Forestville."[13] Albright's response came two days later. "I will try to meet your wishes with regard to posting some troops on the south side of Mine Hill," he replied. "For the present I have ordered tri-weekly patrols from Heckscherville to Swatara."[14] A contingent duly arrived on June 24 in Forestville, where it would be based for much of the summer, protecting the interests of the New York and Schuylkill. The 214th Pennsylvania Regiment was dispatched to quell labor trouble in neighboring Lehigh and Carbon Counties.[15]

The war was over and the military's rationale for intervening in an industrial dispute had evaporated with the demand for coal. But Mars still couldn't tear himself from the arms of Mahantango. The pretext for the latest military intervention was so flimsy that one newspaper couldn't resist some vicious mockery. The *Lebanon Advertiser* ran a story headlined "War in Schuylkill County! Great battle among the Miners! Bannan, of the 'Journal,' Fortified; his man 'Friday' up a tree—Ministers of the Gospel leading charges! 10,000 Irish infantry in arms!" The ensuing article reported, "Several thousand have been killed. The Irish are murdering everybody. The county in general, and the streets of Pottsville in particular, are crowded with blood-thirsty miners who kill all but Irishmen."[16] It was all an elaborate lampoon of the *Philadelphia Inquirer*'s breathless coverage of the strikes, but even as sober a publication as the *American Presbyterian* noted on June 8 that initial reports of violence in the Schuylkill County were "greatly exaggerated."

It was not only on the military front that the Heckschers outflanked the striking miners. There were political maneuvers as well. In mid-May,

even as it worked feverishly to lay the groundwork for the army's intervention, the New York and Schuylkill hired a new lawyer in Schuylkill County.
He was none other than Franklin Gowen, the Democratic district attorney
elected with the overwhelming support of the company's militant Irish
workforce in 1862. It was a wrenching time for Gowen: his two young sons
had taken ill and died early in the year, and his brother George, commander
of the 48th Pennsylvania Volunteers, was killed in battle just a week before
Lee's surrender. "Mr. Gowen, who will take Niemann's place, has accepted
and will soon be with you," Davis wrote to his chief superintendent on the
West Branch. "He is represented to be a gentleman and very competent."[17]

Past labor troubles had become entwined with ethnic and political conflicts. The New York and Schuylkill was determined that this time around
politics would not be a part of the equation. And so, one of the county's
leading Democrats signed on with its leading coal company; meanwhile
the army's enlisted men spent their days protecting its property and pick-
ing berries, and their officers spent their nights being wined and dined by
coal operators.

It was all a little too cozy for the striking mine workers. They complained to anyone who would listen that the wage cuts at the root of the
strike were part of a plot to drive up the price of coal by cutting its supply.
"The real object in calling in the troops," it was widely believed, "has been
merely to cover up these sinister designs on the market."[18] Some miners
did more than mutter into their glasses of porter. There was always hell to
pay when the military came marching into the coal fields, and in the summer of 1865 the bill quickly came due. As in the case of James Bergen and
James Shields, it landed in the lap of an Irish soldier.

In July, Peter Monaghan, a Union Army veteran, got into a scrape with
Tom Barrett, a hell-raiser from Big Mine Run who was already on the lam
from an assault charge. By the time Barrett was done shooting, Monaghan
had a new hole in his clothes, though miraculously none in his body. A
squad of soldiers took Barrett into custody a few days afterward and tossed
him in the county prison. He was later shot dead while trying to escape—at
least that's how the killing was reported by the man responsible, Constable Joe Heisler, Tower's old deputy in dragooning the West Branch.[19]

As the Barrett case made clear, the violence was by no means limited
to the strike, or the strikers. It seemed to leach out of the mines into the
mainstream of society, like the sulfur-laden water from the collieries that
tinted the rocks orange in the Schuylkill. Richard Heckscher, the mine
operator who had stayed on after his uncle departed Cass Township in the
winter, pled guilty that summer to charges of assault and attempted rape.[20]

In another case, one of the West Branch committeemen Heckscher and other mine operators had sought to have arrested the year before, Patrick Close, was gunned down along with his brother, Michael, after an absurd argument with some other drinkers over a chair-balancing trick in the widow Grody's Shenandoah shebeen. The culprits were identified as James Brennan and John Delaney, two of Close's former neighbors from Cass Township. Years later a Glen Carbon resident told a Pinkerton spy that the killers were "supposed to belong to the Mollies," and a James Brennan from Cass Township had indeed appeared with Patrick Close on the very same list of committeemen that Henry Dunne wanted arrested.[21] There was as much bad blood in the coal fields as there was cheap whiskey, and they seemed to flow in tandem.

The strike, meanwhile, was crumbling beneath the heels of the 202nd Pennsylvania Volunteers, whose patrols wore a path in the green fields between Forestville and the collieries of Swatara, New Mines, and Heckscherville. The "turbulent," as Albright termed them, were indeed overawed. As early as June 10, the *Miners' Journal* reported that the strikers were willing to go back to work if wages were slashed only 10 or 15 percent, instead of 33 percent, but the mine operators, bucked up the army's bayonets, were in no mood for compromise.[22] The wartime labor shortages that had forced them to settle labor differences in the recent past were over, handing the coal companies an advantage worth far more than a regiment of troops. Now the New York and Schuylkill could return to the old practice of simply crushing strikes and evicting union militants.

"My prediction about the supply of labor seems to have been correct and we will not be at a loss for them as in 1863 and 1864," Davis wrote to Duffield, his West Branch superintendent, in June. "We will maintain our position even if we fail to get out coal. Do not fail to keep Mr. Verner busy at vacating homes, reducing the tenants only to the men on whom the bosses say we can rely."[23]

The strike started to collapse a mine at a time. By the third week in July, it was all but over, except among some diehards in Ashland. "The miners and laborers are generally acquiescing in the reduction of 30 to 40 percent of their wages, in this region," the *Miners' Journal* reported on July 22.*

---

* A look at Luke Mohan's income for the years 1864 and 1865 shows the impact of the cuts on one Forestville mining family: After deducting $600 for taxes, rent, and home repairs, Mohan's take-home pay for 1864 was $274. Amid the strikes and pay cut of the following year, that figure plummeted to just $84. By contrast, the New York and Schuylkill's West Branch superintendent, Duffield, reported after-tax income

The end of the walkout was accompanied by the usual blacklisting, though the practice took on a sharply sectarian tone on the West Branch, where the president of the New York and Schuylkill had talked of ending "the tyranny of the Celts." His representatives in Schuylkill County took that to mean they should fire all the Irish. Davis felt compelled to clarify. "We have misunderstood each other," Davis wrote Duffield in late July. "I never intended to give orders not to employ any Irishman, but on the contrary have avoided an order in such terms. The order was not to employ any man who had heretofore given trouble at our mines or elsewhere if known."[24] The confusion, if that's what it was, came at a bad time for the company's superintendents on the West Branch, for Albright's regiment got its marching orders on July 27, and struck camp in Forestville the next day.

There was always hell to pay when the army marched out of the coal fields, and it was sometimes a mine official who got stuck with the bill, as George K. Smith had discovered shortly after Halloween 1863. On the morning of August 25, less that a month after the 202nd stopped its regular visits to the mine he had supervised for so many years in Reilly Township, David Muir finished his breakfast and set off to work. A small group of men followed. One knocked down Muir with a blow from behind. There was a struggle, and Muir was shot through the heart and stabbed three times.[25] The past had finally caught up with the sixty-one-year-old Scot whose daughter had been warned by strikers in April 1863 that he "would not be anymore" if they got hold of him. He died fifty yards from his home.

Muir's attackers walked down a railroad track after the shooting and disappeared into the woods. The killing took place in front of a large crowd of miners, but none could (or would) identify the attackers. "It was reported that signals had been seen burning that night on the hills, soon after the occurrence," Allan Pinkerton wrote more than a decade later. "It was surmised they were built by confederates, to aid the principals in the murder to make their escape."[26]

This is nonsense, of course. The killing took place in the morning; by night the gunmen were long gone. If there were fires in the hills of Branch Township that night, they were the old celebratory bonfires of the Irish countryside, the sort that were lit after Maj. Mahon was killed. With the Muir murder coming far from the winter holidays that the Mollies favored,

of $2,887 for 1865. *MJ*, Income Returns for South Cass Township, Aug. 19, 1865, and Aug. 25, 1866.

any bonfires that night likely served as a signal that his blood was shed on behalf of the community.

The Muir killing prompted some bluster from the Heckscherville mine superintendent, Henry Hawthorne Dunne. "An Irishman got shot this morning on a canal boat," he wrote Davis in September. "He went on board and demanded the captain's money or life. The captain son's overwhelmed him, went down into the cabin, brought up the captain's gun and shot the robber dead instantly. A few such shots around here and Forestville of this kind would do us a 'POWER OF GOOD.'"[27] Despite a $5,000 reward, no one was ever arrested in the Muir killing.[28] It was a classic Molly murder.

Less than two weeks after Muir was slain, another mine official had a close call, in a case that marked the beginning of a trend—highway robbery. On Friday, September 8, William Pollock, a mine superintendent, was bushwhacked as he and his fourteen-year-old son were taking the $8,000 payroll to Crow Hollow colliery, between Pottsville and Tuscarora. Shot in the back, the superintendent sprang from his carriage and wrestled with his assailant, who beat him over the head with a pistol as Pollock's son rearranged the robber's scalp with the butt end of a buggy whip. By the time all the bloodletting was over, a badly wounded Pollock had managed to hold on to the payroll, and the highwayman had made good his escape. He was described as an Irish miner, which ensured that later writers would describe him as a Molly Maguire. While that is far from certain, there is reason to believe that his career as a criminal ended with a bellyful of buckshot during an attempted robbery a couple of years later.

Less than a week after the attack on Pollock, three highwaymen, inevitably described as Irish, held up Percival Byerly as he drove his carriage from Mount Pleasant in Foster Township to Minersville. After some mutual recrimination that included curses, rock throwing, a knife thrust, and gunshots, Byerly was allowed to proceed on through Cass Township, shaken but apparently unharmed, his purse eleven dollars lighter.[29]

And then for a few months something like calm descended on the West Branch. The draft, the army, and the Heckschers' blacklist had driven many of the most militant from the area for good, or at least for better or worse. Autumn came and went, the turning leaves setting the hillsides ablaze with color. As the days grew shorter, the miners found themselves going out to work in the predawn chill and returning after dark. At Halloween, the boys who picked slate in the coal breakers traded songs for apples as they trick-or-treated from home to home. There was some unrest at Phoenix Park, but the army didn't show up, kicking up dust, and nobody attacked any mine bosses.

The Indian summer couldn't last. Out at New Mines, hell had been duly paid with the blood of Muir for the army's summer sojourn on the West Branch. In Forestville, Heckscherville, and Phoenix Park, there remained an uncollected debt. As winter descended over the scarred anthracite hills, it was time to settle the year's accounts.

The trouble came exactly three years to the day after warning notices signed "Brave sons of Molly" had first gone up at the collieries of Cass Township. On the night of December 5, John Robinson, the watchman at the Forestville colliery, spotted a suspicious character and, fearing that the man was out to burn or steal, asked his intentions. Robinson's answer was a club to the back of the head from one of the man's unseen accomplices. Three weeks later, on the night of December 30, Robinson's suspicions were validated when the New York and Schuylkill company store was burglarized and burned. The store lost its books in the blaze, which doubtless made it difficult for the company to dun the miners who were up to their ears in debt.

Just downstream at the Phoenix Park colliery in Branch Township, the reckoning came on December 27. Phoenix Park was where the name "Molly Maguire" had first been recorded in an industrial dispute, in December 1862, and three years later the hard men showed they had not forgotten the fundamentals of a Whiteboy raid, invading a home around the holidays with blackened faces.

The home belong to Philip Whalen, a retired mine boss with a County Kilkenny name who had the good luck to be gone when four armed men whom the Miners' Journal described, tongue in cheek, as "colored Irishmen" burst into his home, terrorized his wife, and stole $320. The quartet appears to have had a busy day with the mine officials of Phoenix Park—that morning, four men had beaten and shot a Welsh boss named Edwards.[30]

Now that the Mollies had settled their scores in Branchdale, Forestville, and Phoenix Park, only Heckscherville, and Henry Hawthorne Dunne, remained. Dunne, a Protestant gentleman from County Waterford who ran the New York and Schuylkill's Heckscherville mine, had been instrumental in the arrest of the West Branch committeemen the year before, and had evicted miners from their homes to make room for an army of occupation. As 1866 dawned, there was similar trouble brewing. The company was planning a campaign against squatters in Forestville—new evictions to make room for some Belgian miners—and had just purchased a local drinking establishment that it linked to "the bad element." "Our purchase of the Fiddler's Tavern and the plan to get rid of the bad population at Forestville are most cordially approved," Davis wrote Dunne on January 8.[31]

Dunne was well aware of the price to be paid for such conduct—he had begun to vary his route home to Pottsville after being fired at in an ambush. Dunne got a chance to display some of his renowned wit when he encountered Francis P. Dewees, the nephew of Democratic leader Francis Hughes, in a Pottsville pharmacy a day after the letter from Davis.

"Harry, you look as if you might live to be a hundred," Dewees said.

"Upon my soul, I have no idea of dying at present," answered the thirty-eight-year-old Dunne, laughing.

"Well, then, you should be more careful about driving at night," the sober pharmacist rejoined.

"Why, no one would hurt me," Dunne replied.[32]

Whatever his other characteristics, the remark is testimony to Dunne's sense of humor, for the mine boss was well aware that there were some who would like very much to hurt him. But the gun he carried as he commuted to work did him little good the next evening. Dunne was returning home from Heckscherville around 7:00 P.M. when his carriage was stopped by five men on the Minersville Road just outside Pottsville. The evening of January 10 was a cold one, and Dunne, wearing heavy fur gloves, was unable to draw his pistol. His attackers, warm with whiskey, had no such difficulty. They shot Dunne four times and dragged him from his carriage.

Three Minersville residents on their way to a skating party in Pottsville's West End happened upon the scene and heard Dunne shout, "I am murdered." One of the attackers approached the skaters' carriage and threatened to blow out the driver's brains if he did not move on. As the party sped off toward Pottsville, they heard two more shots. Dunne was dead. The killers, laughing, headed off toward Minersville—and Cass Township.[33]

The authorities quickly took into custody a number of Cass residents—William Lynch, John Horan, John Burns, Jr., Andrews Adams, and James Conner of Heckscherville; Denis Harkins and James McGum of Thomaston; and John Kelly and Daniel Malloy, for whom no residence was given. But the witnesses could not tie them to the crime—the gunmen were strangers—and no charges were ever brought in the case.[34]

Dunne's slaying left five children orphaned and Schuylkill County's coal establishment badly shaken. Another outbreak of highway robberies in Cass Township did nothing to calm nerves. On New Year's Eve, Joseph Harner, a Northumberland County farmer, had been held up by five men on Broad Mountain and relieved of $40, his watch, and a pistol that he had the good sense not to use. A few days later at Mine Hill Gap, a band of robbers took $170 from Joseph Newlin, a driver for the Yuengling brewery.[35]

Bannan was exasperated. Calling for a mass meeting to address the "reign of terrorism," he blasted lax law enforcement and warned that a "band of secret assassins," a deadly efficient "secret oath-bound organization," was behind the attacks. A well-attended meeting in Pottsville called by Bannan and leading coal operators just five days after the Dunne slaying, adopted a resolution that implicitly linked the violence to the West Branch labor committees—and a secret society behind them. "There has been established among us a system of unlawful interference with the workings of collieries, which attempts to control by violence both the property of capitalists and the labor of workingmen, the tendency of which is to drive away capital and deprive labor of employment. It is charged with great probability that a secret organization exists which is the author of these illegal acts."[36]

The meeting ended with a call for action to restore order. A week later, Bannan published a plan for a county police force "assisted as far as possible by the businessmen of the county and completely backed up by a regiment of picked cavalry." He urged readers to petition the state legislature for the creation of this homegrown military unit. The New York and Schuylkill, as usual, was acting more quietly behind the scenes. On January 23, the company's president helped establish a committee to lobby Harrisburg for legislation establishing a special police force.[37]

State officials received further incentive to act on April 2, the day after Easter, when two strangers appeared at George W. Cole's colliery in Mahanoy Township, asking for the outside boss. The men they approached, Cole's son and his superintendent, T. Lewis, grew wary and gave evasive answers. One of the strangers drew a pistol and shot Lewis in the face. The mine boss survived, but one of the attackers, Patrick Doolan, was killed in the ensuing melee. Hundreds of people came to view the body, but no one recognized the dead man, whose body was buried in a culm bank at the mine. The other suspect, who gave his name as Patrick Johnson, was quickly freed on $1,000 bail, and apparently disappeared. A few days after the shooting, several friends from Minersville made the trek across Broad Mountain to exhume Doolan's body and return it there for burial, though the local priest refused to have it interred in the church cemetery.[38]

The posting of $1,000 bail for Johnson and the odyssey of Doolan's corpse raise the possibility that there was an organization behind the attempt to murder Lewis. The refusal of a Christian burial for Doolin suggests that the organization may have been the Mollies, which had been condemned in the strongest terms by Archbishop Wood and local priests.

It may be no coincidence that a Minersville area mine superintendent had been killed by strangers only a few months before. If the Dunne and Lewis shootings were part of a failed murder swap between Mahanoy and Minersville Mollies—each providing unrecognized gunmen to kill the other's target—it would explain why a stranger from the West Branch crossed Broad Mountain to gun down a Mahanoy Township mine superintendent. And such arrangements would recur among the Mollies in the 1870s.

Nine days later, after the attempt to kill Lewis, the legislature approved the creation of the Coal and Iron Police, a paramilitary force that was to function as an army of occupation for generations, replacing the soldiers who had patrolled the county during and just after the war. During the debate about the bill, one state lawmaker from Schuylkill County suggested that coal companies themselves were the problem. "They have aggravated these men to desperation, and taken from them lease rights of land on which some of them had built houses, worth from one to three thousand dollars," said Rep. John M. Crosland. "A woman was turned out of doors in the absence of her husband, and stood in the pelting rain, holding an umbrella over her children, and the neighbors did not dare take them in, lest they themselves should be turned out in like manner, that being the penalty threatened."[39]

But the legislature wasn't interested in the problems of people evicted in the pouring rain when the coal companies that owned the mineral rights to the land sank mine shafts directly beneath their houses. On April 11, 1866, it voted to allow the coal companies to create a private police force that one historian described as "a close approximation to feudal retainers." Indeed, Henry George, a radical social critic familiar with both the Pennsylvania coal fields and feudalism in the Irish countryside, drew a direct comparison between the two. "The coal and iron police are suggestive of Ireland to anyone who has seen that unfortunate country while landlordism was yet in strength," he wrote in 1886. "Their functions on the coal estates are a combination of those performed for the Irish landlords by the 'rent warner,' the 'process server,' the 'emergency man,' and the Royal Irish Constabulary. They are the spies, informers, collectors, writ-servers, and guards of their employers, licensed always to carry arms and make arrests."[40] Like Ireland, the anthracite region had been reduced to the status of a colony—an internal one—and like all colonies, an army was needed to keep the natives down. With its military protection gone, the coal industry had created one of its own.

The commanders of that army were the mine superintendents—nearly every one of them in Schuylkill County gained a commission in the new police force and led a unit at his colliery.[41] Its general was none other than Col. Henry Pleasants, former commander of the 48th Regiment, who was named general superintendent. Joe Heisler, Tower's loyal deputy during the West Branch draft troubles, rose to chief. A scant few days before the legislature approved the Coal and Iron Police Act, Heisler had been charged with killing Tom Barrett, the inmate from Butler Township who Heisler said was trying to escape. Acquitted of murder in June, Heisler rose quickly in the ranks of the Coal and Iron Police.[42]

Less than a week after the new police force was created, new labor trouble erupted at the New York and Schuylkill mines when workers struck over a wage reduction of one dollar a week. But by this point, the company viewed strikes as an opportunity to reshape its workforce. "During the strike I anticipate that many of our miners and perhaps laborers may leave us," Davis wrote his West Branch superintendent. "If so keep the houses vacant . . . If after we resume we have a number of vacant houses at each colliery we will be more likely to get good men to fill them. In fact I am persuaded we should adopt this policy permanently even though it result for the present in our getting out less coal."[43]

The quest for "good men" was at the center of a debate that spring among executives of the New York and Schuylkill about whether company police, company houses, and company stores were sufficient to keep their West Branch colony pacified. Duffield felt something more was needed: company souls. To that end he assiduously courted a new Catholic priest whom he considered sufficiently tough on the turbulent, though Davis questioned the value of the investment. "Am glad you make so good report about the new priest. We will cultivate him," the company president wrote his superintendent. "I do not however agree with you that it would pay us to invest in such men. We have too much Catholic among us now and we can control them better by officers of the law when we get them than by priests, however belligerent they may be."[44]

Later that year, after a new purge of its payroll, the company hired a Protestant minister, Rev. John Long, to tend the churches it hoped to fill with Protestant miners in Heckscherville, Forestville, and New Mines.[45] "If our plans are successful," wrote the company president, "am sure his presence will be the means of collecting a population on the property more reliable than those who now give us so much trouble."[46]

The West Branch was now a colonized island in the midst of the Commonwealth of Pennsylvania where the coal company controlled everything, right down to the clergy. When miners walked out of the pits into the streets of Heckscherville and Forestville, the company owned the hills above them, the dirt beneath them, and damn near everything in between. The only exceptions were a few hard men who continued to fight back in the old way. And their struggle was beginning to take a toll on the New York and Schuylkill, even at its moment of triumph.

The reversal of fortune became evident in the fall of 1866, just six months after the creation of the Coal and Iron Police. In early October, the New York and Schuylkill shut down its Forestville mine for a few weeks, ostensibly because of a surplus of coal, but in reality to punish the Forestville mine workers for refusing to accept its demands. By the end of the month, company executives were talking about further shutdowns, not as retaliation, but as a financial necessity. For months the company had been willing to lose money to purge its workforce. Now it was paying the price. "The prospect for the future does not look very bright," Davis wrote. "We must stop some of our collieries and sell some of the production. The latter we must do even below market rates."[47]

The company had a mortgage to meet, the price of coal was falling, and the militants of the West Branch were preventing the New York and Schuylkill from slashing its costs to a point where mining would be profitable. By February 1867, all its mines except the Black Heath in Cass were closed. Davis explained the situation succinctly in late January: "We can take out a large amount of coal if we can sell it at a fair price, but $3 a ton at Schuylkill Haven does not pay with wages at the prices they were in 1866."[48]

By June it was all over. The company defaulted on its mortgage and ceased operation, selling assets to meet its obligations. To be sure, labor costs were not the sole cause of the company's difficulties. Demand was off, prices were down, and debt was high. But the cause mattered little to the hundreds of West Branch mine workers who by then had been out of work for months. Many began to migrate to the middle coal fields, where there was plenty of work in towns like Girardville, Shenandoah, and Mahanoy City.

And with them went most of the Mollies. The unemployment that accompanied the collapse of the New York and Schuylkill completed the job that the draft, military occupation, and blacklisting had begun. The "turbulent" were driven away, drifting over Broad Mountain like so many embers from a wildfire. They included several men who would lead the Molly Maguires in the first half of the 1870s—Barney Dolan, Pat Hester, Michael Lawler, and Patrick Tully, to name a few.

Tully left in the fall of 1865, amid the ongoing blacklisting of union militants. Lawler, whose name appeared on a May 1865 Foster Township list of deserting draftees, departed in January 1868. Philip Nash, whose arrest Dunne had sought in 1864 as a leader of the labor committee at his Heckscherville mine, turned up a decade later as a leading Molly in the Finger Board section of Butler Township.[49] Some Mollies went much farther. A witness in a murder trial testified that Daniel Kelly, an infamous killer and informer also known as Kelly the Bum, left the anthracite region in 1866 "to go with the Fenians"—an Irish American paramilitary group that mounted an unsuccessful invasion of Canada in June of that year.[50]

With the mines closing, a handful of Mollies turned to other ways to get money. On March 15, William H. Littlehales, superintendent of the Glen Carbon Coal Company, was gunned down in Cass Township, after traveling through Coal Castle on his way to Glen Carbon. The motive is supposed to have been robbery—his watch and pistol were taken, and Littlehales had regularly used the route to transport the payroll for his colliery. In Pottsville that day he had decided not to take the $8,000 payroll with him, but to return for it the following day.[51]

The motive in the Littlehales case may have been robbery, but the victim was everything the hard men of Cass Township had come to hate—the son of an Englishman and a staunch member of the rear guard of the 48th Regiment, in which his brother served. Littlehales had been a Foster Township delegate to political meetings of "Union men" shortly after the war. He ran a company store. He was an Anglo-Saxon Protestant mine boss and an active Republican, in a region where such men had used troops against their Irish Catholic employees. And so he died on the side of a road at age thirty-two, his eyes shot out, according to one story, because the superstitious killers feared that the last thing a dead man saw would remain reflected there.[52]

No one was ever brought to trial in the case, but a Pinkerton operative, identified only as W.R.H., reported years later that the killing was the work of Barney Dolan's gang.[53] Dolan, as we have seen, was the committeeman who directly challenged Richard Heckscher a few years earlier. He was still in Cass Township in 1865, but by October 1868, with the Forestville mines closed, Dolan had joined the exodus over Broad Mountain and become a Molly leader in Foster Township, where he opened a bar in Big Mine Run, the Preston Hotel. In 1867, the same year as the Littlehales killing, Dolan had been elected as the county leader of the Hibernian Society, after either a remarkably quick rise in the organization or, what seems more likely, years of participation in south Cass. He was also active in local politics, serving as a township judge of elections.[54] Allan Pinkerton described him as a large, muscular man with a "habit of smooth, sweet talk," two traits important to bar owners and local politicians in the rough-and-tumble Schuylkill County of the post–Civil War era.[55]

By 1870, Dolan's personal wealth stood at $4,000, and he owned real estate worth another $2,400—quite a turn of fortune for a man whose after-tax income was just $240 in 1865.[56] But he certainly did not make his money from the Littlehales killing, and the Pinkerton operative's hearsay is the only report to directly link him to serious violence. Dolan never stood trial for a Molly Maguire crime.

A week after the Littlehales killing, an Irish bar owner in Mahanoy Township opened fire on four men trying to break onto his place, killing Patrick Stinson of Glen Carbon. Stinson had been suspected but never charged in the attempted robbery of the mine superintendent Pollock.[57] The next night, four Irishmen invaded the home of a man named either Henry Rapp or Raub, an old farmer in Union Township, which borders Butler Township to the northeast. The victim went to a neighbor, Jacob Johnson, for help, and when the two returned, Johnson was fatally shot and Rapp was wounded.[58]

The violence sparked a predictable response. There were new condemnations in the *Miners' Journal*, new mass meetings in Pottsville, new calls for action by coal operators, new debates in the legislature. As in Ireland, better policing and a tougher court (one controlled by the governor, not the "ring" of Democratic elected officials in Pottsville) were seen as the solution to secret society violence. In the spring of 1867, after a delegation of fifty leading citizens from Schuylkill County visited Harrisburg to plead for help, the legislature considered creating a special criminal court for Schuylkill County with the sole authority to impanel grand juries, and a new countywide force responsible to the governor rather than local authorities.[59]

Debate about the constitutionality of the measures was heated. "You propose to oust the officers selected by the people and introduce martial law there," complained Sen. William A. Wallace, a Democrat of Clearfield County. Sen. Samuel J. Randall, a Philadelphia Democrat, said he saw no need for so extraordinary a measure: "That crime exists and has existed in the County of Schuylkill I do not pretend to deny. But that it exists to the fabulous extent stated by persons who have communicated with Senators, I do positively deny."

Among those who had communicated with the senators was an unidentified Schuylkill County resident whose letter cited the killings of Muir, Dunne, and Littlehales as the work of the same group. "They are formed into a secret organization called Molly Maguires, where their plans and plots are made, and the person selected to execute them," the author wrote. "If they refused the penalty is death. Their system is perfect, for by it they prevent the coal operators from discharging the bad men, as the superintendents would not dare to discharge one of them, or he would surely be the next man murdered. Hence they have such perfect control that in many cases they have stopped the works until the mines were filled with water."[60]

Only the criminal courts bill was signed into law. It didn't stop the robberies. The following year there were several other attempted payroll heists, two within a day of each other. On October 16, 1868, the Swatara mine superintendent J. Claude White escaped an ambush on the road from Llewellyn as he transported the payroll to the mine. There is strong reason to believe the attempted robbery was the work of Hibernians—an informant later testified that Pat Hester, the Locust Gap bodymaster, told him of his disappointment about botching the White robbery: "Hester said he lost a thing down the mountain, but there's a good thing in hand yet." The "good thing" yet in hand involved another payroll carried by a mine superintendent in neighboring Columbia County who was not so lucky as White. And this time there were arrests and a trial that offered a wealth of insight into the relationship between the Hibernians and highway robbery.

On the morning of October 17, Alexander W. Rea, forty-five, set out from his home in Centralia to his Coal Ridge colliery, located between Locust Gap and Mount Carmel. He never returned. The following day, the alarmed citizens of Centralia conducted a search and found Rea's body about a mile and a half west of the town, off a public highway. He'd been shot six times and robbed.

Several suspects were indicted the following year, including Hester, the local tax collector; Thomas Donahue, an Ashland saloonkeeper; and Michael Prior of Branchdale. Most if not all were later implicated in the attempted robbery of Claude White. Donahue, the only one brought to trial, won acquittal in February 1869. The charges against the remaining defendants were dropped, and there the case languished for seven years.[61]

In 1876, Capt. Robert J. Linden, a Pinkerton operative on loan to the Coal and Iron Police, paid a call on an inmate in the Schuylkill County prison he suspected of involvement in the Rea murder. Daniel Kelly, aka Manus Cull, aka Kelly the Bum, was serving time for robbery, and was at first reluctant to talk. When Linden dropped hints that he'd be indicted for Rea's murder upon his release, Kelly decided to cooperate.

He told authorities that the plot to rob Rea had been hatched in Donahue's Ashland saloon on Friday, October 16, by Hester and nine other Hibernians—Billy Muldowney, Patrick Tully, Peter McHugh (the leader of the Columbia County Hibernians), Ned Skiverton, Brian Campbell, James Bradley, Jack Dalton, Roger Lafferty, and himself. It wasn't taken up at an official meeting of the order—this sort of thing never was, Kelly said. It was more of a private arrangement between the bodymaster and some trusted buddies, or "butties" as they were known in the coal fields.

The conspirators were all Irish speakers, and at least three were former residents of the West Branch region—Lafferty had lived in Forestville before moving north under the alias of Johnston. Hester was living in Reilly Township in 1860 and had a history of violence dating at least to 1855, while Tully had been an active Hibernian in Glen Carbon around the time of the Littlehales slaying there. The latter two were both from Molly Maguire strongholds in Ireland—Hester had left Roscommon in 1848, and Tully had left Cavan in 1844.[62]

The conspirators' objective on October 16 was the $18,000 payroll they believed Rea would be transporting to his mine the next day, for Saturday was the usual payday in the anthracite region. What the ten men didn't realize was that Rea's colliery was an exception to the rule— the superintendent was parceling out the pay to his employees that very day, even as the ten plotted to steal it. After a long night of drinking they set out for an ambush. Two dropped out along the way—the lame Muldowney and Hester, who said he needed to go to Shamokin to purchase some material to repair his home. Before parting company with the eight, Hester lent Kelly his pistol, saying it was more reliable than the one Kelly possessed.

The ambush was laid on the road from Centralia to Mount Carmel, with the eight remaining gunmen discussing what they would do if Rea was accompanied by his son. It was agreed that if the father were killed, the boy would be given a horse and allowed to return home. That settled, one of the gunman—Bradley—was dispatched to Centralia; he returned with food and whiskey. Dalton, the only man who knew Rea, was sent a short way down the road to Centralia and ordered to give a signal when the superintendent passed in his buggy.

Five other men waited by a water barrel on the side of the road, while McHugh and Kelly stationed themselves fifty yards west of the barrel, in case Rea eluded the first party. When the mine superintendent's carriage passed, Dalton gave the sign, and the men at the water barrel halted Rea. Kelly and McHugh hurried down the road as Rea alit from the carriage. Facing seven pistols, he wordlessly handed over his pocketbook and watch.

"What are we going to do with this man?" asked Kelly, breaking the silence.

"I'll not be hunted through this world by any man," replied McHugh, opening fire. Rea stumbled off the road into the bushes but fell wounded after a distance. As he lay face down, Tully finished him off with a shot behind the ear. The men divided the fifty or sixty dollars Rea had on him and set off in different directions. Hester, the mastermind, would get nothing but a length of rope, and that nearly a decade later.[63]

The Rea killing marked the end of an era. For several years thereafter, the anthracite region experienced the closest thing to peace it had known since 1862, when Molly Maguire violence was resurrected on the West Branch amid mine strikes and Civil War draft resistance. When the Civil War ended, that movement had concentrated on avenging coercion by the government and mine officials, then moved on to highway robberies of those mine officials, and finally, to general larceny. The trend spread over Broad Mountain into the middle coal fields with the West Branch residents who fled the military occupation, were purged from the payroll of the New York and Schuylkill during the postwar strikes, or left unemployed when the company shut down. In the middle coal fields, the movement took root among the West Branch refugees and a new wave of Irish immigrants.

The violence ended, for the time being, with the Rea killing and the trial that followed, but it would be wrong to suggest that the cease-fire was the solely result of law enforcement measures like the creation of the Coal and Iron Police or the new criminal court. A much more important factor came into play in 1868: the founding of the Workingmen's Benevolent Association, a union for mine workers of all nationalities that was firmly dedicated to the redress of grievances through collective bargaining, not coffin notices and gunfire.

15   The Road to Black Thursday

Well, we've been beaten, beaten all to smash,
And now sir, we've begun to feel the lash,
As wielded by a gigantic corporation
Which runs the commonwealth and ruins the nation.
       —"After the Long Strike"

Oddly enough, the destruction of the Molly Maguires in the 1870s in no small part resulted from the reluctance of a West Branch Irishman to avenge the killing of a Hibernian. At the beginning of the decade, the victim, Edward Cosgrove, twenty-four, was laboring in a Reilly Township mine and living with a relative, Henry Cosgrove, an Irish-born miner with eight children of his own. Edward eventually struck out on his own, moving over Broad Mountain to Shenandoah, where he joined the local AOH lodge. On August 11, 1873, he was gunned down by a Welsh tough, Gomer James, who was arrested, tried for murder, and acquitted.

Escaping judicial punishment for violence against an Irishman could be very dangerous in Schuylkill County, as evidenced by the fate of another Welshman, John Reese, in 1846. Sure enough, there was soon talk among the Mollies about killing James in retaliation, and the task of organizing the job fell to the Shenandoah bodymaster, Michael Lawler, late of Glen Carbon.

But Lawler dawdled. When called to account for the delays, he complained that "it was not his fault that James was not killed, as Cosgrove's own cousin backed out, when he was the man appointed to do the deed, and of course after Cosgrove's cousin backed out all the others would not do it." Lawler's inaction led to his removal as bodymaster, triggering a chain of events that allowed a detective to deeply penetrate and destroy the entire neo-Ribbon movement in the anthracite region.[1] But the groundwork for the Mollies' decline had been laid by two related developments that made the organization increasingly irrelevant. The first was the rise of a modern labor movement. The second was the culture clash that labor movement triggered on the West Branch, which led many there, like the Cosgroves of Reilly Township, to turn their back on the old ways of the Molly Maguires.

The first industry-wide union of anthracite miners was formed largely because business interests overplayed their strong hand in Harrisburg. The Pennsylvania legislature, especially the Senate, had largely been in the deep pockets of the anthracite corporations since 1833, when senators who investigated the rivalry between individual entrepreneurs and big companies opted against legislating limits on the latter. By 1848, that control was being contested to some degree by Schuylkill Hibernians, whose political activity had, in the words of one admirer, prevented workers from having "their honest earnings filched from them by corporate aristocracies . . . whose armies besiege our Legislature and monopolize legislation."[2]

Two decades later, the fight for control of the statehouse was still going on, and the Hibernians were still deeply involved in politics, as the Rea killing made clear. Pat Hester, who was among those first charged in the case, was a supervisor and tax collector in Mount Carmel Township, which put him in a position to hire miners for road repair work. Kelly the Bum, who eventually turned state's evidence in the case, testified that he had canvassed for Hester on behalf of a state legislature candidate. Kelly said he was well taken care of with food, drink, and a little money when he "traveled around, from here to there, to help elect one of these Mollies."

Michael Graham, a Hibernian who lived near Mount Carmel and was charged as an accessory after the fact in the Rea case—he had bought Hibernian leader Peter McHugh's gun for fifteen dollars—was, like Hester, a former township tax collector and supervisor. He was taken into custody on election day 1868 at the polling place for Mount Carmel, which just happened to be his home and bar.[3] That same year, Pat Dormer was elected a Schuylkill County supervisor.

But for all their activity on the local level, the Hibernians hadn't crimped the coal companies' control of the legislature. Indeed, in 1866, the same year that the legislature approved creation of the Coal and Iron Police, the Senate killed two important mine-safety bills that had been approved by the House because the rate of accidental deaths was soaring in the mines. One would have required the governor to appoint four anthracite mine inspectors—two for Schuylkill County and two for Luzerne

County. The other would have required mine operators to enclose with fences any entrances to the pits or air holes into which a pedestrian might stumble.[4]

In 1867, the industry finally went too far. That year, over the objections of mine operators, the legislature approved an eight-hour day, but business lobbyists succeeded in adding a clause that the law did not apply to contract workers, effectively leaving the issue to the discretion of employers. Some mine operators insisted that their hours and wages would remain unchanged, and that any workers remaining on the job after July 1, 1868, when the law was to take effect, would be assumed to have agreed to this "contract." Other mine officials insisted that a pay cut would accompany an eight-hour day.[5]

In the Mahanoy Valley, over Broad Mountain from the West Branch, the coal companies chose the latter course. Their concerted action was made possible by the formation the year before of a trade association, which was said to maintain a blacklist that prevented miners from going to work for new employers unless they had the consent of their old ones.[6] That form of serfdom was bad enough, but in late June, Mahanoy Valley mine workers learned that their employers were planning to cut their pay as a result of the shorter day. They angrily stomped out of the pits, and labor unrest spread throughout the county as they engaged in the familiar tactic of marching from colliery to colliery. But in July came something new—a meeting in Mahanoy City attended by twelve to twenty thousand miners that ended in calls for a countywide union. The nucleus of the new union was the Workingmen's Benevolent Association of St. Clair, a town north of Pottsville, where John Siney had led a successful strike the year before.[7]

Siney was an Irish immigrant born in 1831 in Queen's County, just as the Whitefeet were raising hell with landlords and mine owners. His father was a potato grower active in land agitation who was said to have harbored "patriots who lost favor with the English-controlled constabulary." When John Siney was just five years old, the family was evicted and moved to the English mining center of Wigan.[8]

There, the younger Siney underwent the transformation from peasant child to industrial worker. He became involved in the labor movement, organizing a local brick makers union and serving as its leader for seven years. He emigrated to the United States in 1863, a year after his wife's death, and found work in a mine at St. Clair.[9] Speaking with Siney at the July mass meeting in Mahanoy City was John Welsh of Forestville, who came from a similar background. He was born in the Ulster border county of Down in 1839, and his family fled the famine for England, where he worked in the coal mines. Welsh, a Civil War veteran, was to have a profound influence on the labor movement in the anthracite region—and by extension on the emergence of a new working-class culture in Cass Township that coincided with the decline of the Molly Maguires there.

Siney, Welsh, and several other Irish and British miners formed the Workingmen's Benevolent Association, a countywide organization to "gather the workmen into a fraternal and beneficial association, remove the bitterness existing among them, break up the class prejudices that were a fruitful source of many of their sufferings, and to educate them to a higher plane of moral and intellectual life."[10]

The leadership's first job was to lend the union a degree of respectability. A band of striking miners had marched from Locust Gap and Mount Carmel to the Mahanoy Valley and then the West Branch before heading off to the northern coal field in Luzerne County to enlist support for the eight-hour strike there. Rumors were filtering back that the marchers were exacting "donations" of food and drink at stores, bars, and farms along the way. Such behavior was typical of mummers and Molly Maguires in the Old Country, and it is hard to believe that the West Branch labor committees of the Civil War–era would have had a problem with it. But the leadership of the new union was determined to do away with the old ways and address their grievances in a manner befitting industrial workers, not peasants. While coal executives fumed that "the eight-hour raiders" were the "scum of the Molly Maguires," the union leaders created a fund to make good the losses of farmers, innkeepers, and merchants.[11]

The union's achievements in the 1868 strike were limited—in September, Schuylkill County miners won higher pay, but not a shorter day. Though its success with the coal operators was less than complete, the new approach that the union represented brought miners to its banner in droves. On March 17, 1869, in a meeting in Hazleton, the Schuylkill County Workingmen's Benevolent Association was expanded to include representatives from all six counties of the anthracite region.[12] An industry-wide union was born that St. Patrick's Day, and its president was John Siney.

Two months later, the Pennsylvania state legislature legalized labor unions. (It would be another three years before they won the right to strike, ending the threat of conspiracy charges, so long as they didn't interfere with those who continued working.)[13] Growing worker solidarity and political clout were quickly matched by a consolidation of corporate power. Following the lead of the Mahanoy Valley mine operators, coal companies in four other parts of Schuylkill County had formed trade associations in

1868, and on November 19, 1869, those associations came together in the Anthracite Board of the Trade of the Schuylkill Coal Region.[14]

The first test of strength came in the state legislature, where the union successfully pressed for passage of a mine-safety bill that required state inspections of collieries. The measure, signed into law on April 12, 1869, was the first such law in the country, but the union's victory was less than complete—the measure applied only to Schuylkill County. In the Senate, which had killed a similar bill just three years before, union-supported attempts to broaden the legislation to cover all coal mines had been killed by Samuel G. Turner, a coal dealer from Luzerne County. He hadn't even bothered to read the legislation but felt comfortable talking about why it wasn't needed in Luzerne. "I can now remember but one instance where firedamp explosions resulted in injury to miners in the county," said Turner, referring to combustible mine gases.[15]

Less than five months later, he had reason to regret those words. On September 6, the greatest mine disaster in American history until then killed more than one hundred workers in the Steuben shaft of the Nanticoke Coal Company in Avondale, Luzerne County. A coroner's jury found that sparks from a furnace at the bottom of the shaft had set fire to wooden brattices above it, but that didn't stop mine officials from spreading the word that Irish arsonists were to blame—the mine had just reopened after a strike.

Siney appeared on the scene and made a speech that seared the souls of many who heard it, including a young Irish American named Terence Vincent Powderly. "You can do nothing to win these dead back to life," Siney told the crowd. "But you can help me to win fair treatment and justice for living men who risk life and health in their daily toil."

Powderly went on to lead the Knights of Labor, but he never forgot the charred bodies of the miners being pulled from the pits, the mother he saw kneeling in silent grief over the body of her boy, or Siney, "standing on the desolate hillside at Avondale," daring to talk about justice in the realm of King Coal. "When I listened to John Siney, I could see Christ in his face and hear a new Sermon on the Mount," Powderly recalled. "I thereby resolved to do my part, humble though it might be, to improve the condition of those who worked for a living."[16]

Powderly was not the only overnight convert. Sen. Turner suddenly saw the light and championed a mine-safety law, but his political career was as dead as the men of Avondale. The miners turned their back on him in the next election, and Turner, a Democrat, lost. In the postwar era, he was only one of several Democrats who were more than willing to do the bidding of the coal companies.

In the spring of 1869, while Turner was blocking mine-safety measures, the Reading Railroad appointed as its acting president Gowen, the Democratic former Schuylkill County district attorney who signed on with the New York and Schuylkill after the war. Gowen, who never managed to prosecute the killers of James Bergen but did have Bergen's widow hauled into court for running a shebeen, always had a keen understanding of where power lay, and how to cozy up to it. In 1863, it lay with those Cass Township Democrats who had helped elect him, the Molly Maguires. In 1869, it lay with the coal companies.

Gowen quickly moved to exponentially increase the railroad's power by entering the mining business on a sweeping scale, transforming the Reading from a shipper of coal into the main producer of it in the Schuylkill field. With Gowen's assumption of power, the principals were all in place for a climactic power struggle between Siney, Welsh, and the union on the one hand, and Gowen and the Anthracite Board of Trade on the other.

To understand how that struggle played out on the West Branch, it is important to turn to another, smaller clash, one between the culture in which the Mollies were rooted—old, Gaelic, and peasant—and an emerging working-class ethos profoundly influenced by the rise of Workingmen's Benevolent Association.

Culture Clash on the West Branch

In a sense, the culture clash between those trying to recreate the Irish peasant way of life and those trying to assimilate had always played out in Cass Township. That conflict provided the context for the slaying of James Bergen, whose repeated enlistments in the military betrayed an unmistakable urge to assimilate.

The difference, after 1867, was that those who wanted to leave behind the old ways gained the upper hand. A curious calm descended on the West Branch that year as the echoing footfalls of Littlehale's fleeing killers faded into the hills around Glen Carbon. He was at the end of a long line of men to be killed there by a small band of Irish gunmen, in the classic Whiteboy style.

To understand why the West Branch assassinations ended—and why the Cosgrove family wanted no part of any new ones—consider an anecdote about Reilly Township, where they lived, that was related in 1957 by Harry Murphy, an eighty-year-old former official of the United Mine

Workers. It concerns a young man who turned his back on the Mollies and the Gaelic culture of which they were part and parcel: "Me father told me about this. He went to a dance one night near Branchdale. Women and men in working clothes were dancing to Irish tunes played by an old Irish fiddler. The other dancers were talking Irish, which me father couldn't understand. The fiddler was a friend of me father's and he called him outside and said, 'They're all Mollies having this dance,' and the two of 'em, my father and the fiddler, they dusted out of the place."[17]

All over the West Branch, young men were turning their back on the Molly Maguires and the peasant mind-set and lifestyle that produced them. In part this was because many Mollies had turned their back on the West Branch, fleeing wartime military occupation, relentless postwar purges of union militants, and unemployment. Their departure and the subsequent arrival of the WBA opened new cultural horizons for young second-generation Irish Americans, whose perspectives were no longer limited by the dark, lowering clouds of Irish history. Their language was English, not Irish. Their music was the regimen of a band, not a freewheeling fiddle. Their hero was not a mythical Irishwoman, but a very real neighbor, John Welsh, a Civil War veteran who had taken a leading role in the union, which saw as one of its prime responsibilities the elevation of the miners' intellectual life.

One of the best examples of the new outlook was the Forestville Literary Society, which rose—and fell—with the union. Founded around 1870 for "the promotion of all classes of the community," the society instituted a constitution "based upon the parliamentary laws observed and adopted by the W.B.A. of Schuylkill County." Like the union, the group encompassed young men of all nationalities, but second-generation Irish Americans were in the majority. If members like James Lynch and Terrance O'Connor were typical, their parents had supported the government during the war.

Lynch's father, William, a mine worker who had emigrated from Cavan before the famine, had contributed to a fund for the relief of sick and wounded soldiers. He had a son, Edward, in the service. Like Welsh, O'Connor's father, James, was a famine immigrant from Ulster and a war veteran. He had served in a militia unit, the Schuylkill Guards of Minersville, for three months after the opening of hostilities.[18]

Before it collapsed in 1876, after the union was crushed, the literary society embodied all the lofty ideals of the WBA, featuring readings, poetry, dialogues, and debate. Many members were mine laborers who had observed the labor tumult of the Civil War from their perches in the towering coal breakers, where boys as young as ten separated anthracite from slag. The labor orientation of the literary society is clear in such debates as "Resolved: That suspension [a strike] is a benefit." That topic speaks volumes about conditions in the mines, but another shows that these young men had their sights on horizons more distant than the next coal breast: "Resolved: That the professions offer a better opening to a young man than mercantile or mechanical pursuits."

The literary society was part of a larger working-class cultural renaissance—a Forestville music group was formed about the same time, by members of some of the same families, including Jim Lynch and Terrance O'Connor's brother James.[19] With band practices and formal rules of debate, the young mine workers were imposing on themselves a degree of regimentation that mimicked the discipline of the union, and was utterly at odds with the informal gatherings and barroom debates that had long been the rule on the West Branch. The war itself must have played an important role in this new discipline—Welsh was by no means the only Cass resident who had spent time in the Union Army, internalizing the values of teamwork.

A remarkable degree of energy, optimism, and organization was required for the new cultural pursuits, and the Workingmen's Benevolent Association deserves much of the credit—a state report from the early 1870s found that the union gave "direction in the right way to the superabundant vigor and vivacity of youth."[20] It is not hard to picture the young men of South Cass, after a day of backbreaking labor, heading down the road for the Forestville School House, lines of verse or logic or music running through their heads, as Mine Hill towered above, a deeper black against the night sky. At the door to the tavern at the crossroads, the hard men doubtless pointed and laughed over their porter, and perhaps did worse as the young debaters and musicians passed. They could laugh all they wanted, but their day was all but done, at least on the West Branch.

When a Pinkerton spy visited Glen Carbon in October 1873, an informant told him that he "had not heard anything of the Molly Maguires for some time, he believed that most of the members had left." To be sure, some Hibernians stayed, clinging to the old ways even as they adjusted to the new. Luke Mohan's son, Thomas, was active in both the AOH and the labor movement, running for secretary of the county miners' union in 1874.[21] But he was never implicated in any crime, demonstrating that a Hibernian and union man did not necessarily a Molly make.

In a history of the Mollies published a scant few years after the last were hanged, Dunne's companion the night before his murder, Francis Dewees, offered a twofold explanation—motive and opportunity—for the shift in the organization's locus from the southern anthracite field to the middle one. The opportunity was simple—the war stimulated demand for coal, which led to the development of the middle coal fields when the Mine Hill and Schuylkill Railroad was extended from the West Branch over Broad Mountain to the Mahanoy Valley.[22] The motive Dewees cited was a bit more complex—a feud within the Irish community, between natives of County Kilkenny and some other counties in Ireland. According to Dewees, the Kilkenny men were once well represented in the Mollies of Cass Township but region-wide found themselves in the minority overall, and eventually left or were forced out, forming a rival group called the Sheet Irons or the Chain Gang. "In the course of time the Kilkenny men became the most powerful in that section of the county," he wrote of the West Branch. "And the great majority of the 'Mollies' in Cass and adjoining townships, finding that retaliation followed very quickly any outrage upon a Kilkenny man, beat a retreat and settled in force over the Broad Mountain and in the Mahanoy Valley."[23]

Dewees's thesis has a few points in its favor. The lists of West Branch union activists whom the coal operators wanted arrested in the Civil War were indeed rife with names straight out of County Kilkenny, like Brennan. The Mollies did fade south of the mountain. And there was a conflict between Mollies and Kilkenny natives in the Mahanoy Valley during the 1870s. But there is little or no evidence that the Mollies were driven en masse from the West Branch in the 1860s by a more powerful group of Irish thugs. There is, on the contrary, ample documentation of the flight of many union activists and draft opponents from the West Branch amid military occupation, postwar purges by employers, and mine shutdowns— factors that Dewees ignores.

His explanation becomes plausible if that flight is taken into account, if we assume "Kilkennymen" was a something of synonym for "experienced mine workers," and if the simple geographic feud he cites is subsumed into a larger cultural clash. Because Kilkenny had a long history of anthracite mining, immigrants from there had more experience and rose more quickly in the workforce. They assimilated faster than did immigrants from other Irish counties. The forced flight of many of the most hard-core Mollies during and after the war may have tipped the scales in Cass Township in favor of the more experienced, more assimilated miners, encouraging others members of the order to join their brethren over the mountain.

The shift was clear in "What Makes Us Strike?" a Schuylkill County ballad from the 1870s that is structured as a conversation between a miner and an inquisitive visitor to the county:

"How far to Pottsville?" Stranger, did you say?
I guess it's 'bout a dozen miles away,
Straight out in that direction—o'er the hill.
"Do any Mollies lie in wait to kill?"
Oh, no, You're south of the mountain,
And murdering Mollies, sir, you needn't count on.
You see we're civilized on this side,
And do not deadly weapons hide

No Mollies lie in wait to kill, "because you're south of the mountain"—
Broad Mountain—and "we're civilized on this side." The ballad goes on to
explore the causes of labor unrest in the coal region—"the work is hard,
we oft get hurt, and sometimes lost, pard." Reading Railroad President
Franklin Gowen is damned as "the great conspirer against our price, our
liberties, our rights, and the instigator of one-half our fights." Significantly,
the miner turns down the offer of a drink—"Some miners like their whiskey, but I don't./In fact, to tell the truth, I can't afford it." The entire composition is designed to portray the miners of the southern anthracite field
as sober, hardworking, and independent, to counter the notion that they
were "lazy, bloody, reckless men" who emerged from the pits only "to burn
a breaker, kill a boss, or fight." It ends with a rather plaintive plea: "And
mind, tell them we're like other men."[24]

Another ballad, "The Phoenix Park Colliery," sheds some light on the
transformation of the workforce at the mine where armed Irishmen were
first heard to use the term "Molly Maguire," in December 1862. The lyrics
are undated, but were certainly written after 1870:

For three hard months I worked there
And divil a cent I drew;
I walked right into Minersville
And swore Bill Brown I'd sue.[25]

Any West Branch Irishman who preferred lawsuits to coffin notices
was one who had made the transformation from shovel-wielding peasant
to American industrial worker. Indeed, an October 12, 1879, retrospective
in the *New York Times*, after the last of the Mollies was hanged, described
the early members of the order as "peasant-miners" among whom "local
prejudices, customs and modes of thought and action survived the passage
across the ocean." The Mollies, the *Times* said, "transferred to the American
coal operators their old hostility to the Irish landlords, and the conflicts

which everywhere seem inevitable between employer and employed were thus additionally embittered by much of the hatred of the Celts for their Saxon conquerors, by Roman Catholics for a Protestant ruling class, and by tenants on precarious leases for their landlords, who, they firmly believe, have robbed them of their birthrights." But by the 1870s, the heavily Irish workforce of the West Branch, which had been in the United States for decades, was on their way to becoming much like "other men" in that they relied on an industrial union, rather than neo-Ribbonism, to advance their economic interests.

That is not to say the new generation of Irish mine workers were the sober, docile workers Bannan had always wanted. "The Phoenix Park Colliery" contained lines like "remember boys, when payday comes / You'll all know how to fight." And when an officer of the Forestville band, William J. Dormer, chiseled his name deep into a rock near the West-West Falls, he and his butties made sure to carve images of beer kegs and bottles beside it. The Workingmen's Benevolent Association could not prevent drunken payday brawls, but it did offer a way to redress grievances that fell short of killing the mine superintendent or burning the company store.

The decline in Molly Maguire violence in the West Branch after 1867 cannot be understood outside the context of the new miners' union. The speed with which the Workingmen's Benevolent Association spread throughout the anthracite region bespeaks a growing maturity and class consciousness on the part of the region's mine workers. Molly Maguire violence was a toxic by-product of the long and painful process by which Irish peasants transformed themselves into American industrial workers, and that transition was more advanced in the West Branch than it was anywhere else. Irish mine workers there had moved from the disorganized strike of 1842 to the short-lived Bates union of 1849 to the Ribbon-influenced local labor committees of the Civil War to the modern type of labor union that the WBA constituted in 1868–69.

As the workforce matured and assimilated, Gaelic declined in Cass Township, the inevitable result of death, the shrinking use of Gaelic in Ireland after the famine, and the fact that newer immigrants from Gaelic-speaking areas of Ireland like West Donegal were settling elsewhere—in the booming middle coal fields, or at the eastern end of the lower coal fields, around Coaldale in Schuylkill County and Summit Hill in Carbon County.

For example, Peter McHugh, a Gaelic speaker convicted in the Rea killing, came to the United States in 1864 from West Donegal and eventually settled in the middle coal fields; Daniel Kelly, another Gaelic-speaking Donegal native who arrived in 1865, spent much of his time wandering the middle coal fields. And two men convicted for Molly Maguire killings in the mid-1870s, James Roarity and Alexander Campbell, were both born in the Irish-speaking area around Dungloe, Donegal, and arrived in the United States in 1869 and 1868, respectively, with Roarity settling in Coaldale and Campbell in Summit Hill.[26]

With a fresh infusion of Gaelic speakers—the oxygen that the Molly Maguires needed to survive—these areas would be the focus of secret society activity in the 1870s. Not coincidentally, the towns "north of the mountain" in the middle coal fields—Shenandoah, Girardville, Mahanoy City, and Big Mine Run—were founded much later than those of the West Branch, so the community's experience in labor relations was as shallow as the new mine shafts.

In the West Branch collieries, which grew deeper every year, there was a corresponding depth of experience in mining and sophistication in labor relations. A quarter century of labor unrest had taught most miners of the West Branch that something more than Ribbon muscle was needed— namely, a multiethnic, centralized union powerful enough to confront the operators at the negotiating table and in the legislature. The few who clung to the Molly Maguire approach were reduced to the odd election-day beating or act of industrial sabotage. They would have quickly become totally irrelevant, and this story would have had a vastly different ending, had not one of those acts of sabotage incurred the wrath of the Reading Railroad. For the Reading brought in detectives, and Michael Lawler's downfall allowed one of those detectives unprecedented access to the secrets of the society.

The Rise of King Coal

The long, sad story of the anthracite labor troubles of the 1870s has been exhaustively documented elsewhere, and it will receive only brief treatment here, for the denouement involved many individuals and incidents from the Civil War era.[27] When Gowen took control of the Reading Railroad, he quickly learned that the key to profits was the uninterrupted shipment of coal. This lesson was underlined in April 1870, when the company's railcars rattled to a halt after the Anthracite Board of Trade locked out the mine workers of the Schuylkill field to force the union to accept a pay cut. Gowen brokered a compromise, one-year agreement that was quickly accepted by the union, for the workers of the Northern Field in Luzerne and Lackawanna Counties had stayed on the job, thereby undermining the strike. Early the next year, the union won some minor gains in a new contract that was quickly ratified. It seemed, for a moment, that the industry had achieved a degree of stability, at least in the Schuylkill field.

That, of course, was an illusion. The trouble began in the Northern Field, where workers had stayed on the job for high pay during the 1870 strike, then been hit with a drastic wage cut just after Gowen's compromise had ended the southern strike. On January 10, 1871, the northern WBA quit the pits in an attempt to win back what was lost, and they appealed to the southern miners to join them. Siney opposed the move, but was voted down by militants who saw an opportunity to at last end a debilitating regional rift and create an effective, industry-wide organization.

It very nearly worked. Within a month, many coal operators were ready to accede to the union's demands. But they had not counted on Gowen. The railroad president, angered by what he viewed as the union's betrayal, raised his freight rates 100 percent, making it impossible for any mine operator who had settled with the union to resume shipping. The action spurred widespread outrage, and hearings on the issue were held in March by the Pennsylvania State Senate, a body certain to give the Reading a sympathetic ear. Sure enough, Gowen was allowed to deflect questions about the rate increase and place the union on trial at the hearings, with sly insinuations that it was somehow linked to "an association which votes in secret, at night, that men's lives shall be taken, and that they shall be shot before their wives, in cold blood."

The strike collapsed the following month when the union accepted an offer of arbitration. Among the four labor leaders who argued the union's position in the arbitration proceedings was Michael Lawler.[28] After three strikes in three years, Gowen concluded that the railroad needed to monopolize not only the transportation of coal, but its production and distribution as well, borrowing a page from the corporations that controlled the northern anthracite fields.

To achieve a monopoly, Gowen had to overcome several obstacles. His railroad's state charter barred it from mining operations, so the legislature would have to be finessed. The independent mine operators who still dominated the Southern Coal Field would then have to be either bought out or brought to heel. And last but by no means least, he would have to crush not only the new mine workers union, but also the Hibernian order, that longstanding locus of labor militancy among the Irish.

The legislature proved the lowest hurdle to Gowen's ambitions. In January 1871, he sought to create a front company through a friendly lawmaker, who drew up a bill chartering the Franklin Coal Company, inserting in fine print a provision granting the Reading the right to own coal lands. An opponent in the Pennsylvania State Senate, Esaias Billingfelt, smelled a rat and grilled the sponsor about who was behind the measure. When the sponsor finally admitted that it was the Reading, the Senate struck the provision.

Gowen was undeterred. He began buying coal lands under his own name and convinced friends of the company to do the same, promising he would take the property off their hands at a 6 percent profit once he had straightened things out in the Senate. They didn't have long to wait. Six months later, Gowen tried the front-company ploy again, seeking a charter for the Laurel Improvement Coal Company that would have given the Reading the right to own coal lands. Once more Sen. Billingfelt ferreted out the truth, and the offending provision was struck by a margin of three votes. The Senate then adjourned for lunch, and the chicanery began in earnest. When senators returned, three opponents of the Reading were mysteriously absent, and one had changed his mind. The morning's vote was reconsidered, the provision favoring the railroad reinserted, and, this time, the Reading won.[29]

Outraged independents accused the company of bribery. "Whilst I believe the majority of our legislators are not proverbial for their mental acumen, I never supposed they were such a set of consummate asses as to confer extraordinary privileges, so sadly subversive to the interests of their constituents, upon corporations without compensation to themselves," wrote one leading independent operator, Benjamin B. Thomas. In language that echoed the dire words of the Senate's debate over coal corporations some thirty-five years before, he warned that the Reading and the Legislature were in cahoots to crush the independents and subjugate workers, "rendering the idea of representative government a scoff and a byword." Bannan damned the underhanded way the bill was passed, and complained that "the Reading Railroad Company are now master of the situation," though he blamed the union for this sorry situation.[30]

The future was now clear for the independent coal operators of the Schuylkill region. Squeezed by the union on the one hand and the Reading on the other, many sold out to the railroad, which bought more than sixty-five thousand acres of coal land in 1871. By 1874, that number had risen to more than one hundred thousand acres, and by the end of the following year, the buying spree had left the company and its Laurel Run subsidiary, now renamed the Philadelphia and Reading Coal and Iron Company, with a bonded debt of $75 million.[31]

A continuous supply of coal was now vital if the company was to pay off the debt; to guarantee that supply, the company would have to subjugate its workers. That meant smashing the two organizations that the workers re-lied on for succor and support—the Workingmen's Benevolent Association and the Ancient Order of Hibernians, as the group became known after 1870. For that job, the Reading turned to the Pinkerton Detective Agency.

The Pinkertons

It is somehow fitting that the Pinkertons, who would ring down the curtain on the Mollies in such dramatic fashion, made their entrance in Glen Carbon, near the wellspring of both the West Branch and the secret society.

In the first part of October 1873, Allan Pinkerton, the founder of the renowned detective agency, traveled to Philadelphia to meet with Gowen. According to Pinkerton's sensational and self-serving account of the case, the Reading president told him, "The coal fields are infested by a most desperate class of men, banded together for the worst purposes—called by some, the Buckshots, by others, the Molly Maguires—and they are making sad havoc with the country. It is a secret organization, has its meeting in out-of-the-way places, and its members, I have been convinced ever since my residence in Pottsville and my connection with the criminal courts as District Attorney in the county of Schuylkill, are guilty of a majority of all of the murders and other deeds of outrage, which, for many years, have been committed in the neighborhood."[32]

The trouble in Glen Carbon involved the burning of a coal breaker and the dispatch of an empty railcar down the track. When Pinkerton sent in two detectives—identified in reports only as S.M. and W.R.H.—their main concern seemed to be reports of tampering with the railroad switches and signals. One was told by a resident that most of the Mollies had moved on. Among those who remained were Jim Brennan, Jim Whitmore, and "Mc-Cluskey," the resident said.* The Mollies were still active in politics—a coal operator, Martin Brennan, confided to S.M. that he had just been badly beaten by a Molly, Jim Burns, "because he did not vote the same as Burns." Not everyone was so forthcoming. The detectives talked with carpenters who were building a wooden chute to help quench the fire in the slope, but "they seemed to be afraid to express any opinion as to the origin of the fire." They queried a fireman at the nearby Taylorsville colliery about who had sent empty railcars down the track, but couldn't get any satisfactory answers.[33]

---

* Brennan's name suggests that not all the West Branch Kilkennymen had abandoned the Molly Maguires.

Pinkerton quickly realized that another type of detective—one who would blend in a little better—was needed. The ideal candidate would be a Catholic native of the Ulster borderlands with an intimate knowledge of the region's violent peasant secret societies. Pinkerton just happened to have such a man in his employ in Chicago—James McParlan, who was born in 1844 in the parish of Mullaghbrack, just north of Markethill in County Armagh. It was the very spot, oddly enough, where the precursors of the Protestant Peep O'Day Boys had planned their depredations against local Catholics in the barn of the "widow M'P—n" in the 1780s, leading to the formation of the Defenders.[34] There does not seem to be any doubt, however, that McParlan's family was Catholic, and in the black famine year of 1847 his parish priest fulminated about the causes of the disaster then sweeping the land. Rev. Thomas Hanley cited worldliness, inactivity, Sabbath-breaking, and neglect of church ordinances, before coming to what he considered the worst:

> *Murder*, that most treacherous and damnable of crimes—treacherous, for the assassin walks abroad wearing the day-light robe of charity and peace—salutes you by the way—engages in conversation—watches his opportunity—plies his secret dagger—effects his deadly purpose—then flies back to his hiding place, glutted, but marked with blood—damnable, for if there is one more than another, who, should he die unrepenting and unforgiven, shall suffer the extreme of hell's torment, and hell's punishment, it will be the assassin, who, unprovoked, and with cool and calculating premeditation, way-lays his fellow-man, and sends the innocent victim to an unmerited and untimely grave.[35]

McParlan, as Pinkerton quickly discovered, was every bit as appalled by secret society violence as his old parish priest, but had a far better understanding of its origins, for he recognized that the Molly Maguires were in many ways a symptom of the famine, not its cause. When Pinkerton asked him on October 8 to write a report on the origins of the Mollies in Ireland, McParlan took just two days to produce a remarkably detailed seven-page document that pointed directly to the potato blight: "Some of the people in the provinces of Ulster and Connaught resolved not to starve," he wrote. "They immediately organized under the name of Molly McGuire."[36] He said the organization spread to England, Scotland, and the United States when it was suppressed in Ireland, and had been renamed the Ancient Order of Hibernians, though he seemed somewhat at a loss about why Pinkerton would be so interested in the topic. "I presume by the time you have got this read you will get tired as most of it or in fact all of it may not be very interesting to you," McParlan added in a postscript to his boss.

He could not have been more wrong. Pinkerton was fascinated with the subject, and McParlan's report convinced him that the Ulsterman was perfect for a very special assignment in the anthracite region. McParlan seems to have had one other qualification—it appears that as recently as 1870, he had been working as a Chicago barkeep, experience that would stand him in good stead in the saloons and shebeens of Schuylkill County.[37] He agreed to go undercover and infiltrate the Mollies. On October 27, McParlan entered Schuylkill County under the guise of a counterfeiter named James McKenna who was on the run for a murder in Buffalo, New York.

It was an oddly quiet time in the hard coal fields. With the union taking up miners' grievances, the Hibernians had stood down from their roles as avengers. The Mollies had not killed anyone since December 1871, when Morgan Powell, a Welsh mine boss in Summit Hill, Carbon County, had been gunned down. In Schuylkill County, there had been only one murder since Barney Dolan took over as county delegate of the AOH in 1868—that of Patrick Burns, a Tuscarora mine boss who was killed on April 15, 1870.

McParlan's real work began in November, when he toured the west end of the county as a tramp, stopping in Swatara, a mining village on the edge of the West Branch region that had been the site of much trouble during the Civil War. Finding no signs of Molly Maguire activity, he doubled back toward Pottsville, taking refuge from a snowstorm in a Minersville tavern, and sharing a conversation with Hugh Mohan, who was the state secretary of the Emerald Beneficial Organization, a rival to the AOH.

That conversation aroused some suspicion when McParlan returned to Pottsville and stopped in the Sheridan House, a Centre Street saloon run by the former county commissioner and reputed Molly leader Pat Dormer, a gray-haired veteran of the Hibernians. McParlan impressed Dormer by dancing a jig, singing the Molly Maguire ballad, and winning a barroom brawl. But one of the hard men, Daniel Kelly, aka Kelly the Bum, had his doubts, wrote Allan Pinkerton, who recorded the following conversation in *The Molly Maguires and the Detectives*:

> "Didn't I see you at Minersville, not long ago, in company with Hugh Mahan?"
>
> "Sure, and may you did! You might as well as not, at laste, fur I war wid him, at tat place, only the last month sometime!"

Kelly scanned the face of the detective sharply for a second, and then resumed:

"Do you chance to belong to the Emeralds? The benevolent society of that name is what I mane!"

"No I do not!"

"Well, I know Mahan to be a mimber, and he's been making himself very free wid lashings of people, herebouts, within the past few weeks, inviten them to join, and I didn't know but that you were wan."[38]

With any doubts about his membership in a nonviolent Irish benevolent society laid to rest, McParlan went on to further ingratiate himself with Dormer. In January 1874, he made an even better contact, when Dormer introduced him to Lawler, the Shenandoah bodymaster, mine contractor, and former Glen Carbon resident. When the conversation turned to reports that the Reading planned to import five thousand workers to break the union, Lawler showed he could bluster with the best of them. "You must know that I am a man of learning and some sound sense and know the workings of this region," the bodymaster boasted. "And if President Gowen undertakes to do this—in place of requiring the State Militia to protect those new men in the mines and protect his breakers, shafts and depots from the torch—he will require them all to protect his own life."[39]

McParlan's reaction must have impressed Lawler, who told the detective that if times were not so hard, he would hire him. In fact, Lawler did something much better, taking the newcomer under his wing and inducting him into Shenandoah lodge of the Ancient Order of Hibernians on April 15, 1874. With a ready supply of cash to keep his hard-drinking butties in booze, McParlan steadily rose in their esteem. (At one point early on he was introduced by a Pottsville publican as "one of the old school"—a sure sign of respect in an organization that was itself a throwback.)[40]

Much has been written about accusations that McParlan served as an agent provocateur during his years undercover. Regardless of what he did or did not do to prevent specific acts of bloodshed, a few points are certain. The first is that Molly assassinations had been reduced to little more than a memory at the time McParlan joined the Hibernians. The second is that within months of his induction, longtime Hibernian leaders who had kept a lid on violence were removed, a process in which the detective played at least some small part. The third is that they were replaced by men more willing to spill blood.

On April 17, two days after McParlan became a Hibernian, the *Miners' Journal* dismissed as "totally without foundation" reports of a murderous secret organization of miners. "There might have at one day existed a society known as the 'Molly Maguires,' the object of which was revenge for fancied wrongs to any of its members," the paper opined. "But whether it is kept up now is more than we can say."[41]

A Molly Maguire ballad about McParlan recorded in the 1930s struck much the same note:

> He came among these people
> At a very quiet time
> And bragged himself to be a plotter
> In a most atrocious crime . . . [42]

One factor in the decline in violence was the leadership of West Branch veterans like Barney Dolan, the county delegate, and Michael Lawler, the Shenandoah bodymaster, who did their best to rein in a rambunctious rank and file. In addition to stalling the revenge killing of Gomer James, Lawler prevented another Wildgoose Lodge when he sidetracked a plan to burn down a mine patch where two Mollies had been beaten, and then shoot its inhabitants as they fled the blaze.[43] And as the *New York Times* put it, "Barney Dolan was a man who sought to rule rather by 'moral suasion' than by brute force."[44]

But Lawler and Dolan were ousted soon after McParlan joined the order. Allan Pinkerton went to some pains in *The Molly Maguires and the Detectives* to refute the notion that McParlan acted as an agent provocateur, but a close reading of his account suggests that if nothing else, the detective was an agent of change. While he may not have deliberately provoked violence, his efforts to gain a better perch within the organization to do his spying seem to have had a domino effect that contributed to the violence.

There are perils in trying to sort out the internal politics of a secret society well over a century after the fact, but Pinkerton's account suggests that the key to the situation lay in McParlan's friendship with Frank McAndrew, an illiterate native of County Mayo who wanted to succeed Lawler as Shenandoah bodymaster. Lawler at first appeared reluctant to induct McParlan into the Hibernians, fearing another vote for his rival. But then McParlan promised to help Lawler get an even better position—county delegate. When the detective promised "to do his utmost to put Lawler in Dolan's position," the former chuckled with satisfaction and promised to make McParlan a member at the very next meeting.[45]

McParlan was as good as his word. When, in July, Dolan had Lawler ousted for refusing to avenge the Cosgrove killing, McParlan helped McAndrew become bodymaster. All this turbulence proved highly advantageous to McParlan. Because McAndrew could not read or write, the detective was appointed secretary of the lodge at a July 15 meeting, a move that gave him cover to gather information, write it down, and move around.

When the secretary of the Pennsylvania AOH visited the bar of Tom Fisher, the Carbon County Hibernian leader, McParlan put in a bad word about Dolan. McParlan agreed with others that Dolan should be banned from the organization for life for cursing a bishop. Dolan was indeed expelled, on August 31, and in a telling passage, Pinkerton notes that while Dolan was stunned by the decision, it came as no surprise to the detective. But Lawler's hopes to replace Dolan had been dashed, and Jack Kehoe, the Girardville bodymaster, was named county leader in his stead.[46]

Dolan's departure ended one of the quietest periods of the Molly era. During his six-year tenure as leader of the Schuylkill Hibernians, there had been just one murder, and that far from his headquarters in Big Mine Run. It is true that he had Lawler removed as Shenandoah bodymaster for not avenging the Cosgrove killing, but that may have simply been a convenient excuse to get rid of an inconvenient rival. The *New York Times* noted, years later, that "during his term of office the county had a season of comparative immunity from the startling crimes which mark its history before and since."[47] Indeed, while Dolan was a union committeeman in Forestville during the Civil War, there were no murders there, either. To be sure, a company store was burned and a guard beaten, but the New York and Schuylkill mine bosses in Forestville escaped the fate of their counterparts in Branchdale and Heckscherville.

At least one contemporary Schuylkill County observer believed the violence that marked Kehoe's reign was part of a strategy by the new county delegate to a establish a contrast with his predecessor. "Kehoe, acting on the assumption that Dolan had been cowardly and weak in his direction of the order, endeavored to contrast with such former policy his own boldness and daring," Francis Dewees wrote in 1877, while Kehoe was still alive.[48]

McParlan made note of all the changes in the AOH, sending regular reports to Pinkerton, who forwarded summaries to Gowen. And the Ulsterman wasn't the only Pinkerton spy in the anthracite region. There were several others—P. M. Cummings, William McCowan, and one identified only as R.J.L. (probably Robert J. Linden)—monitoring the union. While the violence of the Mollies was at this point little more than barroom bluster, there was plenty of activity to report on the labor front.

In October 1873, as Pinkerton was dispatching spies into the anthracite field, Siney, the head of the anthracite mine workers' union, was organizing a national convention of mine workers in Youngstown, Ohio. A nationwide miners' union was born at the convention, with Siney as its president. He promptly resigned as leader of Workingmen's Benevolent Association, in a move that helped spark acrimony between the new organization, the Miners' National Association, and the WBA, which was often referred to as the state union. (Many of the old combatants were moving on—Benjamin Bannan sold the *Miners' Journal* to his old acolyte, Robert H. Ramsey, that same year.)[49]

In April 1874, John Welsh of Forestville was elected president of the Workingmen's Benevolent Association. The *Miners' Journal* praised his "clear, discerning judgment"—an astonishing turnaround from the days when Bannan had suggested that Cass Township needed to be cleansed of Irish Catholic union members.[50] Welsh would need all the judgment he could muster. As 1874 drew to a close, a titanic battle loomed between coal operators insisting on a deep wage cut and a union determined to protect its gains. There was no bargaining this time—the companies, which had been stockpiling coal, simply announced a wage cut of 10 to 20 percent. The union's position was weakened when the mine workers of the Northern Field accepted the pay cut. On January 5, his back to the wall, Welsh formally announced a strike. It was clear that if the WBA lost, it would be shattered.

All through the long, cold winter and into the spring, the union held firm in what came to be known as the Long Strike. Mockery was used to stiffen the spines of anyone considering a return to work—in late May, the Pinkerton operative R.J.L. reported that "two rough-looking men" had entered the bar at the Ashland Hotel: "They were said to be miners, distributing snide poetry and ballads, but their real purpose being to sound the men, and prevent them from going to work."[51] When mockery didn't work, there were other means available. McParlan reported on May 10, 1875, that three Shenandoah-area Mollies had "proposed to call a meeting of a few of the Molly Maguires of No. 3 and Loss Creek, and to destroy those men who were to work at the W. Shenandoah Colliery, and also to destroy their homes."

Hibernians had been union enforcers since the Civil War, but with the advent of the WBA, they were acting without sanction. That is not to say a few rank-and-file union members did not appreciate their efforts. "Some miners who do not live up to the rules of the State Union are very much afraid of the Mollie Maguires," a detective reported in May 1874, referring to the WBA. "Others who are favorable to the State Union also favor the Mollie Maguires, saying that many a man joins the State Union for fear of the Mollie Maguires."[52] Even Welsh, the WBA leader who helped redirect the West Branch from its bloody course, saw some value in the Mollies' fearsome reputation. In a speech to Shenandoah strikers reported by McParlan, the union leader "referred to some of the newspapers branding all the miners as Molly Maguires . . . and said this was all the better, as it would keep black sheep away."[53]

The union and leading Hibernians tried to apply political pressure, joining in an Anti-monopoly Convention in Harrisburg on March 4 that sought to unite independent coal operators and miners in opposition to Reading Coal and Iron. Among those attending were Lawler and Hugh Mohan of Minersville, who was named secretary of the proceedings.[54] But it was all for naught. Snide songs could not fill the bellies of children weak with hunger, barroom plots did not budge the Reading, and political pressure failed to faze Gowen. He was starving the strikers into submission. "Hundreds of families rose in the morning to breakfast on a crust of bread and glass of water, who did not know where a bite of dinner was to come from," one historian wrote. "Day after day, men, women and children went to the adjoining woods to dig roots and pick up herbs to keep body and soul together."[55]

The union did not die quietly. When bands of strikers, headed by a drum corps with flags flying, descended on Mahanoy City on June 3 to free some imprisoned comrades and shut down mines, a spectacular burst of violence ensued. And the Mollies were in the vanguard. Philip Francis, a Welsh union member who took part in the march, described the scene in a memoir. "First, we marched to the jail to get some miners out who were in jail for being too rough in the city. The police and eighteen citizens were there all armed to defend it. It was then and there that I first saw Jack Kehoe, a leading Mollie, with his pistol in hand, arguing with the police at the jail door. At times they would place their pistols at each other's breast." According to Francis, a gun battle was avoided only after a magistrate agreed to bail for the union men.[56]

As the strikers left the jail with their freed comrades, they headed toward the Little Drift mine, intent on shutting it down. They were confronted by a deputy sheriff, who read them the riot act, backed up by the Mahanoy City police and a civilian posse. When an overexcited deputy whom Pinkerton identified as "Tim Jolley" fired into the crowd, mayhem ensued. Both sides began shooting, and those strikers who were not armed tossed rocks and manhandled any policemen and posse members they could get their hands on. Among the most prominent combatants on the union side were Kehoe's brother-in-law, James "Friday" O'Donnell of Wiggans Patch, who "did some rapid shooting," and Friday's housemate James McAllister, whose brother was married to O'Donnell's sister. McAllister "received a cut in the head" while throwing rocks at the officers, according to Pinkerton.[57]

Among the casualties on the law enforcement side were two members of a newly formed state militia unit, the Silliman Guard, which had close connections to the town's law enforcement apparatus. William Enke, a magistrate, posse member, and private in the militia unit, was injured in the head by a rock, while Henry Leitenberger, a policeman and fellow guardsman, was gravely wounded by a gunshot, but not before he cut down several strikers.[58] The Francis memoir tells how, after the crowd picked up a man he identified as Ellison and passed him over their heads, it next turned it attention to Leitenberger: "I could see LIGHTENBERGER's eyes and his firm chin. He backed away about twenty feet, placed both elbows to his side and began shooting rapidly. There was no need to aim. We stood so close together. Every shot found its mark. After every shot we could hear cries of 'Oh! Oh!'"

In addition to Enke and Leitenberger, several other men with close ties to the Silliman Guard appear to have played prominent roles on the law enforcement side that day. The man Francis identified as "Ellison" was most likely the Mahanoy City police chief, Elias Whetstone, who was the father of a Silliman Guardsman, John Whetstone. Henry Lochman, a policeman who was wounded in the leg, was the next-door neighbor of another Guardsman, Henry Zimmer. Finally, the trigger-happy "Tim Jolley" who Pinkerton said started the riot by firing into the crowd was almost certainly another member of the Silliman Guard, Jim Jolley. (No one named Tim Jolley appears in the 1870 or 1880 census for Mahanoy City.)[59] When it was all over, the union men, acting much like a labor militia, "formed in line and marched defiantly through town, headed by music."[60]

The bloody riot marked the death knell of the strike, but the Kehoe clan's clash with members of the Silliman Guards would come back to haunt the anthracite region before the close of the year. Welsh announced a formal end to the strike on June 14, 1875, citing "the keen pangs of hunger." Joe Patterson, the secretary of the union, recalled the bitterness of the defeat. "Famine drove the men into submission. It was a terrible thing to submit to a 20 per cent reduction," he wrote. "Evil days had come. We went to work, but with iron in our souls."[61] Benjamin Bannan, who had always hated unions, lived to witness the demise of this latest one, but just barely. He died on July 29, 1875, at age sixty-eight, just as the last wave of Molly violence was getting under way.

With the union broken, many mine bosses retaliated against those who had been in the forefront of the labor struggle, which meant that many Irishmen found themselves blacklisted. The choices were simple and hideously familiar for those who had fled the Irish famine thirty years before—migrate, fight, or starve. John Welsh, for one, had to move to western Pennsylvania for a time to find work.[62] There were plenty of others in the same situation, and for those who could not or would not move, fighting seemed a better option than starving. As a result, Molly violence returned with a vengeance.

In the seven years between the founding and destruction of the regional union, the Molly Maguires had been involved in four murders. In a two-month period after the Long Strike ended, Molly gunmen killed six individuals, most of them mine bosses or law enforcement officials. Benjamin Yost, a Tamaqua policemen, was gunned down on July 5. A month later, on August 4, the Mollies killed Thomas Gwyther, a Girardville justice of the peace, and finally closed accounts with Gomer James, the killer of Cosgrove. (The James killing would in short order decimate the leadership of the organization, for a dispute about who should get the blood money for the murder had to be decided by a panel of bodymasters, all of whom were later convicted as accessories after the fact.) On September 1, Thomas Sanger, a Cornish mine boss, and his friend, William Uren, a miner, were killed; and on September 3, it was the turn of John P. Jones, a Welsh mine superintendent, in Lansford, Carbon County.

McParlan had seen it all coming. "Now you can see yourself how this is, and what I predicted at the time of the suspension—'that if the Union would fail there would be rough times,'" he wrote on September 2. Under the union, "each man got his turn," he said. "But now the Irish are discharged or if not they are put to work at some place where they can make nothing . . . There was very little killing whilst the union stood, but now it is quite the reverse."[63]

His report as an undercover detective for the corporation responsible for the situation was simply a more articulate version of the letter from a Mahanoy City Molly published in the *Shenandoah Herald* one month later. "I am aginst shooting as much as ye are," the letter read. "But the Union is Broke up and we Have got nothing to defind ourselves with But our

Revolvers and if we dount use them we shal have to work for 50 cints a Day . . . I have told ye the mind of the children of the Mistress Molly Maguire, all we want is a fare Days wages for a fare Days work, and thats what we cant get now By a Long shot."[64]

The struggle was waged with ballots as well as bullets. Kehoe, the Schuylkill County AOH leader and the constable of Girardville, signaled his displeasure with the coal establishment that fall by working to undermine Cyrus Pershing, the Democratic candidate for governor who just happened to be the senior judge of Schuylkill County Court. Kehoe's work on behalf of the Republican incumbent, John Hartranft, was only modestly effective—he delivered Girardville and West Mahanoy Township, and can hardly be credited with Pershing's defeat.[65]

Kehoe's embrace of the governor has been portrayed as a cynical attempt to curry favor with an official who had the power to pardon. (Some local officials associated with the Hibernians were facing embezzlement accusations, and three Mollies had recently been arrested in the Jones killing—the Tamaqua bodymaster, James "Powderkeg" Kerrigan; and two Mount Laffee men, Edward Kelly and Michael J. Doyle.)[66] But if Kehoe was trying to curry favor with powerful officials on behalf of accused Mollies, snubbing the local Democrat who presided over the court that would try them seems an odd course. Rather, it may be that his work on behalf of Hartranft simply demonstrated the degree to which the political alignments of the Civil War era had become irrelevant. With a Democrat like Gowen running the Reading, and a Democrat like Pershing running the courts, the conflict was no longer one that pitted Irishmen, Catholics, Democrats, and union members against Anglo-Saxons, Protestants, Republicans, and mine owners. Now it was simply the coal companies and their allies versus the workers and theirs.

Kehoe soon had more immediate worries than the election results. On December 10, vigilantes invaded the home of his in-laws, the O'Donnells of Wiggans Patch, between Mahanoy City and Gilberton. Charles O'Donnell never stood a chance—he was dragged outside and shot fifteen times. His sister, Ellen McAllister, who was several months pregnant, died of a single bullet wound to the chest. Their mother, Margaret O'Donnell, escaped with a mere pistol-whipping. Luckier still were two other inhabitants of the house—James "Friday" O'Donnell and Ellen's husband, James McAllister, who both got away.

It was the sort of attack that was common in Ulster from the 1790s right through to the 1990s: masked killers armed with pistols and inside information, gunning down victims in their home in the wee hours of the morning. The identity of the attackers was never determined for certain, but the home's occupants had been included in a list of Molly Maguires that the Pinkertons had circulated in the area. And a note found on the scene the next day read, "You are the murderers of Uren and Sanger." Perhaps as important, Friday O'Donnell and James McAllister had been active participants in the June 3 riot in Mahanoy City that injured several members of the Silliman Guard. The only man ever taken into custody in what became known as the Wiggans Patch Massacre was the militia unit's second in command, Frank Wenrich, on the word of Margaret O'Donnell, Kehoe's mother-in-law. But he was quickly released.

A Mahanoy City burgess and butcher, Wenrich displayed a curious sign on his Centre Street shop in the year of the vigilante killing. It featured a giant eye, flanked by the words "meat market." It was an odd symbol for a butcher, but a near-perfect match for the logo of San Francisco's famed vigilance committee—and that of the Pinkerton Detective Agency. William Enke, Wenrich's fellow Guardsman who was wounded in the June 3 riot, was a professional sign and coach painter.[67]

Wenrich also had business dealings with Reading Coal and Iron. Just a couple of weeks after the butcher's arrest in the Wiggans Patch killings, a coal company official who lived just two doors away from Wenrich's commanding officer in Mahanoy City wrote a curious note to Reading Coal and Iron's immensely powerful land agent, Frank Carter. Wenrich had "Mahanoy Township orders amounting to about one hundred and Seventy Five Dollars. Can you pay them or don't you want to have anything to do with them?"[68] The note from Thomas L. Hess may have been a simple accounting question, but it is worth noting that Wenrich's business was in Mahanoy City, a separate municipality from Mahanoy Township, which included Wiggans Patch.

The note also opens a window on a web of interlocking business relationships involving officials of Reading Coal and Iron, the Silliman Guard, and members of Mahanoy City's business elite and judiciary. In addition to Carter's duties as land agent for the coal company, he was a close business associate of E. S. Silliman, the man who bankrolled the Silliman Guards. Carter was secretary of the Mahanoy City Water Company, of which Silliman was president. The two were also founding directors of the First National Bank, and part owners of the *Mahanoy City Gazette*. George Troutman, the lawyer who represented Wenrich in the Wiggans Patch case, was, like Silliman, a director and officer of the Mahanoy City Gas Company.

Silliman was the treasurer of the Fidelity Building and Loan Association; the commander of the Silliman Guard, the architect and builder John Schoener, was a director.

Another set of ties involves the Citizens Fire Company, No 2. Like the militia unit, it was founded by Silliman, and at the time of the Wiggans Patch killings its foreman was Schoener. Schoener rose to that position after the killing of the fire company's previous foreman, George Major, the chief burgess of Mahanoy City, who was gunned down during a Halloween night riot with a rival, largely Irish American fire company, Humane. The killing was blamed on the Molly Maguires, and the Silliman Guard was founded a few months after Major's death.[69]

If the June 3 riot gave members of the Silliman Guard a direct, personal motive for the attack on the O'Donnell home six months later, the web of ties among the town's business elite, civic leaders, and law enforcement officials may help explain why no one was ever brought to justice in the case. The Wiggans Patch murders on December 12, 1875, were the very last in a long line that stretched all the way back to the killing of James Bergen in his Coal Castle home nearly thirteen years earlier, close to a winter holiday. Though this time, of course, the Mollies were the target.

In a sense, Wiggans Patch marked not just a closing, but also a convergence. It was as if the two polar opposites of the parade tradition, the rowdy mummers and the disciplined militiamen, had developed violent, extralegal adjuncts—Mollies and vigilantes—who met in the middle, and there did battle in a naked class war. In a weird sort of inversion, the Molly leader Jack Kehoe had marched in Mahanoy City on June 3 at the head of something akin to a labor militia; six months later, a leader of a Mahanoy City militia unit stood accused of acting like a Molly assassin at the home of Kehoe's in-laws in Wiggans Patch. The folk justice of the Mollies, it appears, had been matched tit for tat by the vigilantism of the militiamen, flip sides of the same extralegal coin.

In January the Mollies suffered another blow. Archbishop Wood of Philadelphia, the leader of the county's Roman Catholics, reissued his pastoral letter of 1864 that had condemned the Molly Maguires. This time, however, he added the words "otherwise the Ancient Order of Hibernians" after "Molly Maguires," and excommunicated the lot. But the most alarming development for the Hibernians also came in January, when Doyle went on trial for the Jones killing, and Kerrigan turned informer. He implicated Alexander Campbell, the AOH treasurer in Storm Hill, in the Jones case, and a host of other Hibernians in the Yost, Sanger, and Uren killings.

There was another round of arrests, and rumors began to circulate that an informer had penetrated the order. Suspicion fell on McParlan, and he tried to bluff his way through. But he soon discovered that he was being stalked by a number of Mollies, including Philip Nash, who may well have been the Civil War labor committeeman in Cass Township. On March 7, 1876, McParlan came in from the cold, ending one of the most dramatic undercover assignments in American history.

With McParlan safe, the arrests picked up. In Cass Township, where it had all begun fourteen years before, the Forestville bodymaster went on the run. Frank Keenan, a Queen's County native, had been one of several bodymasters indicted for conspiracy for taking part in the discussions about who should get the reward for the Gomer James killing. A Pinkerton report said that Thomas Mohan, Luke's son, had taken over as bodymaster in Forestville, with James O'Leary as secretary.[70]

Lawler, embittered by his expulsion for dawdling on avenging Edward Cosgrove, turned informer in the Sanger–Uren case, saving his neck and inspiring a derisive ballad, "Muff the Squealer":

"Now I'll commence," he says, "me whole story to tell
When I go back to Shenandoah, I'll be shot sure as hell."
"We'll send you to a country where you're not known so well."
"Bejabers, that's good," says Muff Lawler.[71]

The society was crumbling. In April, at a convention in New York, the national AOH expelled all its chapters in Schuylkill, Carbon, Columbia, and Northumberland Counties. When Kehoe, the Schuylkill County leader, was rounded up on May 6 with ten others, the organization was effectively dead.

Now came the matter of burials.

The Day of the Rope

Officials in Schuylkill and Carbon Counties turned over much of the task of prosecuting the Molly Maguires to the Reading Railroad and other major coal companies. Gowen himself served as one of the lead prosecutors. In the first big trial, for the Jones slaying, the state's evidence was presented by none other than that old Civil War scourge of the Buckshots and Mollies, Charles Albright, who was now a lawyer for the Lehigh and Wilkes-Barre Coal Company, Jones's employer. He appeared in court in his army uniform and with his sword. Francis Hughes, the Schuylkill

County Democratic leader during the war, like Gowen had become a lawyer for the Reading Company, and he, too, served on the prosecution. Judge Pershing, the Democratic candidate for governor in 1875 whom Kehoe had worked so hard against, presided over several trials, including Kehoe's.

In fact, the great Molly Maguire trials of the 1870s allowed the coal establishment to finally lay to rest the bitter partisan feuds that had riven it during the Civil War era, giving rise to secret society violence. In effect, the leaders of the two parties buried the hatchet deep in the flesh of the Molly Maguires. Doyle, Kelly, and Campbell were convicted and sentenced to death in the Jones murder, as was Thomas Munley, a Gilberton Hibernian, in the Sanger–Uren killings. The coal establishment, smelling blood, pressed on with a frenzy of arrests and trials. When the railroads wrapped up the cases stemming from the poststrike wave of violence, they moved on to older cases from the Civil War era—sometimes because new evidence had emerged, and sometimes because the cases offered a convenient excuse to hang an inconvenient Irishman.

The murder trial of Jack Kehoe fell into the latter category. Kehoe had already been convicted and sentenced to fourteen years in prison in assault and conspiracy trials.* But Gowen was not satisfied, so he dredged up the 1862 death of Frank Langdon, the Audenried mine foreman. The crime was fifteen years old and probably did not rise to the level of first-degree murder—Langdon had been beaten with sticks and stones on a booze-soaked summer Saturday, which hardly suggested malice aforethought, and his inept doctor may have been as responsible as anyone for his death. There was also considerable doubt that Kehoe was even at the scene of the beating. But the prosecutors, who included Gowen and Albright, saw the trial as a way to eliminate Kehoe once and for all, and to link the Molly Maguires to the labor movement. Albright asked James Shoveland, a defense witness, if the miners union for which he was secretary in 1862 was known as the Buckshots, a synonym for the Mollies. "The coal operators put that name on the union then," he replied. Then Albright asked him if

---

* In the assault trial, McParlan seemed right on the border of perjury, if not over it, when he was asked, "Prior to your joining the Ancient Order of Hibernians, did you have any knowledge of their organization?" "I did not; I had no knowledge, only what I had gathered up throughout the county," replied the detective, whose seven-page report to Pinkerton, written before he ever entered the anthracite region, had specifically linked the AOH to the Mollies. *Report of the Case of the Commonwealth v. John Kehoe*, 70.

Kehoe had been in the union. "He must have been; he was a miner," said Shoveland.[72]

Kehoe was found guilty in January 1877 and Judge Pershing sentenced him to hang. On the same page that the *Miners' Journal* reported the verdict, it carried a one-paragraph item that another Mollie convicted of murder, "Yellow Jack" Donahue, had confessed to killing Langdon. Donahue reported that "for a long while he was haunted by the murdered man, and had to go to New York to get the spell removed."[73] It's hard to say what is more chilling about the tale—its echoes of the Molly Maguire ballad, in which the murdered Bell comes back to haunt his killer, or the fact that the *Miners' Journal* gave just three sentences to the news that someone other than Kehoe had confessed to killing Langdon.

The ramifications of the Molly trials quickly spread far beyond the anthracite region. The week of Kehoe's conviction, workers in New York denounced the press in Pennsylvania as the hirelings of the mine owners and condemned the prosecution of the Irish miners. The *Miners' Journal* headline read "New York Workingmen Making Asses of Themselves." In February, a mass meeting of workingmen in Philadelphia to protest the prosecution of the Mollies struck an ominous note, with one warning that "the people were fast drifting into a condition where revolution would be necessary" to defend their rights against monopoly.[74] That same month, Pat Hester, Peter McHugh, and Patrick Tully were convicted in the 1867 murder of Alexander Rea, the mine boss killed in an aborted highway robbery on the road to Centralia.

A little over a year later, in the spring of 1878, James McDonnell and Charles Sharpe were convicted in the November 1863 killing of mine operator George K. Smith. Charles Mulhearn, a Tamaqua Hibernian who had turned state's evidence, testified that Smith's killers were all Mollie Maguires or Buckshots. "It had three names," he said of the Ancient Order of Hibernians. "It was called the Mollie Maguires and Buckshots."[75]

The hangings, meanwhile, had begun in spectacular fashion. Ten men went to the gallows on June 21, 1877, a date close enough to the summer solstice to suggest some kind of pagan sacrifice. On Black Thursday or "the day of the rope," as it came to be called, Campbell, Doyle, Kelly, and "Yellow Jack" Donahue were hanged in Mauch Chunk; and Munley, James Roarity, Hugh McGehan, Thomas Duffy, James Carroll, and James Boyle in Pottsville. It was the largest mass hanging in the history of the Commonwealth, but it did nothing to stem the tide of industrial strife. In fact, it only contributed, as Reading Coal and Iron officials acknowledged. "There is general uneasiness at all the collieries where there are Irish workmen,"

Henry Pleasants reported the day before the hangings. "There will be little or no work tomorrow." A week later he wrote of "a universal feeling of restlessness" among the miners. "The Irish are very poor and having given their last dollar toward the defense and burial of the Mollies are left without enough to eat," he wrote. "They blame our company for the hanging of innocent men and their hatred for our company is very great at present." Their hatred, in fact, was so great that it trumped their hunger—in an eight-day period from June 20 to June 27, strikes had crippled the Elmwood, Ellengowen, Knickerbocker, Mahanoy City, North Mahanoy, and Shenandoah collieries.[76]

The trouble soon widened. In the weeks after the hangings, the Great Railroad Strike of 1877 erupted, and the miners of Summit Hill, Campbell's hometown, joined in, carrying bread on polls. It was a bit of symbolic protest that had boded ill for landlords during the agony of the famine years in the Ulster borderlands, and it proved a reliable barometer of the depth of feelings in the newest crisis.[77] Amid gunfire and flames, the railroad strike spread from Baltimore to Scranton, Pittsburgh, St. Louis, and San Francisco in the bloodiest class conflict the nation had ever known. In an echo of the Wiggans Patch killings, a vigilance committee in Scranton killed two Irishman when it opened fire on a crowd of strikers on August 2, trying to quell what a *New York Times* headline labeled "The Working Men's War." Efforts to arrest the killers were blocked by a National Guard unit—and then the vigilantes *became* a National Guard unit. Newspapers and state officials justified the killings by claiming the victims were "filled with the spirit of Molly Maguire" or by suggesting that they may have actually been Mollies.

A group of men and boys who marched into Mahanoy City to quite literally drum up a strike were promptly dispersed by a posse, and their leaders were arrested. The forces of law and order were determined to avoid a repeat of the drubbing they'd received just two years earlier at hands of Kehoe and his followers.[78] When the authorities finished breaking what came to be known as the Great Strike, the railroads and the Commonwealth returned to the task at hand—hanging Irish miners.

Hester, McHugh, and Tully went to the gallows in Bloomsburg on March 25, 1878, for the Rea murder. Tully had already admitted his guilt and implicated Hester. The Associated Press reported that McHugh expressed remorse on the scaffold, saying that he wouldn't have ended up there if he had taken good advice. Tully read a confession, too. The condemned were among the few people present to conduct themselves with dignity. The sheriff was staggering drunk, an intoxicated onlooker fell to his death from the roof of a nearby hotel, and a thirteen-year-old girl was crushed when the shed she was standing on collapsed.[79]

Kehoe worked frantically, and in vain, to escape the fate Gowen had ordained for him. To prevent Gov. Hartranft from pardoning Kehoe, the railroad president introduced testimony that he would do just that, forcing a denial from the governor. In a jailhouse interview, Kehoe delivered a bitter condemnation of Gowen as a man whose "whole course as president of the Reading road has shown him to be a man of restless, arbitrary ambition, with such grasping tendencies that no obstacle, however sacred, was ever allowed to interpose between him and his end." He accused Gowen of destroying the prosperity of the region by striving for a monopoly financed by British gold, subverting the legislature, buying out or bullying the independent coal operators, and destroying the Workingmen's Benevolent Association.

"I believe he started out with the intention of breaking up our organization as soon as he bought the mines," Kehoe said. "He broke the Labor Union first . . . Of course he was aware of this Hibernian Society, and he was afraid that they would kill him, because he deserved to be killed."[80] To the end, Kehoe maintained his innocence in the Langdon case. Standing on the scaffold in Pottsville on a snowy December 18, 1878, he reasserted it one last time. "I am not guilty of the murder of Langdon," he said in a clear, loud voice. "I never saw the crime committed; I knew nothing of it." Then the trap was sprung, but the fall did not break his neck—Kehoe, once the high constable of Girardville, died slowly of strangulation, the rope gashing his face in his death throes.[81]

Of all the botched, ugly execution spectacles, none were quite as bad as the two that followed Kehoe's. James McDonnell and Charles Sharpe had been convicted in the Civil War–era slaying of mine superintendent George K. Smith. It was the Molly murder with the strongest overtones of Old World mummery—committed within days of Halloween, by men who invaded the Smith home in costume or disguise. They had been scheduled to die on the same day as the Schuylkill County delegate, but their lawyers had won a reprieve until January 14, 1879. They sought a second reprieve in Harrisburg the day before the executions, to allow a review of the case by the Supreme Court of Pennsylvania. The governor promised a decision the next morning.

The execution was scheduled to take place between 11:00 A.M. and 3:00 P.M. At 10:25 A.M., the sheriff knocked on the doors of the condemned men's cells to let them know it was time. At 10:30, the governor decided to grant the reprieves, and at 10:37, the news was received at the Mauch Chunk telegraph office. A telegraph messenger dashed off to the prison, where Sharpe and McDonnell were by now making their last statements, both proclaiming their innocence in the death of Smith (though McDonnell acknowledged his guilt in another killing). The two kissed crucifixes as priests whispered words of consolation. White caps were drawn over their heads.

At the door to the prison, where McDonnell's wife and children were weeping loudly, the telegraph messenger rang for admittance, only to be ignored, probably on the assumption that he was a distraught relative. Thirty seconds later, McDonnell and Sharp dropped into eternity. The former died instantly, but the latter struggled violently. In the hush that accompanied his death throes, the ringing of a bell was heard, and the breathless messenger was let in with his news—half a minute too late.

Bedlam ensued. McDonnell's brother, standing at the foot of the gallows where his brother still twisted, shouted, "This is murder. There hang two innocent men and their murderers are in this crowd." The sheriff, instead of cutting down the wrongly hanged, took the time to inform the crowd of the contents of the telegraph. "Gentlemen," he announced, "this is a dispatch reprieving the two men till Monday, the 20th. It is marked received at the post office at 10:37." By the time he was done, Sharp had stopped struggling. The sheriff turned toward the swaying bodies and said, "I am as sorry as anyone. It is too late to be helped. Where is the undertaker?"

In response came more loud allegations of murder from relatives of the dead men, who accused the sheriff of hastening the executions because he knew a reprieve was at hand. The sheriff tried to shift blame for the timing of the execution to the priests. "I did not name the hour," he said. "To Fr. Bunce I said that when he was ready the execution should go on. He could have stayed with the men, praying with them till two o'clock, had he chosen to do so."

That nearly prompted a riot amid the agitated observers, but Fr. Bunce acted quickly to defuse the situation. "It was I who told him the men were ready," he told the crowd. "Stand back, I say, and be silent." The crowd obeyed. The *New York Times* headline said it all: "Thirty Seconds Too Late."[82]

There were two more executions—one in Pottsville two days later, on January 16, and another in Sunbury on October 9. With twenty Molly Maguires now in the grave, the Reading's triumph seemed complete. It had gained a monopoly on the production of coal in the lower anthracite region, crushed the miners' union, and exterminated the leadership of the local Hibernian societies.

But like the New York and Schuylkill's earlier triumph on the West Branch, the Reading's victory was a Pyrrhic one. Gowen could not pay off the debt from his extensive purchases of coal land. The Reading went into receivership in 1880, and Gowen was forced out as president the following year. His repeated efforts at a comeback failed, and Gowen finally gave up on December 13, 1889. He secluded himself in a Washington hotel room, pulled out a gun and, in morbid imitation of his old enemies, killed a mine official—himself. It was twenty-seven years to the day since strikers had invaded Phoenix Park, shouting a name to rival Nemesis as the goddess of retribution: Molly Maguire.

16

What comes out of the mountain
Where men first shed their blood?
—William Butler Yeats, "The Death of Cuchulain"

And so it ended, or so it would seem. The dark and turbulent stream of Molly Maguire violence, loosed by the sectarian passions of one son of Ulster, Benjamin Bannan, had been dammed by the cold financial calculations of another, Franklin Gowen, just as the Schuylkill is dammed in that shaded hollow high above Forestville. But there is nearly always runoff from a dam, and so the stream survives, at times a mere trickle, at others something resembling its companion, the West Branch, which still runs free from Glen Carbon to Coal Castle, between the scarred hills of Irish Valley. And to some degree the Molly tradition, that confluence of folk justice and folk drama, survived as well—in the coal region and far beyond.

More than a century after McParlan broke up the Mollies, two of the most feared and powerful labor leaders in eastern Pennsylvania were rough-and-tumble Irishmen from Schuylkill County with intimate ties to a secret organization of Ulster gunmen. One of them, John Morris, a vice president of the International Brotherhood of Teamsters, was dubbed the "last of the Molly Maguires" on the eve of the twenty-first century when a raid on his union local uncovered enough guns and ammunition to equip a small army. Morris was a key fund-raiser for the Irish Republican Army, but the weapons were not destined for Northern Ireland, where peace had been declared the year before. Enemies in the Teamsters said Morris planned to use the arsenal to disrupt the 2000 Republican National Convention in Philadelphia. Morris, the grandson and namesake of a convicted Molly, said that was nonsense—he was merely planning a strike.[1]

And he wasn't the only Pennsylvania labor leader of that ilk.

John McCullough, who grew up in the Minersville area, became a legend in Philadelphia's blue-collar neighborhoods as he transformed an anemic roofers' local into the shock troops of the city's building trades unions. Born in 1919, the son of a coal miner, McCullough spent part of his youth laboring in the collieries. By age fifteen, he was riding the rails during the Depression. In and out of trouble with the law (he was arrested in Philadelphia in 1936 as an "incorrigible"), McCullough joined the marines in 1941 and served in the Pacific. After the war McCullough moved to Philadelphia, married, and found work as a roofer. As one newspaper put it, "Soon, the unionism that had been so much a part of his early life, that had imbued every part of life in Minersville, came to the fore."[2]

In 1959, McCullough was elected business agent of Local 30 of the Roofers' union, which had just three hundred members. Two decades later, it had 1,500 members and a cherished tradition of violence against nonunion contractors. On June 5, 1972, 1,000 roofers and other members of the building trades stormed a nonunion construction site in Valley Forge near the banks of the Schuylkill and caused $400,000 in damage. The attack was not unlike the 1862 assault on the Phoenix Park colliery outside McCullough's native Minersville. Like the Mollies, McCullough helped to insulate the United Union of Roofers from legal difficulties by a deep involvement in Democratic Party politics.[3]

Morris had a similar resume. A native of Mahanoy City, he moved to Philadelphia during the war—a childhood hand injury kept him out of the military—and found work as a shipping clerk at Lit Brothers department store. There he organized his first strike, gaining a pay raise after stuffing live pigeons into the sleeves of fur coats during a sale—a stunt that sent blue-haired customers fleeing in horror when they tried on the coats.

Morris went on to become one of the most militant Teamsters in the nation from his base as president of Local 115 in Northeast Philadelphia. He specialized in organizing small, low-wage workplaces, often harassing strikebound companies with pounding music from a flatbed truck—a sort of charivari straight out of the raucous (and musical) strike parades of the 1840s.

In 1994, when the battle-scarred firebrand had risen to vice president of the Teamsters, a federal magistrate in Philadelphia filed a sixty-six-page report detailing a pattern of violence by Local 115 in five labor disputes over the previous two years. And the assaults were not limited to strikes. In October 1998, five members of the local were charged with beating protesters when President Bill Clinton visited the city. Morris, then in his seventies, was in the thick of it all.

But the most astounding charges came a year later, after Morris had alienated the international's president, James P. Hoffa, by supporting a rival. When a 1999 raid uncovered shotguns, pistols, ammunition, and helmets, the international ousted him as president of the local. Morris's enemies in the union said he planned to use the arsenal against the Republican convention in Philadelphia the following summer. *Time* magazine ran a profile under the headline "Last of the Molly Maguires."[4]

After Northern Ireland erupted in gunfire and flames in the late 1960s, both Morris and McCullough took active roles in raising money for the Irish Republican cause. The move was hardly surprising. For anyone with knowledge of anthracite history, the latest cycle of violence in Ulster was all too familiar—political and economic repression by a Protestant establishment, violent resistance by a Catholic underclass, military occupation, a campaign of assassinations by the Irish Republican Army, and a vicious backlash by vigilantes.

At $100-a-plate ham-and-cabbage dinners, McCullough not only raised money for the IRA but coordinated the activities of other sympathizers throughout the Mid-Atlantic region. He was especially influential with Irish American union officials, a key base of support for the rebels. McCullough was so influential, in fact, that his murder by the Mafia on December 16, 1980—he had challenged a mob-controlled union while organizing workers at Atlantic City's new casino industry—caused considerable consternation among IRA arms smugglers.[5] (Morris, too, had made enemies in the mob—in 1979, the year before McCullough was killed, the government disclosed that a wiretap had picked up a conversation in which a mobster said he wanted to kill Morris for refusing to sell out his membership during a wage dispute.)[6]

After McCullough's murder, Morris carried on his work for Irish Republicans. In a 1998 banquet by the Philadelphia chapter of Irish Northern Aid, an important fund-raising group for the cause, the Teamsters leader was a guest speaker along with prominent IRA veterans like Gerry Kelly and Joe Cahill. Morris regaled them with stories about the Mollies, and "was supportive and generous again this year, as from the beginning."[7]

The Fall of King Coal

Arguably "Molly Maguire," like "Mafia," describes as much a mind-set as a secret society—in this case a bred-in-the-bone conviction that the deck is stacked against the little guy, and that corporate executives operate according to their own law, usurping government powers, manipulating public institutions, and coercing (and even killing) their opponents in pursuit of private profit. A corollary is the idea that collective violence and intimidation are a justifiable if not exactly legal way to help even the odds.

This was far from a universal mind-set among the anthracite Irish. Even in their heyday, the Mollies constituted only a small subset of the region's Irish population. But Jack Kehoe neatly summarized this view of the world in a jailhouse interview before his execution: "Mr. Gowen had scarcely gotten warm in his seat as president of a carrying company before his idea of empire began to take shape. Knowing the profits of coal-mining . . . he determined to monopolize the mining as well as the carrying of coal. So he organized the Philadelphia and Reading Coal and Iron Company under a bogus charter, 'yanked' through the Pennsylvania Legislature under a concealed name, which gave unlimited powers to the company to do everything almost." More than 120 years later, Morris offered an echo of that mentality that was a precise as it was concise. "Corporations do what they want," he told the *New York Times* in 1993. "And there's nothing the people can do about it."[8]

The careers of men like Morris and McCullough show just how long the Molly Maguire mind-set survived after the mass hangings of the nineteenth century. It persisted, in part, because the feudal conditions that gave rise to it survived in Pennsylvania well into the 1930s, when the two Philadelphia labor leaders were young men. A world in which the coal monopoly could use the legislature to gain "unlimited powers" to "do everything almost" was not a world in which the law was going to be accorded too much respect.

And that eventually proved the undoing of King Coal—the mining monopoly met its doom during the Great Depression precisely because it could not get anyone to respect the laws it had so long manipulated. When an army of unemployed laborers literally undermined corporate profits in the 1930s by digging their own mines on coal company land, stealing anthracite by the ton, neither county nor state officials would stand up for the property rights of Reading Coal and Iron. Formed into a self-defense organization that bore more than a passing resemblance to the old Ribbonmen and Mollies, the bootleg miners fought eviction with violence, through local units that came to one another's aid, settled disputes, and raised money for legal defense.

It was no coincidence that Minersville and Mahanoy City, those old bastions of Molly Maguire, were centers of the bootleg coal trade. When a researcher, Michael Kozura, interviewed a number of old bootleggers in 1990, nearly every one brought up the Mollies, unbidden. A Minersville woman whom Kozura thought was in her nineties told him, "If you want to learn about bootlegging, you'ld better find out about the Molly Maguires first."[9]

How the power of the coal companies was eventually broken is a tale of labor organizing, political activism, and direct grassroots action. On the West Branch, the labor organizing never died, though it did not always bear fruit. The painful lessons that the Civil War era taught the miners paved the way for the region's transformation into a bastion of industrial unionism. After the war, the West Branch region was in the forefront of nearly all subsequent labor struggles, from the Workingmen's Benevolent Association in the late 1860s and 1870s to the Miners' and Laborers' Amalgamated Association and the Knights of Labor of the late 1880s, to the United Mine Workers of the 1890s and beyond.

When an effort was made to resurrect the WBA in 1880, Cass Township led the way. "A significant step was taken last week at Forestville, in the western part of Schuylkill County, in the revival of the old Working Men's Benevolent Association, which was crushed out by Mr. Gowen in 1875," the New York Times reported. "The new lodge numbers nearly 100." The effort failed, but thirteen years later, the first UMW local in Schuylkill County was organized in Forestville. One member was John Fahey, a labor organizer who brought thousands of eastern European mine workers into the fold, paving the way for the UMW's success during the great strike of 1902.[10]

In response to Irish industrial militancy, the coal companies began to import large numbers of Slavic, Hungarian, and Italian immigrants to the coal fields in the 1870s and 1880s. The Celtic flavor of Cass Township's southern precinct was diluted by the influx, but the northern precinct— the Heckscherville Valley—remained an Irish bastion right down to its brogues. (John F. Kennedy won an astonishing 96.6 percent of the more than four hundred votes cast there in the 1960 presidential election.)[11]

On the West Branch and throughout the coal region, the newer immigrants were greeted with disdain, and sometimes with rocks, but in time their willingness to take on the coal companies came to match—and surpass—that of the Irish. It was with grudging wonder that one Irishmen followed his Italian and Hungarian coworkers out of the pit in an 1897 strike, muttering, "Holy Mother, is it miself that's quittin' fer the shallow faced spalpeens? [itinerant laborers]."

A short time later, on September 10, 1897, three hundred Slavic strikers marched on a colliery in Lattimer, Luzerne County. Fahey, the UMW organizer, had warned the strikers to be extremely cautious, so they marched unarmed under an American flag. It offered no protection when 150 sheriff's deputies opened fire, killing at least nineteen of the marchers and wounding thirty-two.* There was one other casualty—the coal companies' long-standing effort to keep their work forces divided by ethnicity.[12]

The outcry over the massacre may have helped stay the coal company's hand during two epic battles over the next five years. After a strike in 1900 that demonstrated the union's success in organizing workers of all nationalities, the United Mine Workers launched a climactic showdown with the coal monopoly in 1902. After 140,000 mine workers walked out of the pits, the entire Pennsylvania National Guard was dispatched to the anthracite region, to complement three thousand Coal and Iron Police and one thousand private detectives, or deputies. The strike was far from peaceful along the West Branch—on August 4, in an odd echo of the bad old days, William Purcell, a union leader at Phoenix Park, was assassinated in front of a crowd of bystanders. The gunman, "supposed to be deputy," escaped as the witnesses stood dumbfounded.[13] A month later, on September 3, a dynamite blast wrecked the home of a Coal Castle man who kept working during the strike, along with Patrick Bergen's pub next door.[14] But there were no Lattimer massacres or assassination campaigns against mine officials. Shutting down the industry for more the five months, the strike prompted federal intervention that ended with a pay raise and shorter day for the miners.

After 1902, the United Mine Workers became a fixture in the hard coal region. But like so many others in the region, it was a short-lived victory for the miners, for the anthracite monopoly had already sown the seeds of its own demise. During World War I, anthracite production could not meet demand, so many customers turned to other fuels. That trend accelerated during the 1920s, thanks to a series of bitter strikes.

By the time the Great Depression struck, the industry was already in a deep hole, and it continued to dig furiously. As mines closed, unemployed workers in the Southern Field simply plunged their shovels into the sides of mountains, opening illegal mines on coal company land. When the Coal and Iron Police dynamited shut their "dog holes," the bootleggers formed a union and fought back with help from Communist Party organizers. There were councils of the unemployed and marches by the hungry.

---

* The deputies were represented at a coroner's inquest by George Troutman, the same lawyer who represented Frank Wenrich after the vigilante killings at Wiggans Patch twenty-two years earlier. *New York Times*, Sept. 24, 1897, "The Shooting at Lattimer." The sheriff and the deputies were acquitted at a later trial, despite evidence that most of the dead strikers had been shot in the back.

And at the center of it all was Minersville, the West Branch's main town, now dominated by Ukrainians, Lithuanians, and Russians. "During the 1930s, Minersville contributed a large number of leaders to the popular movements in the anthracite fields and always raised more money and sent more people to rallies and marches than other, comparable communities," one history of the region noted. One factor, the authors concluded, was the town's history of social activism and labor struggles, including the Mollies.[15] Regardless of whether it was a direct legacy of the Mollies, Minersville's militancy certainly said something about the continuing influence of immigrant peasant solidarity in an industrial setting. In a twisted way, the bootleg mines marked a return to Bannan's old Jeffersonian vision of small, independent coal operators working in harmony with their employees—a dream the Reading Railroad had dashed in the 1870s.

Just as the creation of the Coal and Iron Police had helped consolidate King Coal's power, so did that force's decline help pave the way for the decline of the monopoly. Gov. Gifford Pinchot refused to grant new commissions in the force after Coal and Iron policemen murdered a union activist in western Pennsylvania in 1929. "No longer may they have aides who roam at will about the counties, arresting as they move," the *New York Times* noted on November 24, 1935. "Guards are now limited to company properties."

Those properties were still extensive, and Reading Coal and Iron, on whose land 65 percent of the illegal mining took place, dynamited nearly 1,200 "dogholes" in the first eleven months of 1933, but the bootleggers simply opened four thousand more. A more effective response was prevented by the political power of the organized bootleg miners and their supporters. In a story headlined "Coal Bootleggers in Political Bloc," the *New York Times* quoted from a confidential report by Reading Coal and Iron: "County, State and local elected officeholders cooperate with the bootleg miners in every possible way, blocking at every turn efforts by the coal companies to combat the bootlegging of coal." The illegal industry had become, in the words of *The Atlantic*, "big business."[16]

Government officials were loath to intervene, fearing bloodshed and mass starvation. The corporations had ruled with absolute power for over half a century, making so many enemies that when the crisis struck, no one in the anthracite region was willing to speak on their behalf. As Gov. George Earle, a Democrat, toured the coal fields in December 1935, bootleg miners, clergymen, bankers, lawyers, and editors "dinned a hymn of hate against the seven coal corporations which own 85 per cent of the hard coal sources on this side of the world," the *New York Times* reported. "Never a word was said for the tax-ridden and debt-ridden companies" facing the loss of half their market. Instead, local and state officials argued for a moral economy. Thomas Evans, the sheriff of Schuylkill County, told Earle that bootleggers had a moral if not a legal right to earn the living the companies had denied them by closing mines. Earle, refusing to act against the miners, called the issue "the greatest conflict between moral and property rights in the history of the state."[17]

As far as the governor was concerned, the companies had brought the disaster on themselves. "They brought these people into the coal region, let them build their homes and churches, and then closed down the mines to concentrate their operations so that they could make bigger profits. They made millions of dollars from the labor of these men who are now unemployed. They can't let them starve." Denouncing company towns and company stores as "economic serfdom," Earle said that "such conditions are symbolic of a feudalism from the Dark Ages, which has no place in modern life."[18]

And it didn't help the industry that the lieutenant governor of Pennsylvania was Thomas Kennedy, an anthracite Irishman who happened to be secretary–treasurer of the United Mine Workers. The coal industry was so desperate that it purchased tear gas in bulk, hoping to "bomb" all the illegal mines in a single night, and then balked due to legal and humanitarian concerns.[19]

Thus little was done to impede what was almost certainly the most massive campaign of theft in the history of the United States in terms of sheer bulk. In 1935, it was estimated that between four and six million tons of anthracite were being stolen annually. Sold at a steep discount, the lost coal cost the mining companies up to $32 million a year. The losses created a descending spiral—in dire financial straits, the coal companies closed more mines, which simply created more bootleg miners, worsening the cycle.[20]

When Reading Coal and Iron finally declared bankruptcy in February 1937, it blamed bootleg mining.[21] With the downfall of the last antagonist in the Molly troubles, feudalism had finally ended in the anthracite region, though its aftereffects would linger. The approach of World War II finally brought concerted action by Pennsylvania officials against illegal mining—state troopers closing the dogholes fought a pitched battle against bootleggers in the summer of 1941.

With the state and the United Mine Workers turning against them, their ranks sapped by the war, and their own union divided, the bootleggers saw their support among local officials erode during the war. In an eerie echo of the issue that helped give rise to the Mollies eighty years earlier, a state legislator complained that a higher portion of men were being drafted in bootlegging strongholds, and that draft boards were specifically targeting bootleggers for conscription.[22]

The war's end brought on a sharp decline in both legal and illegal mining. The number of workers employed by Schuylkill County coal companies plunged from 19,000 in 1945, to 12,000 in 1950, to 6,900 in 1960. By 2008, the industry that once ruled the region was so diminished that it had a hard time dissuading the Schuylkill County commissioners from switching from coal to gas heat at the courthouse where the Mollies were tried.[23]

Assessing the Mollies

The legacy of a violent secret society is by its very nature difficult to discern, which is why the Mollies have often been portrayed as dead ends in the evolution of the American labor movement, colorful Neanderthals, intriguing as a footnote perhaps, but of no lasting importance or influence. The fact that at the dawn of the twenty-first century a top leader of one of the nation's most powerful labor organizations was being labeled the "last of the Molly Maguires" argues otherwise.

But exactly who and what were the Molly Maguires of Pennsylvania? Descriptions of the group during the two decades from 1857 to 1877 in many ways evoke the Indian fable of the blind men trying to describe an elephant by feel alone—one, touching a leg, proclaims that an elephant is like a pillar; another, grasping the trunk, says it is like a snake; a third, touching the tusk, says it is like a spear.

Thus, in 1857, when the name first spread through American newspapers, the Molly Maguires were perceived as members of an Irish Catholic secret society devoted to Tammany-style machine politics within the Democratic Party, with no hint of murder or labor activity.

Just over five years later, during the Civil War, they were seen as union thugs willing to use violence and anonymous threats to win higher wages and control the way the mines were worked.

As the war dragged on, the name was increasing associated with violent resistance to the draft.

When their underground union was broken by the military at the end of the war, the Mollies were linked first to retaliatory killing of mine officials who aided the crackdown, and then cast as highwaymen out to rob mine superintendents of payrolls.

During the 1870s, the Mollies were seen as leaders of a corrupt local political machine, self-appointed labor enforcers and, after the collapse of the Long Strike, a gang of assassins, taking vengeance on mine officials.

Just as the blind men's descriptions of an elephant were neither wholly wrong nor wholly right, none of the above descriptions of the Molly Maguires, taken alone, gives the whole picture. It's important to remember that the Mollies' cousins in Ireland filled exactly the same range of roles, serving at various times and in various places as a fraternal order, a counterweight to anti-Catholic bigotry, a rural trade union, a political machine and, last but by no means least, a band of assassins.

The neo-Ribbonmen of Pennsylvania did much the same. As far back as the 1840s, after gaining a charter from a Ribbon group based in the north of Ireland, leaders of the Hibernian society in Schuylkill County were involved in anticorporate politics, an effort to mediate a strike, and the defense of an Irishman sentenced to die in a Whiteboy-style murder. There was no question about whether this activity on the political, labor, and legal fronts was sanctioned by the leadership of the order—during the period in question the national organization was headquartered in the county.

After the headquarters moved to New York in 1853, the Hibernian movement in Schuylkill County took a militant turn. Pat Hester and Pat Dormer were charged with assault in March 1855, as militiamen singing Orange Order anthems broke strikes, arresting Irish Catholic miners en masse. In 1857 Bannan complained of the Hibernians' St. Patrick's Day banquet becoming overtly partisan. Six months later, he wrote about "Molly Maguires" taking over the Democratic Party at the local level in eastern cities.

By 1862, it appears that the Hibernians had moved from offering to mediate strikes to organizing them. And in December of that year, "Molly Maguire" became a battle cry for strikers at Phoenix Park. A few weeks later came the Whiteboy-style killing of James Bergen. The anthracite region's neo-Ribbon movement had clearly moved beyond defending convicted murderers to actually organizing assassinations.

For the Mollies, murder was politics by other means. Labor activity and draft resistance were intertwined strategies for defending the Irish community, because that community largely consisted of exploited mine workers, and the draft was being used to punish them for standing up to the coal operators.

The role of the Hibernians and Mollies changed over time as the group adopted different ways to protect and advance its members' interests, which ranged from employment to common crime. But if conspiratorial violence is what eventually came to define a Molly Maguire, it's worth noting that such violence did not emerge until Bannan attempted to use the extraordinary powers of conscription to bludgeon his political and economic opponents—Irish Catholic union Democrats of the West Branch—into the maw of the bloodiest war the nation has ever known.

Molly Maguire leaders all countenanced violence, or the threat of it, but to varying degrees. Barney Dolan could bluster with the best of them, as his confrontation with Heckscher showed, but he seems to have generally shied away from shedding blood. Michael Lawler likewise did his best to head off some of the worst excesses, pursing peaceful means as a negotiator for the union and a delegate to the antimonopoly convention. Pat Hester, while a skillful politician, was implicated in assault, murder, and attempted robberies. And though Jack Kehoe may or may not have played any significant role in the Langdon killing, his reign as the Schuylkill County leader of the AOH was without question the bloodiest of the Molly era.

But if the four differed on the level of violence they were willing to employ, they had much else in common. Aside from their Irish background and membership in the AOH, all four were politically active bar owners. More important, all were willing to do battle with the coal industry, and they rallied others to do the same: Kehoe at the head of a labor march in Mahanoy City in 1875, Lawler as a delegate to the antimonopoly convention that same year and as a union negotiator in 1871, Dolan as a labor leader in Forestville during the Civil War, and Hester as the mastermind of attempted robberies of mine payrolls. Kehoe, Lawler, and Dolan were fighting for the common good of mine workers, while Hester was clearly acting toward self-enrichment.

The different roles played by these four in particular, and the Mollies in general, suggest that the organization was not so much a dead end in the labor movement as a vital part of the complicated process by which the transplanted Irish peasants of the anthracite region were over time transformed into American industrial workers. The labor union the Mollies sponsored during the Civil War was an intermediate step between Ribbonism and a modern labor organization, an attempt to mold a traditional mode of peasant defense to industrial conditions. When violence was not being threatened, committeemen negotiated in the open. When they felt the need to resort to illegal intimidation, the anonymity of the Irish countryside returned. The coal operators' use of conspiracy law against trade unionists in the late 1850s ensured that the only way for a union to survive in the area in the early 1860s was to retain elements of a Ribbon conspiracy.

The brutal fact is that the clandestine use of force by some members of the Union Benevolent Society during the Civil War helped the union succeed where its forerunners had failed in 1842 and 1849. In a meaningful way, the union raised the living standards of the anthracite mine workers, who went from being among the worst paid industrial workers in the country just before the war to among the best paid in the latter stages of the war, with some working on contract making up to $250 a month.[24] The organization survived three years of furious attacks before finally succumbing to what could be fairly described as a counterconspiracy by the mine owners and the government.

In short, had the Hibernian Benevolent Institution not given birth to the Union Benevolent Association during the war, it is difficult to believe the Workingmen's Benevolent Association would have been such a success just three years after the war. The wartime union taught miners both the benefits of collective bargaining—their wages soared to levels unheard of in the industry's history—as well as the limitations and perils of secret society anonymity.

Were the Mollies acting as Irish peasants with a Gaelic mind-set or American industrial workers with a degree of class consciousness when they went to war with Bannan, the Heckschers, and other coal operators? The formal name of their union and the inclusion of some non-Irish miners in leadership positions suggest the latter, but the widespread use of "Molly Maguire" and anonymous threats point to a workforce still very much in the process of transition. Ribbon tradition certainly played a role.

In the end, perhaps, what matters most is the Mollies' impact.

Just as the Scots–Irish, influenced by their experiences in Ulster, brought to the American frontier a predilection for brutality toward natives that set a lasting pattern, so too did the Molly troubles pioneer a long trail of blood in American labor relations. The postwar killings of West Branch superintendents led directly to the creation of the nation's first private industrial army, the Coal and Iron Police. Sabotage of Reading Coal and Iron property on the West Branch led directly to the introduction of Pinkertons, first as spies, and then as a supplement to the Coal and Iron Police.

The use of such private police to break the Long Strike blazed a path that led directly to open class warfare between Pinkertons and the steel strikers in Homestead, Pennsylvania, in 1892. Private detectives and private guards would play an ongoing role as mercenaries in Appalachia's mine wars, from the 1920 gun battle involving Baldwin–Felts detectives in Matewan, West Virginia, to the bullet-riddled contest in the late 1970s between the United Mine Workers and Blue Diamond Coal Company in Stearns, Kentucky. The mass violence of the Long Strike also broke ground for the Great Railroad Strike that convulsed the nation in the summer of 1877, a mere three weeks after the mass hangings of Molly Maguires. It is hard to imagine that the rioters, who made the Reading Railroad a particular target, were not a least partly motivated by anger at the company's outsized role in the case.

Given Ireland's long experience with secret societies and the volatile mix of ethnic and social tensions in the anthracite region, it is easy to conclude that the reemergence of the Molly Maguire there during the Civil War troubles was to some degree inevitable. But that easy conclusion ignores the role of individuals. Perhaps events might have taken a different course had not fate intervened, with the death, shortly before the Civil War, of an entire cadre of Irish political leadership on the West Branch: the Mohan brothers in Minersville and Cass Township's John Kelly and Patrick O'Connor. These were the men who had long mediated between the Irish peasant mind-set in the hills, with its emphasis on anonymous collective action, and the wider world of Schuylkill County, where the capitalist ethos reigned. And who is to say whether the second round of Molly Maguire violence would have even occurred had not Jack Kehoe replaced Barney Dolan as the leader of Schuylkill County's Hibernians.

The very fact that there was a three-year gap in Molly assassinations in the 1870s, instead of one continuous campaign, may say something about the question of leadership. While there were plenty of beatings and breaker burnings throughout the thirteen-year period from 1863 to 1875, there were no cold, calculated killings between the death of Morgan Powell in Carbon County in December 1871 and that of Frederick Hesser in Northumberland County in December 1874. That period just happens to encompass not only Dolan's reign as head of the Schuylkill County Hibernians, but also Pat Hester's two-year-and-seven-month sentence in Eastern Penitentiary, which began in August 1872. (A native of County Roscommon, where Mollies didn't hesitate to take on the Catholic Church, Hester had been convicted of riot for assaulting a priest who tried to bar the burial of a Molly in a Catholic cemetery.)

If one turns from sweeping social movements to the history of a single family, the evolution from Irish peasant to American worker is just as evident. Consider the microcosm of the Mohan family. The first family member to turn up in the records, Charles Mohan, came to the United States in 1827 from Fermanagh and settled in Minersville, working as a miner and, later, as a politician and innkeeper. He seems to have had several brothers in the area—"Luke Mochan," a native of Fermanagh, was listed as living in Minersville in 1845. Luke named one of his sons Philip, and a Philip Mohan had been named a ringleader of the polling place riot in Llewellyn in 1848, when Cass was being created from Branch Township. The family was politically active—the final settlement between Cass and Branch Townships was reached at the home of Charles's son, John Mohan, a Minersville civic leader, on November 23, 1861. In 1870, Luke Mohan was living in Forestville, with sons Thomas and Philip. Thomas was active in the Hibernians and the union. A Pinkerton report dated August 30, 1876, named Thomas Mohan as the AOH bodymaster at Forestville. "He has all the books and papers since Frank Keenan left," it said. And just four years later, another Pinkerton agent reported that P. J. Mohan of Forestville—Thomas's brother, Philip—had served as secretary at a meeting designed to resurrect the Workingmen's Benevolent Association.[25] Here then is the history of Cass Township in a single surname—its bearers hailing from south Ulster, midwifing the violent birth of an Irish political enclave, leading the local branch of the Ancient Order of Hibernians and, finally, working to revive an industrial union.

Just as coal is created from peat pushed underground and subjected to tremendous pressure, so were American workers made of Irish peasants, and industrial union members of Mollies. The peasant solidarity that served as the bedrock of the Molly Maguires became the industrial solidarity that served as the foundation of the WBA, and, later, the United Mine Workers. On the West Branch, the anonymous bloodletting of the Mollies had been discarded in favor of the open methods of the WBA even before conspiratorial violence was removed as an option by McParlan and the Pinkertons. The transformation was internal, the choice deliberate, the result a commitment to industrial unionism that burned as hot as anthracite itself.

In the Wake of the Mollies

As a fundamentally modern movement that sought sweeping change, industrial unionism marked a radical departure from the stubborn conservativism, the wholesale resistance to change, that had been a hallmark of the peasant, Gaelic worldview of the Molly Maguires. As the miners' union took root in the 1870s, it opened the door to the emergence in the coal region of a number of fundamentally modern Irish nationalist movements.

In early 1876, as the anthracite AOH was under siege, a letter to one prominent Irish Republican, John Devoy, underlined growing support in the coal region for Clan na Gael, an American fund-raising organization for Irish revolutionaries. "We are very glad to get a footing in the coal region, where hitherto all kinds of *so-called* Irish societies have held ground to the exclusion of the only *really Irish* society of which I have any knowledge," wrote Dr. William Carroll, the chairman of Clan na Gael's leadership body.[26]

The anthracite region also played a prominent role in the formation of the American Land League when agitation for land reform heated up in Ireland in the 1880s. Terence Powderly of the Knights of Labor, elected mayor of Scranton in 1878, became of a leader of the American league, bringing the luminaries of the Irish land reform movement—Charles Stuart Parnell, Michael Davitt, and John Dillon—to the hard coal fields to raise money for the cause. (Davitt was even inducted into the Knights.)[27]

In the late 1880s, when the Knights of Labor and the Miners' and Laborers' Amalgamated Association were mounting the most successful challenge to the coal companies in more than a decade, a reformed Hibernian movement reemerged in the southern coal fields. It was then, and would remain, what it had always claimed to be—nothing more than an Irish American fraternal and benevolent society. Firmly under clerical control, the AOH reestablished chapters in many of the old Molly strongholds, including Branchdale, Heckscherville, Minersville, Summit Hill, Mount Carmel, Locust Gap, Shamokin, Pottsville, Shenandoah, Mahanoy City, Girardville, New Philadelphia, and Ashland.[28]

The reconstituted Hibernians were not the only ones parading through the streets of those coal towns—for a time, the mummers and fantasticals lingered as well. Into the early twentieth century, the fantasticals were still showing up around the holidays, but the replacement of mandatory militia service with National Guard volunteers eliminated their main complaint and robbed them of their political edge. That much was clear from their choice of a commander.

"On Christmas afternoon a special train on the Central Railroad of New Jersey rushed into Mauch Chunk, and brought with it Santa Claus and an escort of 50 fantastics," the *Pottsville Evening Chronicle* reported on December 29, 1886. "The train stopped at the Mansion House depot where old Santa was met by a procession of 400 fantastics." With Santa Claus replacing Santa Ana, adult fantasticals were fast marching toward irrelevance. Between the Civil War and the early twentieth century, the tradition was increasingly the province of the younger set, sometimes acting on their own, and sometimes serving as a children's adjunct to larger parades.

Johnny Boyle was just nine years old when, "dressed in fantastic costume," he was gunned down on New Year's Eve, 1876, because his group had disturbed some homeowners in Mount Pleasant. But the parades were no longer limited to the Christmas and New Year's holidays. In the late 1950s, John Bowman, then eighty-nine, recalled for a folklorist that as a boy he had joined fantastical festivities, wearing his sister's dress for the George Washington birthday parade in Schuylkill Haven.[29]

In 1895, the Columbia Fire Company in Shenandoah organized a fantastical parade for the Fourth of July, and Mahanoy City was staging a similar event for New Year's, 1899.[30] After Labor Day became an official federal holiday in 1894, it too became a focus for anthracite fantasticals and mummers. When Mother Jones joined the United Mine Workers for a labor parade in Carbondale in early September 1901, they were followed by an afternoon parade of young fantasticals: "Two bands and a hundred youngsters in old-fashioned suits of as many varieties as were wearers composed the column."[31]

Eventually the tradition died out everywhere except Philadelphia and Ashland, a longtime locus of Molly Maguire activity. The exact origins of the parade in Ashland are obscure. It is said to have grown from traditions dating to the mid to late nineteenth century. Certainly there were Irish shivarees in Ashland as far back as the Civil War, when Bridget Munks prosecuted five men for the "horse fiddle" concert to which they subjected her on the night before her wedding. But because the Ashland parade is teamed with a reunion of former residents of the town, it is hard to know whether its mummery is homegrown, influenced by the Philadelphia parade, or perhaps both.

The Ashland Boys Association Mummers Parade was held, significantly, on Labor Day weekend, a holiday more important to industrial workers than to peasants. The 1925 march must have been particularly interesting, for the longest strike in the history of the anthracite industry had begun on September 1, and that parade was the first in which there is any explicit mention of mummers in local newspapers.[32] The tradition continues. On September 3, 2011, after a two-year hiatus, the mummers again marched from Ashland's Eureka Park. "String band members had many little children—and a few adults—dancing energetically in the band's uniforms," the local newspaper reported.[33]

In Philadelphia, the fantasticals were simply reabsorbed into the mummer tradition from which they had sprung. As the tradition was dying out in the hinterlands of Pennsylvania, mummery was undergoing a resurgence in the state's biggest city. The 1859 legalization of masquerades, and by association mummery, certainly played some part in this, but the war that began just two years later must have been a major factor. There had always been a paramilitary element to the mummers (or "shooters," as they called themselves). The first parade of shooters had been held during the War of 1812 by an informal "home guard" of boys too young to serve. And while the mummers in the decades that followed could be raucous and unruly, the years after the Civil War were marked by a new degree of discipline. In some ways it was imposed—civil authorities banned the spoofing of politicians and policemen, required parade licenses, and flooded the streets with police.[34] But part of the new discipline was internal.

As in the West Branch, where young men instilled with the wartime values of teamwork and discipline turned away from the raucous ceili to the more regimented music of the formal band, so the young mummers of Philadelphia increasingly turned from informal home visits to more elaborate musical marches in the postwar era. There were neighborhood parades by 1877, and the military overtones were only enhanced as the mummers grouped themselves into "brigades" and "divisions."

The seeming contradiction between the tradition's rural European roots and its popularity in an American urban center at the forefront of nineteenth-century industrialization can be resolved if mummery is viewed as a cultural component of the internal transformation that marked the making of Philadelphia's working class. To this day the parade remains the most visible manifestation of the city's blue-collar culture. And if you looked closely enough in the 1990s, you could spot among the string bands, comics, and fancy brigades some trucks from Local 115 of the Teamsters union, which was led by Johnny Morris. When it came to maintaining the old connection between Mollies and mummers, Morris was true to the last, and the last of the true.

The West's Awake

Pennsylvania was not the only place where the Molly Maguire story continued to influence the labor movement. Some of the wildest battles of the Old West were fought not between ranchers and sod busters or cowboys and Indians, but between union mine workers and the management of hard-rock mines in states like Idaho and Montana. Irishmen from the anthracite region had been heading west for decades before the denouement

of the Molly Maguire struggle—the *Miners' Journal* had complained of riotous behavior by Coal Castle residents heading to the iron mines of Lake
Superior as early as 1853—but the Long Strike and the repression that
followed offered a fresh impetus for the westward migration.[35]

In 1877, more than twelve years after his wife's epic trek to Washington on his behalf, John Donlin of Carbon County packed up his family of
five and moved to the area around O'Neill, Nebraska. The town was settled
by John O'Neill, a die-hard Fenian and Union Army veteran, who while
sitting in a Burlington, Vermont, jail after his third effort to invade Canada, "conceived the idea of establishing the Irish from the Eastern mining
cities on the farms of the Middle West." In Nebraska, the Donlins built a
log homestead on Eagle Creek, where Mrs. Donlin kept her treasured portrait of Lincoln, the man who had given her breakfast, train fare home,
and her husband's freedom. "Do you wonder that I loved him?" she would
ask visitors.[36]

Other anthracite Irishmen headed to the mining centers of the booming West. Mike Hurley, a Shenandoah Molly implicated in three killings—
those of Uren, Sanger, and James—turned up a decade later in Gunnison,
Colorado, committing suicide after his arrest.[37] In heavily Irish Butte, Montana, the headquarters of the militant Western Federation of Miners, or
WFM, former residents of Pennsylvania constituted one the largest seg-
ments of the population, with the hard-coal counties contributing a stream
of Irish miners. They brought with them experience not only in working
underground, but also in fighting one of the most oppressive industrial sys-
tems in the nation.[38]

It was private detectives, though, who most effectively cast the long
shadow of the Molly Maguires over the western mine fields. That is apparent in the experiences of two Pinkertons who worked together tirelessly to
undermine the labor movement in the West, Charles A. Siringo and his
boss, James McParlan. Pinkerton had been so impressed with McParlan's
work in the anthracite region that in 1877 he wrote a sensational, self-
serving, and, at least in terms of the dialogue, semi-fictional, account of it,
The Molly Maguires and the Detectives. McParlan was eventually promoted
to the detective agency's Denver bureau, adding a "d" to his last name along
the way.

In Denver, he found an admirer—Siringo. The latter's memoir, *A Cowboy Detective*, was prescient in combining the two great heroes of American popular culture—the former from the nineteenth century, the latter
from the twentieth. But Siringo's account of an undercover assignment
with a militant miners' union in Coeur d'Alene, Idaho, so closely mirrors

Pinkerton's *Molly Maguires and the Detectives* that one must conclude that Siringo was either a literary fraud or a remarkably apt student of McParlan, who gave him the Coeur d'Alene assignment in 1891.

Just as McParlan became a secretary of an AOH chapter, so Siringo becomes the secretary of a union local. He is forced to take "an iron-clad 'Molly Maguire' oath" that he would never turn traitor to the union, which he says was led by "a desperate lot of criminals of the Molly Maguire type." They are Irish, of course. And just as McParlan's nemesis was "Black Jack Kehoe," so Siringo is nearly undone by "Black Jack," a union tough from the Nevada town of Tuscarora, another name straight out of Schuylkill County.

Like his hero, Siringo relies on bravado to counter accusations that he is a spy. The strike degenerates into mass violence, and is eventually broken by federal troops. Siringo narrowly escapes, as McParlan did, and his testimony as a star witness leads to the conviction of eighteen leaders—just shy of the twenty men hanged in Pennsylvania after his mentor broke up the Mollies.[39]

While the details of Siringo's tale bears suspicious similarities to Pinkerton's account of McParlan's time in Pennsylvania, the broad outline is indisputable. He did infiltrate the miners' union and his testimony did lead to convictions. Whatever embroidery Siringo may have added, it is clear that the Pinkertons under McParlan were working from a Molly Maguire template in Coeur d'Alene.

The degree to which McParlan viewed subsequent Pinkerton cases through the lens of his Molly Maguire experiences became clear when, more than a decade after the Coeur d'Alene troubles, the former governor of Idaho was assassinated. Frank Steunenberg had asked President McKinley "to call forth the military forces of the United States to suppress insurrection in Shoshone County" during the strike. It was the sort of thing that had invited retaliation in the anthracite region, often around the holidays, and sure enough, a bomb blew Steunenberg into the next world on December 30, 1905.

The Steunenberg killing was no Whiteboy-style execution—the timing near New Year's was purely coincidental and the killer was not Irish—but McParlan reacted as if he were back in Schuylkill County when the Pinkertons were brought into the case. Before even interviewing the chief suspect arrested in the case, a union operative named Harry Orchard, McParlan had concluded that Orchard was working on behalf of an inner circle in the leadership of the Western Federation of Miners. After briefing

Orchard on the favorable treatment that Daniel Kelly, or Kelly the Bum, had received for informing in the Molly Maguire case, McParlan extracted a confession that implicated the WFM's leaders—Charles Moyer, the union president; Big Bill Haywood, its legendary secretary–treasurer; and George Pettibone, a former member of the union's executive board. In the words of the historian J. Anthony Lukas, "The official text of the confession bears not only the imprint of McParland's Molly Maguire theories, but of his notions, already outlined to Orchard, about parallel WFM skullduggeries."[40]

McParlan arranged the arrest of the three in Colorado and their extralegal extradition to Idaho, setting up a spectacular trial in 1907. Here, as in Pennsylvania, the mining companies underwrote the cost of prosecution, though their role was not nearly so naked as it had been in the anthracite region. The chief difference this time around was the strength of the defense team, led by none other than Clarence Darrow. Haywood, Moyer, and Pettibone were acquitted, which says no more about their innocence than the conviction of Jack Kehoe says about his guilt. As in Pennsylvania, the joint machinations of the mining companies and the Pinkertons so muddied the waters of justice that whatever lay at the bottom of these cases may forever remain obscured.

There is one other odd footnote that connects the Mollies with the Steunenberg case, involving an Irish American mine worker from the West Branch who headed west in the wake of the Long Strike. Hugh Mohan, whose friendly chat with McParlan in his family's Minersville tavern nearly ruined the detective's undercover mission against the Mollies, moved to California in the spring of 1877, finding work as a newspaperman in San Francisco. He married and had a daughter, Louise, though by the time she was four the marriage had dissolved. When her mother remarried, Louise adopted the surname of her stepfather—Sheridan Bryant. As the journalist Louise Bryant, Mohan's daughter became a formidable advocate for leftist causes (and Irish revolutionaries) in the twentieth century.[41]

She married a man who was in some ways remarkably like the father she never really got to know, the politically active journalist and labor spokesman John Reed. Both Bryant and Reed wrote eyewitness accounts of the Russian Revolution, though her *Six Red Months in Russia* was overshadowed by his *Ten Days That Shook the World*. Reed was a confirmed leftist and close friend of Big Bill Haywood—so close, in fact, that when the latter died in 1928, half of his ashes were buried next to those of Reed beneath the Kremlin Wall in Moscow. It's hard not wonder what Reed would have made of his father-in-law's chance run-in with the undercover McParlan, and the suspicions it raised with the Kelly the Bum—the informer McParlan cited to build a case against Haywood.

Capt. Moonlight and Capt. Mummer

Just as the Pennsylvania Mollies were written off as a dead end of the labor movement, the same view is often held of their cousins, the agrarian secret societies of Ireland. In histories of the 1798 uprising, the United Irishmen are given full prose portraits, while their Defender allies are sketched in quick, broad strokes, if at all. The successors of the Defenders—the Rockites, Ribbonmen, and Mollies—are lucky to garner more than brief notice in more general works on nineteenth-century Ireland.* And when they are mentioned, the peasant secret societies' complicated struggle on behalf of a dying way of life is sometimes oversimplified as a conflict between Irish peasants and absentee English landlords.

In fact, Molly Maguire survived the famine, even if many of her children did not. The name popped up in Irish-speaking western Donegal in the 1850s and 1860s, as the introduction of Scottish sheep in the 1850s by market-minded landlords impinged on the commons that tenants had traditionally used for grazing their own cattle. The result was a "sheep war" that pitted tenants against the landlords and the government between 1857 and 1863. The extent to which the tenants were organized under Molly's banner has been the subject of much debate. After all, the main landlord involved, John George Adair, was the nephew of that peerless propagandist of the propertied, William Steuart Trench, who tended to see Mollies where there was little evidence of them.[42]

That is not to say there were no Mollies in west Donegal. Longtime residents of the area, looking back in 1961 on stories about the Mollies, described for the Irish Folklore Commission a group that not only regulated land use, but also set prices and interfered with weddings in the old strawboy style. "They didn't want anybody to take advantage of the poor by overcharging," reported one. "Even some of the shopkeepers were afraid of them, and they daren't charge a penny over the market price . . . for these reasons at the start a whole lot of people had a certain amount of respect for them. In the end they became very cruel and they did things like what is going on in Africa," such as raking their victims' skin with wool cards and rough stones.[43]

The notion that the Mollies initially enjoyed popular support, only to descend into cruelty, was echoed in McParlan's report on the secret society

---

* The *Evolution of Irish Nationalist Politics* by Tom Garvin is a welcome exception.

to Pinkerton in 1873. After describing the Mollies' efforts to aid victims of the potato failure, McParlan insisted that following the famine, "instead of performing the simple Acts of taking from the rich & giving to the poor the[y] commenced hostilities something after the fashion of the Kuklux Klahn," killing landlords' agents and bailiffs and "any unoffending neighbor who might not coincide with their views." He went on to describe in gory detail the tortures to which their victims were subjected—being stripped naked and forced to walk barefoot for miles on a cold night while being whipped by a man on horseback—before concluding that the Mollies eventually became "one of the most formidable organizations for Rapine & Murder ever existed in Ireland."[44] The comments were made before McParlan was assigned to investigate the Mollies in Pennsylvania, so the detective had no obvious motive to exaggerate. What is striking in both descriptions is how far abroad a native of Ulster feels the need to range for an apt comparison—Africa or the Ku Klux Klan. Michael Davitt, a Land League leader of the 1870s and 1880s, spoke in the same vein when he described "outrages of a shocking kind" perpetrated by the Mollies.[45]

While the Mollies did persist after the famine, and doubtless inflicted many of same brutal punishments they used before and during the years of the great hunger, this talk of a movement turning increasingly savage stands in stark contrast with the historical record, which shows that Mollies and Ribbonmen were evolving into the more respectable Ancient Order of Hibernians. While the Ribbonmen still pulled off a spectacular murder now and again—the 1878 assassination of Lord Leitrim, for example—their level of agrarian killing never again approached that of the famine era.

In the one notorious case from that era where the name Molly Maguire was mentioned—the killing of an informer in the 1882 murders of London's chief secretary and undersecretary for Ireland in Dublin's Phoenix Park—the link was not to the Hibernians of Ireland, but to the O'Donnells of Wiggins Patch. After one of the Phoenix Park killers, James Carey, turned informer and helped hang five of his compatriots, he was killed on a passenger ship off South Africa. Arthur Conan Doyle used the case as the inspiration for the Sherlock Holmes novel *The Valley of Fear*, because the accused, Patrick O'Donnell, was a first cousin of the Schuylkill County O'Donnells, and had lived in the United States for years until 1882. It is believed some of his time was spent in Wiggins Patch. A letter writer told the Rochester, New York, *Post-Express*, "He is the man I knew in the Pennsylvania coal regions. He was the chief of the Molly Maguires then."

O'Donnell cited his experience in the United States to justify the killing of Carey, saying they had both drawn weapons in an altercation. "I came from a part of America where people don't wait to inquire into a man's intention's when his pistol is against your forehead," he said. The Phoenix Park murders had been arranged by an Irish Republican splinter group, the Invincibles, and Carey's widow testified at O'Donnell's trial that he told her immediately after the killing that he "was sent to do it." But it is far from clear that Carey's killing was part of the wider Invincibles conspiracy. When he was hanged on December 17, 1883, Patrick O'Donnell became the ninth person to die as a result of the Phoenix Park case—and the fourth member of the O'Donnell/Kehoe clan since 1875 to face an execution-style death in mid-December.[46]

Just as Patrick O'Donnell was an old Molly turned militant Republican, many of the old strongholds of the Molly Maguires had become major centers of Irish Republican activity. In 1878, the five counties where the Irish Republican Brotherhood boasted the greatest strength were Monaghan, Cavan, Sligo, Roscommon, and Leitrim. The reason was simple. In the wake of its failed uprising in 1867, the IRB (or Fenians), which had been largely based in cities and towns, began to show greater interest in rural issues, such as the abolition of landlordism. By the 1870s, magistrates were reporting that Fenianism had merged with Ribbonism in areas like Cavan, Westmeath, and Meath.[47]

That merger, and the subsequent alliance of the Fenians with parliamentarians like Charles Stuart Parnell, lent the land reform struggle a degree of success unseen in Irish politics since O'Connell's efforts on behalf of Catholic liberation a half century before. Much of Parnell's success in abolishing the worst excesses of the landlord system stemmed from the realization on both sides that the alternative to constitutional reform was "Capt. Moonlight"—a synonym for Molly Maguire, Capt. Rock, and all the other noms de guerre used by Irish peasant rebels over the years. The movement's most effective weapons were not murder but obstructionism in Parliament and boycotting in Ireland. Landlords who violated the rules of the Irish countryside and tenants who took the farms of the evicted were to be utterly shunned by the rest of society, "left severely alone," in the words of Parnell.

In the wake of the successful land war of the late 1870s and early 1880s, and the subsequent disgrace of Parnell in a sex scandal, revolutionary republicanism and the increasingly conservative rump of the Ribbon movement parted ways. With its reason for being—the land issue—largely eliminated by reform of the land system, the latter evolved into a reactionary Catholic political machine in Ulster under the banner of the Ancient Order of Hibernians. Profoundly sectarian, the AOH fulfilled two traditional roles of a Catholic secret society in Ulster—as counterweight to the Orange Order and as political bullyboys, this time for John Redmond's Irish Parliamentary Party.

The Mollies had always opposed change, and their quarrel with improving landlords stemmed from the fact that those landlords were the prime agents for change in mid-nineteenth-century Ireland (along with mass starvation). Parnell's parliamentary successes and other reforms paved the way for the end of landlordism—and once the landlords ceased to be landlords, the Mollies ceased to be Mollies, for in the zero-sum game of Ulster politics, mass movements are defined by their enemies. As the Mollies were transformed into the AOH, the group's new enemies were the new agents of change—feminists, labor unions and militant Republicans.

The Hibernians violently disrupted suffragist meetings in the early 1900s and served as strikebreakers (a role that would have stunned their anthracite cousins) during the climactic 1913 labor showdown in Dublin between the Employers' Association and the Irish Transport and General Workers' Union.[48]

But the biggest threat to the AOH came not from Orangemen, suffragists or union members but from the rise of Sinn Féin and the militant Republican movement that it represented. If the leadership of Sinn Féin and the Irish Party sometimes cooperated, the situation at the grass roots could be a bit testy, as was discovered by Bulmer Hobson, a Belfast Quaker and rising star of the Irish Revolutionary Brotherhood in Belfast. When Joseph McGarrity, a Philadelphia businessman active in Clan-na-Gael, offered to rent Hobson a farm he owned in his native Carrickmore, County Tyrone, Hobson felt obliged to decline in January 1910. "Our boys down there think I might have trouble with the AOH and trouble with Father Short," he wrote. "If the AOH objected I could not get a man or a horse for a day's work in the district."[49]

Nearly thirty years after the first boycott, the weapon was being wielded by the remnants of Ribbonism against Irish nationalists. But the tide would soon turn. With the opening of World War I, progress stalled on the Irish Party's decades-old reason for being, a Home Rule bill that would have given Ireland self-government within the British empire. The separatists of the Irish Republican Brotherhood sensed an opportunity, energized by the threat of wartime conscription, which had galvanized the Defenders in 1793 and the Pennsylvania Mollies of the early 1860s. The brotherhood played on the same theme—death, resurrection, and renewed combat—that had lent the mummers play its subversive undertones, and the struggle of the Irish Mollies its powerful emotional symbolism.

In his famous 1915 eulogy for the renowned Fenian Jeremiah O'Donovan Rossa, the Gaelic-speaking poet and IRB leader Patrick Pearse intoned, "Life springs from death, and from the graves of patriot men and women spring living nations." That is precisely the message sent by the Mollies when they claimed that their movement was founded at Ballinamuck, the grave of the 1798 uprising.

Pearse put his words into action less than a year later. As military director of the IRB, he scheduled an insurrection for a major holiday, Easter, 1916. As the date drew near, there were compelling reasons to put it off, for the British government had learned of the plan. But for Pearse, who was entranced with the notion of blood sacrifice, an Eastertide rising to resurrect the Irish nation was a symbol too precious to abandon. After some mixed signals from the rebel leadership forced a delay, the rising took place on Easter Monday. As a military operation, it failed spectacularly; central Dublin was left a smoking ruin and the British promptly executed Pearse and other leaders. But as a nationalist anthem, written in blood and punctuated by the roar of firing squads, the rising proved the most rousing rebel song Ireland had ever heard. It breathed new life into the Republican movement's political wing, Sinn Féin, and its military wing, the Irish Republican Army.

By 1919 the old Molly strongholds of Longford, Cavan, Leitrim, and Roscommon had the highest per capita Sinn Féin membership in Ireland. Longford, where Ballinamuck is located, led the way with between six hundred and one thousand Sinn Féin members per ten thousand people.[50]

Then came revolution. In the hills of Leitrim, the cradle of the Mollies, the IRA leader Ernie O'Malley found refuge during the war for independence among the Gaelic-speaking country folk, whose acceptance of rebels was conditioned by decades of resistance to the landlords. Like Yeats, O'Malley was haunted by the black pig of legend, hunting it on the back roads of Roscommon. He never found it, except in the war and strife—the last great battle of the Gaels against their oppressors—that had always been associated with the creature.[51]

Nearly one hundred and twenty five years after the defeat at Ballinamuck, the Gaels finally won.

As Molly faded, so too did her twin, Capt. Mummer, in part because people could not tell one from the other. The confusion had begun long before. Mary Leadbeater, who as a child in 1772 was scared witless by the mummers of Kildare, noted that in later years "the Whiteboy Act frightened the mummers as much as they had frightened others, and put a stop to their proceedings." A century later, in 1872, a writer from Belfast noted that the police disapproved of mummers, for anyone encountering such a band on a dark road would think "that the days of Whiteboyism had returned."[52]

By the end of the decade, the days of Whiteboyism had returned to some extent, with the Land War of 1879–82. The disturbances, Ireland's last great agrarian insurrection, contributed significantly to the decline of the mummer and wren boy tradition in the Ulster borderlands. This was especially true in Leitrim, which was one of the most disturbed counties during that period.

A twentieth-century resident of Leitrim told the Irish Folklore Commission that "about the eighties of the last century the mummers were abolished by the authorities. There was curfew them times and you were supposed to get a pass to go out after nightfall. It was the time of the Land League when the country was disturbed. Disguises were forbidden as well as people going about in crowds. So the mummers died out."[53]

In the 1940s, Thomas O'Flynn of Drumsna, Roscommon, told the Irish Folklore Commission, "Leitrim 60 years ago was a hot-bed of secret societies, and unfortunately the bands [of wrenboys] sometimes belonged to rival ones, which frequently led to violent fights. This, to my mind, led to the destruction of the custom." An old-timer in Edgeworthstown, Longford, recalled hearing that wren boys there had feared prosecution under the Whiteboy Act.[54]

The authorities had good reason to suspect a link between wren boy activity and subversion during the Land War of the 1880s. One issue that especially grated on tenant farmers was that they were banned from hunting on the land they rented—all game belonged to the landlord, who employed gamekeepers to prosecute "poaching," even if it amounted to little more than a tenant farmer fishing for salmon. This was why foxhunting, so popular with the handholding class, became a particular target for the Land League in December 1881.

On December 26, the traditional day for "hunting the wren," thousands of peasants gathered near Nenagh, in North Tipperary, for a "people's hunt" or "Land League Hunt," defying both the landlords and an entire regiment of troops that had been called out specifically to prevent the event. Holding up Land League banners and poles carrying the game they had killed, the marchers—led by a band—paraded past the troops and the constabulary (who had decided that discretion was the better part of valor).

This was the "hunting of the wren" writ large, a defiant display of the continuing power of the old link between peasant revels and peasant rebellion.[55] But the close identification between the festive groups like wren boys and subversive groups like the Mollies and the Land League, which had once lent legitimacy to the latter, was now clearly helping to undermine the legitimacy of the former.

New troubles brought a further decline in collective merrymaking. In the mumming heartland of Ballymenone in south Fermanagh, the war for independence after the Easter Rising took a heavy toll on the ancient tradition. No one wanted a group of masked men banging at the door on a winter night in the middle of a civil war. The constabulary stopped mummer processions and demanded permits. A custom that sought to bring the community together couldn't survive a conflict that divided not only Catholics and Protestants, but also the IRA and the AOH.

After the war mummery made a comeback, at the behest of some older Republicans who wanted to heal the split in Ballymenone. The revival lasted until World War II, when the custom once again went into sharp decline. Through the long, dark winter night of the Troubles, the combat play lived only in the memory of the community's older residents, but since the violence has ebbed, Capt. Mummer has made a limited return to Fermanagh.[56]

There were many reasons for the decline of festive groups like the wren boys and mummers, but the trend cannot be fully understood outside the context of their link to secret societies and agrarian violence. Yet as the folk revels faded, so too did the recognition of their connection to the darker side of rural traditions. What seemed obvious to a nineteenth-century observer like William Wilde is now understood only dimly, if at all.

Today the connection is visible mostly in literature and formal drama, perhaps most notably in James Joyce's *Ulysses*. Glassie, the folklorist who studied the Ballymenone mummers, cites a "remarkable parallel" between the combat play and the scene in which Stephen Dedalus is felled by Pvt. Carr. "There is an accidentally provoked battle in which the names of St. George and St. Patrick, the colors orange and green, are evoked," he writes. "Stephen, cast as Ireland's representative, is goaded to revenge by dead Irish heroes and by Ireland in her old woman personification. He is knocked down by a foul-mouthed, red-coated English soldier and lies as if dead until he is revived by Bloom."[57]

An even more striking parallel, in view of the 1916 rebellion, comes in the very middle of that passage:

Dublin's burning! Dublin's burning! On fire, on fire!

(*Brimstone fires spring up. Dense clouds roll past. Heavy Gatling guns boom. Pandemonium. Troops deploy. Gallop of hoofs. Artillery. Hoarse commands. Bells clang. Backers shout. Drunkards bawl. Whores screech. Foghorns hoot. Cries of valour. Shrieks of dying. Pikes clash on cuirasses. Thieves rob the slain . . .*

Joyce moves seamlessly from a scene that evokes the Easter Rising to a vision of dead men rising to fight again:

The midnight sun is darkened. The earth trembles. The dead of Dublin from Prospect and Mount Jerome in white sheepskin overcoats and black goatfell cloaks arise and appear to many. A chasm opens with a noiseless yawn. . . . It rains dragons' teeth. Armed heroes spring up from furrows. They exchange in amity the pass of knights of the red cross and fight duels with cavalry sabers: Wolfe Tone against Henry Grattan, Smith O'Brien against Daniel O'Connell, Michael Davitt against Isaac Butt, Justin M'Carthy against Parnell . . . [58]

The men Joyce summons from the grave to fight another battle are armed champions, as are the mummers. They fight in amity, as do the mummers. They use swords, in single combat, like mummers. The scene has been interpreted as a vision of the Apocalypse, but amid its layers of meaning, a nod to mummery and its links to rebellion seems clear. Throughout the novel, which was written as the Easter Rising and the War for Independence unfolded, the character Buck Mulligan makes frequent references to mummers. Mulligan calls Dedalus "the loveliest mummer," a "mournful mummer," and a "peerless mummer," and adds that he has "conceived a play for the mummers."[59] In a novel known for its leaping wordplay and investment of names with deeper meaning, Buck's formal name is Malachi Mulligan. It evokes "Mickey Mulligan," a mumming character, like Mary Ann McMonagle, Molly Masket and, just possibly, Molly Maguire.

Fittingly, for a movement founded where folk drama met folk protest, theatrical presentations about the Mollies and their ilk provoked uproars on both sides of the Atlantic as the twentieth century drew to a close. In Ulster, Vincent Wood aroused the ire of Irish Republicans with his play *At the Black Pig's Dyke*, which examined the links between mummers and rebel gunmen in the Ulster borderlands over several generations. Supporters of the IRA complained that the play made their movement seem atavistic. When the Druid Theater's production of the play came to Derry, a group of local theater people decided to attend—and stage their own ending. As the play drew to close, several protesters wearing Union Jacks beneath straw clothing leapt to the stage. As they tried to make the point that the play was anti-Republican, some of the real actors fled, fearing an actual attack by Protestant loyalists. Newspapers labeled the affair a riot, but in a sense the protesters were doing nothing more than mummers had done for generations: tailoring the mumming play's denouement to fit the audience.[60]

In Pennsylvania, dramatic reenactments of Molly Maguire episodes likewise led to protests. In 1994, when the Historical Society of Schuylkill County and the county Bar Association restaged the Kehoe trial before a modern jury, some of his descendants complained, the United Mine Workers talked of picketing the event, and telephone threats led Kutztown University to bar the participation of its students, who were to have served on the jury. It was an episode any red-blooded Molly would have savored—anonymous intimidation, with the powers that be in Pottsville muttering darkly about acts of terror by the militants in the hills. This time around Jack Kehoe was acquitted.[61]

The mock trial was merely the first skirmish in what became an ongoing conflict over Molly Maguire–era reenactments designed to boost tourism in the region. Four years later, in 1998, the Schuylkill County Visitors Bureau had to shelve plans to reenact an 1874 riot in Mahanoy City after objections by residents. And Kehoe's great grandson, Joe Wayne, bitterly criticized the reading of three condemned Mollies' last words by amateur actors standing on a gallows, before a noose, as part of a "Molly Maguire Weekend" event at Tamaqua's summer festival. "They were going to re-enact hangings," said Wayne, who helped secure a pardon for his great-grandfather in 1979. "How do you do that tastefully?"[62]

Today the old Carbon County prison where four Mollies were hanged on the summer solstice has become a tourist attraction in Jim Thorpe, or Mauch Chunk as the old-timers still call it. On weekends, people pour in to see the hand print in Cell 17 that was supposedly left by a condemned Molly. The folklorist George Korson relates that before Alexander Campbell, a Donegal native, was led to the gallows from that cell, he proclaimed his innocence to the sheriff. Then Campbell ground his right hand into the dirt and grime of the cell floor, and dragging his ball and chain after him, smacked his hand high on the wall.

"There is proof of my words," he is reported to have said. "That mark of mine will never be wiped out. There it will remain forever to shame the country that is hanging an innocent man." The handprint defied all efforts by the sheriff to remove it, and it was drawing tourists as far back as the

1930s, Korson wrote.[63] (It's hard not to wonder whether the two circumstances were related.) Decades later, the hand print is still there, a smudged, grimy image remarkable not only for the resilience of the legend behind it, but for its resemblance to that dark and enduring symbol of Campbell's native land: the red hand of Ulster.

If history belongs to the winners, legend belongs to the losers.

Notes

Introduction: The Fountainhead

Epigraph. Richard Lalor Sheil, *Sketches of the Irish Bar*, vol. 2 (New York, 1854), 68–69.

1. J. Bennett Nolan, *The Schuylkill* (New Brunswick: Rutgers University Press, 1951), 3.

2. Tonnage figure and closing date from the *Pottsville Republican*, May 24, 1998.

3. George Korson, *Black Rock* (Baltimore: Johns Hopkins University Press, 1960), 389–90.

4. Recording, Library of Congress, George Korson Collection, AFC, 2003/001: SR67.

5. George Korson, *Minstrels of the Mine Patch: Songs and Stories of the Anthracite Industry* (Philadelphia: University of Pennsylvania Press, 1938), 38–41, 48–53.

6. Eugene Victor Debs, "Looking Backward," *Appeal to Reason*, Nov. 23, 1907, quoted in *Debs: His Life, Writing, and Speeches* (Girard, Kan.: Charles H. Kerr, 1908), 283–85. In their magisterial *The Growth of the American Republic*, Samuel Eliot Morison, Henry Steele Commager, and William E. Leuchtenburg wrote that the Mollies gave Americans "their first premonition of class warfare" (vol. 2; Oxford: Oxford University Press, 1969, 96).

7. Recording, Library of Congress, Korson Collection, AFC, 2003/001: SR67.

8. Francis Percival Dewees, *The Molly Maguires: The Origin, Growth, and Character of the Organization* (Philadelphia, 1877). Dewees was the nephew of one railroad lawyer who served as a Molly prosecutor, Francis W. Hughes, and on page 48 he thanks another, Charles Albright, for sharing some of his files.

9. Debs, *Debs: His Life, Writing, and Speeches*, 283–85; also, Anthony Bimba, in *The Molly Maguires* (New York: International Publishers, 1932), offers a Marxist analysis of the Molly troubles.

10. Charles A. McCarthy, *The Great Molly Maguire Hoax* (Wyoming, Pa.: Cro Woods, 1969); Patrick Campbell, *A Molly Maguire Story* (Jersey City, N.J.: Templecrone Press, 1992).

11. Donald L. Miller and Richard E. Sharpless, *The Kingdom of Coal: Work, Enterprise, and Ethnic Communities in the Mine Fields* (Philadelphia: University of Pennsylvania Press, 1985), 137.

12. Kevin Kenny, *Making Sense of the Molly Maguires* (Oxford: Oxford University Press, 1998); Grace Palladino, *Another Civil War: Labor, Capital, and the State in the Anthracite Regions of Pennsylvania, 1840–1868* (Urbana: University of Illinois Press, 1990).

1. "A Slumbering Volcano"

Epigraph. James Bonwick, *Irish Druids and Old Irish Religions* (1864; repr., New York: Sterling, 1986), 90. The "Daome-Shi" apparently refers to the "daoine sidhe," Irish for "fairy people."

1. Korson, *Minstrels of the Mine Patch*, 156; *Scientific American* 8, no. 22 (Feb. 12, 1853): 108; *Miners' Journal* (hereafter *MJ*), Aug. 1, 1879, reprinted in *New York Times*, Aug. 3, 1879.

2. Anthony F. C. Wallace, *St. Clair: A Nineteenth-Century Coal Town's Experience with a Disaster-Prone Industry* (New York: Alfred A. Knopf, 1987), 265, 270–73.

3. Sherman Day, *Historical Collections of the State of Pennsylvania, Containing a Copious Selection of the Most Interesting Facts, Traditions, Biographical, Anecdotes, etc., Relating to the History and Antiquities of Every County* (Philadelphia, 1843), 613; *MJ*, Aug. 1, 1879; *Scientific American* 11, no. 14 (Dec. 15, 1855), 108.

4. The watercolor is in the Kennedy collection of the Historical Society of Pennsylvania in Philadelphia.

5. Lady Wilde, "The Holy Well and the Murderer," in *Ancient Legends, Mystic Charms, and Superstitions of Ireland, with Sketches of the Irish Past* (1919; repr., Mineola, N.Y.: Dover, 2006), 70–71; Korson, *Minstrels of the Mine Patch*, 156–57.

6. Payne's trip to Ireland is recounted in a souvenir pamphlet by St. Kieran's Catholic church in Heckscherville published in 1918; the similarity between Pennsylvania anthracite and Kilkenny coal is discussed by H. Benjamin Powell in "The Pennsylvania Anthracite Trade, 1769–1976," *Pennsylvania History* 47 (Jan. 1980).

7. *Kilkenny Moderator*, Nov. 30, 1831.

8. J. H. Beers, *Schuylkill County, Pennsylvania: Genealogy – Family History– Biography*, vol. 2 (Chicago, J. H. Beers & Co., 1916), 974.

9. *MJ*, June 25, 1853; Schuylkill County Coroner's Index, County Courthouse, Pottsville, Pa. *MJ* identified the victim as John Berger, but that appears to have been a typographical error—there was no John Berger listed in the Cass Township census for 1850, though there was a John Bergen, the son of a James Bergen. The county coroner listed the victim as John Bergen, and reported that the

inquest took place in the home of James Bergen—a different James than the man killed in January 1863.

10. *MJ*, May 21, 1853.

11. Ibid., May 20, 1854.

12. Dewees, *Molly Maguires*, 324–26; *New York Times*, Dec. 26, 1888.

13. I. Daniel Rupp, *History of Northampton, Lehigh, Monroe, Carbon, and Schuylkill Counties* (Harrisburg, Pa., 1845), 296.

14. *MJ*, June 1, 1861.

15. U.S. Census, 1860, Cass Township, Schuylkill County, Pa.

16. Samuel B. Bates, *History of Pennsylvania Volunteers*, vol. 1 (Harrisburg, Pa., 1869), 50.

17. Sheriff's docket, December session, 1861, Schuylkill County Courthouse, Pottsville, Pa.; *MJ*, Dec. 14, 1861.

18. Military record, James Bergen, National Archives, Washington, D.C.

19. *Captain James Wren's Civil War Diary*, ed. John Michael Priest (New York: Berkley Books, 1991), 68.

20. Bates, *History of Pennsylvania Volunteers*, 1193.

21. *Captain James Wren's Civil War Diary*, 34.

22. *Philadelphia Inquirer*, May 9,1862; Records of the Reserve Brigade, 1st Division of Pa. Militia, During the Riots of Schuylkill County, 1862, Record Group 19, Pennsylvania State Archives, Harrisburg; *MJ*, July 5, 1862.

23. Alexander K. McClure, *Old Time Notes of Pennsylvania*, vol. 1 (Philadelphia, John C. Winston Co., 1905), 546; Palladino, *Another Civil War*, 98.

24. Thomas Bartlett, "An End to Moral Economy: The Irish Militia Disturbances of 1793," *Past & Present* 99 (May 1983): 49–51.

25. Curtin to E. M. Stanton, Oct. 22, 1862, in *War of the Rebellion: A Compilation of the Official Records of the Union and Confederate Armies*, ser. 1, vol. 19, pt. 2 (Washington, D.C., 1887), 468; *Philadelphia Inquirer*, Oct. 25, 1862.

26. *MJ*, Oct. 1, 1853, for scores of shebeens; Microfilm Roll 189, Schuylkill County Clerk of Courts, Pottsville, Pa.

27. *MJ*, Jan. 7, 1863.

28. Records of the Office of the Quartermaster General, RG 92, Entry 628, Headstones for Civil War Veterans, Reel 2, National Archives, Washington, D.C.; Schuylkill County Coroner's Index, County Courthouse, Pottsville, Pa.

29. *MJ*, Jan. 17, 1863.

30. Ibid. for details on shooting; kinship from Patrick O'Connor's tombstone, St. Vincent's old cemetery, Minersville, Pa.; polling place from *MJ*, Oct. 6, 1862; elected auditor, *Emporium*, Mar. 11, 1853; ran tavern, Cass Township tax book, 1859–67, Schuylkill County Courthouse, Pottsville, Pa.

31. Military records, John and Thomas Curry, National Archives, Washington, D.C.

32. J. H. Battle, *History of Columbia and Montour Counties* (Chicago, 1887), 429.

33. Dewees, *Molly Maguires*, 52; J. Walter Coleman, *The Molly Maguire Riots* (Richmond, Va.: Garrett and Massie, 1936), 47.

34. *New York Times*, Nov. 7, 1863; transcript of *Commonwealth v. McDonnell*, Carbon County Courthouse, Jim Thorpe, Pa.

2. The Black Pig's Realm

Epigraph. William Carleton, "The Irish Shanahus," *Irish Penny Journal*, May 29, 1841.

1. T. W. Rolleston, *Myths and Legends of the Celtic Race* (1911; repr., New York: Dover, 1990), 129; Michael Dames, *Mythic Ireland* (London: Thames and Hudson, 1992), 170.

2. Jonathan Bardon, *A History of Ulster* (Belfast: Blackstaff Press, 1992), 11–12; E. Estyn Evans, *The Personality of Ireland: Habitat, Heritage and History* (Dublin: Lilliput Press, 1992), 27–28.

3. James Bonwick, *Irish Druids and Old Irish Religions* (1894; repr., New York: Barnes & Noble Books, 1986), 121–22, 161; J. A. MacCulloch, *Religion of the Ancient Celts* (New York: Charles Scribner's Sons, 1911), 79, 146–47; Rolleston, *Myths and Legends of the Celtic Race*, 85.

4. "The Plain of Adoration," translated from Irish by John Montague in Chris Maguire's *Bawnboy and Templeport: History, Heritage, Folklore* (Bawnboy: Chris Maguire, 1999), 34.

5. MacCulloch, *Religion of the Ancient Celts*, 80; Bonwick, *Irish Druids and Old Irish Religions*, 134.

6. Ward Rutherford, *Celtic Mythology: The Nature and Influence of Celtic Myth—from Druidism to Arthurian Legend* (New York: Sterling, 1990), 112.

7. Joe McGowan, *Echoes of a Savage Land* (Cork: Mercier Press, 2001), 347.

8. Seumas MacManus, *The Story of the Irish Race* (Greenwich, Conn.: Devin-Adair, 1991), 43; the version mentioning Samhain is in the Book of Fermoy, pp. 72–80.

9. William Wilde, "The History of the Rise and Progress of Medicine in Ireland," *London Medical Gazette* 6 (1848): 303. In Irish mythology, the Tuatha were an ancient race that occupied Ireland before the Celts, and later became closely associated with the fairies. According to Wilde, "the fairy mythology of Ireland" sprang from the Tuatha and another ancient race. His wife, Lady Wilde, wrote, "It is believed by many people that the cave fairies are a remnant of the ancient Tuatha de Dananns." See Lady Wilde, *Ancient Legends, Mystic Charms, and Superstitions of Ireland*, 93, 337. The Wildes were the parents of Oscar Wilde.

10. George Bennett, *History of Bandon* (Cork, 1869), 419: "a lot of the disaffected in this kingdom banded themselves together—as Fairies, Redboys, Whiteboys, Levellers."

11. Henry Glassie, *All Silver and No Brass: An Irish Christmas Mumming* (Philadelphia: University of Pennsylvania Press, 1983), 5–6, 16–17; Rutherford, *Celtic Mythology*, 140–41.

12. Henry Glassie, *Passing the Time in Ballymenone* (Philadelphia: University of Pennsylvania Press, 1982), 116–18.

13. Ibid., 174, 626–27.

14. Bardon, *History of Ulster*, 13–14; Henry Frederic Reddall, *Fact, Fancy, and Fable* (Chicago, 1889), 436.

15. Bardon, *History of Ulster*, 56–57.

16. Kerby A. Miller, *Emigrants and Exiles: Ireland and the Irish Exodus to North America* (Oxford: Oxford University Press, 1985), 19.

17. Evans, *Personality of Ireland*, 30–31.

18. Kevin Whelan, "An Underground Gentry," in *Irish Popular Culture, 1650–1850*, ed. James S. Donnelly, Jr., and Kerby A. Miller (Dublin: Irish Academic Press, 1998), 118, 130–32.

19. Terry Eagleton, *Heathcliff and the Great Hunger* (London: Verso, 1995), 29; R. F. Foster, *Modern Ireland, 1600–1972* (London: Penguin, 1988), 36.

20. Eagleton, *Heathcliff and the Great Hunger*, 140.

21. Miller, *Emigrants and Exiles*, 119–22; Glassie, *All Silver and No Brass*, 157.

22. De la Tocnaye, "Promenade d'un Francais dans l'Irlande," quoted in Robert Kee, *The Most Distressful Country* (London: Penguin, 1972), 171.

23. Michael Beames, *Peasants and Power: The Whiteboy Movements and Their Control in Pre-famine Ireland* (New York: St. Martin's Press, 1983), 7.

24. Donald E. Jordan, Jr., *Land and Popular Politics in Ireland: County Mayo from the Plantation to the Land War* (Cambridge: Cambridge University Press, 1994), 54–55.

25. Samuel Lewis, *A Topographical Dictionary of Ireland*, vol. 2 (London, 1837), 382.

26. Samuel Clark, *Social Origins of the Irish Land War* (Princeton: Princeton University Press, 1979), 76.

27. George Hill, *Facts from Gweedore*, quoted in Evans, *Personality of Ireland*, 96; see also p. 101 of Evans.

28. Gerard MacAtasney, *Leitrim and the Great Hunger* (Carrick on Shannon: Carrick on Shannon & District Historical Society, 1997), 95.

29. Conrad Arensberg, *The Irish Countryman* (London: Macmillan, 1937), 72–75.

30. James O'Neill, "Popular Culture and Peasant Rebellion in Pre-famine Ireland" (Ph.D. diss., University of Minnesota, 1984), 220–21. O'Neill borrowed

the reciprocity/right to subsistence concept from a study of landlord–tenant relations in Southeast Asia, James Scott's "Exploitation in Rural Class Relations: A Victim's Perspective," *Comparative Politics* 7, no. 4 (1975): 489–532.

31. Sean Connolly, "Elite Responses to Popular Culture, 1660–1850," in *Irish Popular Culture*, ed. Donnelly and Miller, 22.

32. Kevin Danaher, *The Year in Ireland* (Cork: Mercier Press, 1972), 24–27.

33. Ibid., 78, 101–3, 138, 154; Sir William Wilde, *Irish Popular Superstitions* (New York: Sterling, 1995), 44.

34. E. Estyn Evans, *Irish Folks Ways* (New York: Devin-Adair, 1957), 277; Glassie, *All Silver and No Brass*, 114–15; Danaher, *Year in Ireland*, 211.

35. Glassie, *All Silver and No Brass*, 115–16.

36. Danaher, *Year in Ireland*, 242.

37. Ibid., 243–49; Evans, *Irish Folk Ways*, 279.

38. Alan Gailey, *Irish Folk Drama* (Cork: Mercier Press, 1969), 9–15.

39. Glassie, *All Silver and No Brass*, 25, 85.

40. From survey of one hundred mummers scripts, Ulster Folk and Transport Museum, Cultra.

41. Gailey, *Irish Folk Drama*, 68.

42. Ibid., 73–74, 90.

43. McGowan, *Echoes of a Savage Land*, 317–19.

44. Glassie, *All Silver and No Brass*, 134.

45. Gailey, *Irish Folk Drama*, 30.

46. Glassie, *All Silver and No Brass*, 100.

47. Hugh Brody, *Inishkillane: Change and Decline in the West of Ireland* (New York: Knopf Doubleday, 1974), 26–27.

48. Glassie, *All Silver and No Brass*, 127, 110; Glassie, *The Stars of Ballymenone* (Bloomington: Indiana University Press, 2006), 25, 27.

49. Bonwick, *Irish Druids and Old Irish Religions*, 203.

50. Danaher, *Year in Ireland*, 188; Irish Folklore Department, University College Dublin, Manuscript 1458, p. 6; McGowan, *Echoes of a Savage Land*, 11–14.

51. *Ordnance Survey Memoirs of Ireland*, vol. 40: *Counties of South Ulster 1834–8* (Belfast: Institute of Irish Studies, 1998), 133; Danaher, *Year in Ireland*, 250.

52. O'Neill, "Popular Culture and Peasant Rebellion in Pre-famine Ireland," 147.

53. Wilde, *Irish Popular Superstitions*, 61, 62.

3. The Secret Societies

Epigraph. Report from the Select Committee on Outrages (Ireland), Minutes of Evidence (London, 1852), 80.

1. Raymond Murray, *The Burning of Wildgoose Lodge* (Monaghan: Armagh Diocesan Historical Society, 2005), 1, 171, 176.

2. Ibid., 86; Miller, *Emigrants and Exiles*, 213; Tom Garvin, *The Evolution of Irish Nationalist Politics* (Dublin: Gill and Macmillan, 1981), 38.

3. "Wildgoose Lodge," in *Tales of Old Ireland*, ed. Michael O'Mara (Secaucus, N.J.: Castle, 1994), 40.

4. Seamus Heaney, "Station Island," in *Seamus Heaney: Selected Poems, 1966–1987* (New York: Farrar, Straus and Giroux, 1990), 185.

5. R. Shelton Mackenzie, *Bits of Blarney* (Chicago, 1884), 167.

6. Richard Lalor Sheil, with R. Shelton Mackenzie, *Sketches of the Irish Bar*, vol. 2 (New York, 1854), 143.

7. Beames, *Peasants and Power*, 23–25; Bardon, *History of Ulster*, 206–8.

8. Beames, *Peasants and Power*, 26–29.

9. W. S. Trench, *Realities of Irish Life* (London, 1867), 39.

10. Quoted in John William Knott, "Land, Kinship, and Identity: The Cultural Roots of Agrarian Agitation in Eighteenth- and Nineteenth-Century Ireland," *Journal of Peasant Studies* 12, no. 1 (1984): 99.

11. Michael Davitt, *The Fall of Feudalism in Ireland* (London, 1904), 38.

12. Paul E. W. Roberts, "Caravats and Shanavests: Whiteboyism and Faction Fighting in East Munster, 1802–1911," *Irish Peasants: Violence and Political Unrest, 1780–1914*, ed. Samuel Clark and James S. Donnelly, Jr. (Madison: University of Wisconsin Press, 1983), 82–83; Arthur Young, *A Tour of Ireland with General Observation on the Present State of That Kingdom Made in the Years 1776, 1777 and 1778* (Cambridge: Cambridge University Press, 1925), 23; James. S. Donnelly, Jr., *Captain Rock: The Irish Agrarian Rebellion of 1821–1824* (Madison: University of Wisconsin Press, 2006), 88–89.

13. Beames, *Peasants and Power*, 50, 54, 66.

14. G. C. Lewis, *On Local Disturbances in Ireland, and on the Irish Church Question* (London, 1836), 284.

15. Michael Beames, "Rural Conflict in Pre-famine Ireland: Peasant Assassination in Tipperary, 1837–1847," *Past & Present* 81 (Nov.): 85, 86.

16. Roberts, "Caravats and Shanavests," 66, 92.

17. Beames, *Peasants and Power*, 66–67; Lewis, *On Local Disturbances in Ireland*, 136; Clark, *Social Origins of the Irish Land War*, 84.

18. Definition of "boy," Glassie, *All Silver and No Brass*, 153; Knott, "Land, Kinship, and Identity," 99–100; R. F. Foster, *Modern Ireland, 1600–1972* (London: Penguin, 1988), 408.

19. Lewis, *On Local Disturbances in Ireland*, 239; see also Young, *Tour of Ireland*, 23.

20. O'Neill, "Popular Culture and Peasant Rebellion in Pre-famine Ireland," 285.

21. Wilde, *Irish Popular Superstitions*, 60.

22. Frank Peel, *Spen Valley: Past and Present* (Heckmondwike, 1893), quoted by Norman Simms in "Nedd Ludd's Mummers Play," *Folklore* 89, no. 2 (1978):

170–71; see also Kirkpatrick Sale, *Rebels Against the Future: The Luddites and Their War on the Industrial Revolution* (Reading, Mass.: Addison-Wesley, 1995), 133.

23. Eric Hobsbawm and George Rude, *Captain Swing: A Social History of the English Agricultural Uprising of 1830* (New York, W. W. Norton, 1975), 109, 111, 113.

24. Peter Sahlins, *Forest Rites: The War of the Demoiselles in Nineteenth-Century France* (Cambridge: Harvard University Press, 1994), 61–96.

25. David Williams, *The Rebecca Riots* (Cardiff: University of Wales Press, 1986), 54, 202, 236–37; David J. V. Jones, *Rebecca's Children: A Study of Society, Crime and Protest* (Oxford: Clarendon Press, 1989), 196–250.

26. Charles Wilkins, *The History of the Iron, Steel, Tinplate and Other Trades of Wales* (Merthyr Tydfil: Joseph Williams, 1903), 178.

27. Sahlins, *Forest Rites*, 30, 80; E. P. Thompson, *Customs in Common: Studies in Traditional Popular Culture* (New York: New Press, 1993), 528–29.

28. Edmund Hayes, *Crimes and Punishments; or, An Analytical Digest of the Criminal Laws of Ireland* (Dublin, 1837), 149–77. The first of the laws to be specifically labeled a Whiteboy Act was passed in 1776.

29. Beames, *Peasants and Power*, 33; Thomas P. Power, *Land, Politics and Society in Eighteenth-Century Tipperary* (Oxford: Oxford University Press, 1993), 178–79; Jon Banim; *The Peep O'Day; or, John Doe* (Dublin, 1865), 26; Patrick D. O'Donnell, *The Irish Faction Fighters* (Dublin: Anvil, 1975), 48.

30. *Sessional Papers of the House of Lords*, vol. 21: *State of Ireland in Respect of Crime*, pt. 4 (London, 1839), 1375–79.

31. Wayne G. Broehl, *The Molly Maguires* (Cambridge: Harvard University Press, 1964), 31–32; Gailey, *Irish Folk Drama*, 10.

32. Evans, *Personality of Ireland*, 108.

33. Kevin Whelan, *The Tree of Liberty: Radicalism, Catholicism, and the Construction of Irish Identity, 1760–1830* (Notre Dame: University of Notre Dame Press, 1996), 39.

34. *Impartial Account of the Late Disturbances in the County of Armagh* (Dublin, 1792), quoted in *Peep O'Day Boys and Defenders: Selected Documents on the Disturbances in County Armagh, 1784–1796*, ed. David W. Miller (Belfast: Public Record Office of Northern Ireland, 1990), 11.

35. James G. Leyburn, *The Scots-Irish: A Social History* (Chapel Hill: University of North Carolina Press, 1962), 191; Miller, *Emigrants and Exiles*, 152, 155.

36. Bardon, *History of Ulster*, 177.

37. Ibid., 210–12: Maurice R. O'Connell, *Irish Politics and Social Conflict in the Age of the American Revolution* (Philadelphia: University of Pennsylvania Press, 1965), 72–75.

38. Bardon, *History of Ulster*, 214–16.

39. Miller, *Emigrants and Exiles*, 169–70.

40. Miller, *Peep O'Day Boys and Defenders*, 13.

41. Tom Garvin, "Defenders, Ribbonmen, and Others: Underground Political Networks in Pre-famine Ireland," *Past & Present* 96 (Aug. 1982): 138, 142.

42. Bardon, *History of Ulster*, 224–25; Sir Henry McAnally, *The Irish Militia, 1793–1816* (Dublin: Clonmore and Reynolds, 1949), 50, 60–61; Thomas Bartlett, "An End to Moral Economy: The Irish Militia Disturbances of 1793," *Past & Present* 99 (May 1983): 58; William Edward Hartpole Lecky, *A History of Ireland in the Eighteenth Century*, vol. 2 (London, 1892), 221.

43. Bartlett, "An End to Moral Economy," 49–50.

44. Ibid., 52–56; Lecky, *History of Ireland in the Eighteenth Century*, 217, 219.

45. Seamus Heaney, "Requiem for the Croppies," in *Seamus Heaney: Selected Poems*, 17.

46. Thomas Pakenham, *The Year of Liberty: The Great Irish Rebellion of 1789* (New York: Random House, 1969), 324–26.

47. Wilde, *Irish Popular Superstitions*, 59–60; Kyla Madden, *Forkhill Protestants and Forkhill Catholics, 1787–1858* (Montreal: McGill-Queen's University Press, 2005), 96–97.

48. Garvin, *Evolution of Irish Nationalist Politics*, 37–40; Lewis, *On Local Disturbances in Ireland*, 128.

49. Joseph Lee, "The Ribbonmen," in *Secret Societies in Ireland*, ed. T. Desmond Williams (Dublin: Gill and Macmillan, 1973), 31.

50. Garvin, *Evolution of Irish Nationalist Politics*, 41; Garvin, "Defenders, Ribbonmen, and Others," 146; Beames, "Rural Conflict in Pre-famine Ireland," 132.

51. Outrage Papers (hereafter OP) for County Leitrim, 1846, National Archives, Dublin.

52. Garvin, "Defenders, Ribbonmen, and Others," 148–49.

53. John O'Dea, *History of the Ancient Order of Hibernians and Ladies' Auxiliary*, 2:772; Beames, "Rural Conflict in Pre-famine Ireland," 129; Garvin, *Evolution of Irish Nationalist Politics*, 38; Garvin, "Defenders, Ribbonmen, and Others," 146.

54. A. M. Sullivan, *The New Ireland*, vol. 1 (London, 1877), 71. He grudgingly allows that the Ribbon Society also viewed itself as political organization.

55. Bardon, *History of Ulster*, 303–4.

56. Report of James McParlan to Allen Pinkerton, Oct. 10, 1873, Reading Railroad Collection, Hagley Museum and Library, Wilmington, Del. For New York City, see Michael A. Gordon, *The Orange Riots: Irish Political Violence in New York, 1870 and 1871* (Ithaca: Cornell University Press, 1993).

57. OP, County Longford, 1839.

58. Garvin, "Defenders, Ribbonmen, and Others," 149; OP, County Longford, 1839.

4. Land and Politics

Epigraph. Philip H. Bagenal, *The American Irish and Their Influence on Irish Politics* (London, 1882), 7.

1. Kevin O'Neill, *Family and Farm in Pre-famine Ireland: The Parish of Killeshandra* (Madison: University of Wisconsin Press, 1984), 38–39; Bardon, *History of Ulster*, 252, 253.

2. *Her Majesty's Commission of Inquiry into the State of the Law and Practice in Respect to the Occupation of Land in Ireland* (hereafter Devon Commission), Minutes of Evidence, vol. 2 (Dublin, 1845), 274–75.

3. Thomas Campbell Foster, *Letters on the Condition of the People in Ireland* (London, 1846), 31–32; O'Neill, *Family and Farm in Pre-famine Ireland*, 36.

4. W. Steuart Trench, *Realities of Irish Life* (London, 1868), 76–77.

5. *Irish Peasants*, ed. Clark and Donnelly, introduction to sec. 2, "Land and Religion in Ulster," 149; Foster, *Letters on the Condition of the People in Ireland*, 130.

6. O'Neill, *Family and Farm in Pre-famine Ireland*, 23.

7. Ibid., 8, 15.

8. Ibid., 101; Miller, *Emigrants and Exiles*, 237–38.

9. O'Neill, *Family and Farm in Pre-famine Ireland*, 24, 41–42, 52, 117; Miller, *Emigrants and Exiles*, 208, 230–31.

10. Michael Hurst, *Maria Edgeworth and the Public Scene* (London: Macmillan, 1969), 82.

11. Foster, *Letters on the Condition of the People in Ireland*, 23.

12. Fergus O'Farrell, "The Ballinamuck 'Land War,' 1835–39," *Teathbha: Journal of the Longford Historical Society*, Mar. 1983.

13. Ibid.

14. Ibid.

15. Ibid.; OP, County Longford, 1835, 1836.

16. K. Theodore Hoppen, *Elections, Politics and Society in Ireland, 1832–1885* (Oxford: Clarendon Press 1984), 380–90.

17. OP, County Longford, 1836, 1837.

18. O'Farrell, "Ballinamuck 'Land War,'"; OP, County Longford, 1838.

19. OP, County Longford, 1839.

20. O'Farrell, "Ballinamuck 'Land War,'"; OP, County Longford, 1839.

21. OP, County Longford, 1836, 1838; Danaher, *Year in Ireland*, 154.

22. MacManus, *The Story of the Irish Race*, 76; Bardon, *History of Ulster*, 92, 109; Kee, *The Most Distressful Country* , 58.

23. Peadar Livingstone, *The Monaghan Story* (Enniskillen: Clogher Historical Society, 1980), 181, 182.

24. Ibid., 185, 186; James Godkin, *The Land-War in Ireland* (London, 1870), 365.

25. Livingstone, *Monaghan Story*, 187; Godkin, *Land-War in Ireland*, 365.

26. Trench, *Realities of Irish Life*, 284, 285.

27. Bardon, *History of Ulster*, 245, 246; Foster, *Letters on the Condition of the People in Ireland*, 304.

28. Livingstone, *Monaghan Story*, 198, 203; Broehl, *Molly Maguires*, 46, 47; Godkin, *Land-War in Ireland*, 365, 366.

29. Garvin, *Evolution of Irish Nationalist Politics*, 38–39; Garvin, "Defenders, Ribbonmen, and Others," 148–49.

30. Broehl, *Molly Maguires*, 48–49; Godkin, *Land-War in Ireland*, 366.

31. Trench, *Realities of Irish Life*, 58.

32. *Ordnance Survey Memoirs of Ireland*, vol. 40: *Counties of South Ulster, 1834–8* 140, 148; author's survey of the texts of one hundred mummers plays, Ulster Folk and Transport Museum, Cultra.

33. Trench, *Realities of Irish Life*, 58, 76, 77.

34. Broehl, *Molly Maguires*, 46.

35. Trench, *Realities of Irish Life*, 59–64, Broehl, *Molly Maguires*, 54.

36. Broehl, *Molly Maguires*, 56; Trench, *Realities of Irish Life*, 67–72.

37. Devon Commission, Minutes of Evidence, vol. 2, 890–938.

38. Godkin, *Land-War in Ireland*, 359–61; *New York Times*, Jan. 6, 1869; introduction to the Shirley Papers, Public Records Office of Northern Ireland, Belfast, 2007, 22.

39. Trench, *Realities of Irish Life*, 65, 66.

40. OP, County Monaghan, 1843.

41. Devon Commission, Minutes of Evidence, vol. 2, 1000.

5. The Molly Maguires

Epigraph. Allan Pinkerton, *The Molly Maguires and the Detectives* (New York, 1877), 77.

1. OP, County Cavan, 1845.

2. *Extracts Made by Colonel McGregor, from the Police Reports, Stating the Particulars of the Principal Homicides in Ireland, in the Years 1845 and 1846*, printed by the House of Commons, Apr. 2, 1846.

3. *The Nation*, Dec. 28, 1844.

4. National Archives, Dublin. The description of Molly and the attack that followed appear in the 1845 Outrage Papers for County Leitrim; the names of all the victims appear in a Nov. 11, 1846, memorial from the victims seeking government aid to emigrate that is part of the Leitrim Outrage Papers for 1846. The four prosecuted Michael Bradley and Thomas Kiernan, who were sentenced to exile from Ireland, or "transportation" as "members of an illegal conspiracy well known at that time by the name Molly Maguires." Other details appear in "Abstracts of the Police Reports of Some of the Principal Outrages in the

Counties of Tipperary, Limerick, Leitrim and Roscommon in the Year 1845," *British Parliamentary Papers on Ireland* 35 (1846): 75.

5. Devon Commission, Digest of Evidence, p. 388, on desperation of Leitrim tenants; pp. 406–7 on ten-to-twelve acres needed to support a farmer; p. 395 on the size of farms in Leitrim and Cavan.

6. Ibid., Digest, pp. 809, 803.

7. O'Neill, *Family and Farm in Pre-famine Ireland*, 38.

8. *Armagh Guardian*, Dec. 3, 1844.

9. Danaher, *Year in Ireland*, 188–89.

10. *Armagh Guardian*, Dec. 3, 1844.

11. OP, Leitrim, 1845, Return of Outrages, District of Ballinamore.

12. Devon Commission, Extracts of Evidence, 324–29.

13. OP, Leitrim, 1845, Return of Outrages.

14. Ibid., Clements, Feb. 7.

15. Robert Tracy, introduction to Anthony Trollope's *The Macdermots of Ballycloran* (Oxford: Oxford University Press, 1989), xvi.

16. Beames, *Peasants and Power*, 144; *Armagh Guardian*, Feb. 4, 1845; *Extracts Made by Colonel McGregor*; OP, Cavan, 1845.

17. Maguire, *Bawnboy and Templeport*, 63; OP, Leitrim, 1845.

18. Lady Wilde, *Ancient Legends, Mystic Charms, and Superstitions of Ireland*, 108.

19. "Parliamentary Intelligence," *Times* of London, Feb. 24, 1846.

20. OP, County Cavan, 1846; *Anglo-Celt*, Feb. 1, 1850.

21. Richard McMahon, "The Madness of Party: Sectarian Homicide in Ireland, 1801–1850," *Crime, History and Societies* 11, no 1 (2007): 83–112.

22. OP, Cavan, 1845.

23. Kenny, *Making Sense of the Molly Maguires*, 312.

24. John B. Cunningham, "The Investigation into the Attempted Assassination of Folliot Warren Barton near Pettigo on 31 October, 1845," *Clogher Record* 13, no. 3 (1990): 125–28; March 5, 1846, letter from Ribbon Detection Society to Lord Enniskillen, Correspondence of the 3rd Earl of Enniskillen, Enniskillen Papers, Public Records Office of Northern Ireland, Belfast.

25. OP, County Fermanagh, 1846.

26. Cunningham, "Investigation into the Attempted Assassination of Folliot Warren Barton," 130–31, 145. The threat invoking the McLeod killing was reported in The Anglo-Celt, a Cavan newspaper, on July 24, 1846.

27. OP, Cavan, 1847.

28. OP, Cavan, 1846.

29. Ibid., Leitrim, 1846.

30. OP, Cavan, 1846; Foster, *Letters on the Condition of the People in Ireland*, 20; OP, Leitrim, 1846.

31. OP, Leitrim, 1845.

32. Knott, "Land, Kinship, and Identity," 100.

33. OP, Donegal, 1846.

34. Ibid., Leitrim, 1845.

35. O'Dea, *History of the Ancient Order of Hibernians and Ladies' Auxiliary*, 2:770–71; Michael Davitt, *The Fall of Feudalism in Ireland* (New York: Harper and Brothers, 1904), 43.

36. OP, County Armagh, 1846.

37. Paul Bew, *Land and the National Question in Ireland, 1858–82* (Atlantic Highlands, N.J.: Humanities Press, 1978), 35.

38. Foster, *Letters on the Condition of the People in Ireland*, 323–24.

39. OP, Leitrim, 1846.

40. Ibid., Armagh, 1846.

41. Ibid., Cavan, 1846.

42. *Roscommon and Leitrim Gazette*, Aug. 9, 1845, quoted in Beames, *Peasants and Power*, 92.

43. OP, Leitrim, 1846.

44. *Roscommon and Leitrim Gazette*, Mar. 8, 1845, quoted in Beames, *Peasants and Power*, 79.

45. OP, Roscommon, 1846.

46. Foster, *Letters on the Condition of the People in Ireland*, 20.

47. OP, Cavan, 1846; Leitrim, 1845.

48. OP, Roscommon, 1846; Longford, 1846; Hoppen, *Elections, Politics and Society in Ireland*, 382.

49. OP, Cavan, 1845.

50. Foster, *Letters on the Condition of the People in Ireland*, 324; Sept. 12, 1845, statement of account for the Ribbon Detection Society, Correspondence of the 3rd Earl of Enniskillen, Enniskillen Papers, Public Records Office of Northern Ireland, Belfast.

51. OP, Donegal, 1846.

52. *Dublin Evening Post*, June 3, 1845, quoted in Samuel Clark, *Social Origins of the Irish Land War* (Princeton: Princeton University Press, 1979), 65.

53. Beams, *Peasants and Power*, 193, 78; excommunication report in Desmond Norton, *Landlords, Tenants, Famine: The Business of an Irish Land Agency in the 1840s* (Dublin: University College Dublin Press, 2006), 106.

54. *The Nation*, Jan. 25, 1845.

55. Ibid., June 7, 1845.

56. OP, Leitrim, 1845.

57. Michael Doheny, *The Felon's Track* (Dublin: M. H. Gill & Son, 1920), App. 1, "Thomas D'Arcy M'Gee's Narrative of 1848," 174.

58. Stephen J. Campbell, *The Great Irish Famine* (Strokestown: Famine Museum, 1994), 50.

59. James Robert Scally, *The End of Hidden Ireland: Rebellion, Famine and Emigration* (Oxford: Oxford University Press, 1995), 70, 76.

60. Ibid., 5.

61. Ibid., 31, 72, 102.

62. OP, Roscommon, 1847.

63. Scally, *End of Hidden Ireland*, 97, 98.

64. OP, Roscommon, 1847.

65. Quoted in MacAtasney, *Leitrim and the Great Hunger*, 31.

66. Campbell, *Great Irish Famine*, 47.

67. Scally, *End of Hidden Ireland*, 60; Campbell, *Great Irish Famine*, 44.

68. Scally, *End of Hidden Ireland*, 39.

69. Campbell, *Great Irish Famine*, 47, 48.

70. On display at the Famine Museum, which is located in Mahon's former home in Strokestown.

71. *The Nation*, Nov. 6, 1847.

72. Campbell, *Great Irish Famine*, 49; Peter Duffy, *The Killing of Major Denis Mahon* (New York: HarperCollins, 2007), 243, 250, 301.

73. Edward O'Reilly, *An Irish–English Dictionary* (Dublin, 1864), 344.

74. McGowan, *Echoes of a Savage Land*, 325.

75. OP, Leitrim, 1845; Cavan, 1847.

76. Irish Folklore Commission, University College Dublin, Manuscript 1458, p. 343.

77. Ibid., Manuscript 1089, p. 69.

78. From a survey of one hundred mummers texts, Ulster Folk and Transport Museum, Cultra.

79. Gailey, *Irish Folk Drama*, 49, 61; Alex Helm, *The English Mummers' Play* (Woodbridge: Suffolk, D. S. Brewer, 1980), 31, 67, 69, 120; Alex Helm, *Eight Mummers' Plays* (Aylesbury: Ginn & Co., 1971), 43–45, 48–50; R. J. E. Tiddy, *The Mummers' Play* (Chicheley: Paul P. B. Minet, 1972), 227.

80. Helm, *Eight Mummers' Plays*, 29–34; Tiddy, *Mummers' Play*, 225; see also the survey of mummers plays available at the Ulster Folk and Transport Museum, Cultra.

81. O'Dea, *History of the Ancient Order of Hibernians and Ladies' Auxiliary*, 2:771–72; Broehl, *Molly Maguires*, 28; *The Molly Maguires: A Thrilling Narrative of the Rise, Progress, and Fall of the Most Noted Band of Cut-Throats of Modern Times*, Tamaqua, Pa., pamphlet ca. 1877, author unknown, p. 4.

82. Campbell, *Molly Maguire Story*, 66; David W. Miller, "Armagh Troubles," in *Irish Peasants*, ed. Clark and Donnelly, 165. For the quotation, see Accession

No. 1520, Box 979, Reading Rail Road Collection, Molly Maguire Papers, Hagley Museum and Library, Wilmington, Del.

83. Asenath Nicholson, *Annals of the Famine in Ireland* (Dublin: Lilliput Press, 1998), 118.

84. Beames, *Peasants and Power*, 100.

85. Broehl, *Molly Maguires*, 29.

86. Foster, *Letters on the Condition of the People in Ireland*, 23.

87. OP, County Cavan, 1845.

88. O'Dea, *History of the Ancient Order of Hibernians and Ladies' Auxiliary*, 2:771.

89. Thomas Pakenham, *The Scramble for Africa: White Man's Conquest of the Dark Continent from 1876 to 1912* (New York: Random House, 1991), 677.

90. Quoted in Eagleton, *Heathcliff and the Great Hunger*, 16.

91. *Weekly Freeman's Journal*, Sept. 18, 1847, quoted in *The Famine Decade: Contemporary Accounts, 1841–1851*, ed. John Killen (Belfast: Blackstaff Press, 1995), 151; James J. Clancy, *The Land League Manual* (New York, 1881), 18.

6. Brotherly Love

Epigraph. "The Coal Trade of Pennsylvania," *North American Review* 42 (1836): 248; Bimba, *Molly Maguires*, 66.

1. On background of Bannans, see Ella Zerbey Elliott, *Blue Book of Schuylkill County* (Pottsville, Pa.: Republican, 1916), 160–61; for Gowens, see Marvin W. Schlegel, *Ruler of the Reading: The Life of Franklin B. Gowen* (Harrisburg, Pa.: Archives Publishing, 1947); for Mohans, see Samuel T. Wiley, *Biographical and Portrait Cyclopedia of Schuylkill County* (Philadelphia, 1893), 689. Bannan has often been described as coming from Welsh lineage, but Elliot's account, the earliest on the subject, makes clear that his father was an Ulster Protestant; her description of his grave in an Episcopal cemetery in Douglassville, Pennsylvania, was confirmed by the author.

2. W. W. Munsell and Co., *History of Schuylkill County, Pa., with Illustrations and Biographical Sketches of Some of Its Prominent Men and Pioneers* (New York, 1881), 121, 131.

3. Elliott, *Blue Book of Schuylkill County*, 160–61; Wallace, *St. Clair*, 67; Munsell, *History of Schuylkill County*, 268, 293.

4. Clifton C. Yearley, Jr., *Enterprise and Anthracite: Economics and Democracy in Schuylkill County, 1820–1875* (Baltimore: Johns Hopkins University Press, 1961), 66.

5. Advertisements in *MJ*, July 9, 1842; Mar. 30, 1839; Nov. 23, 1833.

6. Ibid., Mar. 21, 1838; Mar. 27; July 9, 1842.

7. Kevin Kenny, "Nativism, Labor and Slavery: The Political Odyssey of Benjamin Bannan," *Pennsylvania Magazine of History and Biography*, Oct. 1994.

8. Schlegel, *Ruler of the Reading*, 1–5.

9. Ibid., 6–10.

10. Wiley, *Biographical and Portrait Cyclopedia of Schuylkill County*, 689; U.S. Census, 1850 and 1860, Minersville, Schuylkill County, Pa.; *MJ*, Mar. 25, 1843; *Pottsville Emporium*, Feb. 20, 1847, Munsell, *History of Schuylkill County*, 167; *MJ*, Mar. 23, 1850.

11. Hugh J. Mohan, E. H. Clough, and John P. Cosgrave, *Pen Pictures of Our Representative Men* (Sacramento, 1880), 96. I am indebted to Mary V. Dearborn, author of *Queen of Bohemia: The Life of Louise Bryant* (Boston: Houghton Mifflin, 1996), for sharing this material.

12. Rupp, *History of Northampton*, 509; U.S. Census, 1850, Coal Township, Northumberland County, Pa.; 1860, Foster Township, Schuylkill County; 1870, Cass Township; *Index to the Miscellaneous Documents of the House of Representatives for the First Session of the Forty-Fifth Congress* (Washington, D.C.: Government Printing Office, 1877); *Nutting v. Reilly*, testimony of Luke Mohan, 688–89.

13. *MJ*, Sept. 11, 1874; Report of Aug. 30, 1876, Molly Maguire Papers, Society Collection, Historical Society of Pennsylvania, Philadelphia; Report of Mar. 5, 1880, Reading Collection, Molly Maguire Papers, Knights of Labor Folder, Hagley Museum and Library, Wilmington, Del.

14. *Report of the Committee of the Senate of Pennsylvania, upon the Subject of the Coal Trade* (Harrisburg, Pa., 1834), 8–9.

15. Palladino, *Another Civil War*, 19, 22.

16. Ibid., 37.

17. Wallace, *St. Clair*, 453.

18. *Report of the Committee of the Senate of Pennsylvania*, 11.

19. Ibid., 68–69.

20. Ibid., 82.

21. Ibid., 72–73.

22. Palladino, *Another Civil War*, 46–47.

23. Ibid., 29–31.

24. Ibid., 54.

25. *MJ*, Mar. 27; July 9, 1842.

26. Rupp, *History of Northampton*, 499–550.

27. Miller, *Emigrants and Exiles*, 152–53; Leyburn, *Scots–Irish*, 171, 228, 232.

7. The Hibernians

Epigraph. O'Dea, *History of the Ancient Order of Hibernians and Ladies' Auxiliary*, 2:885.

1. Eli Bowen, *The Coal Regions of Pennsylvania* (Pottsville, 1848), 67; *MJ*, Mar. 24, 1832.

2. O'Dea, *History of the Ancient Order of Hibernians and Ladies' Auxiliary*, 2:884.

3. Tyler Anbinder, *Nativism and Slavery: The Northern Know Nothings and the Politics of the 1850s* (Oxford: Oxford University Press, 1992), 9–10; Maureen Dezell, *Irish America: Coming into Clover* (New York: Random House, 2002), 54.

4. *New York Times*, Dec. 26, 1888.

5. Miller, *Emigrants and Exiles*, 329; Richard N. Rosenfeld, *American Aurora: A Democratic-Republican Returns* (New York: St. Martin's Griffin, 1997), 135, 637.

6. O'Dea, *History of the Ancient Order of Hibernians and Ladies' Auxiliary*, 2:885–86.

7. M. R. Beames, "The Ribbon Societies: Lower-Class Nationalism in Pre-famine Ireland," *Past & Present* 97, no. 1 (1982): 133; Garvin, "Defenders, Ribbonmen, and Others," 148.

8. A.O.H. Extracts, Selected from Propaganda Literature of John O'Dea, National Secretary, Balch Institute, Philadelphia, 36.

9. "Great Fire in Pottsville," *New York Herald*, Sept. 12, 1848; *Laws of the General Assembly of the Commonwealth of Pennsylvania* (Harrisburg, 1852), 648.

10. Beers, *Schuylkill County, Pennsylvania*, vol. 2, p. 14.

11. Eliza Zerbey Elliott, *Old Schuylkill Tales* (Pottsville, 1906), 156.

12. Bowen, *Coal Regions of Pennsylvania*, 67; *MJ*, Mar. 25, 1848.

13. O'Dea, *History of the Ancient Order of Hibernians and Ladies' Auxiliary*, 2:886.

14. *MJ*, Mar. 24, 1838.

15. Ibid., Oct. 10; Oct. 17; Oct. 24, 1840.

16. Ibid., Mar. 23, 1840.

17. Ibid., Mar. 20, 1841; Mar. 19, 1842.

18. *Emporium*, Feb. 20; July 17, 1841; *MJ*, Mar. 27, 1841.

19. *Emporium*, July 10, 1841; Feb. 26, 1842; Angela F. Murphy, *American Slavery, Irish Freedom: Abolition, Immigrant Citizenship, and the Transatlantic Movement for Irish Repeal* (Baton Rouge: Louisiana State University Press, 2010), 84–87.

20. *The Liberator*, May 13, 1842; *Emporium*, Mar. 12, 1842.

21. *The Liberator*, May 13, 1842.

22. Reprinted in ibid.

23. Ibid., May 27, 1842.

24. *Boston Pilot*, reprinted in ibid., Aug. 5, 1842.

25. *Freeman's Journal*, June 4, 1842, reprinted in *The Liberator*, July 15, 1842.

26. Munsell, *History of Schuylkill County*, 53.

27. Yearley, *Enterprise and Anthracite*, 168–69.

28. *Emporium,* July 23, 1842.

29. O'Neill, *Family and Farm in Pre-famine Ireland,* 47.

30. *MJ,* July 30, 1842.

31. *Emporium,* July 16, 1842.

32. *MJ,* July 23; July 9, 1842.

33. Ibid., July 16, 1842.

34. Ibid., July 30, 1842.

35. *Emporium, MJ,* both July 23, 1842.

36. *MJ,* Aug. 6, 1842.

37. *Emporium,* Dec. 24; Dec. 31, 1842.

38. *The Liberator,* Aug. 12; Sept. 2, 1842.

39. Ibid., Oct. 7, 1842.

40. Record Group 110, E-3050, Letters Sent, 10th District Pa., 1863–65, Alonzo Snow affidavit, Feb. 1 1864, National Archives, Washington, D.C.

41. Joseph Henry Zerbey, *History of Pottsville and Schuylkill County,* vol. 5 (Pottsville, Pa.: J. H. Zerbey Newspapers, 1934–35), 2078–79.

42. *MJ,* May 19, 1849.

43. *Emporium,* Mar. 30, 1848.

44. *MJ,* Oct. 10, 1840.

45. *Emporium,* Apr. 1, 1843.

46. *Anthracite Gazette,* Aug. 31, 1844.

47. *MJ,* Nov. 16, 1844.

48. Miller, *Emigrants and Exiles,* 248.

49. *Emporium,* Aug. 8, 1840; *MJ,* Apr. 11, 1843; Rupp, *History of Northampton,* 499–536. On Ribbonmen in Ballycastle, see *Edinburgh Review,* Jan. 1899, 171; on United Irish activity in Ballycastle, see de La Tocnaye, quoted in Bardon, *History of Ulster,* 228.

8. Another Ulster

Epigraph. Allan Pinkerton, *The Molly Maguires and the Detectives* (New York, 1877), 77.

1. Wallace, *St. Clair,* 315–20.

2. *Emporium,* Jan. 27; Feb. 3, 1848.

3. Dewees, *Molly Maguires,* 21.

4. William A. Gudelunas, "The Rise of the Irish Factor in Anthracite Politics, 1850–1880," Occasional Paper No. 3, Pennsylvania Ethnic Heritage Studies Center, University of Pittsburgh.

5. U.S. Census returns of Cass Township in 1850 and 1860 show a number of children born in Nova Scotia to natives of Ireland; advertisements in *MJ,* Mar. 27; May 14; July 9, 1842.

6. Grace Palladino, "The Poor Man's Fight: Draft Resistance and Labor Organization in Schuylkill County, Pa., 1860–1865" (Ph.D. diss., University of Pittsburgh, 1983), 69, 72, 74.

7. Korson, *Minstrels of the Mine Patch*, 14–15.

8. Anthracite book field notes, Box 13, Dec. 8, 1939, Record Group 23, Pennsylvania State Archives, Harrisburg.

9. Ibid., Box 12, July 27, 1939.

10. Interview with Cass native Kitty O'Connor, Feb. 1995.

11. Field notes for "Folklore and Customs" by John S. Carroll, Box 12, Record Group 13, Pennsylvania State Archives, Harrisburg; *MJ*, May 5, 1849.

12. Field notes for "Folklore and Customs," Box 12, Record Group 13, Pennsylvania State Archives, Harrisburg.

13. Thompson, *Customs in Common*, 493, 521–23; Evans, *Personality of Ireland*, 286.

14. Korson, *Black Rock*, 251–52.

15. *MJ*, June 11, 1864.

16. "Folklore and Customs," Box 12, Record Group 13, Pennsylvania State Archives, Harrisburg.

17. Phoebe E. Gibbons, "The Miners of Scranton," *Harper's New Monthly Magazine*, Nov. 1877, 917.

18. "Folklore and Customs," Box 12, Record Group 13, Pennsylvania State Archives, Harrisburg.

19. Ibid.; Rupp, *History of Northampton*, 18; Gibbons, "Miners of Scranton," 916.

20. "The Labor Troubles in the Anthracite Region," in *Miscellaneous Documents Read in the Legislature of the Commonwealth of Pennsylvania During the Session Which Commenced on January 6, 1874*, vol. 1 (Harrisburg, 1874), 306.

21. Miller, *Emigrants and Exiles*, 326.

22. Zerbey, *History of Pottsville and Schuylkill County*, 409.

23. *MJ*, Mar. 18, 1848.

24. *Emporium*, Mar. 18, 1848.

25. Zerbey, *History of Pottsville and Schuylkill County*, 409.

26. U.S. Census for Cass Township, 1850.

27. *MJ*, June 29, 1850.

28. *Emporium*, Mar. 11, 1853; *MJ*, Mar. 26, 1853; Sept. 26, 1863; the Primrose location of the tavern becomes clear from the testimony of his sons Michael, John, and James and in *Nutting vs. Reilly*, both in *Index to the Miscellaneous Documents of the House of Representatives for the First Session of the Forty-Fifth Congress*, 714–16.

29. *MJ*, Mar. 25, 1854.

30. U.S. Census, Cass Township, 1860; Schuylkill County Coroner's Index, County Courthouse, Pottsville, Pa.

31. U.S. Cass Township, 1850; *Emporium*, Mar. 11, 1853; *MJ*, Oct. 6, 1860; tombstone, St. Vincent's Old Cemetery; Cass Township tax records in Schuylkill County Archives.

32. Arthur Lewis, *Lament for the Molly Maguires* (New York: Harcourt Brace and World, 1964), 13–14.

33. *Emporium*, Dec. 21, 1848; Rupp, *History of Northampton*, 520.

34. *MJ*, Nov. 11, 1848.

35. William A. Gudelunas, Jr., and William G. Shade, *Before the Molly Maguires: The Emergence of the Ethno-Religious Factor in the Politics of the Lower Anthracite Region, 1844–1872* (New York: Arno Press, 1976), 54.

36. *MJ*, July 2, 1853.

37. Gudelunas and Shade, *Before the Molly Maguires*, 60; *Emporium*, June 19, 1847.

38. *MJ*, Nov. 6, 1852, quoted in Palladino, "Poor Man's Fight."

39. Gudelunas and Shade, *Before the Molly Maguires*, 55.

40. Kenny, "Nativism, Labor and Slavery," 330–33.

41. On the lack of social mobility among Irish mine workers during this period, see Wallace, *St. Clair*, 133–40. On social mobility in the Heckscher collieries, see Palladino, *Another Civil War*, 61.

42. *MJ*, Oct. 1, 1853; Sept. 29, 1855; *Emporium*, Nov. 1, 1856.

43. Zerbey, *History of Pottsville and Schuylkill County*, 409; *MJ*, Jan. 12; Jan. 19, 1850.

44. *MJ*, Apr. 23, 1853. Italics are Bannan's.

45. *Emporium*, Apr. 13, 1848.

46. *MJ*, Mar. 24; Mar. 31; Apr. 6, 1855.

47. *MJ*, Apr. 28; May 5, 1855.

48. Casebook, December session 1853–March session 1857, Charlemagne Tower Papers, Butler Library, Columbia University, New York.

49. *MJ*, Apr. 21; May 26; June 2, 1855.

50. Ibid., May 12; May 19; June 9, 1855.

51. Anbinder, *Nativism and Slavery*, 18; Kenny, "Nativism, Labor and Slavery," 345–51.

52. *MJ*, Sept. 20, 1855, quoted in Kenny, "Nativism, Labor and Slavery," 351.

53. Kenny, "Nativism, Labor and Slavery," 351–52; Anbinder devotes all of Chapter 7 in *Nativism and Slavery* to the divisive effect of the slavery issue on the Know Nothings.

54. *MJ*, Dec. 29, 1855.

55. Alfred E. Shoemaker, "Fantaticals," *Pennsylvania Folklife* 9 (Winter 1957–58): 29; *MJ*, Jan. 4, 1851; Mar. 3, 1855.

56. Charles E. Welch, *Oh! Dem Golden Slippers: The Story of the Philadelphia Mummers* (New York: Nelson, 1970), 27.

57. Susan G. Davis, *Parades and Power: Street Theatre in Nineteenth-Century Philadelphia* (Berkeley: University of California Press, 1986), 104, 109.

58. Munsell, *History of Schuylkill County*, 106.

59. Davis, *Parades and Power*, 58–64.

60. Ibid., 71, 78, 80–81, 93, 103–4.

61. Ibid., 107.

62. Ibid., 84; Elizabeth Pleck, "The Making of the Domestic Occasion: The History of Thanksgiving in the United States," *Journal of Social Science* 32, no. 4 (1999): 773–89.

63. Shoemaker, "Fantasticals."

64. Joseph J. Holmes, "The Decline of the Pennsylvania Militia," *Western Pennsylvania Historical Magazine*, Apr. 1974, 208, 209.

65. *MJ*, May 28; June 11, 1853.

66. Davis, *Parades and Power*, 209.

67. *MJ*, Jan. 2, 1858.

68. Palladino, *Another Civil War*, 56.

69. *MJ*, Jan. 5, 1877; Shoemaker, "Fantasticals," 30–31.

70. AOH Extracts, Selected from Propaganda Literature of John O'Dea, National Secretary, Balch Institute, Philadelphia, 36.

71. *Emporium*, Feb. 20; Mar. 20, 1847.

72. Ibid., Aug. 17; Aug. 31, 1848.

73. AOH Extracts, Selected from Propaganda Literature of John O'Dea, National Secretary, Balch Institute, Philadelphia, 36; *MJ*, Jan. 5, 1850; Mar. 25, 1854.

74. *New York Times*, Dec. 26, 1888.

75. *MJ*, Mar. 21, 1857.

76. Ibid., Oct. 3, 1857.

77. Davis, *Parades and Power*, 151.

78. *MJ*, Oct. 10. 1857; reprint from the *Chicago Journal* in the *Albany Evening Journal*, Oct. 10, 1857.

79. Borda to Tower, Apr. 7, 1857, Charlemagne Tower Papers, Butler Library, Columbia University, New York

80. Quoted in Palladino, *Another Civil War*, 56–57.

81. *MJ*, May 22; May 29; June 12; June 19, 1858.

82. Schlegel, *Ruler of the Reading*, 7–9.

83. Wallace, *St. Clair*, 68–69.

9. Resurrection

Epigraph. William Butler Yeats, "The Second Coming," in *Michael Robartes and the Dancer* (Churchtown, Dundrum: Chuala Press, 1920), reprinted in

Selected Poems and Three Plays of William Butler Yeats, ed. M. L Rosenthal (New York: Collier, 1986), 89.

1. *MJ*, Apr. 27; July 21, 1861; Arnold Shankman, "Francis W. Hughes and the 1862 Pennsylvania Election," *Pennsylvania Magazine of History and Biography* 95 (1971): 384–85.

2. *MJ*, Apr. 27; May 25, 1861; Civil War Veterans Card File, Pennsylvania State Archives, Harrisburg.

3. *MJ*, Mar. 22, 1862.

4. Alonzo Snow affidavit, Feb. 1, 1864, Record Group 110, E-3050, Letters Sent, 10th District Pa., 1863–1865, National Archives, Washington, D.C.

5. *New York Times*, Apr. 26, 1863, regarding the strike fund and the organization's secret society aspect.

6. G. O. Virtue, "The Anthracite Mine Laborers," *Bulletin of the Department of Labor* 13 (Nov. 1897): 732; *MJ*, Jan. 2, 1864.

7. *MJ*, Feb. 28, 1863.

8. Andrew Roy, *A History of the Coal Miners of the United States* (Columbus, Ohio: 1907), 72.

9. U.S. Census for Reilly Township, Schuylkill County, 1860, p. 389; *Commonwealth vs. Patrick Hester, Peter McHugh & Patrick Tully* (Sunbury, Pa.: J. E. Eichholtz, 1877) 440.

10. Heckscher to Tower, Feb. 1, 1864, Record Group 110, E-3050, Letters Sent, 10th District Pa., 1863–1865, National Archives, Washington, D.C.

11. *Philadelphia Inquirer*, May 7; May 9, 1862.

12. Ibid., May 8, 1862.

13. *MJ*, May 10, 1862; Larry B. Maier, *Rough and Regular: A History of Philadelphia's 119th Regiment of Pennsylvania Volunteer Infantry, the Gray Reserves* (Shippensburg, Pa.: Burd Street Press, 1997), 4.

14. *New York Times*, Apr. 26, 1863; James W. Latta, *History of the First Regiment Infantry, National Guard of Pennsylvania (Gray Reserves)* (Philadelphia: J. B. Lippincott, 1912), 753.

15. *Philadelphia Inquirer*, May 9, 1862.

16. Hewitt to Tower, Feb. 2, 1864, Record Group 110, E-3050, Letters Sent, 10th District Pa., 1863–1865, National Archives, Washington, D.C.

17. Record of the Reserve Brigade of the 1st Division of Pa. Militia During Riots of Schuylkill Co., 1862, Record Group 19, Pennsylvania State Archives, Harrisburg.

18. *MJ*, May 10, 1862.

19. Ibid., May 17, 1862.

20. Ibid., June 21, 1862.

21. *Every Evening and Commercial* newspaper (Wilmington, Del.), Dec. 19, 1878.

22. *MJ*, July 3, 1862; June 6, 1863; Sheriff's Department Records for *Commonwealth and Thomas Crowe v. David Kelly, William Kelly, Laurence Flynn*, in Schuylkill County Courthouse, Pottsville, Pa.

23. Mark E. Neely, Jr., *The Fate of Liberty* (New York: Oxford University Press, 1991), 52.

24. Ibid., 56.

25. Ibid.

26. *MJ*, Jan. 7, 1863.

27. Bannan to Curtin, Sept. 23, 1862, Record Group 19, Office of the Adjutant General, General Correspondence, Pennsylvania State Archives, Harrisburg.

28. Ibid., White to Curtin, Sept. 24, 1862.

29. Ibid., Myers to Curtin, Sept. 12, 1862.

30. Neely, *Fate of Liberty*, 57.

31. *MJ*, Oct. 4; May 10, 1862.

32. Shankman, "Francis W. Hughes and the 1862 Pennsylvania Election," 390.

33. *New York Times*, Aug. 31, 1862. The paper said the Schuylkill County trouble was in "North and South Gap Townships," but no such municipalities existed. It clearly meant the North and South Precincts of Cass Township.

34. *MJ*, Oct. 11, 1862.

35. Ibid., Oct. 18, 1862.

36. Lewis, *Lament for the Molly Maguires*, 29.

37. *Philadelphia Inquirer*, quoted in *New York Times*, Nov. 2, 1862.

38. *Philadelphia Inquirer*, Oct. 27, 1862.

39. *Philadelphia Inquirer*, Oct. 24, 1862.

40. *War of the Rebellion*, ser. 1, vol. 19, pt. 2, p. 468.

41. *MJ*, Oct. 25, 1862.

42. *War of the Rebellion*, ser. 1, vol. 19, pt. 2, p. 473.

43. *Philadelphia Inquirer*, Oct. 27, 1862.

44. *War of the Rebellion*, ser. 1, vol. 19, pt. 2, p. 479–80.

45. McClure, *Old Time Notes of Pennsylvania*, vol. 1, 547–49.

46. Charles Loeser Papers, vol. 33, pp. 42, 43, Historical Society of Schuylkill County, Pottsville, Pa.

47. Davis, *Parades and Power*, 156.

48. Heckscher to Tower, Feb. 1, 1864, Record Group 110, E-3050, Letters Sent, 10th District Pa., 1863–1865, National Archives, Washington, D.C.

49. *MJ*, Oct. 25, 1862; Sept. 26, 1863.

50. *Philadelphia Inquirer*, Oct. 25; Oct. 27, 1862.

51. John T. Ridge, *Erin's Sons in America: The Ancient Order of Hibernians* (New York: Ancient Order of Hibernians 150th Anniversary Committee, 1986), 50.

10. "Brave Sons of Molly"

Epigraph. Pinkerton, *The Molly Maguires and the Detectives*, 77.

1. *MJ*, Mar. 14, 1863.

2. Hewitt to Tower, Feb. 2, 1864, Record Group 110, E-3050, Letters Sent, 10th District Pa., 1863–1865, National Archives, Washington, D.C.

3. *MJ*, Dec. 20, 1862.

4. Iver Bernstein, *The New York City Draft Riots* (New York: Oxford University Press, 1990), 26–27.

5. Schlegel, *Ruler of the Reading*, 9–10.

6. *MJ*, Jan. 17, 1863. (Copies of the newspaper for 1863 are missing from microfilm records, but are available in a bound volume at the Library of Congress.)

7. *MJ*, Mar. 14, 1863.

8. Ibid., Feb. 28, 1863.

9. Ibid., Mar. 14, 1863.

10. Accession No. 1520, Box 979, Reading Rail Road Collection, Molly Maguire Papers, Hagley Museum and Library, Wilmington, Del.

11. Ferry to Schultze, Mar. 18, 1864, Record Group 393, E-4612, Letters Received, National Archives, Washington, D.C.

12. Hewitt to Tower, Feb. 1, 1864, Record Group 110, E-3050, Letters Sent, 10th District Pa., 1863–1865, National Archives, Washington, D.C.; *MJ*, Mar. 21, 1863; O'Dea, *History of the Ancient Order of Hibernians and Ladies' Auxiliary*, 1:514.

13. "The Coal Trade" column, *MJ*, Mar. 14, 1863; *New York Times*, Apr. 26, 1863.

14. "The Coal Trade" column, *MJ*, Mar. 21, 1863.

15. Heckscher to Tower, Feb. 1, 1864, Record Group 110, E-3050, Letters Sent, 10th District Pa., 1863–1865, National Archives, Washington, D.C.

16. *New York Times*, Apr. 26, 1863.

17. Reprinted in *MJ*, Apr. 4, 1863.

18. *MJ*, Mar. 23, 1863.

19. *New York Times*, Apr. 26, 1863.

11. Mars in Mahantango

Epigraph. Couch to Curtin, Aug. 6, 1863, Record Group 393, E-3050, Letters Sent, 10th District Pa., 1863–1865, National Archives, Washington, D.C.

1. Hal Bridges, *Iron Millionaire: The Life of Charlemagne Tower* (Philadelphia: University of Pennsylvania Press, 1952), 71–75; Lucy C. White, "The Youth of Charles Sumner," *The Galaxy*, Dec. 1877.

2. Tower to Col. James Fry, May 25, 1863, Record Group 110, E-3050, Letters Sent, 10th District Pa., 1863–1865, National Archives, Washington, D.C.

3. Ibid., Tower to Stanton, May 12, 1863.

4. Ibid., Tower to Curtin, June 12, 1863.

5. *War of the Rebellion*, ser. 3, vol. 3, p. 332.

6. Tower to Bomford, June 16, 1863, Record Group 110, E-3050, Letters Sent, 10th District Pa., 1863–1865, National Archives, Washington, D.C.

7. Ibid., Letters Received, Fry to Tower, June 27, 1863.

8. Palladino, *Another Civil War*, 109–11.

9. Tower to Emanuel Whetstone of Tamaqua, June 13, 1863, Record Group 110, E-3050, Letters Received, 10th District Pa., 1863–1865, National Archives, Washington, D.C.

10. Ibid., Letters Sent, Tower to Bomford, June 16, 1863.

11. Ibid., June 25, 1863.

12. Ibid., July 7, 1863.

13. *MJ*, July 11, 1863.

14. Tower to Ernst, July 15, 1863, Record Group 110, E-3050, Letters Sent, 10th District Pa., 1863–1865, National Archives, Washington, D.C.; Tower to Fry, July 18, 1863.

15. Ibid., Letters Received, Bomford to Tower, July 21.

16. *War of the Rebellion*, ser. 3, vol. 3, p. 562.

17. Couch to Curtin, Aug. 6, 1863, Record Group 393, E-3050, Letters Sent, 10th District Pa., 1863–1865, National Archives, Washington, D.C.

18. Reprinted in the *New York Times*, Aug. 16, 1863.

19. Tower to Bomford, July 7, 1863, Record Group 110, E-3050, Letters Sent, 10th District Pa., 1863–1865, National Archives, Washington, D.C.; Tower to Bomford, Aug. 11, 1863.

20. Ibid., Tower to Bomford, Aug. 14, 1863.

21. Neely, *Fate of Liberty*, 151, 153.

22. *Daily Patriot and Union of Harrisburg*, Aug. 24, 1863.

23. Tower to Fry, Aug. 20, 1863, Record Group 110, E-3050, Letters Sent, 10th District Pa., 1863–1865, National Archives, Washington, D.C.; Tower to Heisler, Aug. 21, 1863; Tower to Bomford, Aug. 24, 1863.

24. Ibid., Tower to Fry, Sept. 26, 1863.

25. Ibid., Sept. 30, 1863.

26. Ibid., Tower to Gilbert, Nov. 7; Nov. 28, 1863

27. Ibid., Tower to Gilbert, Dec. 4, 1863; Tower to Ramsay, Oct. 19, 1863.

28. Ibid., Tower to Fry, Nov. 7, 1863; Tower to Oliphant, Nov. 28, 1863.

29. Philip Francis, "Seventy Years in the Coal Mines," privately published memoir posted at http://seventyyearsinthecoalmines.org/.

30. Dunne affidavit, Feb. 1, 1864, Record Group 110, E-3050, Letters Sent, 10th District Pa., 1863–1865, National Archives, Washington, D.C.

12. "A Damned Hard Hole"

Epigraph. The Ancient Irish Epic Tale Táin Bó Cúalnge, trans. Joseph Dunn (London: David Nutt, 1914), 199.

1. Testimony of E. H. Rauch, Trial of Peter Dillon, Record Group 153, Records of the Proceedings of the United States Army General Courts-Martial, Cases NN1478, National Archives, Washington, D.C.

2. Palladino, *Another Civil War*, 99.

3. Testimony of Patrick Shannon, trial of Peter Dillon, Record Group 153, Records of the Proceedings of the United States Army General Courts-Martial, Cases NN1474, National Archives, Washington, D.C.

4. Ibid., testimony of Frederick Berger in trial of Hugh Brislin.

5. Ibid.

6. Ibid., testimony of Charles Scrimshaw, trial of Peter Dillon.

7. *New York Times*, Nov. 7, 1863.

8. Testimony of George Heycock, trial of John McCool, Record Group 153, Records of the Proceedings of the United States Army General Courts-Martial, Cases NN1474, National Archives, Washington, D.C.

9. Shankman, "Francis W. Hughes and the 1862 Pennsylvania Election," 385.

10. Rauch to Yohe, June 10, Record Group 110, E-3050, Letters Sent, 10th District Pa., 1863–1865, National Archives, Washington, D.C.

11. Ibid., June 19, 1863.

12. Ibid., July 15; July 22, 1863.

13. Trial of Peter Dillon, Record Group 153, Records of the Proceedings of the United States Army General Courts-Martial, Cases NN1478, National Archives, Washington, D.C.

14. Ibid.

15. Transcript of *Commonwealth v. James McDonnell*, Apr. 1878, Carbon County Courthouse, Jim Thorpe, Pa.

16. Yohe to Gilbert, Oct. 22, Record Group 110, E-3050, Letters Received, 10th District Pa., 1863–1865, National Archives, Washington, D.C.

17. Trial of Peter Dillon, Record Group 153, Records of the Proceedings of the United States Army General Courts-Martial, Cases NN1478, National Archives, Washington, D.C.

18. *New York Times*, Nov. 7, 1863.

19. Scott to Lincoln, Oct. 31, 1863, Record Group 110, E-3050, Letters Sent, 10th District Pa., 1863–1865, National Archives, Washington, D.C.

20. Record Group 393, E-4612, Letters Received, Sigel to Schultze, Jan. 25, 1864.

21. Testimony of Allen Craig, Record Group 153, Records of the Proceedings of the United States Army General Courts-Martial, Cases NN1478, National Archives, Washington, D.C.

22. *New York Times*, Feb. 5, 1864.

23. Trial of Owen Gallagher, Record Group 153, Records of the Proceedings of the United States Army General Courts-Martial, Cases NN1478, National Archives, Washington, D.C.

24. Ibid., Gallagher and Dillon trials.

25. Transcript of *Commonwealth v. James McDonnell*, Carbon County Courthouse, Jim Thorpe, Pa.

26. Tower to Fry and Tower to Gilbert, Nov. 7, 1863, Record Group 110, E-3050, Letters Sent, 10th District Pa., 1863–1865, National Archives, Washington, D.C.

27. James W. Geary, *We Need Men: The Union Draft in the Civil War* (DeKalb: Northern Illinois University Press, 1991), 109.

28. *War of the Rebellion*, ser. 3, vol. 3, p. 1006.

29. Ibid., 1008–9.

30. Couch to Townsend, Nov. 13, 1863, Record Group 393, E-4606, Letters Sent, National Archives, Washington, D.C.

31. Rauch to Yohe, Nov. 16, 1863, Record Group 110, E-3050, Letters Sent, 10th District Pa., 1863–1865, National Archives, Washington, D.C.

32. Record Group 94, Turner–Baker Papers, Turner 2950, Microfilm M-797, Roll 76, National Archives, Washington, D.C.

33. Ibid.

34. Couch to Townsend, Dec. 22, 1863, Record Group 393, E-4606, Letters Sent, National Archives, Washington, D.C.

35. Ibid., Couch to Sigel, Nov. 14, 1863.

36. Ibid., Couch to Gen. Lilly, Nov. 24, 1863.

37. Ibid., Couch to Maj. Gen. H. W. Halleck, Dec. 10, 1863.

38. Ibid., Letters Received, Albright to Sigel, Dec. 3, 1863.

39. Ibid., Letters Sent, Rauch to Couch, Jan. 22, 1864.

40. Ibid., Letters Received, Ryerson to Couch, Feb. 22, 1864.

41. Record Group 153, Records of the Proceedings of the United States Army General Courts-Martial, Cases NN1478, National Archives, Washington, D.C.

42. Ibid.

43. Ibid.

44. Capt. J. C. Hullinger to Maj. John L. Schultze, June 9, 1864, Record Group 110, E-3050, Letters Received, 10th District Pa., 1863–1865, National Archives, Washington, D.C.

45. Ibid., July 9, 1864.

46. Excerpts from Nov. 1, 1864, letter by James McHenry, published in the *Columbia Democrat*, Dec. 3, 1864.

47. Arnold M. Shankman, *The Pennsylvania Antiwar Movement, 1861–1865* (Madison: Fairleigh Dickinson University Press, 1980), 154–55.

48. *New York Times*, Oct. 9, 1864.

49. Nellie Snyder Yost, *Before Today: The History of Holt County, Nebraska* (O'Neill, Neb.: Miles Publishing Co., 1976), 410–11.

50. Headquarters, Department of Pennsylvania, to Adjutant General, U.S. Army, Washington, D.C., Record Group 110, E-3050, Letters Sent, 10th District Pa., 1863–1865, National Archives, Washington, D.C.

13. "A Howling Wilderness"

1. *MJ*, Jan. 16, 1864.

2. Archbishop Woods's temporal letter, Jan. 19, 1864, Archives of Philadelphia Archdiocese.

3. Tower to Sigel, Jan. 16, 1864, Record Group 393, E-4612, Letters Received, National Archives, Washington, D.C.

4. Dunne affidavit, Feb. 1, 1864, Record Group 110, E-3050, Letters Sent, 10th District Pa., 1863–1865, National Archives, Washington, D.C.

5. Ibid., Heckscher to Tower, Feb. 1, 1864.

6. Ibid., Tower to Ramsey, Feb. 6, 1864; Schlegel, *Ruler of the Reading*, 91.

7. Lt. Col. Carlisle Boyd to Capt. H. F. Beardsley, Mar. 15, 1864, Record Group 393, E-4612, Letters Received, National Archives, Washington, D.C.

8. Ibid., Ferry to Couch, Mar. 27, 1864.

9. Tower to Ramsey, Feb. 6, 1864, Record Group 110, E-3050, Letters Sent, 10th District Pa., 1863–1865, National Archives, Washington, D.C.; *Carbon Advocate* (Pa.), June 10, 1876, Robert Ramsey obituary; *MJ*, Feb. 13, 1864.

10. Palladino, *Another Civil War*, 152.

11. *MJ*, Feb. 20, 1864.

12. *Freeman's Journal* (N.Y.), June 30, 1877.

13. *Genealogical and Biographical Annals of Northumberland County, Pennsylvania* (Chicago: J. L. Lloyd & Co., 1911), 541; *Pottsville Emporium*, Mar. 11, 1853.

14. U.S. Census, 1860, Cass Township, Schuylkill County, Pa.

15. Ferry to Couch, Mar. 25, 1864, Record Group 393, E-4612, Letters Received, National Archives, Washington, D.C.

16. Ibid., Boyd to Beardsley, Mar. 15, 1864.

17. *MJ*, Feb. 20, 1864.

18. Ibid., Jan. 2, 1864.

19. Tower to Boyd, Feb. 23, 1864, Record Group 110, E-3050, Letters Sent, 10th District Pa., 1863–1865, National Archives, Washington, D.C.

20. Boyd to Beardsley, Mar. 15, Record Group 393, E-4612, Letters Received, National Archives, Washington, D.C.

21. John L. Blackman, Jr., "The Seizure of the Reading Railroad," *Pennsylvania Magazine of History and Biography* 112 (1981): 50–52.

22. *MJ*, July 16, 1864.

23. Blackman, "Seizure of the Reading Railroad," 50, 54, 55.

24. Ibid., 54.

25. Leo Ward, "It Was Open, Defiant Rebellion," *Civil War: The Magazine of the Civil War Society*, Mar.–Apr. 1991, 61–62.

26. *MJ*, Aug. 15, 1863.

27. Ibid., Mar. 5, 1864; Ward, "It Was Open, Defiant Rebellion," 61–62.

28. Boyd to Beardsley, Mar. 15, 1864, Record Group 393, E-4612, Letters Received, National Archives, Washington, D.C.

29. Tower to Ferry, Apr. 11, 1864, Record Group 110, E-3050, Letters Sent, 10th District Pa., 1863–1865, National Archives, Washington, D.C.

30. *MJ*, Mar. 12; Mar. 19, 1864.

31. Bowen to Gilbert, May 13, 1864, Record Group 110, E-3050, Letters Sent, 10th District Pa., 1863–1865, National Archives, Washington, D.C.

32. Bowen to Hullinger, Aug. 18, 1864, Record Group 393, E-4612, Letters Received, National Archives, Washington, D.C.

33. Tower to Gilbert, Mar. 9, 1864, Record Group 110, E-3050, Letters Sent, 10th District Pa., 1863–1865, National Archives, Washington, D.C.

34. Ibid., Historical Report on Draft in 10th District, Bowen to Fry, May 20, 1865.

35. Ibid., Letters Received, Foley to Fry, Jan. 17, 1865.

36. *MJ*, June 11, 1864; Tower to Fry, Apr. 7, 1864, Record Group 110, E-3050, Letters Sent, 10th District Pa., 1863–1865, National Archives, Washington, D.C.

37. *MJ*, Jan. 21, 1865.

38. See http://www.arlingtoncemetery.com/wwduffield.htm.

39. *MJ*, Jan. 21, 1865.

40. Broehl, *Molly Maguires*, 68.

14. Parting Shots

Epigraph. Henry George, "Labor in Pennsylvania II," *North American Review* 143, no. 358 (1886): 273.

1. *MJ*, May 27, 1865.

2. *War of the Rebellion*, ser. 1, vol. 46, pt. 3, p. 743.

3. *MJ*, Apr. 29; May 6, 1865.

4. *New York Times*, June 12, 1865; *MJ*, May 13; May 27, 1865.

5. Davis to Duffield, Apr. 26, 1865, Charles A. Heckscher Company Papers (hereafter Heckscher Papers), Moses Taylor Collection, Manuscript Division, New York Public Library, vol. 716.

6. Ibid.; *MJ*, May 20, 1865; *New York Times*, June 12, 1865.

7. Davis to Smith, May 15, 1865, Heckscher Papers, vol. 716.

8. Ibid., Davis to Dunne, May 27, 1865.

9. Ibid., Davis to Duffield, May 31, 1865.

10. *War of the Rebellion*, ser. 1, vol. 46, pt. 3, p. 1220.

11. *Civil War Sketchbook and Diary* (Huntingdon, Pa.: Huntingdon County Historical Society, 1988), 64–65, 79–80. The book combines the diary of Pvt. Philip Bolinger and the sketches of Sgt. Henry Hudson, both of Company K, 202nd Regiment, Pennsylvania Volunteers.

12. Davis to Duffield, May 31, 1865, Heckscher Papers, vol. 716.

13. Ibid., Davis to Albright, June 10, 1865.

14. Ibid., vol. 715, Albright to Davis, June 12, 1865.

15. *Civil War Sketchbook and Diary*, 68; *New York Times*, June 12, 1865.

16. *Lebanon Advertiser*, June 14, 1865.

17. Davis to Duffield, Schlegel, May 16, 1865, Heckscher Papers, vol. 716.

18. *New York Times*, June 12, 1865.

19. *MJ*, July 22, 1865; Apr. 7, 1866.

20. Ibid., June 10, 1865.

21. Ibid., May 6, 1865; Pinkerton report dated Oct. 15, 1873, in Molly Maguire Collection, Reading Rail Road Papers, Hagley Museum and Library, Wilmington, Del.; Dunne affidavit, Feb. 1, 1864, Record Group 110, E-3050, Letters Sent, 10th District Pa., 1863–1865, National Archives, Washington, D.C.

22. *Civil War Sketchbook and Diary*, 68–70; *MJ*, June 10, 1865.

23. Davis to Duffield, June 22, 1865, Heckscher Papers, vol. 716.

24. Ibid., Davis to Duffield, July 22, 1865.

25. *MJ*, Aug. 26, 1865.

26. Pinkerton, *Molly Maguires and the Detectives*, 67.

27. Dunne to Davis, Sept. 18, 1865, Heckscher Papers, vol. 716.

28. *MJ*, Sept. 2, 1865.

29. Ibid., Sept. 16, 1865.

30. Ibid., Dec. 16; Dec. 30, 1865; Jan. 6; Jan. 13, 1866.

31. Heckscher Papers, vol. 718.

32. Dewees, *Molly Maguires*, 58.

33. *MJ*, Jan. 13, 1866.

34. Ibid., Jan. 20, 1866.

35. Ibid., Jan 6, 1866.

36. Ibid., Jan. 13; Jan. 20, 1866.

37. Davis to C. Little, Jan. 24, 1866, Heckscher Papers, vol. 718.

38. *MJ*, Apr. 7; Apr. 14; Apr. 28, 1866; *Molly Maguires*, pamphlet, 9.

39. George Bergner, *Pennsylvania Legislative Record, 1866* (Harrisburg, Pa.: Printed at "the Telegraph," 1866), 459–60.

40. J. P. Shalloo, *Private Police, with Special Reference to Pennsylvania* (Philadelphia: American Academy of Political and Social Science, 1933), 60; George, "Labor in Pennsylvania II," 273.

41. Wallace, *St. Clair*, 246–47.

42. *MJ*, Apr. 7; June 16, 1866; report of Supt. Franklin, Apr. 28, 1875, Molly Maguire Collection, Reading Rail Road Papers, Hagley Museum and Library, Wilmington, Del.

43. Davis to A. B. Gorgas, Apr. 16, 1866; Davis to Duffield, Apr. 21, 1866, Heckscher Papers, vol. 718.

44. Ibid., Davis to Duffield, Mar. 22, 1866.

45. Ibid., Dec. 26, 1866.

46. Ibid., Davis to Verner, Dec. 27, 1866, vol. 717.

47. Ibid., Oct. 3, 1866; Davis to Duffield, Oct. 26, 1866.

48. Ibid., Davis to John Tucker, Jan. 24, 1867.

49. *Commonwealth v. Patrick Hester, Peter McHugh & Patrick Tully*, 440–441, 444–45; list of members of the AOH, Molly Maguire Collection, Reading Rail Road Papers, Hagley Museum and Library, Wilmington, Del.; *Report of the Case of the Commonwealth v. John Kehoe, et al. . . . for an Aggravated Assault and Battery with Intent to Kill Wm. M. Major* (Pottsville, 1876), 95–96; Nash turns up as a twenty-year-old in the 1860 U.S. Census for Cass Township, and as a thirty-year-old in the 1870 U.S. Census for Butler Township.

50. *Commonwealth v. Patrick Hester, Peter McHugh & Patrick Tully*, 667.

51. *MJ*, Mar. 23, 1867.

52. Ibid., Aug. 26, 1865; Mar. 23, 1867; Lewis, *Lament for the Molly Maguires*, 39.

53. Report from Pinkerton operative W.R.H. dated Jan. 16, 1874, in Molly Maguire Collection, Reading Rail Road Papers, Hagley Museum and Library, Wilmington, Del.

54. *Commonwealth v. Patrick Hester, Peter McHugh & Patrick Tully*, 52–53; *MJ*, Aug. 25, 1866 (list of south Cass incomes); Dec. 20, 1878; Feb. 27, 1874; F. W. Beers and A. B. Cochran, *County Atlas of Schuylkill, Pennsylvania* (1875; repr., Vernon, Ind.: Windmill Publications, 1999), 126.

55. Pinkerton, *Molly Maguires and the Detectives*, 161–62.

56. U.S. Census for Butler Township, Schuylkill County, Pa., 1870; *MJ*, Aug. 25, 1866.

57. *MJ*, Mar. 30, 1867; Dewees, *Molly Maguires*, 54.

58. *MJ*, Mar. 30, 1867; Bergner, Appendix to *Pennsylvania Legislative Record*, Mar. 23, 1867, 223.

59. *MJ*, Apr. 13, 1867; Wallace, *St. Clair*, 330.

60. Bergner, Appendix to *Pennsylvania Legislative Record*, Mar. 28, 1867, 222–23.

61. Dewees, *Molly Maguires*, 65–66; *Commonwealth v. Patrick Hester, Peter McHugh & Patrick Tully*, 4, 53, 103, 502.

62. Broehl, *Molly Maguires*, 61; *MJ*, Mar. 29, 1878; Dewees, *Molly Maguires*, 65–66; U.S. Census for Reilly Township, Schuylkill County, Pennsylvania, 1860; *Commonwealth v. Patrick Hester, Peter McHugh & Patrick Tully*, 216, 438–41.

63. *Commonwealth v. Patrick Hester, Peter McHugh & Patrick Tully*, 56–62.

15. The Road to Black Thursday

Epigraph. "After the Long Strike," *Publications of the Historical Society of Schuylkill County*, vol. 4 (Pottsville, Pa., 1914).

1. U.S. Census, Reilly Township, Schuylkill County, Pennsylvania, 1870; Broehl, *Molly Maguires*, 172, 175–78.

2. *Pottsville Emporium*, Mar. 30, 1848.

3. *Commonwealth v. Patrick Hester, Peter McHugh & Patrick Tully*, 354–55, 91–96, 628–29.

4. Wallace, *St. Clair*, 277–78.

5. Harold W. Aurand, "Early Mine Workers Organizations in the Anthracite Region," *Pennsylvania History* 58 (Oct. 1991): 301; Charles E. Killeen, "John Siney: The Pioneer in American Industrial Unionism and Industrial Government" (Ph.D. diss., University of Wisconsin, 1942), 106–8.

6. Killeen, "John Siney," 117–18.

7. Yearley, *Enterprise and Anthracite*, 181–82.

8. Edward Pinkowski, *John Siney: The Miners' Martyr* (Philadelphia: Sunshine Press, 1963), 4–5.

9. Wallace, *St. Clair*, 291.

10. Killeen, "John Siney," 237–39; Yearley, *Enterprise and Anthracite*, 81–82.

11. Killeen, "John Siney," 111; Wallace, *St. Clair*, 291; *MJ*, July 11, 1868.

12. Killeen, "John Siney," 128.

13. Frank B. Evans, *Pennsylvania Politics: 1872–1877: A Study in Political Leadership* (Harrisburg: Pennsylvania Historical and Museum Commission, 1966), 240.

14. Killeen, "John Siney," 118–19.

15. Ibid., 157–59; Wallace, *St. Clair*, 293–95.

16. Terence Vincent Powderly, *The Path I Trod* (New York: Columbia University Press, 1940), 23–24, 35; Wallace, *St. Clair*, 300–301.

17. Korson, *Black Rock*, 356.

18. Zerbey, *History of Pottsville and Schuylkill County*, 415; U.S. Census for Cass Township, 1860, 1870; *MJ*, July 9, 1864; Apr. 25, 1861.

19. Zerbey, *History of Pottsville and Schuylkill County*, 415–17.

20. Report of the Pennsylvania Bureau of Industrial Statistics, 1872–73, quoted in Yearley, *Enterprise and Anthracite*, 188.

21. For "had not heard anything of the Mollie Maguires for some time," see report of Operatives S.M. and W.R.H., Oct, 12, 1873; for Mohan's role as body-master of Forestville AOH, see Aug. 30, 1876, report of Benjamin Franklin, Pinkerton superintendent, both in Molly Maguire Collection, Reading Rail Road Papers, Hagley Museum and Library, Wilmington, Del.; for Mohan's union activity, see *MJ*, Sept. 11, 1874.

22. Dewees, *Molly Maguires*, 45.

23. Ibid., 324–26.

24. Korson, *Minstrels of the Mine Patch*, 219–20.

25. Korson, *Black Rock*, 389–90.

26. Kenny, *Making Sense of the Molly Maguires*, app. 1, 289–95.

27. The best overviews are Broehl, *Molly Maguires*; and Kenny, *Making Sense of the Molly Maguires.*

28. Broehl, *Molly Maguires*, 108–20; Kenny, *Making Sense of the Molly Maguires*, 137–46. Lawler's role is mentioned by Pinkowski, *John Siney*, 81–82.

29. Schlegel, *Ruler of the Reading*, 33–35.

30. Broehl, *Molly Maguires*, 122–24; Kenny, *Making Sense of the Molly Maguires*, 139, 149–50.

31. Broehl, *Molly Maguires*, 127.

32. Pinkerton, *Molly Maguires and the Detectives*, 13.

33. Reports of Operatives S.M. and W.R.H., Oct, 13, Oct. 14, Oct. 15, Oct, 16, 1873, Molly Maguire Collection, Reading Rail Road Papers, Hagley Museum and Library, Wilmington, Del.

34. Miller, *Peep O'Day Boys and Defenders*, 13.

35. Killen, *Famine Decade*, 130–31.

36. Accession No. 1520, Box 979, Molly Maguire Collection, Reading Rail Road Papers, Hagley Museum and Library, Wilmington, Del.

37. Page 100 of the 1870 Census for Chicago, where the detective was living, lists an Irish-born, twenty-six-year-old James McParlan working as a saloon-keeper in the 9th Division.

38. Pinkerton, *Molly Maguires and the Detectives*, 57, 83.

39. McParlan report, Jan. 21, 1874, Molly Maguire Collection, Reading Rail Road Papers, Hagley Museum and Library, Wilmington, Del.

40. Ibid., Jan. 17, 1874.

41. *MJ*, Apr. 17, 1874.

42. Record Group 13, Federal Writers' Project, Box 12, recorded Nov. 3, 1939, Pennsylvania State Archives, Harrisburg.

43. Pinkerton, *Molly Maguires and the Detectives*, 235.

44. *New York Times*, Feb. 10, 1878.

45. Pinkerton, *Molly Maguires and the Detectives*, 139–40.

46. Ibid., 201, 191, 208, 216; Broehl, *Molly Maguires*, 175–76; *MJ*, Dec. 20, 1878.

47. *New York Times*, Feb. 10, 1878, "Crimes of the Mollies."

48. Dewees, *Molly Maguires*, 176.

49. Killeen, "John Siney," 237; Broehl, *Molly Maguires*, 183–84, 170.

50. *MJ*, Apr. 17, 1874.

51. Report of R.J.L., May 30, 1875, Molly Maguire Collection, Reading Rail Road Papers, Hagley Museum and Library, Wilmington, Del.

52. Ibid., McParlan report, May 10, 1875; A.Mc. report, May 15, 1874.

53. Ibid., McParlan report, Feb. 14, 1875.

54. Pinkerton, *Molly Maguires and the Detectives*, 257–58; R. R. Parkinson, *Pen Portraits* (Sacramento, 1877), 96.

55. Andrew Roy, *A History of the Coal Miners of the United States* (1905; repr., Westport, Conn.: Greenwood Press, 1970), 96–97.

56. Francis, "Seventy Years in the Coal Mines," 35. (Francis was not particularly sympathetic to labor violence by mine workers, which he later confronted himself as a mine boss in Tennessee.)

57. Pinkerton, *Molly Maguires and the Detectives*, 335.

58. *New York Times*, June 4, 1875.

59. Record Group 23, Records of the Department of Military and Veterans Affairs, National Guard of Pennsylvania, muster role of 7th Regiment, Company C (Silliman Guards), Nov. 1875, Pennsylvania State Archives, Harrisburg.

60. *New York Times*, June 4, 1875.

61. Killeen, "John Siney," 247; Joseph F. Patterson, "Old WBA Days," *Publications of the Historical Society of Schuylkill County* 2 (1910): 383.

62. Killeen, "John Siney," 250–51.

63. Quoted in Broehl, *Molly Maguires*, 234.

64. Quoted in Kenny, *Making Sense of the Molly Maguires*, 200–201.

65. Gudelunas, "Rise of the Irish Factor in Anthracite Politics."

66. Broehl, *Molly Maguires*, 257.

67. Beers and Cochran, *County Atlas of Schuylkill*, 42A; Munsell, *History of Schuylkill County*, 230; U.S. Census for Mahanoy City, Schuylkill County, Pennsylvania, 1870.

68. T. L. Hess, D&L Agent, to Frank Carter, Land Agent, Jan. 1, 1876, P&RC&I Copy Letters, Mahanoy City, 1875–80, Reading Anthracite Archive, Pottsville, Pa.

69. Munsell, *History of Schuylkill County*, 231–33.

70. Aug. 30, 1876, Molly Maguire Collection, Reading Rail Road Papers, Hagley Museum and Library, Wilmington, Del.

71. Korson, *Minstrels of the Mine Patch*, 267–68. Reading Coal and Iron later rewarded Lawler with work as a miner at its Indian Ridge Colliery, "because it is important that all the men who turned state's evidence should remain in the region and not be driven away by fear of the Mollies or lack of work," Henry Pleasants wrote. Letter to E. Gregory, Girardville district superintendent, July 24, 1877, Reading Anthracite Archive, Pottsville, Pa.

72. McCarthy, *Great Molly Maguire Hoax*, 130.

73. *MJ*, Jan. 19, 1877.

74. Ibid.; *New York Times*, Feb. 13, 1877.

75. *Commonwealth v. James McDonnell*, Apr. 11–13, 1878, Carbon County Courthouse, Jim Thorpe, Pa.

76. June 20; June 27, 1877, Pleasants to George deB Keim, Reading Anthracite Papers, Pottsville, Pa.

77. Page Smith, *The Rise of Industrial America: A People's History of the Post-Reconstruction Era*, vol. 6 (New York: McGraw-Hill, 1984), 175.

78. *New York Times*, Aug. 3; Aug. 9; Sept. 9, 1877; *Report of the Committee Appointed to Investigate the Railroad Riots of July 1877*, Pennsylvania General Assembly, Harrisburg, Pa., 30.

79. Kenny, *Making Sense of the Molly Maguires*, 271; Associated Press report in the Every evening and commercial newspaper, Wilmington, Del., Mar. 25, 1878; *New York Times*, Mar. 26, 1878; Campbell, *Molly Maguire Story*, 181.

80. Barclay and Co., *The Life and Execution of Jack Kehoe*, pamphlet (Philadelphia, 1879), 62–64.

81. *MJ*, Dec. 20, 1878.

82. Associated Press report in the *Every Evening and Commercial* newspaper, Jan. 14, 1879; *Philadelphia Times*, Jan. 15, 1879; *New York Times*, Jan. 15, 1879.

16. Shadows of the Gunmen

Epigraph. Yeats, "The Death of Cuchulain," in *Selected Poems and Three Plays*, 223

1. "Last of the Molly Maguires," *Time*, Dec. 6, 1999; *The Irish People*, Nov. 14, 1998.

2. *Philadelphia Inquirer*, Dec. 17, 1980.

3. Ibid.; *Philadelphia Daily News*, Dec. 17, 1980; *Philadelphia Bulletin*, Dec. 17, 1980.

4. *Philadelphia Inquirer*, Oct. 20, 1994; *Time*, Dec. 6, 1999.

5. Mike Mallowe, "My Life and Times with the IRA," *Philadelphia Magazine*, Mar. 1973; Jack Holland, *The American Connection: U.S. Guns, Money, and*

Influence in Northern Ireland (New York: Penguin, 1987), 88. McCullough is the "union organizer in Philadelphia" to whom Holland refers.

6. *New York Times*, Dec. 12, 1993.

7. *The Irish People*, Nov. 14, 1998.

8. Barclay and Co., *The Life and Execution of Jack Kehoe*, 63–64; *New York Times*, Dec. 12, 1993.

9. Michael Kozura, "We Stood Our Ground: Anthracite Miners and the Expropriation of Corporate Property," in *"We Are All Leaders": The Alternative Unionism of the 1930s* (Champaign: University of Illinois Press, 1996), 215, 233n41.

10. *New York Times*, Jan. 26, 1880; Zerbey, *History of Pottsville and Schuylkill County*, 419.

11. William A. Gudelunas, "The Ethno-Religious Factor Reaches Fruition: The Politics of Hard Coal, 1845–1972," in *Hard Times, Hard Coal: Ethnicity and Labor in the Anthracite Region*, ed. David L. Salay (Scranton, Pa.: Anthracite Museum Press, 1984), 175.

12. Miller and Sharpless, *Kingdom of Coal*, 176, 224, 230–34.

13. *New York Evening World, Washington Times*, both Aug. 5, 1902.

14. *Minneapolis Journal*, Sept. 3, 1902.

15. Miller and Sharpless, *Kingdom of Coal*, 319–20.

16. *New York Times*, Nov. 20, 1936; Louis Adamic, "The Great 'Bootleg' Coal Industry," *The Atlantic*, Jan. 9, 1934.

17. *New York Times*, Dec. 22; Dec. 23, 1936; Apr. 4, 1937.

18. Ibid., Nov. 18; Dec. 20, 1936.

19. Ibid., Sept. 25, 1936.

20. Ibid., Jan. 13, 1935.

21. Ibid., Feb. 27, 1937.

22. United Press International report published in the *Evening Standard*, Uniontown, Pa., Mar. 26, 1943, cited by David Barker and Tom Loughran in an academic paper, "The Ethics of Bootleg Coal," 22.

23. Gudelunas, "Ethno-Religious Factor Reaches Fruition," 171; *New York Times*, June 10, 2008.

24. G. O. Virtue, "The Anthracite Mine Laborers," *Bulletin of the Department of Labor* 13 (Nov. 1897): 731.

25. Rupp, *History of Northampton*, 509; *MJ*, Sept. 11, 1874; U.S. Census for Cass Township, 1870; Report of Benj. Franklin, Pinkerton Superintendent, Aug. 30, 1876, Molly Maguire Papers, Society Collection, Historical Society of Pennsylvania, Philadelphia; Report of Operative T.J., Mar. 5, 1880, Knights of Labor–Pinkerton Folder, Molly Maguire Collection, Reading Rail Road Papers, Hagley Museum and Library, Wilmington, Del.

26. Broehl, *Molly Maguires*, 323.

27. Powderly, *The Path I Trod*, 178, 182.

28. Ridge, *Erin's Sons in America*, 52.

29. Shoemaker, "Fantasticals," 30–31.

30. *Shenandoah Herald*, July 3, 1895; Dec. 30, 1898.

31. *Scranton Tribune*, Sept. 4, 1901.

32. *Allentown Morning Call*, Sept. 3, 2000; *Pottsville Republican*, Aug. 30, 2000.

33. *Republican Herald*, Sept. 4, 2011.

34. Davis, *Parades and Power*, 109, 111.

35. *MJ*, Sept. 3, 1853.

36. Yost, *Before Today*, 4–5, 410.

37. J. Anthony Lukas, *Big Trouble* (New York: Simon and Schuster, 1997), 196.

38. David M. Emmons, *The Butte Irish: Class and Ethnicity in an American Mining Town, 1875–1925* (Chicago: University of Illinois Press, 1989), 16–17.

39. Charles A. Siringo, *A Cowboy Detective* (1912; repr., Lincoln: University of Nebraska Press, 1988), 136, 140–49, 185–86.

40. Lukas, *Big Trouble*, 200.

41. Mary V. Dearborn, *Queen of Bohemia: The Life of Louise Bryant* (Boston: Houghton Mifflin, 1996), 10–12.

42. Kenny, *Making Sense of the Molly Maguires*, 38–41.

43. Broehl, *Molly Maguires*, 31.

44. Accession No. 1520, Box 979, Molly Maguire Collection, Reading Rail Road Papers, Hagley Museum and Library, Wilmington, Del.

45. Davitt, *Fall of Feudalism in Ireland*, 43.

46. Kenny, *Making Sense of the Molly Maguires*, 207–8; *New York Times*, Oct. 4; Nov. 21; Sept. 29; Dec. 17, 1883.

47. Garvin, *Evolution of Irish Nationalist Politics*, 61–63; Bew, *Land and the National Question in Ireland*, 41, 45.

48. *Ireland, 1798–1998*, ed. Alvin Jackson (Oxford: Blackwell, 1999), 189, 193.

49. Seán Cronin, *The McGarrity Papers* (New York: Clan na Gael, 1972), 27.

50. Foster, *Modern Ireland*, 496.

51. Ernie O'Malley, *On Another Man's Wound* (1936; repr., Dublin: Anvil Books, 1979), 78–81.

52. Mary Leadbeater, *The Leadbeater Papers*, vol. 1 (London, 1862), 85; W. H. Patterson, "The Christmas Rhymers of the North of Ireland," *Notes and Queries*, 4th ser., vol. 10 (Dec. 21, 1872): 487.

53. Irish Folklore Commission, MS 1458, p. 345, Irish Folklore Department, University College, Dublin.

54. Ibid., MS 1089, p. 206; MS 1090, p. 207.

55. H. Laird, "'Ride Rough-Shod': Evictions, Sheriff's Sales and the Anti-hunting Agitation," in *Subversive Law in Ireland, 1879–1920: From "Unwritten Law" to the Dáil Courts* (Dublin: Four Courts Press, 2005), 91–95.

56. Glassie, *All Silver and No Brass*, 34–35, Glassie, *Stars of Ballymenone*, 55, 62–63.

57. Glassie, *All Silver and No Brass*, 130.

58. James Joyce, *Ulysses*, Gabler ed. (New York: Vintage, 1986), 488–89.

59. Ibid., 5, 164, 177, 178.

60. Ruairí Ó Brádaigh, "Irish Folk Drama," *Musical Traditions*, Dec. 16, 1998.

61. *Pottsville Republican*, Dec. 5, 1994.

62. *New York Times*, July 4, 1998.

63. Korson, *Minstrels of the Mine Patch*, 252.

Index

CPSIA information can be obtained
at www.ICGtesting.com
Printed in the USA
JSHW031601070323
38608JS00001B/1

9 781531 502959